LOCKHART
AS ROMANTIC
BIOGRAPHER

Is it not enough to have to bear the image in which nature has wrapped me, without consenting to perpetuate the image of an image, as if it were worth contemplating?

PLOTINUS

For what man knoweth the things of a man, save the spirit of man which is in him?

I CORINTHIANS 2 : 11

LOCKHART
as Romantic Biographer

FRANCIS R. HART

Edinburgh University Press

© Francis R. Hart 1971
Edinburgh University Press
22 George Square, Edinburgh

ISBN 0 85224 155 0

North America
Aldine Publishing Company
529 South Wabash Avenue, Chicago

Library of Congress
Catalog Card Number 72-92291

Printed in Great Britain by
R & R Clark Ltd, Edinburgh

PREFACE

'English biography in the nineteenth century,' observes Richard Altick, 'was a rich but unstable compound of history, journalism, eulogy, inspiration, and materials suitable for the study of the mind. How far,' he wonders, 'was it also a form of literary art?' The answers provided by most historians of biography are lukewarm at best. Many rehearse Sir Harold Nicolson's anti-Victorian lamentation: 'Then came earnestness, and with earnestness hagiography descended on us with its sullen cloud.' John Garraty finds 'few really significant developments' in biography in the century after Boswell, and declares a major cause: 'By the forties biography was rapidly descending into complete respectability.' Paul Kendall confirms the diagnosis: 'the cultural-social forces of the age had throttled the development. . . . Biography was silenced; pseudobiography took its place. . . . Whiskers hid the Victorian face no more securely than pseudobiography hid the Victorian heart.' Such caricatures of Victorianism, defunct in better defined areas of literary history, hang on in chronicles of biography.[1]

The assigning of earnestness exclusively to the reign of Victoria is admittedly absurd, and Joseph Reid properly bases his account of biography during the Romantic period on a recognition of the impact of Evangelicalism. He is misguided, I think, to argue a segregation of Evangelicalism from Romanticism and to compartmentalize biography accordingly: 'As Garraty has pointed out, the Romantic movement

v

never really became an issue in biography: the Evangelical movement was already too firmly entrenched.'[2] No interpretation of Romanticism can afford to neglect its relation to the several religious revivals of the early nineteenth century. No reading of biography during the period can ignore the Romantic movement as an 'issue'. If, as Reid says, 'it is unsound to refer to the lives of this period as Romantic biography', then meaningful historical classification will be difficult indeed.

The evidence against Reid's judgement is in his book. The importance of Wordsworth and Carlyle as critics of biography is apparent there. Equally central, Stanfield's *Essay on the Study and Composition of Biography* (1813) has its pervasively Romantic principles, not least that epistemological conception of gusto that Stanfield calls 'the biographic spirit'. Southey and Lockhart, Moore and Scott, are the chief artists; some of their chief subjects – Nelson, Napoleon, Burns, Byron, Scott himself – are potently Romantic personalities. Finally, Reid's own critical principles eventuate in this very Romantic formulation: 'the biographer's image is the highest truth.'[3] How the Enlightenment's positivistic Boswell would have demurred!

My aim in this book is not to challenge Reid's pioneering essay – indeed, it took shape much too early to benefit from his insights. Nor do I mean to generalize about the biography of the period, but rather to further a historical understanding of the genre through close study of one major artist. I have called John Gibson Lockhart a Romantic biographer, and he is, after all, the great and representative biographer of what we still call the 'Romantic period'. But the reader will, I hope, see that there is more to it than this. He will recognize, in Lockhart the biographer, a poetics of personality and spontaneity, a Carlylesque ethic of reverence, a sense of the tragic ambivalence of imaginative vision, an epistemology of knowing by sympathetic self-projection, an artistic commitment to the norms of organic narrative, a sympathy with Scott's ideal of patriarchal community, a devotion to Wordsworth as the greatest of recent English poets and to Coleridge as contemporary Europe's greatest mind, a religious awe at the mystery of the true self, and a cultural view of art and creativity inspired by Friedrich Schlegel. Such are the informing ideas of Lockhart's biography and his biographical theory. If, taken together, they do not warrant the term 'Romantic', then we must indeed despair of the classification. And if we do, then we may see Lockhart instead as the great biographer of the British counter-enlightenment – a term I take to mean virtually the same thing.

Such a classification is evident in the title of my second chapter, '*Peter's Letters* as the Biography of a Culture'. The subtitle has meaning only with reference to Romantic cultural theory, the theory John Stuart Mill saw as the major counter-enlightenment reaction of the 'Germano-Coleridgian school'. *Peter's Letters to His Kinsfolk* (1819) may seem too obscure an item in literary history for the attention I give it. In fact, an introduction to this brilliant and notorious juvenile piece is the best preface to Lockhart the biographer. Moreover, the generic transformation of Goldsmith's Citizen of the World and Montesquieu's Persian into Lockhart's cultural enthusiast Peter Morris parallels the transition in biography from Boswell's Enlightenment to Lockhart's Romanticism. The chapter serves several ends.

The reader who remembers Lockhart only for the *Life of Scott* (and perhaps the Death of Keats) may feel impatience, too, at the extended treatment of the biographer of Burns and Napoleon. Both lives, studied historically, genetically, and formally, show skills less obvious in the massive impersonal structure of the larger work. Both have outlived their obsolescence as history, and as biographical narratives still bear comparison with their contemporary masterpiece, Southey's *Nelson*. Carlyle recognized Lockhart's *Burns* as the poet's first true biography, and I have tested this opinion with reference to early Burns biography in general. If anything, his *Napoleon*, invariably slighted or ignored by Lockhart scholars, is even more impressive.

For the amplitude of my reconstruction of 'The Making of the *Life of Scott*' the justification must be in Lockhart's terms: the interest lies in the detail. The complexity of the book's genesis, method, and form can be discovered only through such intensive study. This one makes abundant use of raw materials still in manuscript. Under such circumstances, a failure of elaboration would be false criticism.

My opening chapter surveys biographical theory in the half-century following Boswell, and out of some definitive contradictions formulates what I take to be the central paradox of biographical theory in the period. The period covers two generations, and Lockhart belongs to the second; but his representative position in its controversies is, I trust, never lost sight of. His shorter biographies – his biographical essays as well, necessarily excluded from this study – are impressive and characteristic responses to contemporary demands for an *art* of biography. And to the art of his masterpiece, the central paradox of Romantic biographical theory is the best key.

'What a slippery set of principles biographical criticism rests upon,' observes Joseph Reid; and the selections in James Clifford's *Biography as an Art* bear him out.[4] The present study began more years ago than its author, his family, and surely his friends are willing to remember, at a time when the criticism of biography had scarcely begun or its lack of principles deplored. Over the years many have aided or encouraged the book at its various stages. The kindnesses of F. W. Hilles, Marion Lochhead, R. L. C. Lorimer, W. M. Parker, the late J. W. Oliver, and the hospitable Mrs Maxwell-Scott of Abbotsford are gratefully acknowledged. To the library staffs of Harvard, Yale, the Ohio State University, the University of Virginia, and most of all the National Library of Scotland, I am much indebted. Several patient readers have carped constructively: Howard Mumford Jones and W. J. Bate; Robert Estrich; Arnold Silver; Albert Friedman and Marshall Waingrow. The encouragement of Ian Jack, James Clifford, and Alan Lang Strout has been invaluable. Without the generous help and guidance of James C. Corson, Edgar Johnson, and Richard Altick, the work could never have been done. The responsibility is mine. Even my willing wife, who has struggled with the manuscript for years, cannot take that weight off my shoulders.

FRANCIS RUSSELL HART
Charlottesville, Virginia
February 1970

CONTENTS

To Lorena L. Hart *and*
Richard D. Altick

1

AFTER BOSWELL.
PARADOXICAL THEORY IN
A BIOGRAPHICAL AGE

. . . this age of personality, this age of literary and political gossiping, when the meanest insects are worshipped with a sort of
Egyptian superstition, if only the brainless head be atoned for by
the sting of personal malignity in the tail. . . . In an age, when
even sermons are published with a double appendix stuffed with
names – in a generation so transformed from the characteristic
reserve of Britons, that from the ephemeral sheet of a London
newspaper to the everlasting Scotch professorial quarto, almost
every publication exhibits or flatters the epidemic distemper.
. . . In an age, when a bashful Philalethes or Philaleutheros is as
rare on the title-pages and among the signatures of our magazines, as a real name used to be in the days of our shy and notice-
shunning grandfathers.
  COLERIDGE, *The Friend*

A personality can only be awakened to life by a personality.
  SCHWEITZER, *The Quest of the Historical Jesus*

1

AFTER BOSWELL.
PARADOXICAL THEORY IN
A BIOGRAPHICAL AGE

I

Boswell,' wrote Leslie Stephen in 1893, 'founded biography in
England as much as Gibbon founded history and Adam Smith political
economy.'[1] John Gibson Lockhart, Boswell's great successor in what
Lytton Strachey called 'the method of enormous and elaborate
accretion',[2] was in essential agreement. His praise, however, was
ambiguous. 'The example once set,' wrote Lockhart in 1831,

'the curiosity of the public having been *so* gratified as to a single
illustrious man, and their satisfaction made so apparent in the boundless popularity of the performance, the evil, if evil it were, was
done, and could not be repaired. . . . From that time a new spirit
animated all this department of composition; and to the influence of
Boswell we owe probably three-fourths of what is *de facto* most
entertaining, as well as no inconsiderable portion of whatever is
most instructive, in all the books of memoirs that have subsequently
appeared.'[3]

But whatever reservations Lockhart felt, he has been fated to survive in
facile juxtaposition, to inhabit sketch and syllabus as chief in the vanguard of the 'Boswell tradition' or prime heir to the 'Boswell formula'.[4]

Many have linked them, from Leslie Stephen's typical reference to
'Lockhart's admirable life . . . next to Boswell's *Johnson*, the best in
the language', to Ian Jack's incisive paragraphs on 'one of the few
biographies that deserve the compliment of comparison with Boswell's'.

George Saintsbury's Lockhart is 'the prince of biographers' whose work 'puts even Boswell on his mettle, and in some respects excels him'. Sir Robert Rait suggests that 'Lockhart's biography has a completeness which Boswell would have envied'; and Sir Harold Nicolson and Sir Herbert Grierson, applying different criteria, draw the same comparison. Long ago, Scott's friend Morritt of Rokeby wrote Lockhart: 'You make men as well acquainted with Scott as ever Jemmy Boswell did with Johnson, and yet neither you or your hero ever suffer from it, as his did.' Yet few have had occasion to note a further bond. Few have recalled them together as 'brither Scots' from adjoining counties in the Lowland West, as 'our old Glasgow Collegians, Boswell and Lockhart', as heritors (together with the biographer from Ecclefechan, Dumfriesshire) of a national tradition biographical in impulse and focus.[5]

The nationalistic pamphlet, the thumbnail sketch, sometimes proves suggestive: 'Since curiosity, a sense of detail, and a strong interest in family and local history have been enumerated as Scots characteristics, it is perhaps not surprising that the two greatest biographies in English should be by Scotsmen.'[6] Such suggestions lead nowhere and everywhere. With no intention of pursuing the biographical impulse through centuries of 'Scots characteristics', I cite the later eighteenth-century Scottish origin of Boswell and Lockhart as an initial clue in a search for the causes of the obsessive biographical self-consciousness, the upsurge of enthusiasm for the genre of biography, which marks the generations they represent and the literary taste we call 'Romantic', and which may also explain the strong Victorian reaction in favour of the characteristic reserve of Britons'.[7]

Such an upsurge did take place, at least in the minds of contemporary observers. A Critical Reviewer refers in 1794 to 'this time when a taste for biography is more than usually prevalent'; an Annual Reviewer affirms in 1804 that 'there is no species of literature which has been received of late with such distinguished favour by the public as biography; nor is this to be wondered at, for it gratifies at once both the most laudable and the most perverse curiosity'. The most voluminous of biographical theorists, James F. Stanfield, writes in 1813 at 'a time when that species of writing is so generally cultivated, and when so many elaborate compositions of the kind are brought before the established literary tribunals', just five years after the popular author of *Marmion* commences a memoir with concern –

'The present age has discovered a desire, or rather a rage, for literary anecdote and private history, that may be well permitted to alarm one who has engaged in a certain degree the attention of the public –' and six years before the biographical dictionarist John Watkins complains: 'Of late years, thanks to the officious zeal of friendship, and the active industry of literary undertakers, biographical memoirs have become as multitudinous, prolix, and veracious as epitaphs in a country churchyard.'[8]

Some found the upsurge dangerous. *The Friend* warned:

'In the present age (emphatically the age of personality) there are more than ordinary motives for withholding all encouragement from this mania of busying ourselves with the names of others, which is still more alarming as a symptom, than it is troublesome as a disease.'

John Foster, one of the most thoughtful of theorists, spoke much of 'this vicious state of an important literary province', and noted 'the present epidemical disease in literature, the custom of making very large books about individuals', which has resulted in a 'swelling fungus type of biography'. And when Stanfield suggested that the 'rage for indiscriminate biographical reading' showed 'the frivolous taste of the present times', he was preparing the way for Boswell's uneasy successor. Lockhart himself christened his *Quarterly* career with his most acid pen:

'The classics of the *papier-maché* age of our drama have taken up the salutary belief that England expects every driveller to do his Memorabilia. Modern primer-makers must needs leave *confessions* behind them, as if they were so many Rousseaus. Our weakest mob-orators think it is a hard case if they cannot spout to posterity. Cabin-boys and drummers are busy with their commentaries *de bello Gallico*; . . . and thanks to "the march of intellect", we are already rich in the autobiography of pickpockets. . . . The mania for this garbage of Confessions, and Recollections, and Reminiscences, and Aniliana, "is indeed a vile symptom".'[9]

The 'march of intellect' and the new popularity of biography were profoundly connected. Noting at the turn of the century that 'the study of biography is a recent taste in Britain', the anecdotalist Isaac D'Israeli saw a change in the direction of philosophical inquiry: 'the human mind became the great object of our inquiry, and to separate the shades of the passions the great aim of the Biographer.' He was describing the same change Lockhart noted in fiction: 'What was darkly hinted by the profound philosophers of old, is now familiarly illustrated by the most popular creations of female fancy; and it is at last universally recognized, that the world of thought is the proper theatre of man.' D'Israeli, expanding on the new science of psychological differentiation, hints at the origin of this biographical and auto-biographical abundance.

'Every man, in whatever department he moves, has passions, which will vary even from those who are acting the same part as himself. Our souls, like our faces, bear the general resemblance of the species, but retain the particular form which is peculiar to the individual.'
The recording of human diversity is endless, and the evidence is as accessible as one's own examined life.

'He who studies his own mind, and has the industry to notedown the fluctuations of his opinions, the fallacies of his passions, and the vacillations of his resolutions, will form a journal to himself peculiarly interesting, and, probably, not undeserving the meditations of others.'[10]
The author of *Rambler 60* and *Idler 84* – who told Boswell, 'There is nothing, Sir, too little for so little a creature as man' – would agree. But D'Israeli's taste for the tulip's streaks and the forest's shades suggests what changes the passing of a generation had made in the uniformitarianism espoused by the humanist 'biographers' of Joseph Andrews and Rasselas.

One need not look hard to explain the biographical taste for psychological particularity. Some cultural historians would cite the collapse of old stabilities in a revolutionary world and the resultant appeal to individual experience as the only ground of value. Less controversial is Evangelicalism's stress on the religious value of introspection and personal commitment.[11] The phenomenon Ian Watt traces as the 'rise of the novel' may be broadened to constitute the rise of a biographical conception of historic and moral reality. Specifically, the tradition of Sensibility celebrated intense self-consciousness, acuteness and subtlety of personal response, as criteria of moral worth; and the related emergence of Gothic romance envisioned a more complex reality of individual experience under the stress of social and spiritual dilemma. Finally, there can be no shortage of explanations in a period which energetically controverted Locke's notions of consciousness and personal identity, or in the age of Kant's Copernican Revolution. Most intellectual activities conspired to generate this new 'age of ideology', with its stress on unique modes of experience and on the primacy in knowing of the appercipient subject.

Perhaps prior to all was the philosopher's recognition that particulars of individual consciousness possess 'the same kind of cognitive significance as any other body of empirical data'.[12] MacLean and others have traced the preoccupation of Enlightenment literature with the history of consciousness to the philosopher considered by the period to be Bacon's logical successor. The admiring Voltaire wrote of John Locke, 'So many philosophers having written the romance of the soul, a sage has arrived who has modestly written its history.' If Locke was responsible for fixing the characteristic Enlightenment conception of philosophy as 'a kind of scientific psychology', or its assumption that (in Hume's words) 'as the science of man is the only solid foundation for the other sciences, so the only solid foundation we can give to this science itself must be laid on experience and observation', then to Locke must go credit for the philosophical milieu in which biography would flourish.[13] But Romantic biography can be understood better as part of a general reaction against the Lockean Enlightenment.

For one thing, 'history' in Voltaire's adulatory phrase does not denote the process we think of. For the Romantic historiographer, right or wrong, 'history' in the true sense was unknown to the Lockean Enlightenment. The historian of psychology reminds us that for all Locke's concern with genesis, he 'does not describe a process that takes place in time; he has no idea of evolution'.[14] For the true Lockean, 'history of mind' could not yet have the meaning it had come to have for the confessor Rousseau by mid-century: 'the unbroken consciousness of my own existence', the successive revelation of 'the extravagances of my heart', the 'certain sequence of impressions and ideas which modify them' – in short, 'the history of my soul'.[15] And clearly, Locke neither alone nor in Hartley's company could account wholly for the complex spiritual evolution recorded in Wordsworth's autobiographical *Prelude*.

In a late Enlightenment context, it makes sense to refer the new biographical rage to the domestic reaction against Locke, significantly among those philosophers who spread the intuitionist philosophy of Common Sense and specifically (in the case of Dugald Stewart) constituted 'the most powerful formative influence upon the principles and tastes of a famous generation of literary Scotsmen'.[16] This was the tradition in 'moral philosophy' that produced such Glasgow collegians as Boswell and Lockhart, and it persisted in Stewart's brilliant successor Thomas Brown when Lockhart arrived in Edinburgh in 1815.

The conservative Lockhart, disciple of Johnson, Burke, and Coleridge, predictably went on record as an enemy of the speculative philosophy of the 'Edinburgh metaphysicians'. But his real quarrel, like that of Coleridge (whom he considered the most brilliant man of his age in Europe), was with the Lockean associationist. His attack was aimed at 'a mode of studying the human mind . . . perhaps better adapted for throwing light upon the intellectual faculties, and upon the association of ideas, than upon human nature in general'. Such study confers merely a 'calculating and mechanical' power – the Burkean Romantic is in evidence here; the Coleridgian in what follows: 'to suppose that man's moral being can ever be subjected to, or swayed by, a power so much lower than itself, is almost as revolting as the theory which refers all ideas and emotions to the past impressions on the senses.'[17]

No one was more insistent on man's moral dignity than the founder of the Common Sense school, Thomas Reid. No one was more deliberately anti-sensationalist: 'The merit of what you are pleased to call *my philosophy* lies, I think, chiefly in having called in question the common theory of ideas.' The mild and benign Dugald Stewart could be as fierce an anti-Hartleian as Coleridge: 'Many absurd theories have, indeed, at different times been produced by our countrymen; but I know of no part of Europe where such systems as those of Hartley and Bonnet have been so uniformly treated with the contempt they deserve as in Scotland.' Describing the anti-Lockean impulse of the Common Sense School, Victor Cousin implies what formative conceptions of human development the Scottish biographer acquired from his teachers in moral philosophy:

'The whole of English and French philosophy in the eighteenth century comes from Locke and its principle is *tabula rasa*. Reid grounded Scottish philosophy on the contrary principle and in so doing he raised himself above his century and from Scotland reached across to Königsberg. Kant in fact proposed, as Reid did, to establish in metaphysics and morals speculative and practical laws which depend on the constitution of human reason itself, laws which are not derived from experience and which alone make experience possible.'[18]

The self is no mere bundle of associated ideas; personal individuality is not to be dissipated analytically into mental states. As Reid says,

'My thoughts, and actions, and feelings, change every moment – they have no continued, but a successive existence; but that *self* or *I*, to which they belong, is permanent, and has the same relation to all the succeeding thoughts, actions, and feelings, which I call mine.'[19] Personal identity is not, as Locke claims, merely consciousness; personal identity is known intuitively – known, Coleridge would say, as the ground of all rational activity. The powers or faculties of the mind are constitutive, and they unfold in 'the gradual progress of man'. Thus, in Reid and his followers, writes W. R. Sorley, philosophy shifts its inquiry from 'the isolated impressions or ideas with which Locke and Hume began' to the experiential context, both subjective and objective: 'The simplest portion of our experience is not separate from its context in this way; it implies a reference to mind and to an objective order.'[20]

The shift is *prima facie* a rationale for biography. And the enthusiasts for biography persisted in their hopes for a new Baconian science of mind. Biography, said Stanfield, could 'collect materials for a moral and intellectual history of man', with Bacon its 'great master'. Lockhart's friend J. L. Adolphus opened his Oxford essay 'Biography' with a long epigraph from the *de Augmentis* and justified the genre in the same Baconian terms: it provided 'new facts in the moral history of man'. No late Enlightenment biographer commenced without some such justification, and no justification slighted such Baconian pretensions. The biographer's business, wrote Robert Bisset, is to collect data: 'Lord Bacon observes that history is either narrative or inductive. . . . Narrative history is the foundation of inductive. We must know particular facts before we can deduce from them general conclusions.' Thus, the biographer's aim was a copious particularity. 'Human nature, like a vast machine,' wrote Isaac D'Israeli, 'is not to be understood by looking on its superficies but by dwelling on its minute springs and wheels.'[21] The omission of any period or portion of a life might be detrimental. Irving was right to give the details of Columbus's early life, conceded Francis Jeffrey:

> 'when the whole grand series of sufferings and exploits has been unfolded, and the greatness of the event, and of the character with which it is inseparably blended, have been impressed upon our minds, we feel how necessary it was to tell, and how grateful it is to know, all that can now be known of the causes by which both were prepared.'[22]

Copious particularity is indispensable. Critics might urge a distinction between the trivial and the significant, but in practice a premature exclusiveness is ill-informed generalization: 'an anecdote, or a circumstance, which may appear inconsequential to a reader, may bear some remote or latent connexion, which a mature reflection often discovers.' It is safer for biographers to give everything 'than to permit themselves the power of rejection'. Better a heavy Birch or a prolix Hawkins 'than that any thing material which concerns a Tillotson or a Johnson should be lost'.[23]

By the same reasoning, the autobiographical mode of biography was to be preferred, for it gave the reader direct access to the particulars. Otherwise, he might expect only the generalizations of another. Adolphus attacked the pre-Boswellian characterologist's 'practice of suppressing the minute and familiar circumstances of a life' and of informing his readers 'only of the opinion which he himself entertains of a man whose conduct he had opportunities of observing'. On this basis Lockhart objected to the historiographer's 'custom of drawing a man's character at full length, when he first introduces him'. The alternative – the autobiographical mode – is to allow the character to present himself, and it is this alternative Lockhart claims for the *Life of Scott*:

'It was my wish to let the character develop itself: and conscious that I have wilfully withheld nothing that might assist the mature reader to arrive at just conclusions, I am by no means desirous of drawing out a detailed statement of my own.'[24]

But this would seem precisely the justification Boswell offers for delaying the collection 'into one view' of Johnson's 'capital and distinguishing features'. The terms are identical: 'The character of SAMUEL JOHNSON has, I trust, been so developed in the course of this work, that they who have honoured it with a perusal, may be considered as well acquainted with him.'[25] Are the great biographers of Enlightenment and Romanticism in fact indistinguishable? If not, then such similarities must be more apparent than real; and this is the case. Both Boswell and Lockhart aspired to copious particularity, and both were subjected to charges of confusing the essential and the trivial. Lockhart's critic Lord Cockburn echoes Boswell's enemies of forty years earlier:

'The author seems to have supposed that no further reason could be required for introducing anything whatever, except that it were true, and related to Sir Walter . . . selfish transactions and paltry thoughts, which were probably immaterial at the time, but are represented in this "Life" as fixed and essential parts of the man.'[26] But for the Enlightenment biographer, the particular truth was an illustration of essential character; for the Romantic, it was an organic symbol in the unfolding of personality. Likewise, both biographers aspired to autobiographical directness; but for one the ideal was dramatic and the character static, while for the other the ideal was narrative and the character dynamic.

We can recognize further the differences between Boswell's and Lockhart's intentions of letting 'character ... develop itself' by noticing Lockhart's addition: 'I am not going to "peep and botanize" upon his grave.' For in this refusal (and its quotation) Lockhart signals his fidelity to tenets of Romantic biographical theory which the Enlightenment Boswell could scarcely have recognized. The Words-worthian echo is natural in one who had early expressed distrust of the 'meddling intellect', of 'that false secondary power / By which we multiply distinctions'. Had the passage been available, Lockhart could only have agreed with Wordsworth's theory of autobiography:

> But who shall parcel out
> His intellect by geometric rules,
> Split like a province into round and square?
> Who knows the individual hour in which
> His habits were first sown, even as a seed?[27]

He might even have agreed with his admirer Carlyle, whose serio-comic pronouncements in *Sartor Resartus* on the biographical quest are in repudiation of Boswell's strenuous positivism:

'What are your historical Facts; still more your biographical? Wilt thou know a Man, above all a Mankind, by stringing-together bead-rolls of what thou namest Facts? The Man is the spirit he worked in; not what he did, but what he became. Facts are engraved Hiero-grams, for which the fewest have the key.'[28]

Even the despised enemy Hazlitt might have struck a responsive Romantic chord: 'Real character is not one thing, but a thousand things; actual qualities do not conform to any factitious standard in the mind, but rest upon their own truth and nature.'[29] In the company of such statements the differences between Boswell's and Lockhart's intentions may be understood.

Boswell's justification for allowing 'character' to 'develop itself' is given in his introduction: (*a*) it gives the liveliest and most perfect image, and (*b*) it avoids partiality or narrowness of view. The premises echo eighteenth-century aesthetic preferences for vividness and generality. 'Instead of melting down my materials into one mass, and constantly speaking in my own person,' Boswell will adopt Mason's 'more lively' autobiographical mode, thereby giving 'an accumulation of intelligence from various points by which his character is more fully understood and illustrated'. Copiousness and autobiographical immediacy, moreover, assuage Boswell's passionate desire to render an exact image of his subject's mind. 'The great lines of characters may be put down,' he complained in 1775. 'But I doubt if it be possible to preserve in words the peculiar features of mind which distinguish individuals as the features of different countenances.' And elsewhere the same frustration: 'it is impossible to clap the mind upon paper as one does an engraved plate, and to leave the full vivid impression.'[30] In the biographer's mind is a static, intricate individuality. The problem is how to communicate it. The attempt is the same gesture of good faith Rousseau makes to the reader of his *Confessions*. Rousseau and Boswell are alike representative Enlightenment characterologists, and Rousseau's terms likewise stress vividness and generality of view:

'I endeavour in all cases to explain the prime causes, in order to convey the interrelation of results. I should like in some way to make my soul transparent to the reader's eye, and for that purpose I am trying to present it from all points of view, to show it in all lights, and to contrive that none of its movements shall escape his notice, so that he may judge for himself of the principle which has produced them.'[31]

Now Rousseau is certainly not vulnerable to Stanfield's later strictures on biographers who slight formative stages and present their heroes in full maturity. Nevertheless, Stanfield's justification for copiousness differs significantly from Rousseau's:

'Unless the subject be followed through its windings, directions, abstractions, advancements, and attainments, so that we may have an intimate as well as comprehensive view of all its bearings and concerns, it is impossible to regard it with sympathy and attention. ... The ... characteristic individuality impressed on the *whole* course of conduct can only raise that interest, which lays hold of the feeling and judgement of the student.'[32]

We are no longer in enlightened search of a single 'principle' or of a dramatic completeness. We are seeking individuality impressed on a *whole course of conduct*; we are striving for intimacy of view as a ground for sympathy, and intimacy is to be gained only through the tracing of intricate development. Classical biography, writes Georg Misch, excluded 'any question of the development of character'. Its concern was with the 'unchanging ego of the fully matured human being'.[33] From start to finish Rousseau's aim is to portray and explain his unique, paradoxical self. His vivid and organic narrative may be remote from Boswell's annalistic drama, but in conception of character it is as close to the idea Misch describes as Boswell's portrayal of the mature Johnson.

The contrasting historicity of Lockhart's Scott is to be detailed elsewhere. Here we may simply cite Ian Jack's summary:

'we see the lame child becoming a boy, the boy becoming a young man with a passion for riding and picturesque excursions, the young man becoming a ballad-collector, the ballad-collector becoming an original writer, and so on to the end.'[34]

The *becoming* is not quite so simple. Just as Rousseau's essentialism often seems compromised by the pessimistic view that character progressively decays, so Lockhart's *becoming* must sometimes be that of the classical Aristotelian: *become what thou art*. The biographer must begin his study, after all, with the mature character. If he writes as the young friend of an older subject (Boswell, Lockhart, Stanley, Trevelyan, and others have done so), then his backward perspective is even more restricted. Yet for the Romantic biographer, conditioned as his understanding must be by his subject's mature character, the ethical emphasis is scarcely Aristotelian. If truth resides in the mature character, then early manifestations are of interest only in connection with that fulfilment. But the Romantic idealization of childhood innocence and piety places the truth elsewhere. The child is father of the man, and the man is tested by his fidelity to that childhood, by his 'natural piety'.

Throughout the early chapters of the *Life of Scott*, where Lockhart's governing theme appears to be the unity of Scott's personality, one may sense this ethical emphasis. Scott survived the process of development in his persistent innocence and gentleness. Having quoted Scott's schoolmate, Lockhart bears witness 'that exactly as the schoolboy still walks before her "mind's eye", his image rises familiarly to mine, who never saw him until he was past the middle of life: that I trace in every feature of her delineation, the same gentleness of aspect and demeanour'.[35]

Changed as well is Boswell's rhetorical concern with the complexity of character. Lockhart's problem is not just that of finding a descriptive language. The rhetorical frustration now merges with the larger sense of the mystery of the true self. Rousseau, like the author of *Idler 84*, is complacent in his assumption of self-knowledge; Wordsworth is not sure; the biographer of Teufelsdröckh pronounces the ultimate mystery of his subject. Stanley's preface to the *Life of Arnold* (1845) echoes Boswell's concern for setting down a vivid and exact image, but with a significant new scepticism:

'Some, indeed, there must be, who will painfully feel the contrast, which probably always exists in the case of any remarkable man, between the image of his inner life, as it was known to those nearest and dearest to him, and the outward image of a written biography, which can rarely be more than a faint shadow of what they cherish in their own recollections – the one representing what he was – the other only what he thought and did; the one formed in the atmosphere which he had himself created – the other necessarily accommodating itself to the public opinion to which it is mainly addressed.'[36]

In such company we can understand Lockhart's own retreat from the analytic complacency of the Enlightenment biographer. His is at once a gesture of orthodox religious humility and an expression of a Romantic distrust of the 'meddling intellect':

'We read in Solomon – "The heart knoweth his own bitterness, and a stranger doth not intermeddle with his joy." . . . Such considerations have always induced me to regard with small respect, any attempt to delineate fully and exactly any human being's character. I distrust, even in very humble cases, our capacity for judging our neighbour fairly; and I cannot but pity the presumption that must swell in the heart and brain of any ordinary brother of the race, when he dares to pronounce *ex cathedra*, on the whole structure and complexion of a great mind, from the comparatively narrow and scanty materials which can by possibility have been placed before him.'[37]

There is a further way to elucidate the differences of meaning between Boswell's and Lockhart's key statements of intention. Boswell's ideal was pictorial and dramatic. In keeping with the genetic emphasis of Romantic logic, Lockhart's was narrative, organic. Karl Kroeber grounds the Romantic 'delight in the narrative mode' in 'basic assumptions about the function of art and the nature of human life'. It reflects, he believes, a concern with 'the synthetic development of actions, with moral behaviour as a temporal process, rather than with the analysis of static situations'. Moreover,

> 'the inherent unity of narrative (in which everything is controlled by the narrator, is the expression of his grasp of events) was precious to these poets. . . . And, finally, we can say that the Romantics were pleased by the definiteness, the palpability of actions represented through narrative.'[38]

Lockhart's method ultimately confirms Kroeber's hypothesis. But the immediate origin of his narrative craft is easier to find. Lockhart became a biographer largely by chance; from his earliest literary aspirations, he was a novelist by choice. His published novels are four: *Valerius* (1821), *Adam Blair* (1822), *Reginald Dalton* (1823), *Matthew Wald* (1824). But his activities as writer and critic of fiction went on throughout his career. It is no accident he is charged with 'fictionalizing'. Like those of Carlyle, another novelist turned biographer-historian, Lockhart's ideas of narrative form, effect, and even 'truth' are governed by the norms of the novel and not, like Boswell's, by those of the forensic dramatist. Lockhart's theory of fiction is richer than his theory of biography, and it is there that we find his fullest conceptions of narrative 'character', 'development', and form.

Much Romantic theory of fiction seems a logical development of Johnson's view that the only interesting history is history of manners. But between *Joseph Andrews* and *Castle Rackrent* (1800), the meaning of the term had undergone a striking change. Fielding's distinction is well-known: 'I describe not men, but manners; not an individual, but a species.' The biographer is distinguished by his generality; his 'facts' are neither the antiquarian's data nor the transcendentalist's hieroglyphs, but the rational empiricist's timeless principles of human nature: 'the facts we deliver may be relied on, though we often mistake the age and country wherein they happened.' As Lockhart uses Boswell's terms with new meaning, so Maria Edgeworth uses Fielding's. Old Thady's narrative has its value in the truth of manners; but manners are local and ephemeral:

> 'Those who are acquainted with the manners of a certain class of the gentry of Ireland some years ago, will want no evidence of the truth of honest Thady's narrative: to those who are totally unacquainted with Ireland, the following Memoirs will perhaps be scarcely intelligible.'[39]

The change is the more marked for the sameness of terms. Fielding and Lockhart both glorify Cervantes for his portrayal of 'manners' as 'the true historian of Spain'. For Fielding, Mariana is 'confined to a particular period of time, and to a particular nation', while Cervantes is the historian of the world in general. For Lockhart, the greatness of *Don Quixote* lies instead in the vivid fullness of its locality, its cultural authenticity, its 'perfect and glowing' picture of national manners.[40] Lockhart, like other Romantic apologists for fiction, frequently prized the novel as the history of manners, cultural history. He shared the time's widespread conviction that 'any variety, any curious aspect, of human existence cried out for its novelist'.[41] For one instance, he urged Washington Irving to undertake novels on the Edgeworth or Scott plan 'illustrative of the present state of manners in the United States of America'. Irving had the priceless *donnée* of cultural inter-play:

'the picturesque mixtures of manners derived from German, Dutch, English, Scottish, Swedish, Gothic, and Celtic settlers . . . the immense interfusion of different ranks of society from all these quarters, and their endless varieties of action upon each other.'

Irving's was 'the true *terra fortunata* of the novelist'.[42]

Lockhart's view of fiction as cultural history is evident in the youth-ful would-be novelist's plans for 'a receptacle of an immense quantity of anecdotes and observations I have made concerning the state of the Scotch, chiefly their clergy and elders. It is to me wonderful how the Scotch character has been neglected.' It is apparent in his collecting of 'any little odd tags, rags, and bobtails of good incidents' to be worked into 'graphical little scenes' for the preservation of Caledonian manners.[43] It is manifest in the Romans of *Valerius*, genre figures in a network of 'social and domestic relations' and in a drama of philo-sophical conflict set in the melancholy milieu of a dying paganism. The picaresque *Matthew Wald* offers a frame for manners survey. The genre pictures, set in significant contrast, are components of milieu: the pretensions of foolish or false peers, the fopperies of Highland hunting lodge and London parliamentary circle, the intellectual rest-lessness of High Street law. *Reginald Dalton*, Lockhart's fullest sketch of contemporary manners, evolves in genre pictures of north country squirearchy, Lake District vicarage, academic Oxford, and high society London. Even in the most psychologically focused of the novels, *Adam Blair*, cultural typology, carefully controlled, is paramount. Mrs

Semple is the epitome of a vanishing natural nobility. John Maxwell the elder is the cultivated Scottish peasant, loyal and pious, a conception central later to Lockhart's interpretation of the Burns milieu. Maxwell represents 'the habitudes and feelings of the religious and virtuous peasantry of the west of Scotland half a century ago' – the milieu within which alone Adam Blair's ordeal has meaning. Lockhart is not merely recording manners, to be sure; his record is informed by a theme familiar to the reader of *The Waste Land*. He has portrayed an ideal past society within which moral tragedy was conceivable. But it is a cultural mimesis he claims at the last: 'I have told a TRUE STORY. I hope the days are yet far distant when it shall be doubted in Scotland that such things might have been.'[44]

The imaginative rendition of milieu and cultural type, dominated by a cultural view of history and morality, marks Lockhart as Romantic novelist and theorist of fiction. Between the representative Enlighten-ment radical and the 'reactionary' of the Germano-Coleridgian school, wrote John Stuart Mill, there arose the epochal idea of culture. If Lockhart differs from the Enlightenment biographer in his anti-analytic preference for organic narrative revelation, he differs as basically in his cultural conception of biographical subject and milieu. And when the novelist crosses the thin line between genres to become the biographer, the same conception of historical authenticity controls biographical recreation. For him, the genres overlap in their fidelity to cultural truth. The world owed Boswell much, he wrote, 'if it were but for having given us, ere it was too late, a complete portrait of the real uncontaminated Englishman, with all his tastes and prejudices fresh and strong about him'. The obligation would be unchanged, he added, 'even if it were possible to consider Boswell's delineation of Samuel Johnson merely as a character in a novel of that period'.[45] If Johnson was a supreme 'manners' figure, so was Scott, and Lockhart thought of them together. 'I am very sincerely rejoiced,' he wrote Peel,

> 'that this last Bust of Scott is in the same collection with Reynolds' last picture of Johnson – and that they are both to be heirlooms in your house for I fancy posterity may be apt to consider the one as the last specimen of the pure Englishman and the other as the *ultimus Scotorum* – so rapidly are the nations now blending.'[46]

Here, rather than in any superficial problem of reticence or palliation, is the significant question of 'truth' in the Lives of Burns and Scott. It may or may not be that 'Boswell had a mind neither original nor powerful enough to distort actual events to fit a preconception or a spiritual need'.[47] Lockhart had that power. It is arguable to what extent Boswell's preoccupation with the moralistic Rambler distorted his vision of Johnson. But it is demonstrable that Lockhart's Scott was indeed preconceived, though not necessarily 'untrue'. Had Scott not existed, Lockhart the novelist as cultural historian would have had to create him. He began the process in *Peter's Letters to His Kinsfolk* (1819). The extent to which he continued in the *Life* is a topic for later speculation.

Meanwhile, if contemporary theory assigned the novel and biography alike the tasks of cultural history, it ceded them superiority in psychological description as well. Reviewing Godwin, Lockhart attributed the rise of the novel to a deepening of interest in psychological events. 'The hero of a modern romance is not the victim either of implacable destiny, or of outward injury; the revolutions of his fate are all engendered within himself . . . ; it is at last universally recognized, that the world of thought is the proper theatre of man.' The 'new species' purports to exhibit 'the internal growth and progress of sentiments and passions, and their conflicts'. It alone is equipped to do so, and therefore, whatever the excellences of drama, the future belongs to the 'romance' of character. Lockhart's praise of Godwin is indicative; his contrast of Godwin and Scott recalls Johnson's contrast of Richardson and Fielding. And the reference to Godwin's 'deep and pathetic knowledge of the human heart', as well as the monomaniacal character of Matthew Wald, identifies Lockhart the novelist with the 'Gothic' strain of Richardsonian sensibility.[48]

Whatever his models, Lockhart's novels evidence an acute inteerst in fine psychological discrimination and in the portrayal of complex and dynamic emotional states. Lockhart had once mourned 'the departed play genius of Britain' – 'the whole art of delineating the delicate mixtures of human character. We have now no specimens of contradictory beings such as Nature makes'[49] – and his novels seek to restore the art and the vision. Most memorable in them are morally complex and unpredictable characters, no longer young and not quite innocent. One thinks of Lascelyne, in *Wald*, never quite the fop or the melodramatic villain that Wald makes him out. One thinks of the Scots solicitor in *Dalton*, capable of all sorts of meanness for the sake of the son, who, torn among love, friendship, and loyalty, is forced to betray him. There is the other father, Catline, repulsively fearful, who suddenly rises to momentary nobility at the end, and shrinks from it as swiftly as does Captain Campbell, in *Blair*, after *he* has bestowed forgiveness on the penitent minister responsible for Mrs Campbell's seduction and death. Most notable, there is Charlotte Campbell herself, the woman of sensibility, who, having loved and lost Blair before, having been his wife's closest friend, having lost most of her worldly respectability, comes back to console him, to recover something of her lost self, unconsciously to win him, to hide from the world of Captain Campbell – who, in short, acts from a complexity of motives of which she has little awareness.

Also prominent are delineations of complex and fluctuating emotional states. Examples may be found in Valerius's attempts to define his feelings in the face of a cruel, melancholy Rome and a new faith which he cannot understand; in the repulsive objectifications of the fallen Blair's moral horror; in the insanely contradictory responses of Wald; and in the interminable surges of familial shame in that young man of feeling, Dalton. The 'new species', for Lockhart, is especially suited to trace 'the internal growth and progress of sentiments and passions, and their conflicts'. And this is what his novels, for all their cultural typology, do.

This is what Lockhart praises in the fiction of others as well. The Mignon of *Wilhelm Meister*, for example, is something of an ideal in narrative characterization:

> 'It is now that the character of this girl begins to develope itself, in a manner the conception of which attests the full mastery of the genius of Goethe. The innocent ignorance and gaiety of childhood begins to be blended with a more than womanly depth of sentiment and passion. . . . The bud expands at once into full flower – and that very moment all its leaves are forever scattered. Jealousy, in short, grows up from the same roots.' [50]

Organically the character 'develops itself'. The phrase means the same when he applies it to biographical narrative. The metaphor of organic development had been invoked as a biographical ideal at the opening of the century:

> 'In contemplating the character of an eminent man, it is delightful to observe the first germination and gradual development of the seed of greatness, to behold it raise its slender growth in the shade of obscurity and retirement, nourished by the dew of instruction, strengthened by the blasts of discipline.' [51]

And speaking in 1818 of Mignon's creator and his autobiography, Lockhart used it for his own definition of biographical characterization as the tracing of a full and organic movement of spirit. 'It was no wonder,' he wrote, that the Germans should

'listen without weariness to the history of a mind from which there had sprung so many wonders. The more minute the details, the more close the descriptions, it was the better for their purpose; for no details and no descriptions could be without their use which might tend to record the gradual development of faculties and ideas to which they owed so much. . . . Let us imagine with what delight we should ourselves peruse an easy and copious biography of any of our own great departed worthies, – or, if the time were come, with what gratitude we should read a minute story of the mode in which the spirit of Scott or Byron had been fashioned.'[52]

The theorist of fiction was father to the Romantic biographer.

The 'minute story' of the fashioning of a spirit must, however, be effectively formed; and here, too, in the mastery of narrative form, Lockhart's experience as novelist and novel critic served the biographer well. To succeed as cultural and psychological portrayal, Lockhart insisted, fiction must succeed as narrative art; and as critic in a period of slipshod imitation and experiment, he had ample opportunity to stress the importance of imagination as a formative power in fiction. The followers of Scott imagined 'that a few scraps of blundered antiquarianism, a prophetical beldame, a bore, and a rebellion, are enough to make a Waverley novel'. The 'Silver-fork' novelists (the Hook-Bulwer-Ward-Disraeli set), second of the prevalent classes of 'brainless as well as heartless novelwrights', had also lost sight of 'the primary principle of all works of art', supposing 'imitation, simply *qua* imitation, will do'. The great formal principle of narrative art is imaginative integrity. In the classics of romance, the 'high faculties of imagination' enabled authors 'to fuse their materials of all kinds into an artist-like unity of form and purpose'. Contemporary 'novelwrights' lack such architectonic power, and the same deficiency shows, said Lockhart, in biographical and historical compilation:

'A note-book of reminiscences and anecdotes, however rich, will no more enable a man of feeble imagination to make a novel, than a collection of state-papers and annual registers will enable a man who has no philosophical grasp and scope of intellect, to produce a history.'[53]

But to understand Lockhart's complex preoccupation with biographical form, we must recognize the heat of contemporary controversy over the use and abuse of biographical materials.

II

When biography acquired prestige as contributor to a new 'science of man', it also acquired champions as a literary genre. But ironically, the new champions found the old 'scientists' wanting in art. Boswell, who had likened his work to the *Odyssey* with the hero 'never long out of sight', would have been dismayed at Sir James Stephen's charge half a century after:

> 'Boswell, the prince of biographers, has well nigh ruined the art of biography. . . . [The] artist must aim at unity of effect, and must therefore bring all the subordinate parts of his design into a tributary dependence on his principal subject.'[54]

To understand Stephen's remark, we must realize that Boswell had assumed not just a princely but a representative status in a general controversy.

'Modern composition,' Stanfield warned in 1813, 'from a superabundance of materials, and from facility of access to them, frequently suffers more under this redundancy than is perceived in the coherent and individual representations of former times.'[55] The prestige of biography has opened new mines and quarries; the art has been left in lumpish hands. The diagnosis is familiar in the twentieth century: 'With us the most delicate and humane of all the branches of the art of writing had been relegated to the journeymen of letters.'[56] The same diagnosis was made in 1799 by a reviewer enthusiastic about 'this pleasing and popular branch of human knowledge'. Of the numerous biographers,

> 'perhaps fewer have excelled than in any other branch of literature. Some have collected facts which they committed to paper without order of selection; . . . Some have been impartial, but have been indolent in research, and destitute of discrimination; while many have brought to their task impartiality, industry, and good sense, but have wanted taste, learning, and skill in composition.'[57]

Carlyle's figure for the journeyman bookmaker in biography is familiar:

> 'Stone is laid on the top of stone, just as it comes to hand; a trowel or two of biographic mortar, if perfectly convenient, being spread in

here and there, by way of cement; and so the strangest pile suddenly arises, amorphous, pointing every way but to the zenith, here a block of granite, there a mass of pipe-clay; till the whole finishes, when the materials are finished; – and you leave it standing to posterity, like some miniature Stonehenge, a perfect architectural enigma.'[58]

The figure had been anticipated in 1801 by a Critical Reviewer who found Malone's *Dryden* 'a ponderous and tasteless mass, composed of sand and stone, and marble, and rubbish, with very little mortar to hold it all together'.[59]

The reception accorded Malone's *Dryden* signals a strong formalist reaction against antiquarian copiousness; the butt was a biographer of whom John Garraty recently said, 'literary artistry and imagination fell before his all-consuming interest in minutiae and his tendency to digress into a dozen obscure byways'.[60] Such was popular derision at Malone's 'laborious trifling and scraps of nonsense'[61] that a satiric pamphlet, *The Essence of Malone*, published in 1800, went into a second enlarged edition the same year. Its comic complaints make a manifesto against formlessness in biography. Its pseudonymous author reflects that

> 'it was reserved for this age to reverse the maxim "that no man was a hero to his *valet de chambre*", by admitting *no other heroes* into the Temple of Genius and Fame. . . . we think it a loss irreparable to our luminaries, and consider them as half "shorn of their beams", unless we can be as minute in their epitome, as the man was in his, who said, "Got up at half-past eight – hands but not face."'

His reaction is less against excessive revelation than against unselectivity and formlessness. From Malone's excesses he formulates ironic new canons for biographers. He recommends copiousness in trifles, indiscriminate inclusion of secondary subjects, and close attention to the 'negative history of a man's life': 'It has been said, "*Ex nihilo nihil fit*"; not such is the Malonian edifice upon that interesting substratum.' And Boswell's significance in all this is indicated by his company in the pamphlet's dedication to

> 'Coryat, Dutch critics, George Steevens, all other Editors of "Shakspere" . . . the Society of Antiquaries – the late facetious, though light moralist, James Boswell, Esq. or those amiable gossips, Mr Spence, Bishop Newton, Mrs Piozzi, and other bluestocking writers of Memoirs.'[62]

C

Lockhart was a generation late to join in the controversy. But his position is easily inferred. As a biographer, he has been subjected to the same charges of formlessness. Yet in 1831 he complained that Scott, in amassing annotative material for his Lives of Dryden and Swift, 'never seems to have even suspected that if information be the first requisite in an annotator, a second, and scarcely, in the case of a voluminous author, a less important one, is compression'.[63] And in his review of Prior's *Goldsmith,* on the eve of publication of *The Life of Scott,* the values of Malone's formalistic critic are evident:

'We could hardly praise too highly the sagacity and patience with which Prior has hunted every hint of information, whether oral or documentary, but he has seldom shown skill in his manner of putting together the results. . . . His episodic chapters on Goldsmith's obscure literary associates and forgotten antagonists should have been first cut down very considerably – and then thrown into so many articles of an appendix; and the new and valuable illustrations of the early career of Burke, which he has crammed head and shoulders into the midst of Goldsmith's story, should have been reserved for another edition of his Life of Burke.'[64]

The formalist reaction behind his criticism may best be seen in three areas of contemporary critical discussion: the increasingly problematical distinction between history and biography; the controversy over the uses of personal letters; and the post-Boswell assessment of conversational anecdote.

The eighteenth century, we are told, 'performed a useful service' in completing the separation of biography and history, or freeing biography 'from the trammels of history proper'.[65] Yet we seem to see the extravagant persistence of the old confusion in Godwin's *Chaucer,* a work which opened the new century and initiated the 'Life and Times' form of such giants as Masson's *Milton.* In fact, the confusion is less old than new.

The most prominent of critics urged the traditional distinction. When public history is unavoidable, says Stanfield, 'the principal figure must be kept ostensibly before us, and care taken that the individual character be never lost in the crowd of surrounding circumstances'. Southey had frequent occasion as a reviewer for upholding the distinction. In Nugent's *Memorials of John Hampden,* for example, the hero is 'mixed up' with 'the view of the times', and 'a more ill-arranged epitome than that view we have seldom seen'. Jeffrey criticizes

Caulfield's biographer Hardy for enlarging upon 'matters of general history, with which Lord Charlemont has no other connexion, than that they happened during his life'. Curran's filial memoirist is likewise at fault: 'The limits of the private and the public story are not very well observed; nor the scale of the work very correctly regulated as to either; so that we have alternatively too much and too little of both.' Scott complains that the central figure in Godwin's *Chaucer* 'is dimly discoverable in the background, obscured and overshadowed by the motley groups of abbeys, castles, colleges, and halls, fantastically portrayed around it'; he can find neither 'unity' nor 'individuality' in 'so whimsical a performance'. He disapproves, too, of Boaden's 'blending the Memoirs of Kemble with an account of the theatre, so general, diffuse, and disproportioned in length to the pages which the life of his proper hero occupies'. The hero is scarcely more than what D'Israeli called 'the senseless phantom of the annalist'; his personal history is cut up 'like the body of an old man cut and ready for Medea's kettle'. Biography must have its own integrity distinct from history.[66]

Lockhart recognized the difficulties inherent in the traditional distinction. With his sense of character in milieu, he saw that any public life 'presses so closely on history, that to draw the necessary line of distinction between the two walks is not the work of ordinary judgement and taste'. The separation is nevertheless a formal necessity. The biographers of Sheridan are at fault 'in writing the Life of Sheridan so much as if they had been composing the political history of his times'. Both works are deficient in biographical matter because

'the stateliness of their historical vein stoops reluctantly to even the occasional record of the personal adventures and domestic habits of their hero, although these were precisely the matters that ought to have occupied the chief part of their attention.'[67]

The biographer of Napier of Merchiston 'has overlaid his memoir with circumstances possessing but the thinnest and most fanciful connexion with its proper subject', and attempted to compensate for an ignorance of Napier's early education with 'the histories and characters of the other afterwards eminent persons who must have been educated at the same time', and 'an account of the origin and primitive institutes of his university'.[68] Biography and general history must be kept distinct for the integrity of both, insists Lockhart:

'A work concentrating the whole interest round an individual, and treating events not in proportion to their actual importance, but to their connection with that one person, can never adequately supply the place of a general history.'[69]

The focus and proportion of biography necessarily distort history. Lockhart faced this dilemma with bold sophistication when he under-took the *History of Napoleon*.

But however general the critics' resistance, new developments in historiographical style and taste complicated the distinction, until the formal integrity of biography became problematic indeed. The develop-ments may be summarized simply: personality became historic in con-ception; and history became increasingly personal. Southey quotes the passage in which Godwin defines historic personality as an individual point of view in a specific milieu:

'We must observe what Chaucer felt and saw, how he was educated, what species of learning he pursued, and what were the objects, the events, the persons successively presented to his view, before we can strictly and philosophically understand his biography.'[70]

Theoretically, personality as conceived by the cultural historian cannot be reconstructed without a full imaginative grasp of the milieu.

Moreover, personality so conceived provided a new range of bio-graphical subjects; as Ian Jack notes, 'People were beginning to realize that they might be interesting because they were 'typical' of some-thing or other, even if they were not famous or exceptionally gifted.'[71] The taste for cultural typology so pronounced in Lockhart was wide-spread. Jeffrey found the *Life of Curran* of limited interest as an individual portrait, but of considerable value as a picture of manners, casting light on 'the national character and state of society in Ireland' and affording 'continual illustrations . . . of their diversity from our own'.[72] The *Life of Sir Astley Cooper* has, says Lockhart, its principal merit 'in the clear light it throws on the actual life – the daily existence – of a first-rate London surgeon'. More than one hundred pages is given to the description of one professional group, the 'body-snatchers': 'We cannot deny that the biographer might justly consider this subject within his province; . . . nevertheless, we must wish the affair had not been dealt with in such detail.' Yet, the 'picture of the traffic' is of interest for cultural history, and therefore its inclusion is justified in a work whose main interest is historical, however biographical its frame.[73] Lockhart's penchant for cultural typology persists to create structural problems even in his great personal biography. Sophia

Lockhart wrote in 1836 of the progress of the *Scott*, 'I am much mistaken if anything in our time will come up to it in interest, style, or as a picture of manners just passing away.'[74] But the new 'personal' element in historical taste confused the biography-history distinction in another way.

When Lockhart wrote to Constable in 1825, 'I am of opinion that much is to be done by throwing the materials of History into the ever attractive form of Biography',[75] he was echoing a general recognition of the convenience of biographical form in non-biographical exposition. Southey conceded that Telford the civil engineer 'was advised to indite his work in some degree biographically, writing in the first person, as more agreeable to the reader, easier to himself, and not requiring classification of subjects'.[76] The decision permits the substitution of personal narrative for impersonal analysis. Lockhart praised Campbell's *Lives of the Chancellors*: 'He has managed to reproduce general history in a series of professional biographies, without almost ever exposing himself to the charge of trespassing beyond the bounds of his avowed province.'[77] The very theorists who insisted on the distinction were finding new reasons to blur it.

The biographizing of history had been a revolution in taste, which found only late expression in Carlyle's assertion that history itself is the sum of innumerable biographies. History otherwise conceived was rendered ineffectual by its decorums. The philosophic historian of the Enlightenment, charged his Romantic critics, conveyed only the reality of his own judicial intellect. Coleridge could find no visible image of the past in Gibbon. Universality and intellectual detachment had robbed Hume, said John Foster, of 'the art of infusing into the scenes a moral interest which shall command the passions'. The past, pronounced Carlyle – the 'bygone ages of the world . . . filled by living men' – is to be understood not by the owl-blind philosophic historian hooting from his tree-top, but by the imaginative participant, roused to concrete sympathetic vision. It is difficult to identify the immediate causes of the revolution in historiography, but one seems to be the growing taste for and availability of memoir, and the consequent recognition of historical value in the very personality of memoir. Jeffrey phrased it best in his reference to

'the great and growing store of those contemporary notices which are every day familiarizing us more and more with the *living character* of by-gone ages; and without which we begin at last to be

sensible, that we can neither *enter into their spirit* nor even understand their public transactions.'[78]
Personal history, history biographized, the unadulterated record of the
immediate pressure of history on a present sensibility, could best do
historiography's work.

The growing taste for memoir was part of a general taste for the
historical picturesque, at once cause and effect of the popularity of
romance in the Waverley mode. Commentators lauded the Pepyses,
the Madame Junots, the diarizing peninsular subalterns for their
graphic minutiae – for 'picturesque truth of detail', for 'those minute
details . . . which History has so often rejected as below her dignity
. . . [which] are indispensable to give life, certainty, or reality to her
delineations'.[79] The picturesque is prized as a mark of authenticity
peculiar to memoir. 'The value of memoirs,' says Croker:

> 'consists in their authenticity; that is, not merely in the *abstract*
> truth of the facts, or in the intrinsic justice of the observations, but
> in their giving the facts and observations as they appeared to, or
> proceeded from, the individual named on their title page.'[80]

The unsophisticated impressions of an eye-witness have the peculiar
value of psychological immediacy, and thus (says Jeffrey), 'are the only
memorials in which the true form and pressure of the ages which produce them are ever completely preserved'.[81] The past as psychological
'form and pressure' must be known dramatically, through description
possessing (says Adolphus) 'that peculiar energy which only experience
can inspire'.[82] The Duchesse d'Angoulême's account of the flight to
Varennes is most authentic; its naivetés of form and logic, says Croker,
'attest its authenticity, and forcibly impress on our minds the cruel
circumstances of perplexity and anxiety under which it was written'.[83]
Lockhart praises Gleig's Peninsular Subaltern for having had 'the good
sense to describe nothing but what he did witness' and yet compelling
himself 'to record not only what he did but what he felt'.

> 'What would we not give to have the great civil war of England . . .
> painted by an eye-witness, with that expansion and picturesque
> truth of detail which this Subaltern has bestowed upon one little
> fragment of the peninsular campaigns.'[84]

The authenticity may well be accompanied by utter unreliability of
fact, even by deliberate falsification. The great contemporary case in
point is cited by Croker:

> 'In the voluminous memoirs dictated by Buonaparte to his followers

at St Helena, many of the facts are notoriously false, and most of the commentaries are studiously delusive; but the memoirs are not, on that account, less characteristic of the author, less entertaining to the casual reader, or less important to the critical history of the man.'[85] Lies or not, the 'personality' is first-hand and authentic. Indeed, 'personality' – the usurpation of truth by the partiality of the eye-witness – is identified with authenticity. The Margrave of Bareth writes her memoirs in 'the vulgar gossiping style of a chambermaid', but half the edification of her book, says Jeffrey,

'consists in the lights it affords as to the character of the writer, and consequently as to the effects of the circumstances in which she was placed: nor is there anything, in the very curious picture it presents, more striking than the part she unintentionally contributes, in the peculiarity of her own taste in the colouring and delineation.'[86]

Partiality and commitment, in repudiation of the Enlightenment historian's ideals, are accepted as inevitable, then cherished as appropriate and authentic. Lockhart calls the vain Mme Junot a 'prying, tattling, and indelicate, but shrewd and clever flirt' who could only be a 'Frenchwoman exactly of this particular class and time'. The triviality of her perspective gives her account a minute clarity impossible for 'maturer observers': 'They give broad sketches of horror – she deals in foregrounds, where every touch is sharp, every rueful detail in relief.'[87]

The first publication of another memoir, one of several from the seventeenth century unearthed during this 'age of personality', occasioned a full discussion of the paradoxical requirements for effective memoir. The discussion illustrates further that memoir was increasingly prized for values which make form in biography undesirable and generic integrity impossible. The reviewers of Samuel Pepys agreed that memoirs are valuable *because* they lack dignity, proportion, form. 'A disposition to idle gossip is an essential ingredient in a memoir-writer.' Pepys is a trustworthy 'mirror of his age' precisely because his 'mind was not formed for the entertainment of expansive generalities'. Had Pepys been able to edit his diary with discrimination, suggests the *Westminster*, the value would have fled:

'the "Memoirs of Samuel Pepys, Esq." would have come forth into the world, invested with a gravity and decorum due to the rank of a "high official situation"; and deprived of all or most of those singular confessions, unconscious exhibitions of character, and pieces of private and ministerial intelligence, which give them a rare and inestimable value.'

Jeffrey recognizes in Pepys' 'credulity' and 'twaddle', a providential fusion of personality and vantage point which insured copiousness. 'The most extraordinary activity, and the most indiscriminating, in-satiable, and miscellaneous curiosity, that ever prompted the researches or supplied the pen of a daily chronicler' are qualities for which Jeffrey would not wish the work 'a page shorter'. Scott concen-trates on the 'character' of the 'unwearied, universal learner – and hence chronicler', and explicitly anticipates Macaulay's Boswellian paradox:

> 'Pepys' very foibles have been infinitely in favour of his making an amusing collection of events; as James Boswell, without many per-sonal peculiarities, could not have written his inimitable life of Johnson.'[88]

Scott's review of Pepys implies how the mixture of history and biography in memoir contributes to the formal dilemmas of the Romantic biographer. He insists that memoirs be published without expurgation. The hint of imperfection, the 'restless suspicion that something has been kept back' by the editor, he suggests, diminishes our confidence in 'the character of his materials'. Not that the 'some-thing' is missed for its informative value; rather, it 'would have rendered the whole more piquant'. Documentary completeness is a dramatic or picturesque value. Excisions even on grounds of moral delicacy may cause 'actual injustice to the characters handled by the author, the self-supplied key to whose character and dispositions is thus mutilated and impaired'.[89] The unconscious self-revelation of memoirist or diarist is not to be impaired by the intrusion of another tone, whether that of editor or biographer.

This important premise is invoked by Lockhart in his praise of another private journal (Sir Jahleel Brenton's):

> 'In every page . . . some charming trait is added to the portraiture of the man, and the religious meditations set down from day to day . . . are so touching in their simplicity that we wonder anybody could have the heart to imbed them in a commentary.'[90]

It determines his attitude towards the editing of Boswell's *Johnson*; everything which gives 'individuality' should be kept in the text, even juvenile verses and legal opinions:

> 'Even these, as presented by Bozzy, give great individuality to the

narration. They keep before us the relative positions of the Doctor and his biographer . . . in all highly illustrative of his good nature and sympathy with his boring friend.'[91] Finally, it helps explain his editorial reserve as biographer in using Scott's diaries. The value of the long 1814 tour journal is in its unconscious personality, he holds, and would only be diminished by the biographical editor's intrusions: 'I question if any man ever drew his own character more fully or more pleasingly than Scott has done in the preceding diary of a six weeks' pleasure voyage.'[92] Yet in its copious substance the journal is almost wholly impersonal. Where, then, is selectivity possible, and how can form be achieved?

The same dilemmas emerge in the controversy over the 'Mason method', the making of 'autobiography' out of private letters. The deliberately self-analytic letter presents no problems; the biographer can recognize and use the relaxed epistolary egocentricity Gibbon described: 'We all delight to talk of ourselves, and it is only in letters, in writing to a friend, that we can enjoy that conversation, not only without reproach, or interruption, but with the highest propriety, and mutual satisfaction.'[93] The difficulty arises with the Romantic anti-rhetorical bias for the 'self overheard', unconscious self-revelation, as more significant and reliable. Personality is sought in the indirect revelations of style. 'The most interesting traits,' wrote Jeffrey, 'are those which are unintentionally discovered, and which the reader collects from expressions that were employed for very different purposes.'[94] Here, the writer reveals what Scott calls the 'various tones of feeling and modes of mind.' Such expressions often occur in letters topically irrelevant. But their 'personality' justifies their inclusion.

That is, inclusion without ostensible abridgement. What Southey calls the 'strong impression of authenticity' in personal documents depends on a dramatic wholeness which extracting or epitomizing would destroy. The document must convey the heat of its occasion, show ideas growing still in the garden of the mind, thoughts captured (says Scott) 'while the gold is yet rude ore'.[95] Macaulay sums up the age's taste for documentary authenticity:

'We love, we own, to read the great productions of the human mind as they were written. We have this feeling even about scientific treatises. . . . What man of taste and feeling can endure *rifacimenti*, harmonies, abridgements, expurgated editions?'[96]

Lockhart agrees that documentary abridgements are intolerable:

'This age has two propensities in literature which have not as yet been *gratified together* – the one is to get at the marrow of the matter without the bone, that is, to have the substance only of what has been written: the other is to have as much as possible of the original Manner of the old writers. Now abridgements hitherto leave the latter of these wishes utterly unsatisfied.'[97]

Maria Edgeworth, writing to Lockhart, similarly associates authenticity with dramatic wholeness. Letters ought not to be published without editing, and yet editing is no remedy: 'Garbling – destroys the value – not only the texture – but the value of wholeness – the integrity – the unity of purpose – sentiment – mind.'[98] This dilemma grew as the editions of letters proliferated, and as the abundance of excellent letters fostered the 'modern fashion' in biography.

The year after his *Cowper* (1803) appeared, Hayley acknowledged the cause of its great popularity by issuing a third quarto of new letters, prefaced by some 'Desultory Remarks on the Letters of Eminent Persons'. The preface emphasizes, in what Jeffrey called these 'genuine Relics of the individual', the 'stamp' of an 'intellectual and personal character'. This 'stamp', said Stanfield, made correspondence the most 'satisfactory materials for biographic composition', and as such it was essential that they display 'the private views, passions, prejudices, and interests' of the subject.[99] For Hayley, Pope's letters were valuable in this respect:

'they exhibit extraordinary specimens of mental power, and a contemplative spirit in very early youth: they show the progress of a tender, powerful, and irritable mind, in its acquaintance with polished life; the delights it enjoyed; the vexations it endured; the infirmities it contracted.'[100]

To Pope's 'elegant . . . universal secrets', Hazlitt preferred 'what is spoken aside, as it were, and without consciousness of being heard'. For him, Gray's letters are 'the finest, perhaps, in our language', and in Cowper's letters 'we see the fluctuations of all his melancholy nature more plainly than in all the biographical dissertations of his affectionate editor'. Moreover, it is a supremely fluctuating epistolary 'nature' that interests Hazlitt most. He gives this impressionistic epitome of the epistolary Horace Walpole:

'He could not get a plain thought out of that cabinet of curiosities, his mind; – and he had no room for feeling – no place to plant it in, or leisure to cultivate it. He was at all times the slave of elegant trifles;

and could no more screw himself up into a decided and solid person-age, than he could divest himself of petty jealousies and miniature animosities.'[101]

The elegant Walpole proved oddly fascinating to Romantic critics who prized spontaneity. No one mistook Walpole's epistolary intentions, least of all Lockhart:

'Lord Lansdowne told me yesterday that his Aunt Ossory told him Walpole called on her daily when they were in town but if anything happened that was of any interest he omitted his visit that he might not miss the pretext for telling it in writing and on such occasions the Gout uniformly had been threatening him.'[102]

Yet Walpole's fame as an epistolary artist grew steadily. Helping to spread it, Scott once more anticipated Macaulay's paradoxical praise of Boswell: 'The peculiarities and even the foibles of Horace Walpole's character, were such as led to excellence in this style of composition.'[103] For Macaulay, Walpole was 'a mannerist whose manner has become perfectly easy to him. His affectation is so habitual and so universal that it can hardly be called affectation. The affectation is the essence of the man. It pervades all his thoughts and expressions.'[104] Croker reviewed Walpole repeatedly as new collections appeared, and in his remarks one can trace the evolution of an attitude toward letters as personal history. He held from the beginning that Walpole was at his best in the avowed personality of the letter form, and by contrast condemned the historical memoirs for their 'personality'. Yet he became aware that, however 'personal' the letters are, 'they constitute, taken altogether, a body of historical evidence to which no other age or country can afford anything like a parallel'. Historical in reference, the letters are of historical interest precisely because personal 'tone' or 'colour' prevails over objective details. By 1843 Croker attributed to such tonal qualities in historical witness the persistence of Walpole's fame. His summary description of the letters locates value in personal tone:

'their brilliancy – sparkling, but cold, like icicles in sunshine – will perhaps rival, in the coarser tastes of the generality of mankind, the sprightly and sensible *causeries* of Madame de Sévigné and the mingled pleasantry and pathos of poor Cowper: the only two letter-writers between whom and Walpole – *magis pares quam similes* – we can admit any propinquity of merit.'[105]

In Lockhart's comments on letter-writers the same models remain supreme, though he may add new candidates – or very old ones:

'Cicero himself,' he writes Croker, 'is surely, with the one exception of H. Walpole, the best letter writer in the world.'[106] Byron is measured by Walpole and Cowper:

> 'He reminds us more frequently of Horace Walpole than of any other of his predecessors; but his vein is thoroughly original; the rapid felicity of the transitions unique; and quite as much as the interfusion of pure and beautiful pathos, not with humour only, as in Cowper, but with highly-polished wit and energetic bursts of declamation.'[107]

The epistolary manner is an index of 'character'. The 'solid worth' of Prior's *Goldsmith* as biography resides 'above all, in the rich mass of the poet's own familiar letters', says Lockhart; and the biographical value of the letters lies not in their information, but in that 'no poet's letters in the world, not even those of Cowper, appear to us more interesting for the light they throw on the habits and feelings of the man who wrote them'.[108] Not every literary nature lends itself to the organic, 'personal' style of the letter; for example, while Thomas Campbell 'might have left behind him, in the shape of letters, a really important addition to his works – a new body of valuable miscellanies', he was actually not

> 'gifted with that nature which abhors a vacuum, and which renders the letters of some of the greatest of authors about the most delightful part of their legacies to the world; that ever glowing necessity of the brain and the blood to which we owe the correspondence of Cicero, Erasmus, Voltaire, Scott, Byron – of Goethe, whose signet bore a star with the words *"ohne hast, ohne rast"*, *without haste, without rest* – and we may safely add by anticipation the name of Southey.'

Nor was the 'glowing necessity' always to be identified with undisciplined energy. In Southey we may miss 'some of those charms of entire ease which we prize in one or two great epistolary collections – that of Swift, for example, who said of himself that when he had begun a letter he never dreamt of pausing "till his elbow was sore"'. But the direction and control had become natural, even as artifice had become natural to Walpole; and 'however frank and manly the substance' of Southey's letters, 'its garb would still have been that of the unwearied penman who instinctively forecast and balanced every sentence'.[109] Hence, the letters project a true portrait, and the portrait would be spoiled by expurgation.

But as the prizing of unconscious epistolary portraiture increased, a reaction had begun, and Southey was one of its leaders. Reviewing Hayley's *Cowper*, Southey objected to the weakness of the scheme as narrative, and read in that formal weakness the irresponsibility of the biographer, whose failure to organize an adequate narrative was an evasion of responsible point of view. Indeed, the autobiographical mode, adopted by Hayley from Mason and Boswell, was an evasion, and 'it will seldom be employed, unless where the biographer is conscious of a paucity of materials for his own share of the work, or of some nice and delicate points in the story, upon which he does not choose to express himself with the responsibility of an author.'[110]

Jeffrey, generally enthusiastic about the epistolary 'scheme', opposed Mason and, specifically, Hayley on practical grounds: 'This book is too long; but it is composed on a plan that makes prolixity unavoidable.'[111] The *Annual Review* alluded in 1805 to 'that lazy, prolix, and indecorous method of composing biography, by printing, without selection or reserve, the correspondence of the person to be celebrated; and thus, as the phrase is, making him his own biographer'.[112] The same year, Scott extended Southey's criticism. Southey's objection to the Mason-Hayley use of letters had been to a 'chequered mode of mingling them entire, with the staple of the writer's narration'.[113] Todd in his *Life of Spenser*, argued Scott, should have printed the Harvey letters as an appendix, rather than thrusting 'large extracts from them into the midst of his own narrative'. Narrative continuity and personal integrity are inseparable: 'The biographer should always study to give his work the appearance of continuity. . . . [His] text ought to be expressed historically, and in the language of the author himself.' Wholesale inclusion of letters confuses point of view and destroys proportion:

'It is extremely awkward to jump from the words of the narrator into those of Spenser, and has, besides, the effect of making one part of the memoir bear a great dis-proportion to the other: for the letter-writer spends much more time in discussing the matter then immediately before him, than the biographer has probably an opportunity of bestowing upon incidents of much greater importance.'[114]

These are the strictures Stanfield quotes in 1813 to support his own reservations.

But Stanfield's comments apply to more than narrative form. They reflect doubts about letters as authentic self-exposure.

'The question which meets us here is – whether a copious insertion of letters, to the exclusion of narrative and reflection, be the best mode of furnishing an exact portrait of human life; or, whether the author, by a careful study of those letters, and, as a result of that study, by giving us the prominent facts, sentiments, and observations, digested into his own language and mode of representation, do not present the likeness in a more genuine and effective manner.'[115]

The 'interesting caveat' attributed by Garraty to Sir Robert Rait – 'A man, writing to an intimate friend, says things that he would not say in print, and these are not necessarily his real or secret thoughts; they are more often the whimsies of the moment' – was voiced as early as 1809, when Scott charged that Burns's letters 'very rarely contain the real opinions of the writer'. An author weighs his views with care before publishing them, but 'the same man usually writes a letter only because the letter must be written – is probably never more at a loss than when looking for a subject – and treats it, when found, rather so as to gratify his correspondent, than communicate his own feelings'.[116]

Recalling the same letters, Wordsworth warned of the difficulty of

'determining what portion of these confidential communications escapes the pen in courteous, yet often innocent, compliance – to gratify the several tastes of correspondents . . . [or] distinguishing opinions and sentiments uttered for the momentary amusement merely of the writer's own fancy, from those which his judgment deliberately approves, and his heart faithfully cherishes.'[117]

Letters may have little reference to any fixed 'character'; Nelson's to Lady Hamilton, protested Croker, 'are the mere records of the transient clouds of his temper, of the passing feelings of his heart, of the peevishness, which an anxious spirit and a sickly frame produced'.[118] Others might respond that such transiences comprise the history of that 'spirit'. But the period kept its concern for the artificiality of epistolary sentiment. Adolphus echoes Johnson when he sums it up:

'the effusions even of the most candid and ingenuous writer, who accustoms himself to expatiate on his own feelings, are not to be considered an unquestionable index of character. In the calm and placid moments of confidential communication, the mind, delighted with its task and with itself, is naturally open to every amiable and disinterested sentiment: then faults and follies are ingenuously avowed; . . . the imagination warms with its own exertion; and the heart, unrestrained for the moment by any sordid passion or low solicitude, indulges in its natural and original bent.'[119]

The 'natural and original bent' of character need not be its truth, just as the 'passing feelings' of a Nelson or the social motives of a Burns may not be indicative of the essential self. The scepticism, grounded in a growing sense of the mystery of identity, is one Lockhart fully shared. Yet he seemed to adopt the epistolary method. Forty-five years after Boswell chose to 'enlarge upon the excellent plan of Mr Mason', Lockhart wrote to Scott of Raeburn that his 'Life of our dear friend Sir Walter' would 'deserve to be called his book, not mine'. In the book itself, he alluded to 'the copious and candid correspondence from which it has been throughout my object to extract and combine the scattered fragments of an *autobiography*'.[120] Little change is suggested, but the reaction had occurred, and its impact on a sophisticated moralist and artist can be realized only through close study of his use of Scott's letters. Then, what appears his monumental neglect of critical admonitions is seen instead as a complex solution to the problem the critics had posed: how to realize the unique value and still avoid the pitfalls of a copious use of letters. The same thing will be found true of his use of conversational anecdote. But on this controversial issue he was more explicit.

In the *Life of Scott* he entered 'a protest once for all against the general fidelity of several literary gentlemen who have kindly forwarded to me private lucubrations of theirs, designed to *Boswellize* Scott'.[121] Garraty ascribes it to a proto-Victorian reticence.[122] But the reticence is found in Stanfield as early as 1813: 'the scrupulous delicacy of modern criticism does not admit the introduction of Dialogue into regular biography.'[123] Why would biographical enthusiasts in this 'age of personality' reject the supreme talent of the 'prince of biographers'? 'Reticence' is an incomplete answer. The rejection of 'Boswellizing' was grounded in epistemological scepticism. Boswell himself had made it inevitable.

The reservation was expressed early. James Beattie offered his warning following the publication of Boswell's *Tour* in 1785. The earliest reviewers of the *Life* followed him in stressing the dangers of misunderstanding. One reviewer asked, 'when every gleaning is collected by one who hung constantly on his lips, and recorded everything which could add to the bulk, where is the clue that could give consistency to the opinions, or guide the most inexperienced enquirer?' Another warned simply, 'What in Dr Johnson was the light and playful sally of the moment, is by his biographer transmitted to posterity.' The *Critical Review* elaborated: 'Authors are exalted or depreciated as the moment of hilarity or gloom was connected with the subject, or as the opinion of the speaker was adverse; and the whole is given as the sentiment of Johnson.' Talk is the creature of mood and occasion. Only judicious selection and compilation can prevent misunderstanding.[124]

Such warnings are the background to Lockhart's rejection. His own sophisticated awareness of conversation as a dramatic phenomenon, conditioned by milieu and specific relationship, is fully expounded:

'To report conversations fairly, it is a necessary prerequisite that we should be completely familiar with all the interlocutors, and understand thoroughly all their minutest relations, and points of common knowledge and common feeling with each other. He who does not, must be perpetually in danger of misinterpreting sportive allusion into serious statement; . . . In proportion as a man is witty and humorous, there will always be about him and his a widening maze and wilderness of cues and catchwords, which the uninitiated will, if they are bold enough to try interpretation, construe, ever and anon, egregiously amiss – not seldom into arrant falsity.'[125]

Lockhart had seen what happened to great talkers of his own period. The greatest, of course, was (said Mme de Staël) an artist in monologue rather than conversation; and the absence of dramatic dimension in Coleridge's case reduced the danger of misunderstanding. But the danger was striking in the case of Byron. For him, the post-Boswell suspicion that every talkative table had its Medwin, its Lady Blessington, its Willis or Basil Hall with notebook on knee, made spontaneity and personal integrity impossible. Byron was 'haunted in his retirement by varieties of the small Boswell or eavesdropping genus, who, as very little penetration must shew him, would take the first opportunity of selling his confidences to the public'.[126] So he cultivated defensive *personae*, turned different facets of self to different listeners. The consequence was obvious to Maria Edgeworth: our passion for 'seeing great minds in undress' will ultimately destroy the use; 'we shall only see minds like Byrons in prepared undress – and shall never get at the real likeness'.[127] Meanwhile, on a South Atlantic island, the age's supreme self-creator was busy exploiting *his* Boswells in the creation of the Napoleonic myth.

Boswell had effected a scepticism as to the reliability of his method by making vivid the dramatic nature of conversation. Invoking the Boswellian model, his admirers returned again and again to the same epithets. Croker used them to attack Fanny Burney: 'her description of Mr Boswell is one of the best in her book. We heartily wish that she had caught more of his biographical style and spirit – at once so accurate and so compressed, so simple yet so picturesque, so dramatic and still so real.'[128] 'Dramatic' and 'picturesque' anticipate Carlyle's insistence on the 'intense pictorial power' by which Boswell made little 'Realities' memorable. They are central in Hazlitt's contrast of Boswell and Spence. Spence's 'curious particulars' lack 'picturesque grouping and dramatic effect': 'We have the opinions and sayings of eminent men: but they do not grow out of the occasion.'[129] They dominate Lockhart's judgement of Coleridge's *Table-talk*:

'Of Boswell we need say nothing, except that his book, in many other respects unrivalled, has this great and almost entirely peculiar advantage, that it presents its talkers, in the strict sense of the word, *dramatically*. Every saying is rendered doubly interesting by our knowledge of the time, the place, the occasion, and of the person or persons addressed.'[130]

Lockhart wrote this while writing the *Life of Scott*. He had learned to appreciate Boswell's use of 'stage directions' or 'the Boswellian sort of accompaniment', but the lesson bolstered his scepticism as to the veracity of stenographic conversational record.

It is not quite clear what Romantic critics meant when they alluded to Boswell's veracity. Hazlitt assumes the character of 'Boswell Redivivus' to introduce the *Conversations of James Northcote*: 'I differ from my great original and predecessor . . . he is supposed to have invented nothing,' whereas his descendant flaunts his literal unreliability: 'I have feigned whatever I pleased. I have forgotten, mistaken, misstated, altered, transposed a number of things.' Yet, from Boswell he has learned the stylistic nature of authenticity: 'I have also introduced little incidental details that never happened; thus, by lying, giving a greater air of truth to the scene.'[131] Others understood Boswell's veracity differently. For Croker, it permitted the art of selection and emphasis. Of an episode in Fanny Burney's diary he wrote: 'The account of this morning visit is spread out over fourteen pages – Boswell would have given all the pith and character of it in two or three.'[132] Carlyle's acceptance of the same qualification is implicit in his verb: 'How the babbling Bozzy, inspired only by love, . . . epi-

D

tomizes nightly the words of Wisdom, the deeds and aspects of Wisdom.'[133] Literal accuracy and truth are not the same.

The truth they prized most in Boswell was the same personal
authenticity cherished in memoir and letter. It is defined by 'Boswell
Redivivus': 'My object was to catch the tone and manner, rather than
to repeat the exact expressions, or even opinions; just as it is possible to
recognize the voice of an acquaintance without distinguishing the
particular words he uses.' Boswell seems to have cared primarily for the
Rambler's sententious substance; his Romantic admirers cared increasingly for the expressive 'tone and manner'. Authenticity of report
implied less a scrupulous regard for the exact word than an acute sense
of the spirit of the speaker, his 'very self and voice'. And the spirit was
to be captured not by the scrupulous auditor but by the sensitive
impressionist.

A skimming through the ponderous compilation of *Coleridge the
Talker* shows a striking dearth of direct quotations, the preponderance
instead of an impressionism which seeks to recreate the experience of
Coleridge the Talker'. Dibdin and others felt 'a SECOND JOHNSON
had visited the earth' and lamented that they 'could not exercise the
powers of a second BOSWELL'. More felt that 'Boswell would have
found his occupation gone at Highgate', because Coleridge defied literal
record. 'I never took a note of Coleridge's conversation which was not
a *caput mortuum*,' Crabb Robinson complained. Sterling spoke of 'the
spirit and flavour and fragrance' of Coleridge's talk, and stenography
could never capture spirit and flavour and fragrance. Even to keep the
caput mortuum of content might be a sin against the sublimity of the
experience. Hamilton felt it 'almost an injury to the sense of grandeur
and infinity with which the *whole* impressed me then, to try to recall
the *details* now'. The true reporter was to be prized for his impressionistic power. Julius Hare wished Sterling had kept an account of Coleridge's conversations, 'for he was capable of representing their depth,
their ever varying hues, their sparkling lights, their oceanic ebb and
flow'.[134] The consequences of such a shift to impressionism will be seen
later, in Lockhart's impressionistic, yet highly dramatic substitute for
'Boswellizing'.

Meanwhile, there were two major factors in his rejection. One was
negative: the distrust of literally reported discourse, apart from its
occasion and milieu, as a reliable self-revelation – and the distrust
applies equally to epistolary discourse. The other was positive: the shift

of attention away from epistolary or conversational substance to the indirect personal revelation of style, tone, 'spirit'. Together the two factors exert a paradoxical influence: they at once discourage direct quotation and demand it; they place major responsibility on the biographer and prevent his exerting it editorially. They suggest what I take to be the central paradox of Romantic biographical theory.

III

The primacy of the 'personal' in biographical material applies as well, in Romantic theory, to the biographer's own part in his creation. The biographer may be humble Baconian compiler-narrator; he may be forbidden conjecture or even commentary. Nonetheless, without the possession of what Stanfield calls the 'biographic spirit', he cannot 'delineate with force and truth'.[135] 'For what man knoweth the things of a man,' asks St Paul, 'save the spirit of man which is in him?' And Albert Schweitzer echoes the idea from the end of the Romantic Century: 'A personality can only be awakened to life by a personality.' The essential premise of Romantic epistemology – the subject knows its object by knowing itself in that object – is basic to Romantic biographical theory.

Boswell might hope 'through an accumulation of intelligence from various points' to avoid the partiality of a single view. His Romantic readers prized the result as uniquely Boswellian. In the critical clamour over Croker's edition of Boswell (1831–2),[136] the real issue is the dominance of the biographer's personality in the experience and rendition of his subject. Croker had dared to proceed on the positivistic assumption that he could 'complete the history of Johnson's Life' by conflating Boswell's text with 'numerous other authentic works connected with the biography of Johnson'. The 'monstrous medley' was altered in the second edition by Wright and Lockhart. Croker, reassuming control in 1848, did not return to the original plan, but never fully repented or restored the Boswellian text. His recent advocate evades the real issue in claiming that 'the practice interferes very little with the reader's ability to follow the course of Boswell's text'.[137]

The real issue for contemporary critics is well put by the modern Romantic Collingwood, attacking Bury's assumption that Gibbon can be updated through footnotes.

'History for him, in the true positivistic manner, consists of an assemblage of isolated facts, each capable of being ascertained or investigated without reference to the others. Thus he was able to accomplish the very strange feat of bringing Gibbon up to date by means of footnotes, adding to the aggregate of knowledge already contained in his pages the numerous facts that had been ascertained in the meantime, without suspecting that the very discovery of these facts resulted from an historical mentality so different from Gibbon's own that the result was not unlike adding a saxophone *obligato* to an Elizabethan madrigal.'[138]

Carlyle's metaphor for personal integrity is even more picturesque. Ridiculing Croker's efforts to stitch 'Hawkins, Tyers, Murphy, Piozzi' into Boswell, Carlyle recalls, 'There is much between the cup and the lip'; but with Croker you cannot be sure 'now when the cup is *at* the lip, what liquor it is you are imbibing; whether Boswell's French wine which you began with, or some Piozzi's ginger-beer, or Hawkins's entire'.[139] To Carlyle's metaphor of flavour, Macaulay adds one of organic growth: 'We know no production of the human mind which has . . . so much of the peculiar flavour of the soil from which it sprang.' Hence Croker's extracts wither like transplanted boughs. Had Boswell himself quoted from Sir John or Mrs Piozzi, he would have been 'guided by his own taste and judgment in selecting his quotations'. Had Hume seen Pepys and Mrs Hutchinson in print, doubtless Hume would have used them. A later editor, argues Macaulay, cannot do so. The analogy serves in Boswell's behalf: 'Hume's history, be its faults what they may, is now one great entire work, the production of one vigorous mind, working on such materials as were within its reach.'[140]

The third of Croker's major reviewers took no public exception to the 'medley'. But in view of Croker's *Quarterly* connection, Lockhart's was not a free hand. From letters to Murray it is plain that Lockhart came to agree with Carlyle and Macaulay, to approve of no deviation from the plan of 'keeping Boswell's text entirely undisturbed', to insist on strict adherence to 'the principle of *saving Boswell entire* in his own station & dignity'. Even the juvenile verses and legal opinions 'give great individuality to the narration'. Bozzy's personality is conveyed by the most trifling editorial gesture, and such bits of evidence 'keep before us the relative positions of the Doctor and his biographer'.[141]

Lockhart's final premise is suggestive. Perhaps Boswell's chief importance for Romantic biographical theory was not in his candour or his dramatic, picturesque style, but rather in his symbolizing of the biographical relationship, its prerequisites of viewpoint and decorums of tone. Lockhart considered the *Life of Johnson* an embodiment of that relationship. Like others, he itemized the Boswellian character: 'the omnivorous curiosity, the unblushing, utterly unconscious indelicacy, the ebullient self-love combined with almost total negation of self-respect, and the perhaps unrivalled *memory*'. But he was more concerned to show how certain features of that character invited in Johnson an extraordinary degree of self-revelation. The work was a function of the 'relative positions' of two personalities, and a testament to 'the sublimest as well as the most beautiful of human sentiments' – the 'friendship of genius'.[142]

The classification implies decorums of tone and perspective. Sympathy, obviously, was demanded; sympathy, for the Romantic theorist, was the prerequisite for all knowledge. The biographer, says Stanfield, 'must enter intimately into the character he would exhibit – he must, for the time, endeavour to see things in the same point of view, and conceive sentiments of the same nature and feeling'; such is of the essence of the 'Biographic Spirit'.[143] The biographer of a distinguished sailor such as Brenton, Lockhart felt, must be 'capable of entering with full zest into details of martial achievement'. By the same reasoning Hobhouse was 'clearly designated' Byron's biographer 'by his sympathy with Lord Byron's opinions' – his ability to sustain imaginatively a kinship in culture and ideology.[144]

But sympathy is not all. In the 'friendship of genius', enthusiasm is to be fused with reverence. It is no accident that Romantic biographical theory opens a century of hero-worship; for here is the origin of Carlyle's idea. Teufelsdröckh assures us, 'Thought without Reverence is barren, perhaps poisonous'; but 'believe not that man has lost his faculty of Reverence', for 'Boswell venerates his Johnson right truly even in the Eighteenth Century'. And Teufelsdröckh is blessed with his Boswellian Heuschrecke, just as the Abbot Samson has his Boswell in Jocelyn, to remind us that 'the manner of men's Hero-worship, verily it is the innermost fact of their existence, and determines all the rest'.[145] Lockhart, the hero-worshipper of Goethe and the translator of Schlegel, had anticipated Carlyle as early as 1818:

'There is something dignified and sacred in human genius. . . . The reverence which we feel for it is an instinct of nature, and cannot be laid aside without a sin. He who is insensible to its influence, has committed sacrilege against his own spirit and degraded himself from the height of his original elevation.'[146]

Veneration, misguided or not, is decorously indispensable. Lord Campbell's personality as a Whig is always before us in his *Lives of the Chancellors*, but

> 'he could no more get rid of it now, even if he were aware of its existence, than he could of his veneration for John Knox or his pride in the Macallamore. It is a part of the man – and he is probably as unconscious of its operation on his judgment as he is of the machinery that circulates his blood.'[147]

Napier of Merchiston's descendant naturally exaggerates his ancestor's merits, but 'the feeling in question inspired the writer to his task, and it is inextricably interwoven with the whole texture of his performance'.[148] Texture, tone, flavour – indispensable terms in the impressionism of the Romantic biographical critic – are correlatives of personality. The decorous biographer's *persona* is rhetorically central and inviolate in his work.

What, then, of the ideals of copious impersonality, the convention after Mason and Boswell of allowing the character to develop itself, the subject to be his own biographer? What of the biographer as humble Baconian compiler of data in the history of a mind? Biographical theory in the half-century following Boswell seems to turn on a major paradox. On the one hand, the method of compendious compilation excludes the biographic personality; on the other, that personality is central and inviolate. In practice, the greatest of Romantic biographers, Lockhart, resolved the paradox; and his mode of doing so, we shall see, accounts for his most controversial features as a biographer: the apparent fusion of formal naiveté and sophisticated editorial art; the application of fiction's methods and effects to an art of the irreducible fact; the licentious use of documents, the freedom with which memoir, letter, and anecdote alike – prized as originals – are unobtrusively manipulated.

The Romantic biographer would not work without voluminous original materials, merely narrating and summarizing. Nor could he work with them, extracting, excerpting, destroying their personal integrity. The solution, then, was to work *through* them, selecting, manipulating, even 'contaminating', to make them accord more closely with his intuitive grasp of his subject. The solution was to Boswellize or Scottize his originals, and having by selection or revision made the self-revelation more true to the essential character than it always seemed in the originals, to arrange his materials, to cause them to evolve in an organic form which would reveal the life as the reticent biographer had conceived and experienced it.

Such a solution would account for some of Lockhart's insistence on the responsibility, ethical and aesthetic, of the editor of private papers.[149] For that insistence demanded more than avoidance of unessential 'personality' and pain to the living, more than syntactical and organizational clarification and compression. Such a solution leads us to a fuller and more technical understanding of the term he uses for such procedures – 'manipulation' – than present connotations allow. It reveals the painstaking art to which he refers by the humble word 'compilation'.

Lockhart considered compilation an art. Of a contemporary *Life*, he wrote: 'Goldsmith happily called one of the arts in which he has never been surpassed, that of "building a book"; but the most studious of his admirers [Prior] does not shine as a compiler.'[150] As the biographer who 'willingly expended' on Scott's behalf 'the time that would have sufficed for writing a dozen books on what will be no more than the compilation of one',[151] Lockhart knew whereof he spoke, when, a few years later, he wrote of the author of *The Lives of the Lindsays* in terms that best describe his own achievement:

'compilation, in the hands of Lord Lindsay, is a very different thing from what we commonly understand by that term. It is a work demanding delicate skill. With him nothing is compiled to save the trouble of composition – every fragment has been studiously chosen – and the whole are so dexterously arranged, and most of them so neatly inlaid upon his own narrative, that we have the charm of variety, without ceasing to lean on our guide or to feel the worth of his guidance.'[152]

2

PETER'S LETTERS
AS THE BIOGRAPHY
OF A CULTURE

. . . an individual who seems to have cared very little how many
enemies he raised up among those who were not personally
acquainted with him. . . . At the same time, a strong and ever-
wakeful perception of the ludicrous, is certainly a prominent
feature in his composition, and his flow of animal spirits enables
him to enjoy it keenly, and invent it with success. I have seen,
however, very few persons whose minds are so much alive and
awake throughout every corner, and who are so much in the
habit of trying and judging every thing by the united tact of so
many qualities and feelings all at once.

    LOCKHART ON LOCKHART in *Peter's Letters to his Kinsfolk*

He seldom remains long in one key . . . a writer, with a keen
sense of the frolicsome, the ludicrous, and the piquant, must be
in perpetual danger of offending, either by the untimely introduction of such mirthful topics, or by their undue prolongation,
or by 'a certain spice' of them remaining behind, even after a
serious, solemn, or affecting appeal has been made to the better
and higher feelings. . . . The current of deeper emotion is too
often checked or diverted. . . .

    LOCKHART ON LOCKHART, reviewing *Reginald Dalton*[1]

2

PETER'S LETTERS
AS THE BIOGRAPHY
OF A CULTURE

'The Society of Edinburgh,' wrote Lord Cockburn of the Athens of the North in the years preceding Waterloo, 'has never been better, or indeed so good, since I knew it as it was about this time':

> 'Its brilliancy was owing to a variety of peculiar circumstances. . . . The principal of these were – the survivance of several of the eminent men of the preceding age, and of curious old habits which the modern flood had not yet obliterated; the rise of a powerful community of young men of ability; the exclusion of the British from the Continent, which made this place, both for education and for residence, a favourite resort of strangers; the war, which maintained a constant excitement of military preparation, and of military idleness; the blaze of that popular literature which made this the second city in the empire for learning and science; and the extent, and the ease, with which literature and society embellished each other, without rivalry, and without pedantry.'

'It continued,' he observed with bitterness, 'in a state of high animation till 1815, or perhaps till 1820' – at which time 'a new race of peace-formed native youths came on the stage but with little literature, and a comfortless intensity of political zeal'.[2] One such youth – peace-formed, son of the minister of Glasgow College Kirk, twenty-one – had much literature, but had too, a political zeal which did indeed prove comfortless to lordly Whigs of Cockburn's class.

Lockhart arrived in Edinburgh in November 1815. He came from three years at Glasgow University and four at Balliol that culminated in a Classics 'first'. He came to read Scots Law, to 'pass advocate' a year later, to 'put on the gown' and (like Alan Fairford) give 'a bit chack of dinner to his friends and acquaintances' and 'tread the boards of the Parliament House . . . with the air of a man wrapped up in Potier and Cujacius', to spend his first three-guinea fee 'in punch and tobacco the same evening' and join other lounging young advocates in 'the daily babble of the briefless' at the part of the Hall which led Peter Morris to christen their 'journeyman days . . . by the simple collective – *Stove-hood*'.[3]

Hogg met Lockhart in these early days and strolled with him in Sir William Hamilton's company on the Leith sands. He recalled 'a mischievous Oxford puppy, for whom I was terrified, dancing after the young ladies, and drawing caricatures of every one who came in contact with him'.[4] The semi-fictitious Shepherd of the *Noctes Ambrosianae* recalled of Lockhart 'the laugh about the screwed-up mouth of him, that fules ca'd no canny, for they couldna thole the meaning' o't'.[5] The 'puppy' was endowed with a ruthless vision of human pretension, of intellectual complacency, which he had brought to a legal-literary culture mostly Whig, to what a more respectable Tory, Andrew Lang, called an 'ice palace' of 'intellectual despots', preening in a place contrived by Nature herself to teach them humility.[6] Or so, at least, Lockhart's *persona* Dr Peter Morris felt. For as he mounted Calton Hill for his first glimpse of Edinburgh, Dr Morris had a vision of the serious Lilliputian irony that was to underlie much of his Edinburgh experience:

'Here there must always be present the idea of the comparative littleness of all human works. Here the proudest of palaces must be content to catch the shadows of mountains; and the grandest of fortresses to appear like the dwellings of pigmies, perched on the very bulwarks of creation.'[7]

Such a view, combined with a talent for satiric exposure, led quickly to notoriety.

'There was,' writes the 'Olympian of Whiggery' already quoted, 'a natural demand for libel at this period.'[8] In such terms, the entrenched Edinburgh Reviewer explained the explosive youth of *Blackwood's Magazine*. As climax of two libellously anti-Whig years of *Blackwood's* there appeared, in mid-July 1819, three startling volumes which Miss Sophia Scott recommended to her former governess:

' I would advise you to read a new book which will be out soon called *Peter's Letters to His Kinsfolk,* being a description of the society of Glasgow and Edinburgh. It is one of the most clever, and at the same time rather severe books that has been written for ages; this is Papa's opinion.'[9]

The Whig daily *Scotsman* welcomed it appropriately as 'little else than a republication of the dullest, most prosing and malignant articles in Blackwood's Magazine', but the complaint of dullness was not general. 'The *literati* were affronted, but the book was read.'[10] Even the struggling young student, Thomas Carlyle, conceded that *'Peter's Letters to his Kinsfolk* . . . will give you some idea of the state of literature in Edinburgh at the time: it was in great vogue three years ago, but is now dead as mutton'.[11] George Gilfillan recalled vividly the 'prodigious sensation' the book created:

'It was so personal – so quizzical – so impudent, and so desperately clever. Its illustrations were so good, and so grotesque withal. And then there was the slightest possible shade of mystification about the fact of the authorship, to give a last tart tinge to the interest. It, accordingly, ran like wild-fire. Steamers and track-boats were not considered complete without a copy. It supplanted guide-books in inns. A hundred country towns, aware that a "chield was taking notes" among them, were on the daily look-out for the redoubtable Peter, with his spectacles – his Welch accent – his Toryism – his inordinate thirst for draught porter, and his everlasting shandry-dan. . . . It became so popular, in Leicester, that Robert Hall actually attacked it from the pulpit.'[12]

There is justice in Cockburn's remark that 'posterity can never be made to feel the surprise and just offence with which contemporaries respond to personal attack'.[13] Lockhart's first biographer, G. R. Gleig, is less just in his claim that he 'can discover no single expression which ought to have rankled in the most sensitive of Scottish minds,' than is W.M. Parker in his excessively severe modern assertion that 'Lockhart satirised and pilloried most of his contemporaries'.[14] Though Scott felt the book 'perhaps too favourable' and wished Dr Morris to return every fifty years 'to record the fleeting manners of the age', Lockhart himself, in that place of many palinodes, the *Life of Scott,* commits the thing to the oblivion of juvenilia: 'Nobody but a very young and a very thoughtless person could have dreamt of putting forth such a book.'[15] Nevertheless, it is fair neither to the book itself nor to the present study to consider *Peter's Letters* an *omnium gatherum* of scurrilous sketches, a mere *jeu d'esprit*.

In the first place, the work is biographical. Its biographical emphasis constitutes its significant deviation from its own genre; indeed, the generic transformation it represents is itself of major importance to biography. In the second place, it calls attention to the biographer's early sceptical flirtation with a popular theory, a fad, of characterology. Again, it displays the creation and use of a complex biographical *persona*, capable of great tonal range from enthusiastic reverence to detached scientific acumen; nor is one *persona* enough, but a second is employed to allow biography by dialogue. The future biographer is present, too, in narrative and anecdotal style, in the power of signifi-cant description, in a sense of epistolary tact and of characterizing tone and manner in individual speech. He is present in architectonic power – the ability to organize the multiple details of Peter Morris's experience into a thematic unity, a comprehensive persuasion. He is present, too, in the controlling themes and in the biographical subjects who embody these themes, Burns and Scott. If Lockhart the cultural theorist preconceived his later biographical subjects, it is to *Peter's Letters* we must go for the preconceptions. Here, both are seen in the light of theoretic issues – the question of a national culture, the cultural value of literary genius – which dominate *Peter's Letters*. Here we see the literary biographer emerging from the theorist of literary culture.

The book has more personal revelations to make, but revelations essential to an understanding of the biographer. They have to do with Lockhart's enigmatic complexity of attitude and tone; Lockhart is described in the work:

'I have seen, however, very few persons whose minds are so much alive and awake throughout every corner, and who are so much in the habit of trying and judging everything by the united tact of so many qualities and feelings all at once.' [III, 134–6]

Reviewing *Dalton* himself four years later, Lockhart notes the same thing – the author 'seldom remains long in one key'. And D. M. Moir, commenting on the same novel, finds such complexity characteristic: 'Mr Lockhart's own, true, genuine style – acute, profound, sparkling, grave, lively, sarcastic, passionate, knowing and imaginative – "every-thing by turns, and nothing long".'[16] This intriguing sensibility, for us perhaps 'metaphysical' in its complexity, must be invoked to define Lockhart's formative influence on *Blackwood's* and to account for his own fate as an ironist at once solemn and flippant, and inevitably misunderstood.

The reciprocally formative influence of Lockhart and early 'Maga' is a topic the later Lockhart would have preferred to avoid. The editor of the stately *Quarterly* and the vice-regent of Albemarle Street, feeling the harassments and inhibitions of his new formality, was anxious to give out that the Blackwoodian wag had been a 'raw boy',

> 'when, arriving in Edinburgh in October 1817 [on his return from a Blackwood-sponsored trip to Germany], I found my friend John Wilson (ten years my senior) busied in helping Blackwood out of a scrape he had got into with some editors of his Magazine, and on Wilson's asking me to try my hand at some squibberies in his aid, I sat down to do so with as little malice as if the assigned subject had been the Court of Pekin.'[17]

Edinburgh partisans of 'Professor Wilson' were unjust in condoning Wilson as an eccentric and shifting the blame onto the 'cool one' of the pair. But Lockhart's early correspondence with Blackwood and Scott suggests that Wilson's erratic behaviour did place considerable editorial responsibility on Lockhart.[18] At any rate, his influence is apparent in Maga's curiously dramatic character.

'One of the attractive novelties of Blackwood,' writes Donald Carswell in an essay on Lockhart more scurrilous than most of 'Ebony's' early pranks, 'was that its most provocative articles appeared over signatures – pseudonyms, it is true, but sufficient to convey an illusion of personality.' These assorted *personae* lived as it were independently; 'the various pseudonyms were not appropriated, but were held by members of the staff jointly and severally, and were frequently exchanged.'[19] Membership in Maga's inner circle demanded the versatility to subject one's style to a pre-established point of view and tonal range. As a result, Wilson's daughter recalls, 'in the early numbers of the Magazine one meets a perfect host of these mythical personages, and the impression conveyed to the credulous reader must have been that contributions were flowing in from remarkable persons in all quarters of the empire'. Her examples make clear to whom the principal credit must go: 'There was really so much variety and individuality imparted to these imaginary characters that it was very difficult to perceive that the same writer was assuming the guises of William Wastle, Esq., and Dr Ulrich Sternstare, and Philip Kempferhausen, and the Baron Lauerwinkel.' Mrs Oliphant and Macbeth, too, ascribe a majority of Blackwood *personae* – 'von Lauerwinkel, Professor Sauer-teig, and others (predecessors and probably progenitors of the immortal Teufelsdröckh)', each 'endowed with a well-defined personality and writing in a characteristic vein and style', to 'the fertile mind of Lockhart'.[20]

Anyone puzzling over Lockhart's enigmatic personality must eventually be struck by the coincidence of certain predominant features of his career. At present we are concerned with the young journalist whose imagination and rhetorical skill allowed him to sustain a multiplicity of *personae*. We are simultaneously confronting a young 'wit' with extraordinary 'adaptive power'[21] in society. We shall be speaking of a man whose adult life was a sequence of strong fidelities to older and more rigid and dominant personalities – Wilson, Scott, Croker. And against such a background, we shall not be surprised to find a literary artist whose mode, biography, demands the projecting and rhetorical sustaining of such fidelities and their appropriate tones and perspectives. We see early a natural inclination which made Lockhart supreme as biographer. He could, while retaining a critical detachment, adopt an appropriate point of view and tone by rhetorical impulse. He could project and animate facets of his own complex sensibility, some of which strongly qualified or contradicted each other.

This impulse seems to have been primarily rhetorical. Of the harshest of his *personae* Mrs Oliphant notes, 'Lockhart put in his sting in a moment, inveterate, instantaneous, with the effect of a barbed dart – yet almost, as it seemed, with the mere intention of giving point to his sentences, and no particular feeling at all.'[22] And Lockhart, conceiving the 'personality' of *Blackwood* satire as akin to the surface 'personality' of the *Dunciad*, wrote later of Theodore Hook that he

'knew little, and could have cared nothing, about those who became the objects of his satire. Exquisitely cruel as it often seemed, it was with him a mere *skiomachy*. Certain men and women were stuck up as types of certain prejudices or delusions; and he set to knocking them down with no more feeling about them, as individual human creatures, than if they had been nine-pins.'[23]

Given this impulse, and with the awareness that the pleasures of *flyting* are traditional in Scottish literary culture, we can account for the dramatic character of early *Blackwood's*.

Of the *dramatis personae* generated by Lockhart's versatility, literary history chooses to remember just one: the infamous 'Z', scourge of King Leigh and the Cockneys. But there were masks for wiser and better attitudes and perspectives. If 'Z' is master of contemptuous invective, of the bellicose sport of *flyting*, 'Wastle' is at the opposite extreme, the harmlessly bigoted arch-Tory Scots antiquarian. Among the spate of German *personae*, Sternstare is the scientifically serious analyst of character, while Lauerwinkel's is the quasi-prophetic utterance of the Enthusiast. But the German hoaxes were more than *ieux d'esprit*.[24]

Edinburgh Germanism did not begin with *Blackwood's*; Scott had belonged to a German study group two years before Lockhart was born. Nevertheless, at a time when the two major reviews, conditioned by their inception *in bello*, preserved a dogged insularity, the Blackwood group – so Morgan and Hohlfeld have concluded – brought into being 'perhaps the most helpful of all British magazines in the introduction of German literature'. For Lockhart, doing battle less against the *Edinburgh Review* than against the sceptical anti-nationalism and dogmatic intellectualism it represented, Germany supplied a battle-field, as well as the transcendentalist vantage point Carlyle shortly exploited, from which to attack a variety of negativisms. Lockhart had already translated Friedrich Schlegel under Blackwood's auspices. He seems to have found there many facets of his own anti-Enlightenment position in criticism and biography. The projection of his most Schlegelian tone was the Baron von Lauerwinkel, who 'speaks with the tolerance and the universal air of Schlegel himself' and is 'the embodiment of the philosophical and meditative spirit of the same nation'. It is he, not the sportively contemptuous 'Z', who attacks Professor Playfair with lofty indignation and philosophic sorrow. For critical undertakings where the Baron was too lofty, there was Sternstare, who represented, says Macbeth, 'the predilection for investigation, and also the grave and heavy humor', of the same nation.[25]

Both were shortly superseded. Lockhart's next invention, a native Briton, combined Sternstare's hobbyhorsical devotion to craniology and phrenology with Lauerwinkel's philosophic enthusiasm. The new *persona*, ideal instrument for Lockhart's purpose and style in cultural observation, was Dr Peter Morris.

It is perhaps needless to look beyond *Blackwood's* for sources of Dr Morris's epistolary survey. Yet his significance as a *persona* can be recognized only in the light of the genre to which Lockhart's work belongs. The tradition was evident to Lockhart's first biographer:

'Of "Peter's Letters" it may suffice to say (we write for the benefit of the present generation,) that, like Goldsmith's "Citizen of the World" and Southey's "Letters of Don Velasquez Espriella", they profess to give the impressions made upon a foreigner by what he saw of men and things during a brief sojourn in a country which was strange to him.'[26]

The genre has not been philosophically defined, and until it is, general classification is bound to oversimplify. Nonetheless, the examples of Montesquieu's Persians and Goldsmith's philosophic Chinese will suggest the Enlightenment genre's conventions and effects. And the example of Southey's Don will suggest the difficulties of adapting a satiric genre of the Enlightenment to the different premises and aims of the Romantic cultural critic.

In praising Montesquieu, Voltaire observes the genre's essential dependence on 'l'air étranger', a potentially ironic, naive detachment in the observer: one puts successfully in the mouth of an Asiatic, satire of our country which would be much less acceptable in the mouth of a compatriot; what is commonplace thus becomes singular.[27] Montesquieu's Usbek, no simple prototypal 'asiatic' but a complex and dynamic character, still expresses the essential posture of the philosophic traveller:

'I spend my life examining. In the evening, I write what I have noticed, seen, or heard during the day. Everything interests me; everything astonishes me. I am like a child whose still sensitive organs are keenly struck by the most insignificant objects.'[28]

And Goldsmith's Lien Chi sees only 'those obvious circumstances which force themselves upon the imagination: I consider myself here as a newly created Being introduced into a new world; every object strikes with wonder and surprise'.[29]

Such an observer can satirize, as it were, by accident. When the commonplace is perceived as the singular by consistent naiveté, discrepancies of ideal and real, of profession and practice, blurred to the habitual eye, are automatically exposed:

'An asiatic who travelled in Europe might well take us for pagans. ... He would see that in another country the government causes an Indian Company to flourish, and that the theologians have declared dividends for actions criminal before God.'[30]

But the Asiatic is no mere *naif*. Supposed representative of an exotic, stable culture, the observer is understood to be humanistic or 'philosophic' in his interests. His attention is focused on essential human nature. Usbek is still the harem despot, but in Europe he becomes the philosophic analyst of civilization. Lien Chi may be charged with reckless discontent at home, but in Europe he is contemptuous of mere external curiosity: 'I esteem, therefore, the traveller who instructs the heart, but despise him who only indulges the imagination; a man who leaves home to mend himself and others is a philosopher.'[31] Finally, the Asiatic, by dint of his cultural remoteness, can be presumed capable of a disinterested reasonability inconceivable in *un compatriote*. Usbek's characteristic purpose is to discern law in the flux of European culture: 'I have seen many governments. It is not like Asia, where the rules of politics are always the same. I have often sought to find out which system of government was most in conformity with human reason.'[32] He learns a wise relativism that liberates him from prejudiced, partial views. Lien Chi, likewise, becomes philosophical:

> 'when I had just quitted my native country, and crossed the Chinese wall, I perceived every deviation from the customs and manners of China was a departing from nature . . . ; but I soon perceived that the ridicule lay not in them but in me; that I falsely condemned others of absurdity, because they happened to differ from a standard originally founded in prejudice or partiality.'[33]

The most superficial understanding of Romantic epistemology suggests the inevitable transformation of such a *persona* in the early nineteenth century. In Lien Chi 'philosophical' implies detached reasonability in the observer and essential generality in the observed. In Usbek cultural relativity is a bewildering idea. The Romantic cultural observer is interested not in philosophical or cultural relativity as an idea or a device, but in the complex reality of cultural diversity. For the reader whose tastes were formed on memoir, diary, and historical romance, the authentication of the cultural observer lay in his closeness to his subject, his partiality for the biases of the milieu he describes or represents. If the observer is to serve as norm, then it will be not as an abstract ideal, but rather as a real cultural prototype. His survey's value will lie in its particularity, its preservation of the ephemeral and the local. He will need to be sympathetically or antipathetically alive to the 'character' or the spirit of what he sees. A culture – like a personality – can be awakened to life only by a personality. This generic transformation was attempted, and the resultant problems are evident in the pseudo-letter-writer called by the *Quarterly* 'our own ingenious Hidalgo Don Manuel de Espriella'.[34]

It is unfair to Southey's book to use it simply as a *locus* of unsolved problems. Of its historical value one can accept Saintsbury's general estimate – 'perhaps, a more accurate picture of English ways in the very beginning of the nineteenth century than exists anywhere else'.[35] As an adaptation of its *genre*, however, it is a curiosity. It has neither the universality of a satiric survey nor the locality of a *Peter's Letters*; its depiction of 'character' is dim whether compared with Goldsmith's social and national types or with Lockhart's personalities, and Don Espriella remains dramatically solitary amid his commentaries. His anecdotes lose their dramatic immediacy to generalization; his comments are *ex post facto*. A church service is not an observation, but *the* English church service abstracted from various implied observations. The epistolary pretence is scarcely preserved. Indeed, the Don explains it away: 'I have thought it better to revise these letters, inserting such matters as further research and more knowledge enabled me to add, rather than to methodize the whole.'[36] Some letters are unabashedly general treatises (the Poor Laws, the state of Catholics in England), and those actually fitted into the itinerary reveal the foreign visitor arriving at a place and immediately launching into a judicious account of its history and institutions.[37] An Edinburgh Reviewer noted this departure from generic convention:

> 'he not only speaks quite familiarly of the names of all the villages and hamlets within his view, but notices, with an accuracy that could only have been attained by a residence in the neighbourhood, many of the changes and alterations that have taken place during a course of years.'[38]

The reviewer notices another factor of primary interest to us – the conception and use of the *persona*. Southey describes the Don as 'an able man, bigotted in his religion, and willing to discover such faults and such symptoms of declining power here as may soothe or gratify the national inferiority, which he cannot but feel'.[39] The Don is neither naive nor 'philosophical'. It is not to Southey's purpose to sustain either a real or a feigned impartiality. His main interest is in institutions of a religious nature, and these arouse the partiality of his heresy-hunting *persona*. But the reader must decide when it is present and when it has been suspended, and the Edinburgh Reviewer noticed the confusion:

' Don Manuel is of course represented as a most zealous member of the Holy Catholic Church, which naturally affords the author an opportunity of filling many pages with lamentations over the miserable heresy which prevails in our unhappy country; but . . . it serves no good purpose either to himself or his reader . . . and harmonizes very ill with the tone of philosophical liberality and intrepid reasoning which is assumed on most other occasions.'[40]

The oscillation seems at first glance akin to that in *Gulliver's Travels*. But Gulliver remains a device subordinate always to the thematically consistent movements of Swift's irony. The Don's complexity, on the other hand, can be rationalized only on the level of characterization and is therefore accidental to Southey's ironic purpose.

Lockhart appears more aware of the need for verisimilitude in the pseudo-letter. Perhaps from Scott's *Paul*,[41] perhaps from Paul's model Walpole, he has acquired the biographer's sense of epistolary tact and form, of what makes the letter a plausible dramatic exchange between two personalities. Peter includes enough casual circumstance to suggest that the letters have their source in unselected experience. He throws out frequent hints that 'life' goes on between the letters, life which for him usually culminates in the gout:

'Were I to send you a literal diary of my transactions, I believe you would not fail to discover abundant room for doubting the authenticity of the MS. I shall therefore reserve the full and entire history of this part of my existence, . . . and proceed in the meantime, as I have been doing, to give you little glimpses and fragments of it, exactly in the order that pleases to suggest itself.' [I, 231]

He throws out frequent reminders, often in personal P.S. or private allusion, that his correspondents have independent existences.

But a more important contrast with Southey's Don, and with the travellers of Montesquieu and Goldsmith, is Peter himself. He is the Romantic counterpart to the philosophic *naïf*. He represents a regional culture, and he comes with a full preconception of the culture he is to observe. Far from being aprioristic madness, his preconception is truer than reality. He comes equipped with a Coleridgian 'idea' of Scotland, not with a philosophic traveller's paradigm of the life according to Nature and the Good Society. He can see present Scottish reality as fallen from its true self. Reminders of that true self – redemptive powers – are at hand in the influence of Burns and the presence of Scott. The deviations Peter observes are not universal principles in the 'manners' sense; they are historically actual, symbolic like Waverley characters of forces in a historical dialectic. As cultural biographer, he sees historic individuals as antagonists in a spiritual war for one country's cultural redemption. Technically, Peter's craniological hobbyhorse makes him ideal as an instrument for graphic description. As the antidote to all that Lockhart found negative and narrowly intellectual in the Scottish character, his nationalism and piety make him equally useful. We may account for these two facets of Peter Morris in order.

On the occasion of Spurzheim's visit to Edinburgh in 1816, all predictions that phrenology would pass with the season ('a mere exhalation of human thought') proved premature. Ten years later, the sceptical *Edinburgh Review* was forced to concede that it still flourished,
'and as our Northern race has not hitherto been supposed to sin on the side of over credulity, we are really something at a loss, and, to say the truth, less proud than surprised, to find that Edinburgh should be the great nursing mother of this brood of Germany.'[42]
Lockhart's attitude seems unambiguous. In April 1816 he wrote to J. H. Christie that he had 'met yesterday at dinner with a Cambridge man, Foster, a craniologist, whom I remember your mentioning last summer. He seems totally cracked, but cleverish withal.' In what must have been one of his first letters as editor of the *Quarterly* (14 December 1825), he wrote to a contributor:
'As to the subject of Phrenology – I am much in doubt and in difficulty. I have always considered the whole affair as quackery but of late circumstances have occurred which wd render it extremely disagreeable for me to have it handled in the way you propose *just at present*. One of the ablest writers in the Q. Review has been converted and has written largely in favour of the Phrenologists.'[43]
And yet, during the later months of 1826, he carried on correspondence with Richard Chenevix, an enthusiastic advocate of Spurzheim, who wrote to announce the imminent arrival in London of Spurzheim himself:
'As I know that he wishes very much to be introduced to you and as you may not be sorry to see the man whose cause you in some measure espouse I have taken the liberty to give him a letter to you. If ever he has an opportunity of exercising his science in your presence upon heads that he has never seen before you will become a total convert.'[44]

The terms imply a degree of tolerance, and one recalls Lockhart's self-description in 'The Mad Banker of Amsterdam' (1818):

> Then touched I off friend Lockhart (Gibson John),
> So fond of jabbering about Tieck and Schlegel,
> Klopstock and Wieland, Kant and Mendelssohn,
> All high Dutch quacks like Spurzheim and Feinagle.[45]

There was reason for Lockhart's interest in the high Dutch quacks – reason beyond the fact that the *Edinburgh Review* had placed itself squarely against the 'science'.[46] Hazlitt uses them in an attack on extreme environmentalism: 'We would sooner go the whole length of the absurdities of craniology, than get into this flatting-machine of the original sameness and indiscriminate tendency of men's faculties and dispositions.'[47] Any enthusiastic student of human character, inclined to believe with Hazlitt in 'a stature of the mind as well as of the body', might well share the choice. Alexander Bain supplies a more immediate reason. The phrenologists, so they claimed, had for the first time set up a system opposed to the 'metaphysicians of mind' – from Aristotle, says Bain, through the Scottish tradition of Hume, Reid, Stewart, and Brown – 'affording new lights in the very perplexing inquiry as to the primitive or elementary faculties and feelings; and as constituting a theory of human character'.[48] It was in this area that Lockhart and Peter Morris found the Scottish 'metaphysicians' wanting: 'their mode of studying the human mind, is perhaps better adapted for throwing light upon the intellectual faculties, and upon the association of ideas, than upon human nature in general' [I, 175]. Phrenology, like Lauerwinkel's Germanism, supplied a critical vantage point.

Lockhart recognized early, too, its value as a critical method. When he did finally publish an attack in the *Quarterly* (1836), his reviewer G. P. Scrope put it bluntly:

> 'There is pleasure . . . in dogmatizing on the character of our neighbour, of understanding the most secret processes of his mind, – and this phrenology has rendered quite easy to persons heretofore considered as remarkable for anything but acuteness and perspicacity. We are willing to believe that some may have assumed nominal belief in the science (!) merely for that air of surpassing knowledge which it gives to the adept.'[49]

As part of a cranio-physiognomist *persona*, 'that air' allowed normative psychology to be carried on behind the pretence of scientific observation.

It gave the observer an emblematic method through which the heads and faces observed symbolized psychological insight and moral judgement. Here, for example, is Buonaparte (observed by Sternstare):
'The organs of causality, observation, and comparison, are sufficient to have made him a philosopher of no common class, if the back part of his head had not pushed him into active life. . . . The organ of ferocity above the ear, is the one which I spoke of as counteracting clemency.'
And here is Cromwell:
'The top of the head is well expanded, and there can be little doubt that Cromwell was sincerely religious, notwithstanding that worldly craft found means to join issue with pious zeal, and to pursue its own ends, without scandalizing the upper state of his brain.'[50]
For as Peter Morris asks, 'after all, what are features unless they form the index to the mind?' [II, 103]. And he cites as precedents 'that wise saying of the wisest of men, which the sceptical wits of the present age are pleased to scorn as much as any of the dicta of poor Spurzheim – "A man may be known by his look, and one that hath understanding by his countenance, when thou meetest him" (Eccles. xiv. 29)' [III, 184]; as well as 'the only great Craniologists the world ever produced', the Greeks, who always considered the head 'in the light of a Form – an object having certain proportions from which certain inferences may be drawn' [I, 288].
Of course, Dr Morris's profession made him a penetrating observer, since the 'practice of a physician is calculated to make him see a good deal into human life' [III, 25]. But his avocational fidelity to Spurzheim explains his possession of the graphic artist's eye:
'The external aspect of the head is all that nature exhibits to us, or intends we should see. It is there that expression appears and speaks a natural language to our minds – a language of which our knowledge is vague and imperfect, and almost unconscious; but of which a few simple precepts and remarks are enough to recall to our recollection the great outlines.' [I, 288]
He urges a programme of training the eye:
'I wish to God some plain, sensible man, with a true Baconian turn for observation, would set about devoting himself in good earnest to the calm consideration of the skulls and faces which come in his way. . . . The person engaged in such a study, I do not at all mean perpetually engaged in it, could not fail to extend his acquaintance

with his own species; for he would be furnished with a stronger stimulus than is common, to be quick and keen-sighted in his scrutiny of individuals.' [I, 88-89]

The method and stimulus for scrutiny supplied by Phrenology is, however, subservient to the critical perspective, which Peter Morris also embodies. His character has been articulated in terms of the book's dominant view of Scotland. The theme is best anticipated by his predecessor in mock-phrenology, Sternstare:

'I am inclined to suspect the Lowland Scots of a meagreness in the enthusiastic and disinterested elements of human nature. They have always been remarkable for a certain cold and unadmiring shrewdness, of which self love is the true foundation. Sawney feels no love of great and beautiful objects for their own sakes, but stands aloof, and measures them with a sceptical eye. . . . Even the metaphysics of this singular race are the metaphysics of littleness, and have never led into the love of beauty, as with most other nations. . . . I have no patience with the love of littleness, which, whoever indulges in, as a great poet observes, "wars against his own soul".'[51]

Upon his arrival, Peter is already emotionally involved; he comes with historical and cultural enthusiasm and veneration for Scotland and Scottish character. His discovery of sceptical littleness and narrow intellectuality, traits fostered by the *Edinburgh Review*, is not the acquisition of knowledge by an alien inquirer, but the betrayal of a deep-rooted anticipation.

Yet Peter Morris could not be a Scot; and since the book was bound to include judicious but sympathetic contrasts of Scotland and England, he could not be an Englishman either. Lockhart's review of 'Miss Spence and the Bagman', two immediate predecessors of Peter in the epistolary survey *genre*, accounts for the rejection of both the 'ignorant calumny of the Cockney' and the uncritical enthusiasm and gullibility of the perfervid Celt.[52] His Welsh nationality may be derived from Matthew Bramble, Smollett's itinerant squire, or merely from Lockhart's Oxford friend, Archdeacon Williams.[53] Whatever the specific source, the purpose of such a selection is clear: Morris is English in his background and yet not English. He has a Scottish mother, from whom he derives some of his expectant enthusiasm. Even if his pride never reaches the degree of ardour observed in Scott reciting Otterbourne:

'the more than martial fervours of his kindled eye, were almost enough to give to the same lines the same magic in my ears; and I

could half fancy that the portion of Scottish blood which is mingled in my veins, had begun to assert, by a more ardent throb, its right to partake in the triumphs of the same primitive allegiance' [II, 304] –
he has 'arrived, at least, without prejudices against that which I should see, and was ready to open myself to such impressions as might come' [I, 7]. He has been a foreigner to both London and Edinburgh, yet with loyalties to both. His most judicious attitude is a wise relativism:
'Instead then of joining in with that senseless spirit of railing, where-with Scotchmen are too often accustomed to talk of the English, and Englishmen of the Scottish Universities, I please myself in thinking that the two institutions have different objects, and that they are both excellent in their different ways.' [I, 39, 204] [54]
Peter's Welsh background allows other complexities of attitude, recognizably those of Lockhart himself. As an Anglican, he is still cap-able of writing with sympathetic admiration of the Kirk. Politically he can align himself with the entrenched Toryism of the South, yet culturally he can, as a fellow Celt, defend the language of the Edinburgh cadies (Gaelic) and speak as sympathetically of that other non-English tradition, Scots. Of more general importance, his residence in Wales permits a distance from both capital cities – in fact, from *the* city – with-out causing his viewpoint to be provincial. Well-versed in city life, he speaks often as the sophisticated pastoralist, the cultural and moral primitivist of a Wordsworthian tenor. For much of his criticism of what urbane Edinburgh symbolizes is based, like Lockhart's anti-Cockney vituperation, on the pastoral attitude that a nation is most true to itself in more 'natural' social structures.

Peter Morris, then, is the embodiment of an enthusiasm for a Scottish heritage which persists and of a criticism of a Scotland untrue to its own national culture. Yet Peter's detachment keeps his conser-vatism within reasonable bounds. That detachment is increased by Lockhart's second *persona*, a kind of 'Man in Black', in whom he satirizes the extreme of Peter Morris's own position, and through whom he causes Peter's experience to evolve by a dialogue with his own extreme Scottish counterpart.

Wastle's uses are many. He augments verisimilitude, giving Peter a partner for the casual life behind the selective epistolary accounts. As a fellow Oxonian, he serves to verify a significant part of Peter's past. He is 'the very person I should have selected to act as my Cicerone in Scotland' [1, 16], giving Peter access to dinners private and public and to prominent individuals and groups. He arrives, for example, in his 'old yellow chariot' insistent 'upon carrying me with him to make my bow at the levee of the Earl of Morton, who has come down as the King's Lord High Commissioner to the General Assembly of this year' [III, 9].

Invaluable as a cicerone, Wastle remains problematical as an informer, for his own bias colours all his contributions to Peter's experience. 'I was always less of a bigot than Wastle,' Peter explains. He cannot rely on Wastle's information and must either reshape Wastle's ways as a guide – 'I soon found it expedient to give my good friend a slight hint, that I wished he could contrive to afford me something else for the main woof of my meditations' – or take advantage of his absences to call on Whiggish gentlemen Wastle scarcely knows: 'I believe, indeed, there is little love lost between him and them – and I wish to see things with my own eyes' [1, 35, 52]. And yet – such is the complexity of perspective allowed by this dramatic interplay – Wastle gives eloquent justification for his own partisanship in terms which cast doubt on Peter's *bonhommie*; and Peter in turn rejects Wastle's self-justification as the self-deception of a bigot.

The biographer of Lockhart recognizes that this dialogue between Tories in 1819 was, in fact, a projection of a conflict in Lockhart's own mind and experience. Lockhart's future in Edinburgh was suspended between the alternatives presented by Scott and the Blackwood group: on the one hand, a liberal, perhaps facile *bonhommie*, and on the other, a sincere but perhaps rigid intolerance. Lockhart was both Dr Morris and his bigoted friend, and neither.

Though Wastle is fictitious, he serves well to illustrate the manner in which the book characterizes individuals. The central people in Peter's experience are not static 'characters'. They grow as a group of personalities as his experience of them deepens, and as his procedure alternates between the descriptive and the dramatic. Wastle plays the cicerone simply as an unnamed friend so that Peter's general view of the city may open the book; he is then named, and in the sketching of his background we learn of Peter's own past. A consideration of his eccentricities evokes a concrete image of his 'natural habitat'; before he is formally described, he and Peter acquire additional concreteness through the dinner episode at his home. Detailed visualization climaxes the imparting to Wastle of substantiality in past and present – and here Dr Morris suspends sympathy to indulge in his physiognomic craft:

'This yellow visage of his, with his close firm lips, and his grey eyes shining through his spectacles, as through a burning-glass, more brightly – the black beard not over diligently shorn – all lurking under the projecting shadow of that strange brim, compose such a physiognomy, as one would less wonder to meet with in Valladolid, than in Edinburgh.' [1, 23]

In his subsequent appearances, there is the same alternation – in style between dramatic and descriptive, in tone between amusement and sympathy. From each location, scene, or opinion in which he is involved, he takes on additional reality; he grows as Peter's experience of him grows; and as Peter's reactions to him develop, so does the continuity of expectancy and response which is Peter.

These techniques of fiction are equally evident in the presentation of historic personages. The two dominant extremes of Edinburgh legal-literary society play commanding roles in Peter Morris's experience: Jeffrey and Scott. But though Scott as symbol and standard haunts the whole book, it is his opposite – the restless intellectual whom Lockhart was perhaps seeking to exorcise from his own personality – who appears more often.

The method by which Peter presents the real Jeffrey avoids the formal 'character'. Yet, in the slightest contextual observations of this visiting student of 'speaking countenances', all things are emblematic of character. The craniologist goes to call on Jeffrey. But before he indulges his genius for physiognomy, he senses Jeffrey as the focal point of an atmosphere:

'I know not how, there is a kind of atmosphere of activity about him; and my eyes caught so much of the prevailing spirit, that they darted for some minutes from object to object, and refused, for the first time, to settle themselves even upon the features of a man of genius – to them, of all human things, the most potent of attractions.' [1, 53]

The portrait that follows is peerless as an illustration of Peter's emblematic impressionism, containing within it the germ of the characterization to follow, conveying psychological analysis within physical description, and suggesting one side of the spiritual conflict that gives the book its thematic structure:

'The lips are very firm, but they tremble and vibrate, even when brought close together, in such a way as to give the idea of an intense, never-ceasing play of mind. There is a delicate kind of sneer almost always upon them, which has not the least appearance of ill-temper about it, but seems to belong entirely to the speculative understanding of the man.' [I, 59]

If the mouth is the centre of the face's 'rapid and transitory expression', the eyes are emblems of a warfare within:

'They disdain to be agitated with those lesser emotions which pass over the lips; they reserve their fierce and dark energies for matters of more moment. . . . With the capacity of emitting such a flood of radiance, they seem to take a pleasure in banishing every ray from their black, inscrutable, glazed, tarn-like circles.' [I, 60]

They suggest the self-condemnation of such denial: 'I think their prevailing language is, after all, rather a melancholy than a merry one – it is, at least, very full of reflection.'

By contrast, Scott is initially disappointing to the craniologist. There is none of the restless energy that stamped Jeffrey's countenance. Instead, the poet is stamped by 'Nature' – by the traditional feelings and collective memories to which he has been sensitively open. They bring his sensibility to his face:

'he happened to quote a few lines from one of the old Border Ballads, and, looking around, I was quite astonished with the change which seemed to have passed over every feature in his countenance. His eyes seemed no longer to glance quick and grey from beneath his impending brows, but were fixed in their expanded eye-lids with a sober, solemn lustre. His mouth (the muscles about which are at all times wonderfully expressive) instead of its usual language of mirth or benevolence, or shrewdness, was filled with a sad and pensive earnestness.' [II, 302]

Both portraits are brief moments in characterizations more dramatic than pictorial. Jeffrey comes to life dramatically in a variety of *milieux* – at his Craigcrook house, at the Burns dinner, at the 'rout' in playful conversation with formidable bluestockings, but most important at the Parliament House. In the presentation of Scott, there is the same fusion of place and personality, the same alternation of scene and picture; but significantly it all takes place in the country at Abbotsford. Peter's visit, based on one or more of Lockhart's, is constructed in such a way that concrete description is skillfully interspersed with illustrative incident which in turn leads Peter to reflect on Scott's significance in Scottish culture, leads back to a renewal of conversation, leads on to further concrete description. Scott is seen amid the association-rich countryside surrounding Abbotsford. Scott appears in various roles, in 'domestic manners', even (by retrospect) at different stages in his development; he is realized as the centre of a whole idyllic way of life. The account of the visit, like Peter's experience of Jeffrey, is constructed so as to justify Peter's reflection on riding away: 'It is wonderful how the mere seeing of such a person gives concentration, and compactness, and distinctness to one's ideas on all subjects connected with him' [11, 547].

Such constructions of pseudo-biographical anecdote to fulfil an expository aim make one of the most interesting aspects of a controversial work. *Peter's Letters* gives actuality to a wholly fictitious observer, then dramatizes as his experience impressions from the experience of his creator, incidents illustrative of historic personages. But since Peter's experience, being fictitious, can be wholly shaped by preconceptions of the people encountered, Lockhart is free to reshape the data of his own experience in accordance with thematic interpretations of personality. The procedure is extreme in this early work; but behind such a theory of anecdote is the same 'unscientific' notion of historical truth which has caused charges of dishonesty to be levelled at his later full-scale biographies. Peter Morris cited precedents in 'all the memoir-writers – and letter-writers – and tourists – and travellers of every nation that ever knew the use of the pen'.[55] Nevertheless, his emblematic constructions were taken as historical fact, evoking such solemn disavowals as that made thirty years later by Jeffrey's biographer:

'A fictitious person of the name of Morris (but who represents a real man, and a powerful writer, and who, in *Peter's Letters to his Kinsfolk,* published in 1819, professes to describe Edinburgh and its neighbourhood,) mentions, as if he had seen it, a Craigcrook scene, where the whole party, including Mr Playfair, who died in July 1819, aged seventy-one, took off their coats and had a leaping match. As the liveliness and individuality of Dr Morris's descriptions have made some of the simple believe them to be all real, it may be as well to say that this is entirely a fancy piece. And, for so skillful a painter, it is not well fancied. It is totally unlike the Craigcrook proceedings, and utterly repugnant to all the habits of Mr Playfair.'[56]

Lockhart's imagination, say those who argue he was not by nature a novelist,[57] operated best when in touch with factual realities. Its essential operation was to penetrate and integrate *given* phenomena. It serves the physiognomist well, allowing him to read character in countenance. But the 'imagination of insight' by which Peter's acute eye penetrates, is used to treat the countenance as an emblem, not simply of idiosyncratic 'humour' or predominant motive but of a mode of life, rooted in region, vocation, and tradition, which the individual represents. Subservient to this cultural view of character, the imagination proceeds from the vividly grasped particular to the construction by inference, in concrete panorama, of the form and texture of the experience which shaped the countenance. There are, for example, the clergymen from all over Scotland, marching to the General Assembly:

'I could easily recognize the inhabitant of a wild and tempestuous region, by his weather-beaten cheek-bones, his loose locks, and the loud and dissonant notes of his voice, if at any time he chanced to speak even to his neighbour. In seeing him, one thinks of the stunted crops of oats, that lie spread in patches upon the desolate hills among which his spire arises. . . . Such as come from good shooting countries, above all, from the fine breezy braes of the North are to be known . . . by a knowing cast of the eye, which seems better accustomed to watch the motions of a pointer, than to decipher the points of a Hebrew Bible.' [III, 22-23]

More characteristic in both severity and sympathy, there are the university students of Moral philosophy. The initial depiction is severe; but the severity is shortly transformed into sympathetic admiration in a full, generic evocation of the Scottish university student's mode of existence:

'all these sorrows of poverty, united with those many sorrows and depressions which the merely intellectual part of a young student's existence must always be sufficient to create – the doubts and fears which must at times overcloud and darken the brightest intellect that over expanded before the influence of exertion – the watching and tossing of over-excitement – the self-reproach of languor – the tightening of the heart-strings – and the blank wanderings of the brain – these things are enough to complete the gloomy fore-ground of a picture which would, indeed require radiance in the distance to give it any measure of captivation.' [I, 194-5]

These illustrations omit, however, the surface feature most aptly suited to Peter's treatment of speaking countenances: the manner of speaking, the conversational emblem itself. The society which he describes, having long since lost its royal court and hereditary nobility, is one aristocratically dominated by three professions – law, church, and education. To portray their leaders is to portray speakers, and one has the feeling that *Peter's Letters* is literally filled with talk.

Literally this is not the case. Direct quotation is limited to the fictitious or semi-fictitious characters (the Ettrick Shepherd, the Philosophical Weaver). For the most part the talk we 'hear' is rather the subtle characterization of tone and style, which, like the craniological pretence, is a flexibly impressionistic means of fusing dramatic presentation with interpretative characterization of the mode of thought and feeling which the manner of speech embodies. As Peter observes of contemporary poets, 'It is, indeed, a very striking thing, how much the conversation of each of these men harmonizes with the peculiar vein of his mind, as displayed in more elaborate shapes' [11, 309].[58]

Illustrations are abundant. In Brown's lecturing, in Lord Hermand's 'hot and choleric style' from the bench, Peter finds opportunities to describe one of the most significant of pathognomic phenomena, the transformation of the face in its passage from repose to the activity of speech. The address of Lord Cockburn to a jury is given, without a word quoted, to set the single master of pathos in contrast with Jeffrey. The meeting of the General Assembly invites Peter's greatest virtuosity to sketch a complete spectrum of ecclesiastical personalities in speech. But most satisfactory is the long sketch of the most celebrated of contemporary Scottish preachers, Dr Chalmers. He is saved for late in the book, the occasion of Peter's trip to Glasgow and the West, because there he can be viewed in his natural *milieu*, because the contrast of religious feeling in East and West is of thematic importance, and because he opens the book's climax.

Chalmers's symbolic importance is first perceived craniologically. His ratiocinative powers are evident in

'the most marked mathematical forehead I ever met with – being far wider across the eye-brows than either Mr Playfair's or Mr Leslie's – and having the eye-brows themselves lifted up at their exterior ends quite out of the usual line – a peculiarity which Spurzheim had remarked in the countenances of almost all the great mathematical or calculating geniuses.' [111, 269]

Thus, he is fully equipped with combative intellectuality for his visits to the 'critical city' of Edinburgh. But ratiocination is subordinate in Chalmers to higher, more comprehensive powers. In his forehead there is

'an arch of Imagination, carrying out the summit boldly and roundly,

67

in a style to which the heads of very few poets present anything comparable – while over this again there is a grand apex of high and solemn Veneration and Love – such as might have graced the bust of Plato himself.'

And his voice and manner of speaking corroborate the testimony of the skull:

'He has a wonderful talent for ratiocination, and possesses, besides, an imagination both fertile and distinct, which gives all richness of colour to his style, and supplies his argument with every diversity of illustration.'

Peter's response to Chalmers is perhaps the thematic centre of the entire book:

'In presence of such a spirit subjection is a triumph – and I was proud to feel my hardened nerves creep and vibrate, and my blood freeze and boil while he spake – as they were wont to do in the early innocent years, when unquestioning enthusiasm had as yet caught no lessons of chillness from the jealousies of discernment, the delights of comparison, and the example of the unimaginative world.'

'Such a spirit' embodies what Peter has come to find, and in such a redemptive response – Carlyle would call it Discipleship – the biographical observer finds at once his appropriate tone and his own highest powers.

The lines of conflict thus resolved in Dr Chalmers have, however, already assumed major significance in the talk of Scott and Jeffrey. Many of the 'pleaders' anticipate Jeffrey's mode of speech. Scott's is anticipated by Mrs Grant of Laggan, who

'had the good sense to perceive, that a stranger, such as I was, came not to hear disquisitions, but to gather useful information; . . . She related, in a very simple, but very graphic manner, a variety of little anecdotes and traits of character, with my recollections of which I shall always have a pleasure in connecting my recollections of herself.' [1, 309]

Scott's conversation, like hers, is not speculative and abstract, but anecdotally concrete. Its store seems infinite; its broad humanity makes it 'of such a kind, that all can take a lively part in it'. It reveals 'the most keen perception, the most tenacious memory, and the most brilliant imagination', which have 'been at work throughout the whole of his busy life, in filling his mind with a store of individual traits and anecdotes, serious and comic, individual and national'

[II, 367]. Jeffrey's receives equally high praise – not of its store, but of its intellectual power:

'. . . The largeness of the views suggested by his speculative under-standing, and the shrewdness with which his sound and close judge-ment seems to scrutinize them after they are suggested – these alone would be sufficient to make his conversation one of the most re-markable things in the world.' [I, 69-70]

Nor does he lack imagination – the contrast with Scott does not lie there. Rather, the contrast is between the store of Nature, the openness and universality of humanity, and the self-sufficient, subtle intellect. Jeffrey is an admirable Spider to Scott's more admirable Bee.

The contrast thus focused in the conversation of the two lions of Peter's expedition underlies his entire experience and gives his book its thematic structure. That structure can best be understood as a battle of Ancients and Moderns against the background of Edinburgh, where 'the proudest of palaces must be content to catch the shadows of mountains' and where 'there must always be present the idea of the comparative littleness of all human works'. For Peter, the Ancients persist as heroic shadows, giants of a former age, in contrast with whom the Moderns are scrutinized in their several kinds of littleness.

Peter Morris has come to Edinburgh at a transitional period when the new is everywhere evident, but the past persists. He comes to observe 'Scottish character' at a time when that character seems un-true to itself and 'Character' itself belongs to the past. He responds enthusiastically to the remnants – the 'huge, strange dwellings' of Lawnmarket and Canongate, which tower above the drab, refined crescents and terraces of the New Town, or to their human counter-parts. They make him 'ashamed of [his] youth' [I, 96-97]. Walking to Henry Mackenzie's house he is 'conscious of an almost superstitious feeling'. In Lord Hermand he sees

'a noble living specimen of a very fine old school, . . . the departure of many of whose peculiarities was perhaps rendered necessary in a great measure by the spirit of the age, but of which it may be suspec-ted not a little has been allowed to expire, which might have been bet-ter worth preserving than much that has come in its place.' [II, 120]

The giants are gone from Bench and Kirk. A remnant of Character is a rare delight, and a strong stimulus to biography:

'In our age, when so much oil is poured upon the whole surface of

F

the ocean of life, that one's eye can, for the most part, see nothing but the smoothness and the flatness of uniformity, it is a most re-freshing thing to come upon some sequestered bay, where the breakers still gambol along the sands, and leap up against the rocks as they used to do.' [II, 109-10]

Though the stimulus appears biographical, Peter's mode of experi-ence, as his 'reviewer' in *Blackwood's* noticed,[59] is philosophical. That mode is characterized throughout by two disappointments. The first looks backward to the Battle of the Books; the second, ahead to the spiritual crisis of Teufelsdröckh. The first is aroused by the pettiness of intellectual complacency, of a restless, carping self-importance; the second, by the 'atmosphere of doubt', the habitual scepticism which, for Peter, is a corollary of that intellectualism, and which, in the mixed moods of the book, translates intellectual folly into spiritual tragedy. These disappointments are the themes which unify Peter's ex-periences and speculations. They embody the anti-enlightenment attitudes which dominate all of Lockhart's work.

In education, for example, Peter pits a fervent classicism against both intellectualism and utilitarianism. He attacks the modern Scot's self-sufficiency, his contempt for history, which, when she 'seizes and expands before us the spirit of great men, great times, and great actions, is in herself alone a true and entire philosophy' [I, 160]. Such attitudes have resulted in a narrower, less humane philosophical 'mode of studying the human mind'. One hears in anticipation the great Victorian educationists when Peter theorizes: 'The power which is conferred by knowledge, is always of a merely calculating and mechan-ical sort, and consists in nothing higher than the adaptation of means to ends' [I, 175-7]. One recalls an earlier English classicism when Peter charges that, under such an educational regimen, the mind is rather sharpened than stored, turned in upon itself, forced into what Johnson and Reynolds knew was a sterile self-sufficiency, and aligned rather with the Spider than with the Bee:

'The style of education and exertion to which he submits, are admirably fitted for sharpening and quickening the keenness of his understanding, but do not much tend to fill his mind with a store of thoughts, feelings, and images, on which it might repose itself, and in which he might possess for ever the means of a quiet and con-templative happiness.' [I, 196]

Nor is the educational theory isolated. A manifestation of the same disappointment is Peter's theory of literature and cultural nationalism, which directs his response to Scottish men of letters, and which provides the clearest anticipation of the biographer of Burns and Scott. Self-sufficiency and abstract intellectuality are, for Peter, inimical to the true man of letters, whose real function is not to invent, but to absorb and embody, and whose participation in human society and openness to human experience are therefore his most essential attributes. Mackenzie the novelist excelled in a 'species of literature . . . in its very essence, connected with any ideas rather than those of secluded and artist-like abstraction' [I, 101]. Peter contrasts the Wordsworthian enthusiasm,[60] 'that of a secluded artist', with the mental universality of Scott, founded in and nourished by an objective world of images, habits, and sympathies. He reflects that a great tradition in painting cannot be born

'till the painters get rid of that passion for *inventing* subjects, which at present seems to predominate among them all. The object of a great painter should be, not to invent subjects, but to give a graphical form to ideas universally known, and contemplated with deep feeling.' [II, 263]

Such art springs only from a 'capacity for the most common sympathies and sensibilities of human nature'; such genius, in its openness to Nature, belongs to the audience whose habits and sympathies nourish it, for it 'is an instrument which he [the artist] himself may not always have the judgement to employ to the best advantage, and which is more safely directed to its mark by the aggregated feelings, I will not say of the multitude, but at least of numbers' [II, 262-3]. Such art and genius are distinctly national in source and appeal. Lockhart had begun his literary career two years before as the translator of Friedrich Schlegel's *Lectures on the History of Literature*. This work, with its conception of the literary artist as an instrument for the awakening and preserving of a nation's cultural self-consciousness, is echoed in Peter's insistence on the artist's sympathetic openness.

'The truth is, that a great national author connects himself for ever with all the better part of his nation, by the ties of intellectual kinsmanship – ties which, in his own age, are scarcely less powerful than those of the kinsmanship of blood, and which, instead of evaporating and being forgotten in the course of a few generations, as the bonds of blood must inevitably be, are only rivetted the faster by every year that passes over them.' [II, 100]

In the propounding of his theory of national culture and genius, Peter's disappointment at Edinburgh's complacent intellectualism is fused with that other disappointment suffered by this enthusiast in his quest for Scottish character. At first he is inclined to believe that analytic scepticism is permanent in a character too inclined to speculation and sarcastic irreverence. But his experience leads him back to an historical view, as well as a regional one at Edinburgh's expense. Wastle accounts historically for the scepticism of Jeffrey's Edinburgh: 'He regards the Scotch philosophers of the present day, and among, or above the rest, Mr Jeffrey and the Edinburgh Reviewers, as the legitimate progeny of the sceptical philosophers of the last age' [II, 128]. They must take the blame for fostering the negative impulse in an enduring *psychomachia* in the Scottish spirit:

'the struggle that seems to be perpetually going on between the sarcastic and reverential elements of their disposition – how bitterly they seem to rejoice in their own strength, when they espy, or think they espy, some chink in the armour of their preacher's reasoning; and then with what sudden humility they appear to bow themselves into the dust, before some single solitary gleam of warm affectionate eloquence.' [I, 41]

Jeffrey has headed a group of thinkers who have 'banished from their own minds a very great part of that reverence for *Feeling* (as abstracted from mere questions of immediate or obvious utility), in the strength and nourishment of which the true old character of England . . . grew', and who therefore can no longer 'understand the value of national experience'. The effect on the public mind has been not just the supremacy of a 'facetious and rejoicing ignorance', but also – and more tragic – the 'encroachment of the spirit of degrading mockery' [II, 135-44].

It is to Wastle that these views are attributed – Wastle, whose zeal and bigotry are always viewed with detachment. But Peter himself is an embodiment of Schlegelian attitudes; his experience, from the texture of a single description to the structure of an entire volume, is integrated in terms of these general antitheses: intellectual arrogance and a pastoral purity of feeling; pompous urbanity and rustic simplicity; restless scepticism and traditional piety. One can find any number of vivid descriptions in which there recurs the same evocation of brilliant, dynamic, yet somehow meaningless and insatiable intellectual restlessness. One can contrast physical descriptions of parts of the city which, by their traditional grandeur and their tragic decay, mock the self-important activity of the living. One can examine the idealized evocations of country life: the depiction of Scott at Abbotsford which closes volume two, and the equally full presentation of the Country Sacrament which climaxes volume three.

Reference to the emphatic locations of these passages suggests the more ambitious claim that the work as a whole, for all its ostensibly haphazard epistolary form, has significant structure. The structure of Peter's experience is the first evidence of Lockhart's skill as a formal artist in biography, of his ability to articulate, through mood and emphasis, the evolving significant pattern in the most diverse of incidents and responses that make up a life.

We might take for illustration the long group of letters in volume one, beginning with the first discussion of David Hume as the '*beau idéal* of the national understanding' and ending in the churchyard on Calton Hill over one hundred pages later. The pages commence with Hume physically portrayed and reflected upon as a representative of national character in defective form. They envision the university as a monument to Hume's influence; they include visits to philosophy lectures and discussions of contemporary education and philosophy – all under the shadow of Hume. In the long letters describing the Burns dinner, Peter's reflections centre on Jeffrey's antagonism toward Burns's memory and the dual deficiency it implies: 'a very lamentable defect, not merely of nationality of feeling, but of humanity of feeling' [I, 114]. The Scotlands of Burns and Hume are at war in spirit, with that of Hume temporarily ascendant. But the providence that governs Peter's experience resolves the conflict otherwise. Peter strolls up Calton Hill with Professor Playfair and comes upon the churchyard where anonymous common humanity and the isolated intellectual, Hume, share the same dust. The human nature in which Burns participated so fully has mingled its ashes 'with Him, whose body had very little share either in his wants or his wishes – whose spirit alone was restless and sleepless, the Prince of Doubters'. Peter imagines one buried there 'who lived, and thought, and breathed in the affections alone . . . close beside one who walked upon the earth, not to feel, but to speculate, and was content to descend into her bosom, with scarcely one ray of hope beyond the dark and enduring sleep of nothingness' [I, 186]. Thus the unit ends – and it is only one illustration of the evolving integrity of Peter's experience.

Significant structure is even more impressive when descried in entire volumes. The book is organized in three long parts. Calton Hill provides Peter, at the opening of the first volume, with a lofty vantage point from which to envision the city as an organic unity. He does so in lines strongly reminiscent of Wordsworth, the poet Lockhart found most congenial:

'the airy bridge – the bright green vale below and beyond it – and skirting the line of the vale on either side, the rough crags of the Castle rock, and the broad glare of Prince's Street, that most superb of terraces – all beaming in the open yellow light of the sun – steeples and towers, and cupolas scattered bright beneath our feet – and, far as the eye could reach, the whole pomp and richness of distant commotion – the heart of the city.' [I, 11]

His vantage point is one of the gigantic natural forms which surround the city with their reminder of 'the comparative littleness of all human works'. The volume that follows is concerned with those works: efforts of restless self-importance, ranging from the seriously thoughtful to the trivially social. At the close we return coincidentally to the physical city: Peter recalls his nightly walks home along Princes Street, on his left a modern city, and on his right 'the eternal rock sleeping in the stillness of nature'. The scene, in which all human ambitions and antagonisms become suddenly irrelevant, brings to his mind the moonlit opening of Goethe's *Faust*, just as his first sight of the restless and intense Jeffrey had evoked the memory of the first sight of Goethe. What closes the volume is an answer to all that Jeffrey and his intellectual city represent. It is an imaginative depiction of the 'weary and melancholy sceptic', Faust:

'The restlessness of an intellect wearied with the vanity of knowledge, and tormented with the sleepless agonies of doubt – the sickness of a heart bruised and buffeted by all the demons of presumption – the wild and wandering throbs of a soul parched among plenty, by the blind cruelty of its own dead affections.' [I, 331-2]

Lockhart leaves it to the reader to recognize the thematic climax.

The second volume opens full upon the restlessness in all its colour and fury in the legal centre of the city, and moves through depictions of a speculative and argumentative society. It then jumps to the discussion of Scottish painters of the day, and this discussion introduces a consideration of human nature in a broader and deeper sense. The questions to which it leads – questions of the national artist in a national culture – prepare for the volume's climax. The trip out of the city is a movement from one world to another by which the first is judged and found wanting; it is a voyage to the home, the locality, and the significance of Scott, providing a focus for the discussion of art and nationality, and a conservative, humane contrast to what has gone before. The depiction is an idyll of neo-feudal primitivism from which we look back upon all that the city contains and represents.

The third volume proceeds similarly, but in the ecclesiastical sphere, from the pomp of the General Assembly, the urbane ecclesiastical world, to the visit to Chalmers. To see Chalmers Peter goes West, and the journey again is significant. Social Glasgow, vulgar, but instinctively cheerful and affectionately humane, is a secular counterpart to the West Country religion of Chalmers, less speculative, more human because simpler and more emotional. Once again Edinburgh's Scotland is judged. The climax is the Country Sacrament, an idyll at once religious, social, and political. Here all ranks join, as, in Peter's reflection, all themes fuse; here he finds the confirmation of the character he has sought, and with Burns more in mind than Scott, he reflects on the necessary conditions for a national culture which would embody such a national character. The climax is the natural conclusion to the entire work.

Peter's Letters is worth attention, not only because it reveals the attitudes and skills that made Lockhart a biographer and includes early perspectives on his future subjects, but also because it remains a singular achievement as a first book. Swift looked back upon the *Tale of a Tub* in awe at the genius he must have possessed to write it. Lockhart, in his supreme diffidence even more merciless to pretension in himself than in others, thought *Peter's Letters* a book that no one 'but a very young and a very thoughtless person could have dreamt of putting forth'.[61]

3

BURNS, LOCKHART,
AND THE
MYTHMAKERS

The posthumous reputation of Burns, more than that of any other British writer, was subjected to a process of falsification which, until the ruthless critical apparatus of twentieth-century scholarship was brought to bear upon it, succeeded in presenting to the world a distorted picture of the poet's earthly tenure. . . . And the myth has become more important than the poetry.

MAURICE LINDSAY

It is impossible to judge impartially a convenient appliance to which we have grown accustomed. The myth is unlike the man; but the man was its basis, and no other could have served. . . . When we consider Burns we must therefore include the Burns Nights with him, and the Burns Cult in all its forms; if we sneer at them we sneer at Burns.

EDWIN MUIR

Myth has a background of reality, and in the foreground steps across an invisible threshold into reality again.

ERIC LINKLATER[1]

3

BURNS, LOCKHART,
AND THE
MYTHMAKERS

I

When Stevenson directed the attention of his idolatrous countrymen to 'Some Aspects of Robert Burns' closer to the feet of clay than to 'Mr Carlyle's inimitable bust', the response was neither grateful nor gratifying. In the bitterness that followed, Stevenson was simply sharing the fate of others who had challenged the public portrait of 'the sweet singer of mice and mountain daisies; of democracy, patriotism, and love; the Ayrshire Galahad who blamelessly loved a lily maid of Astolat named Mary Campbell'. A recent Stevensonian accounts for the wrath of the Burns Cultists:

> 'Burns was – and still is – the Scottish national symbol-deity, a thing Americans can best understand by thinking of Abraham Lincoln. The apotheosis had occurred in the century ornamented by Thomas Bowdler. So the effect of publicly stating that the man who wrote "Had we never loved sae blindly . . ." made a cult of wenching had about the same effect as if American newspapers next February 12 should loudly remind readers that Lincoln was the richest source of dirty stories in Illinois.'[2]

The challengers have nevertheless increased in number and volubility.

They have reason for complaint. The apotheosis of Burns absorbed energies needed elsewhere. Burns, complains a second-generation leader of the Scots Renaissance,

> 'has long since ceased to be merely a Scottish poet, so far as Scots folk are concerned. He has become *the National Bard*, a figure of spiritual

dimensions so mythical as the preposterous physical dimensions attributed to Wallace by the poet Blind Harry. And the myth has become more important than the poetry.'[3]

Poetry has suffered. The Burns Federation

'are manifestly not interested in the living body of Scottish literature but are only a sort of necrophagists, corpse-eaters devouring the symbolic cadaver (the haggis) at their ritual banquet, before hearkening to the prescribed canticles and prayers.'[4]

The Cultists are allied with those hypocrites who in Anglicized apathy oppose everything essentially Scottish, the 'Enemies of Folksong':

'If the history of the Burns Cult in Scotland has largely been the history of a struggle among the Unco Guid and the Holy Willies of the country for the defenceless body of the dead bard, the history of Scottish folksong-ism has been chiefly a determined attempt to take all the guts and spunk, all the ardour, verve, and raucle randiness out of the song of the people, and reduce it to the level of a kirk social.'[5]

However justifiable their bitterness, the iconoclasts are as unfree of dogma and preconception as any Cultist. They, too, reject evidence as false or nonessential; they, too, falsify the baffling complexity of the Burns phenomenon. In their anti-bourgeois primitivism, clearly not derived from the court poets of James IV whose literary cause they espouse, they must, for example, discount Burns's impulse to Anglification, as well as his enthusiastic response to Shenstone, *The Man of Feeling*, and the epistolary mode of Agnes Maclehose.

Such war-cries as those of Hugh MacDiarmid seldom lead to scientific inquiry: 'The Burns Cult must be killed stone-dead – and would be instantly if a single lightning flash of the spirit of Burns were alive in Scotland – home or colonial.'[6] But scientific scholarship has given willing support to the anti-Cultist, in the programme to free Burns from bondage to his 'Victorian biographers'. Formidable forces join to ridicule the image of Burns the early mythmakers are supposed to have fabricated:

'Burns was an Ayrshire ploughman, unlettered but inspired, who suddenly and by the divine afflatus burst into nightingale song. He was promiscuous with women and peopled south Scotland with bastards. . . . But all this disgraceful promiscuity was purged and sanctified and absolved by his wholly uncarnal love for an ethereal creature called Highland Mary. He drank himself to death at an early age, thereby cutting short a career of marvellous promise; he thus came suitably to that Bad End so beloved of Victorian morals. And so on.'[7]

Now that we are no longer fettered by 'Victorian morals', it seems, inquiry may proceed.

This Burns of Romantic and Victorian mythmakers is in part a man of straw. Following the 'full study of the development of the tradition of Burns biography' for which Professor Daiches hopes,[8] the myth itself may well appear to have been nourished by the zestful exaggerations of its attackers. One also questions the optimistic assumption of de-mythologizers that the unique historical personality of a man apotheosized in his own lifetime (the Ploughman Poet, Caledonia's Bard, the amalgam of Pride and Passion, the Natural Genius) can ever be recovered as an objective historical fact. Edwin Muir has cited the naiveté of such a hope:

'He is a myth evolved by the popular imagination, a communal poetic creation. He is a Protean figure; we can all shape him to our own likeness, for a myth is endlessly adaptable. . . . It is impossible to judge impartially a convenient appliance to which we have grown accustomed. The myth is unlike the man; but the man was its basis, and no other could have served. . . . When we consider Burns we must therefore include the Burns Nights with him, and the Burns Cult in all its forms; if we sneer at them we sneer at Burns.'[9]

Confronted with sneers at Romantic and Victorian biography, one wonders at what point dogmatic scepticism becomes self-deluding, self-destroying. What constitutes 'fact' where all contemporary witnesses were involved in the process of making a man into a myth with his own help during his own life? A certain amount of ornamentation, of hagiographic accretion, can be distinguished easily enough. But so varied were Burns's masks as a social, political, and cultural phenomenon that one doubts there is recoverable a nucleus of indubitable fact which was *the* life of Robert Burns.

There arises also a question of procedure in Burns biography. If biography is not just the record, but also the re-creation of the phenomenon of a life, is the value of an anecdote to be identified with its degree of demonstrable veracity? Every biographical phenomenon must be a tissue of partial responses, of indirect or distorted reflections, even myths. Does the biographer err on the side of credulity or dishonesty if he recreates this phenomenological aspect of a life? Does he err if he utilizes the apocryphal anecdote, the oral tradition, for its representative value or even essential truth? In the case of Burns biography, is there an acceptable medium between Mrs Carswell and Dr Snyder? She rejects all scholarly equivocation as improper biographical procedure:

'Where the incidents of the poet's life are obscure I have felt obliged for the sake of a plain narrative to make my choice after prolonged study of all the evidence at my disposal and to relate my finding as definitely as though it were the only one possible.'

Of Snyder's work, one must say with Mark Longaker

'biography which seeks accuracy at all costs is fulfilling only part of its aim. . . . A life filled with this kind of cautious equivocality can do little to bring the reader into touch with the man and his times.'[10]

For Burns circles who accept Snyder and Mrs Carswell as the best introductions, Lockhart's 'graceful' and 'charming' *Burns* can scarcely be rehabilitated. It is no surprise that the ardently anti-Victorian sentiment for Mrs Carswell should reject Lockhart; D. H. Lawrence made the feeling extravagantly clear:

'I read just now Lockhart's bit of a life of Burns. Made me spit! Those damned middle-class Lockharts grew lilies of the valley up their ——, to hear them talk. . . . My word, you can't know Burns unless you can hate the Lockharts and all the estimable bourgeois and upper classes as he really did – the narrow-gutted pigeons. Don't for God's Sake, be mealy-mouthed like them.'[11]

More surprising and damning is the categorical rejection by Dr Snyder, whose position is now accepted *ex cathedra* in numerous derivative accounts. The myth of Lockhart's ubiquitous mendacity is now fixed in Snyder's *Burns*. 'The best that one can say' of Lockhart's *Burns*, says Snyder, 'is that it occasioned Carlyle's review. It is inexcusably inaccurate from beginning to end, at times demonstrably mendacious, and should never be trusted in any respect or detail.'[12] The student of Lockhart's art is accustomed to such incautious condemnations. And, although he would rather turn to the more positive aspects of Lockhart the biographer, he finds such charges and the ease with which they have been accepted an obstacle to be confronted first.

'The most spirited passages in the work,' says Longaker of Snyder's *Burns*,

'are those in which he deplores the inaccuracies of Lockhart. By the time he has finished with his attack on Lockhart's version of the brig *Rosamund* affair (in which Burns, according to his earlier biographers, played an active and picturesque part), we should be very cross at Lockhart for having deluded us into the belief that he was a biographer of reasonable integrity.'[13]

But, while Lockhart comes out worst, Snyder's battle is with the 'romantic biographers' in general, to whom he makes repeated, occasionally vague and harsh allusions. His antagonism seems founded in the assumption made explicit in his reference to Highland Mary:

'early in the nineteenth century, long before the mythmakers had begun their work with Burns, Greenock tradition unhesitatingly identified the grave in which a girl named Mary Campbell had been buried, and, furthermore, knew her to have been the Highland Mary of Burns's lyrics.'[14]

The assumption is that 'early' traditions concerning Burns had been reliable and that error had entered Burns biography through deliberate fabrication by a generation of mythmakers. Even at Burns's death, Snyder concedes, Burns's enemies were doing their dirty work, prior even to Dr Currie's unctuous moralities: 'The very death-notices in the newspapers implied that he had spent his last years in abject poverty and a close approximation to disgrace.'[15] Generally, however, unreliable legend is blamed on the generation following.

The argument for this attribution seems rather circular. On the basis of reports which he rejects as improbable, Snyder generalizes of the Lockhart-Cunningham period of Burnsian inquiry (1828-34) that 'within thirty years there had come into being a very considerable mass of what amounts to little more than idle gossip'. Henceforth, the fact that 'new pieces of gossip' appeared during this period is sufficient reason for rejecting them as improbable. The later reporter may also be guilty by association with Allan Cunningham. 'Honest Allan's' very name suffices: 'Cunningham and other romantic biographers have put into circulation various stories dealing with Burns's enforcement of the law. . . . One had best be sceptical of all such legendary accounts.' Of the building of the Ellisland house, we are given this conjecture as fact: 'Allan Cunningham knew how such an affair should have been conducted, and put into circulation a pleasant legend.' But even in the absence of Cunningham, 'late' entry into 'circulation' is sufficient basis for rejection by 'this sceptical dogmatist'.[16] And in place of the tradition thus denigrated, Snyder invokes his own criterion of probability. If Burns had been as 'probable' as the invocation assumes, he would *probably* never have become the subject of legend and myth.

In the treatment of the sword-cane incident reported by John Syme we can see Snyder's assumptions joined with his editorializing in the treatment of early Burnsians. Of Syme, 'the man who knew him best in his last years', Ferguson has written: 'Syme's deeds and words at the time of Burns's death give as reliable a verdict on the poet's last years as can now be reached.'[17] Of the incident in question, Snyder says Syme 'was well along in years' when he recounted it to Scott. But Syme, born in 1755 and still living in 1829, told Scott the story before February 1809, when Scott published it in the *Quarterly Review* – that is, at most twelve and a half years after Burns's death, and long before he was too 'well along' for clear memory. His story later appeared in slightly different forms. What story has not? What justification is there, then, to conclude 'the probability is that nothing of the sort ever happened'? Certainly not this strikingly circular argument:

'Syme did not "remember" the incident till long after Burns's death, when the myth-making concerning the poet was in full swing and when anyone who had ever seen the poet felt at liberty to exercise his ingenuity in setting afloat new pieces of gossip concerning him.'[18]

Snyder was forced to reverse himself on a comparable incident – the capture of the Brig Rosamond. His original rejection of Lockhart's account is extravagant:

'No more picturesque legend was ever invented by the ingenious brain of a romantic biographer. One has but to visualize the scene to realize its utter impossibility: a smuggling brig "in shallow water" attacked by a squadron of cavalrymen with Burns at their head; boarded, captured, condemned, sold as a prize – and all within twenty-four hours. The whole thing would do full justice to Gilbert and Sullivan.'

Ironically, in this scepticism Snyder had been anticipated by Allan Cunningham. The scepticism of both was invalidated by the discovery, during the 1930's, of two of the documents previously missing. In his reply to H. W. Meikle's 'genial reproof', Snyder conceded that additional evidence might subsequently turn up to verify the whole story but still insisted on Lockhart's 'demonstrable untruth'.[19]

Lockhart was guilty of occasional inaccuracy, and his discretion in representing Burns's sexual athleticism no doubt deserves condemnation by modern standards. But these do not warrant Snyder's wholesale misrepresentation. A minor example is supplied by the account of

'Death and Dr Hornbook'. 'It may be mentioned here', Lockhart writes,

> 'that John Wilson, alias Dr Hornbook, was not merely compelled to shut up shop as an apothecary, or druggist rather, by the satire which bears his name; but so irresistible was the tide of ridicule, that his pupils, one by one, deserted him, and he abandoned his schoolcraft also.'

Wilson, Lockhart reports, moved on to success in commercial Glasgow and was heard in later life to bless the hour he had provoked the castigation of Robert Burns. Snyder says merely, 'Lockhart's statement that the satire actually drove Wilson out of Tarbolton is false, like many other "facts" for which this biographer and his confidential advisor Allan Cunningham were responsible.' He cites as evidence Wilson's letter to Burns asking counsel on a move to Edinburgh. He does not mention the fact that Wilson did leave Tarbolton and go to Glasgow. Nor does he quote the opening of Burns's reply: 'I am truly sorry, my dear Sir, that you find yourself so uncomfortably situated in Tarbolton; the more so, as I fear you will find on trial that the remedy you propose is worse than the disease.' We are left with the *fact*, not mentioned by Snyder, that Wilson found himself too 'uncomfortably situated' to remain in Tarbolton, and went to Glasgow. There is insufficient reason, then, to call Lockhart's statement false.[20]

A more important misrepresentation comes later in Snyder's *Life*. He commences his final section by condemning the early biographers as malicious; they all joined to produce the legend of Burns's drunkenness, 'gross moral turpitude', and final disgrace. 'One after another', he generalizes,

> 'the chroniclers repeated scraps of unsubstantiated anecdote, until there was woven a veritable tissue of falsehood, representing that Burns's life at Dumfries was rendered sordid by alcoholism and debauchery, and that he was "burned out" long before his death.'

He mentions the defence of the poet made by Alexander Peterkin in 1815, and accepts as authoritative the letters of Findlater and Gray which Peterkin published; but 'on the whole', he asserts, 'Peterkin's well-meant defence seems to have produced little change in the contemporary estimate of Burns'. Nowhere does he notice that Lockhart's express claim to novelty in his *Burns* was limited to 'the incidents of his closing years' and that in Lockhart's treatment of those incidents,

Peterkin is amply employed, and the letters of Gray and Findlater are quoted at length. So ready to challenge Lockhart's veracity, he fails to quote Lockhart's extended defence of the poet, which, though not over-credulous, is both judicious and humane.[21]

It is noteworthy that three readers more closely acquainted with the Burns story than Lockhart, none of whom was a mere victim of malicious gossip and the prohibitionism of James Currie, warned Lockhart against over-generosity.

Alexander Young of Harburn conceded that he preferred Lockhart's *Burns* to that of 'my old Schoolfellow Dr Currie', yet added, 'I hope you will do justice to his countrymen, for *he* certainly was the Architect of his own misfortunes.'[22] Young may have in mind the indignant opening of Lockhart's conclusion, a passage one hardly expects from the cold patrician or the malicious mythmaker:

'The great poet himself, whose name is enough to ennoble his children's children, was, to the eternal disgrace of his country, suffered to live and die in penury, and, as far as such a creature could be degraded by any external circumstances, in degradation. . . . In defence, or at least in palliation, of this national crime, two false arguments, the one resting on facts grossly exaggerated, the other having no foundation whatever either on knowledge or on wisdom, have been rashly set up, and arrogantly as well as ignorantly maintained.' [p. 288]

Lockhart refers first to the charge of radical politics, second to the argument that Burns's intemperance and imprudence placed him beyond help.

A liberal (New Licht) Reverend Hamilton Paul, himself ex-biographer of Burns, wrote to urge caution in reliance on Burns's defenders: 'I suspect much allowance must be made for the partiality of friendship and brotherly kindness, where either the Rev. Jas. Gray or Gilbert Burns are concerned.'[23] Perhaps a result of such caution, Lockhart's treatment of his conflicting authorities is a model of conciliation and restraint. The statements of Gray and Findlater come, he asserts, from men 'incapable, for any purpose, of wilfully stating that which they knew to be untrue. Yet we are not, on the other hand, to throw out of view altogether the feelings of partial friendship, irritated by exaggerations such as called forth these testimonies.' The exaggerators themselves are treated with moderation: 'It is scarcely to be doubted that Dr Currie and Professor Walker took care, ere they

G

penned their painful pages, to converse and correspond with other persons than the enemies of the deceased poet' [pp. 239-40]. The third authoritative critic of Lockhart's generosity was Scott. Rather than 'working under the eye of his distinguished father-in-law', as Snyder claims,[24] Lockhart wrote from London for Scott's contribution only when the work was 'far advanced'. This was on the 19th of November 1827; on the 10th of March following, Scott reported, from the eldest son of Burns's Nithsdale landlord, Miller of Dalswinton (no enemy), that when Burns 'came to stay at Dalswinton all night as he often did he used to stipulate for a bottle of brandy in his sleeping room and drink it well nigh out before morning'. Early in June, Lockhart having omitted such details, Scott wrote again: 'I could give you very good authority where you and I seem to differ but you have chosen the wiser and better view and Burns had a right to have his frailties spared especially *post tantum temporis*. All people applaud it.' To his 'Gurnal' Scott had already confided on the 29th of May :

'I have amused myself to-day with reading Lockhart's *Life of Burns*, which is very well written – in fact, an admirable thing. He has judicious[ly] slurd over his vices and follies; for although Currie, I myself, and others, have not said a word more on the subject than is true, yet as the dead corpse is straightened, swathd and made decent, so ought the character of such an inimitable genius as Burns to be tenderly handled after death.'[25]

Such was the response to Lockhart's disagreements with the severe early biographers. Lockhart insisted that Burns's misdemeanours at their most extreme were merely temporary, fitful, 'the aberrations of a man whose moral sense was never deadened', and not 'systematic'. He emphasized that Burns was 'one who encountered more temptations from without and from within, than the immense majority of mankind, far from having to contend against, are even able to imagine' [p. 208]. Of this departure Snyder makes no mention. Instead, he undertakes the dogmatic rejection of the tradition that Burns was ostracized by Dumfries society.

Lockhart gives an anecdote, from 'a gentleman of that country' (MacCulloch), that Burns had been encountered on the wrong side of the street, alone and unwilling to cross. In Lockhart the incident is recounted in a purely political context. Lockhart states that Burns was shunned by the 'local admirers and disciples of the good old King and his minister' for extreme indiscretion in voicing his political sentiments.[26] If even the devoted Mrs Dunlop turned cold at the rampant antimonarchism of Burns's letters, such shunning is scarcely improbable. Lockhart makes no mention of 'personal misconduct' as a cause; he carefully isolates the anecdote. Yet Dr Snyder implies (*a*) that in the specific incident, 'as in many other places, Lockhart was merely drawing upon his imagination'; (*b*) that the tradition of social ostracism is wholly attributable to Lockhart's mythmaking; and (*c*) that the ostracism had been presented, not as an effect of temporary political unrest, but as general moral disgrace.[27] Surely this is misrepresentation. We have been concerned so far with isolated incidents. There is, however, another area in which Snyder's harsh treatment is less easily set aside: the handling of manuscript journals. Here, Lockhart and Cunningham are presented in criminal partnership as 'arch-emendors'.

It is Snyder's 'firm belief that the world owes the most picturesque and the most unreliable of the Burns anecdotes to Allan Cunningham's inventive mendacity', and by Lockhart's 'repeated admission' he was 'dependent to a considerable measure upon information derived from Allan Cunningham'. We are never allowed to forget that Lockhart 'was assisted by Cunningham in the preparation of his *Life*'. Suspected interpolations are either from Cunningham's pen 'or his associate's, Lockhart'. While Lockhart was less given to 'embroidery', 'Honest Allan's fabrications were of a sort that one suspects even as one reads them; Lockhart, with his pretence of absolute accuracy, was harder to detect in the act of falsifying the record'.[28] Early readers discriminated quite differently between Lockhart and Cunningham. Joseph Train, writing to attack Cunningham's scepticism, refers to 'your excellent Life of the bard'. Alexander Young, writing to concede that Currie has been 'greatly surpassed' by Lockhart, continues:

'It was not however the last life of Burns I was destined to read – In a Coffee House in Portsmouth in 1834, a Naval Officer threw down a volume of a life of Burns written by Allan Cunningham, of which I perused several passages that excited in me a great feeling of indignation.'[29]

An account of the inception of Lockhart's work will cast light on Snyder's picture of close collaboration. It was for Constable's Miscellany that Lockhart's *Burns* was announced in 1825. In October Cunningham wrote Scott of his willingness to help Lockhart to 'many little matters which I have treasured up concerning our great rustic Bard which he may exercise his judgment upon if he pleases'. Two days later he made the same offer directly: 'I know some little things connected with his character and his poetry – I can gossip them out to you in a letter if you like; without imagining that I am laying you under any particular obligation.'[30] He gossiped them out. There followed within weeks Lockhart's removal to the duties and burdens of the Murray establishment on Albemarle Street, and the financial disaster which destroyed Constable's firm.

It was not until January 1827, that Constable, attempting to reinstate his business, wrote again. He referred remorsefully to the days of hysteria, and was hoping still for the *Burns* – 'long very much enquired after, and . . . one of the bright stars of my list'. He promised to send some unprinted Burns originals. Lockhart replied, expressing pleasure in the project, but explaining:

'unfortunately, considering the matter as at an end, I had some time ago boxed up all the materials I had collected in London and that in such a way that I fear I cannot without great difficulty get at them for some time. I trust nothing is to prevent my spending the chief part of next summer in Scotland and shall look forward to *Burns* as my work during that time. . . . I have myself attained several trifles of his in M S from various quarters: and curious enough *memoranda* from 2 or 3 friends who recollect the Poet in the flesh.'[31]

In November, Lockhart reported he was 'far advanced with my little book', and Scott saw some 'sheets' the 4th of March following. And yet it was not until the intervening January (1828) that Lockhart thought to call in the aid of his arch-collaborator Cunningham, appealing in terms which reveal (*a*) that he had not been in touch with Cunningham during most of the period of composition, (*b*) that he had not had Cunningham's M S materials before him, and (*c*) that he had received no 'originals' from Cunningham, but a 'gossiping' letter instead:

'I know no apology that wd suffice for the liberty I am taking. The trick is that when you wrote to me 2 years ago a letter, a most valuable and delightful letter, about *Burns*, the arrangement in Constables affairs had rendered it doubtful whether I shd ever return to my Life of our poet. Accordingly yr letter was *too carefully* put by, and I suspect (having searched every box and drawer here for it in vain) sent to Scotland; where I cannot now in the very *hour* of need get at it: in fact my house there is shut up and I cannot if I wd get anybody fit to be trusted with my keys.

May I then beg the very unheard of favour that you wd write me another letter embracing the most material matters?'[32]

If not Cunningham, who were Lockhart's chief sources of supply? In a later article, Snyder sketched a less exclusive genesis. The work was, he conceded, 'inevitably based . . . upon Dr Currie's. . . . But Lockhart, working under the eye of his distinguished father-in-law, was not content merely to rehash old material.' We have already noted that Scott's eye was remote and that his views were essentially rejected. Snyder also mentions Chambers, M'Diarmid, and 'various unpublished journals and letters', presumably those supplied by Constable.[33] He does not mention the Peterkin materials. Nor does he mention Joseph Train, whose notes were sent to Lockhart during the period of preparation, notes gleaned in large part from Grierson of Dalgoner, whose sources were the Burns circle: Richmond, Blane, Lambie, Sillar, 'Clarinda' Maclehose and her son, and Highland Mary's sister.[34] To all these, together with the earlier biographers – Currie, Heron, Irving, Walker, and Paul, Cunningham's was an addition late and slight.

If this was the extent of the Lockhart-Cunningham collaboration, what of the crucial charge against the pair as co-emendors? It has to do with the journal of Burns's second Highland tour, 'some fragments' of which, Lockhart reports, 'have recently been discovered, and are now in my hands' [p. 155]. J. C. Ewing, publishing the journal MS in facsimile in 1927, revealed that the whereabouts of the 'fragments' are unknown, and assumed that the original journal as preserved appears 'to have been transcribed and extended by the Poet at some date subsequent to 1787' and that 'this extended "Journal" came into the hands of John Gibson Lockhart'.[35] Lockhart's reference to 'fragments' implies the existence of no such transcription. Yet Snyder makes a charge out of what is already clearly acknowledged: 'none of this is in the manuscript, or ever was.' From this he simply conjectures that 'it is in Honest Allan's best and most florid vein, and is almost certainly from his pen or his associate's, Lockhart'.[36] In the recent biography by Maurice Lindsay this inference has miraculously become fact and has been extended to include the Border Tour Journal. Of this latter, Ferguson has stated that 'comparison of the original with the printed text reveals no such rewriting and expansion as is charged against Cunningham's text of the Highland journal'. But in Lindsay this becomes 'Burns's *Journal of His Tour in the Highlands* suffered even more than [!] the *Journal of the Border Tour* from the romantic interpolating of Lockhart and/or Cunningham'.[37] Such is the fertility of conjecture among the anti-mythmakers.

Cunningham sent Lockhart a gossiping letter. What other origin could there have been for the 'fragments'? In the first place, the 'interpolations' are near the beginning of the tour. This fact, together with the journal's abbreviated hints such as 'Come over Culloden Muir – reflections on the field of battle – breakfast at Kilravock', suggests that the 'fragments' may indeed represent Burns's commencement of a process Snyder suggests: 'It is apparent that Burns began the Journal with the intention of making his entries somewhat detailed, and of recording his sensations as well as his acts. But after a few days he grew distinctly laconic.'[38] The intention may well have been replaced by the decision to include only markers such as 'reflections on the field of battle', and to reconstruct the reflections and sensations later. In the second place, the 'interpolations' are not 'florid'. There is one exception: the Bannockburn passage. But even if this passage is identifiably in 'Honest Allan's best and most florid vein', it can scarcely have been by Honest Allan: in his own *Life of Burns*, Allan prefers 'the account briefly rendered in one of his letters to all the rapture of his journal', and prints the letter instead.[39]

Lockhart could have written the 'interpolations' himself. If the argument from silence be taken as proof of Lockhart's creation of his documents, then his canon is a remarkable one, including not just Burns's Bannockburn oratory, but also Scott's Ashestiel autobiography and a sizable segment of his correspondence. It is appropriate to quote here his letter to Croker on Lord John Russell's editing of Moore's Diary. He defends the editor's right to suppress.

'That cannot be doubtful. But for it, why an Editor at all? On the other hand there never can be a right to add to what is produced as the letter or diary of another – even to dream that Lord J. R. cd ever confound these questions is quite out of my line.'[40]

But what reason is there for refusing to attribute such a thing as the Bannockburn passage to Burns himself? The reason lies in an anti-romantic preconception of Burns which is hardly consistent with the facts. Some modern biographers are doggedly unwilling to believe Burns capable of such rhetorical posturing as the Bannockburn passage may be taken to represent, even though they know of his theatricality, his taste for gestures in an age of sentimental *poseurs*. Even Thomas Carlyle, having attempted to make unaffectedness one of the distinguishing marks of Burns's greatness, found it necessary to qualify and qualify again. Even Snyder notes Burns's 'life-long habit of sentimentalizing'.[41] One need only turn for corroboration to the opening of the first Commonplace Book, the autobiographical letter to Moore, the Preface to the Kilmarnock edition, the letter to Rev. William Greenfield from Edinburgh, and the letter to 'Clarinda' on his 'constituent elements . . . Pride and Passion'.[42] Snyder concedes that Burns lived in an Age of Sensibility with Thomson, Richardson, Sterne, and Mackenzie, for tutors. Yet he insists that Burns was a laconic, insensitive traveller on the basis of laconic, insensitive journal entries. For example, he discredits Ainslie's image of Burns's posturing at Coldstream as 'an interesting picture, if one is interested in Burns as romantic biographers have tried to represent him' – because 'the poet's Journal . . . contains no evidence of any such hysterical outburst, but shows him acting like a normal man'. Hence,

> 'Ainslie's picture of Burns on his knees in an ecstasy of patriotic fervor is probably apocryphal. He merely crossed the river into England, dined with a friend, discussed French philosophy, slept comfortably, and on Tuesday, May 8, recrossed the river and was again in Scotland.'[43]

Lindsay is equally willing to concede Burns's tendency to exploit posed stylizations of himself. Yet he, too, finds this picture 'as absurd as it is improbable; a mere piece of sentimental Victorian tusherie'. Indeed, Lindsay can accept Burns's assurance in a letter to Robert Muir that 'two hours ago I said a fervent prayer for Old Caledonia over the hole in a blue whinstane, where Robert de Bruce fixed his Royal standard on the banks of Bannockburn', and deny that Burns was capable of the declamatory 'romantic twaddle' of which that prayer would be composed.[44]

Burns was quite capable of it, specifically in his correspondence; and Lockhart's 'fragments' may well have been parts of letters. Lockhart elsewhere speaks of a passage from a letter as from 'the poet's own private diary' [p. 229]. Lockhart's freedom in the 'manipulation' of documents must be acknowledged at once; it was a common procedure which will be discussed later. The invention of an entire passage is quite a different matter.

On matters of editorial accuracy, other concessions must also be made. Transcripts are generally accurate; but the names of correspondents are occasionally confused, dates are occasionally inaccurate, omissions are not always marked, and, on one or two occasions, letters are 'contamina-ted' – that is, conflated – for formal ends such as compression, effective transition, and the avoidance of repetition. Three facts should be noted, however: (*a*) some textual errors were inherited by Lockhart from earlier publications of the material; (*b*) the majority of editorial in-fringements (as we would consider them) occur in passages already available in print and hence are not attempts at deception. Finally, Lockhart's conventions of 'style' are not necessarily of his own choosing. The publisher's control of format is strikingly implicit in an undated note from Lockhart to Ballantyne: 'I certainly do think the brackets are the safest way: but if Mr Constable be very positive, I yield to his judgment. I wd fain, however, have him think twice ere he risks clear-ness for elegance.'[45]

We can return to the implications of Lockhart's handling of docu-ments when we consider the structure of his book. First, we should characterize the conception of Burns that antedated and informed that structure.

II

One might suppose from Carlyle's famous review that Lockhart *had* no individual conception of Burns. Anticipating his strictures on the *Scott*, Carlyle complained that Lockhart was not sufficiently in command of his own subject, that the book 'has less depths than we could have wished and expected from a writer of such power; and contains rather more, and more multifarious, quotations than belong of right to an original production'.[46] Paradoxically the real danger is not of deriva-tive disunity, but of dominant preconception. In *Peter's Letters* Burns, like Scott, had been a focus of various general issues. Against a back-ground of such issues we may identify the themes which made the *Burns* distinctly Lockhart's work.

When the Tory Dr Morris attended one of the earliest of Burns Dinners, Burns's reputation had become a political and cultural battle-ground:

'I well knew before I went, that, as it happened, those gentlemen
who took the chief direction in this affair were all keen Whigs. But I
never considered this as a circumstance of the slightest importance,
nor expected, most assuredly, that it would at all shew itself in the
conduct of the assembly. . . . I was, however, sadly disappointed.'[47]

At its most heated the feuding centered on Wordsworth's 'letter to a Friend of Burns'. To De Quincey it was merely a phase of the Words-worth-Jeffrey war, 'a "craze" . . . on the subject of Burns, which allowed no voice to be heard but that of zealotry and violent partisan-ship'. When Hazlitt joined the attack in a lecture, Crabb Robinson lost his temper and 'was led to burst out into declamations against Hazlitt which I afterwards regretted, though I uttered nothing but the truth'. Still, Wordsworth's letter 'was chiefly instrumental in establishing Burns as a figure of national importance in considerable measure because . . . it was brought forth out of the heat of controversy'.[48] Joining the controversy, Dr Morris's belligerent *Blackwood's* friends found the Heaven-sent Ploughman subordinate in interest to Burns as an historic and ideological force. Ironically, in their hands the Enlight-enment humanitarian became a weapon against the sceptic and the radical. There followed the most pointlessly acrimonious exchange of the entire 'craze'. Wilson probably wrote (*a*) the 'Observations on Mr Wordsworth's Letter' in *Blackwood's* June 1817, attacking the 'officious and egotistical' author as unqualified and unfair; (*b*) the 'Vindication of Mr Wordsworth's Letter' in October, attacking the 'weakness and the malignity' of the 'anonymous Calumniator'; and (*c*) the 'Letter occasioned by N's Vindication'.[49] Lockhart must have been grateful for the alibi that this 'extraordinary "ham"attempted by Wilson on Wordsworth' had occurred during his absence in Germany.[50]

His alibi is meaningful. The German trip was important for his idea of Burns. It produced the English translation of the only book by Friedrich Schlegel to attract international attention – the *Lectures on the History of Literature*.[51] The translation occasioned the *Blackwood's* essay-review which Morgan and Hohlfeld have called 'the most pro-found analysis of the *Literatur* which we have encountered in the magazines', and which Strout has attributed to Lockhart.[52] The review was followed shortly by 'Remarks on the Poetry of Thomas Moore', Lockhart's first discussion of Burns and National Poetry:

'Before any man can become the poet of a nation, he must . . . iden-tify his own spirit with that of his people, by embodying in his verse those habitual and peculiar thoughts which constitute the essence of their nationality. . . . There are few things more worthy of being studied, either in their character or in their effects, than the poems of Robert Burns. . . . Amidst the solitary occupations of his rural labours, the soul of the ploughman fed itself with high thoughts of patriotism and religion, and with that happy instinct which is the best prerogative of genius, he divined every thing that was necessary for being the poet of his country.'[53]

While the reverential excess of these lines belongs to Lauerwinkel rather than to the future biographer, the Schlegelian conception of Burns as national poet retained its influence on the biographer.

Lockhart's review places the same stress on literary nationality and makes the same juxtaposition of religion and nationality as the twin 'established centres' of literary inspiration. It credits Schlegel with having urged the reciprocity of nationality and literature, and with having warred effectively against the evils of 'the philosophy of the last century'. Contrasting Scotland, Lockhart suggests that the ill effects of 'a single generation of abstract reasoners' persist in critical journals whose 'eternal disquisitions have been operating with slow but sure effect in mouldering down all large aggregates of association, which could form centres of gravity of sufficient power to control and regulate the orbits of our feelings'. The effect of Burns on his countrymen – 'meditative in their spirit, proud in their recollections, steady in their patriotism, and devout in their faith' – was to oppose those 'ill effects'. For Lockhart this early, such was Burns's importance:

'the chilling nature of the merely speculative philosophy, which they had begun to cultivate, seemed to threaten a speedy diminution of their fervent attachment to that which was peculiarly their own. This mischievous tendency was stopped by a peasant, and the noblest of his land are the debtors of his genius.'[54]

His importance is identically conceived in the *Life* ten years later, as is evident in the critical remarks about Edinburgh's 'professional metaphysicians' or in the phrases of the conclusion:

'The political circumstances of Scotland were, and had been, such as to starve the flame of patriotism; the popular literature had striven and not in vain, to make itself English; and, above all, a new and a cold system of speculative philosophy had begun to spread widely among us. A peasant appeared, and set himself to check the creeping pestilence of this indifference.' [p. 299]

One facet of the Enlightenment liberal was at considerable odds with the influence of Schlegel. Lockhart could scarcely find the religious side of Burns's nationalistic fervor equal to his political and cultural enthusiasm. Among the elders and ministers of Ayrshire, the castigator of Holy Willie and Holy Fair seemed hardly an anti-enlightenment

force for piety. Perhaps nowhere in his *Burns* is the humane moderation tempering Lockhart's moral severity more apparent than in the
handling of Burns's anti-kirk satire and of the whole question of
Burns's anti-religious influence.

Lockhart is quick to concede that in Ayrshire's 'chosen champions of
the Auld Licht' the reckless young satirist had 'as broad a mark as ever
tempted the shafts of a satirist' [p. 61]. Dean Ramsay has preserved an
anecdote in which Lockhart places the blame for the Holy Willies on
the Auld Licht itself:

'Old Dr Lockhart of Glasgow was lamenting one day, in the presence
of his son John, the fate of a man who had been found guilty of
immoral practices, and the more so that he was one of his own elders.
"Well, father," remarked his son, "you see what you've driven
him to."'[55]

Even so, Lockhart insists, 'Burns has grossly overcharged his portraits'.
This excess he attributes to the 'exaggerated state of party feeling' and
to the liberal ministers who applauded the blasphemous performances
of 'the young and reckless satirist'. Since he knew no liberally educated
company other than these thoughtless abettors, Burns himself is not
to be blamed [pp. 61-66].

Lockhart was readier to blame when Arthur Hugh Clough heard him
speak in 1845 'of the prevalence of infidelity even amongst the country
folk of Scotland, saying that all the small farmers in that neighbourhood were avowed unbelievers. He ascribed it greatly to Burns.'[56] But
that was many griefs and many disappointments later. In 1828
Lockhart finds men older and wiser guilty of encouraging recklessness
in one potentially an ardent and humble Christian. In support, Lockhart
stresses the biographical importance of 'The Cotter's Saturday Night':

'perhaps of all Burns's pieces, the one whose exclusion from the
collection, were such things possible now-a-days, would be the most
injurious, if not to the genius, at least to the character, of the man.'
[pp. 75-76]

But the distinction suggests that the religious question complicated
Lockhart's conception of the national poet. Why would the exclusion of
this poem not be injurious to the man's 'genius' as well as to his
'character'? The poem *is* an extended depiction of the 'national genius'
with which Burns had identified himself, of the 'peculiar way of thinking, and conceiving' which is the 'essence of all nationality' for
Peter Morris as for the reviewer and translator of Schlegel:

'As every nation has its own mental character and constitution propagated from generation to generation, no traditions or poetry can be so congenial to it, as those which originated with itself in early ages, constituting tests of its true bias and genius, and continuing, during the course of its history, to strengthen nature itself by reacting upon the same national temperament which at first produced them.'[57]

Nevertheless, the 'Cotter' is not an authentically Scots poem. The words of Dr Morris explain:

'The most true, the most lasting, the most noble creation by which an independent nation seeks to manifest her spirit and her independence, is her formation and cultivation of an independent speech. . . . Wherein does the essence of a nation exist, if it be not in the character of her mind? and how is that mind to be penetrated or understood, if we neglect the pure and faithful mirror in which of old it has stamped its likeness – her language?'[58]

Lockhart's position on Burns's decision to write in Scots was unequivocal: 'I think it would be doing a service to his fame to place before the public those pieces by which he alone merits his place, apart altogether from his mawkish attempts in the English dialect.' The timid Smolletts and Moores submitted linguistically 'to the prejudices of the dominant nation'; contrast 'the boldness of Burns's experiment' and 'the nature and consequences of the victory in which our poet led the way.'[59] Modern cultural nationalists in Scotland are unaware of the strong, early ally they had in the much maligned editor of the *Quarterly Review*.

The alliance extends beyond the defence of Burns's Scots. Lockhart deplored, as they do, the degeneration of Scots to a provincial dialect. Perhaps for him it was already too late to recall with Cockburn and Ramsay the old Scottish ladies – 'their language, like their habits, entirely Scotch, but without any other vulgarity than what perfect naturalness is sometimes mistaken for', or to recall with Dr Carlyle the times when 'the Scottish dialect was spoken in purity in the low country'. Still, he saw a remnant of the 'pure and classical language of Scotland', and of that remnant he wrote Cunningham:

'I shall never cease to have some difference of opinion w you as to the Scotch tongue – which nobody uses quite to my satisfaction but Sir Walter. Both you and Hogg and I may add both Galt and Wilson seem to me to copy too much the dialects of particular districts – he alone writes what is all over Scotland Scotch National.'[60]

It is this insistence on authentic linguistic nationality that causes him to minimize Burns's debt to Ramsay and Ferguson, and to recall instead 'the days of *Christ's Kirk on the Green*, and *Peebles to the Play*', to attribute to Burns 'depth of inspiration, and a massive energy of language, to which the dialect of his country had been a stranger at least since "Dunbar the Mackar"'.

> 'It was reserved for Burns to interpret the inmost soul of the Scottish peasant in all its moods, and in verse exquisitely and intensely Scottish, without degrading either his sentiments or his language with one touch of vulgarity.' [pp. 116-17]

But the nationality of Lockhart's Burns was more than linguistic. The vulgarization of Scots was a sign of social disintegration; the revitalizing of a truly national society could come only from the peasant because only there did true nationality survive. Here, Lockhart was strongly influenced by the scholar's and translator's knowledge of Spanish literature, as well as by Schlegel, whose high praise of Spain he translated as follows:

> 'no literature has preserved a character of such pure nationality as that of the Spaniards . . . the Spaniards are as rich in ballads as the English and Scotch; but theirs are possessed of certain peculiar excellencies to which the others have no pretension. They are not only popular ballads, intelligible and clear to the vulgar, they are also true national and heroic poems . . . it is always to be regretted when that poetry, whose business it is to keep alive the national feelings of a whole people, assumes a form which adopts it only for the vulgar.'[61]

No doubt under the influence of Schlegel's praise, Lockhart turned, in the early 1820's, to the editing of Cervantes and the translating of Spanish ballads. In the preface of his translations, he invokes the Spanish peasantry as an ideal:

> 'in every other part of the population, the progress of corruption appears to have been no less powerful than rapid and the higher we ascend in the scale of society, the more distinct and mortifying is the spectacle of moral not less than physical deterioration.'[62]

His anti-aristocratic view of the breakdown of national culture is by no means restricted to Spain. It has already appeared in Peter Morris's idealizing of the Scottish lowland peasantry:

> 'It is in rustic assemblages like these that the true characteristics of every race of men are most palpably and conspicuously displayed,

and it is there that we can best see in multiplied instances the natural germs of that which, under the influence of culture, assumes a prouder character, and blossoms into the animating soul and spirit of a national literature.'[63]

It is to reappear when Lockhart comments on the disintegration of Highland society, and the degenerate aristocrat. He speaks through the Shepherd in the forty-sixth of the *Noctes Ambrosianae*: 'if the gentry lose the land, the Highland anes at any rate, it will only be the Lord's righteous judgment on them for having dispossessed the people before them.' He comments in a *Quarterly* review of the Gaelic poet Rob Donn Mackay:

'The short-sighted chieftains, meanwhile, who have been systema-tically banishing their affectionate kindred for the sake of increased rentals, are already beginning to share the doom of their victims. Avenging justice is pressing on them "nec pede claudo!"'[64]

There is every reason to believe that he speaks through the lines of the anonymous 'Canadian Boat Song':

> When the bold kindred in the time long-vanished
> Conquered the soil and fortified the keep,
> No seer foretold the children would be banished
> That a degenerate lord might boast his sheep.[65]

Given such a concern with social disaffection and disintegration, it is easy to see why Lockhart saw Burns chiefly as a force for human solidarity within a national *milieu*. In such terms he concluded his *Burns*:

'whosoever sympathized with the verse of Burns, had his soul opened for the moment to the whole family of man. If, in too many instances, the matter has stopped there – the blame is not with the poet, but with the mad and unconquerable pride and coldness of the worldly heart – "man's inhumanity to man". If, in spite of Burns and all his successors, the boundary lines of society are observed with increasing strictness among us – if the various orders of men still, day by day, feel the chord of sympathy relaxing, let us lament over symptoms of a disease in the body politic, which if it goes on, must find sooner or later a fatal ending: but let us not undervalue the antidote which has all along been checking this strong poison.' [p. 303]

But it was not just Burns's influence that was social. The man himself was essentially a social phenomenon, a shock and a challenge to society, a test of its cultural authenticity. It is as a social phenomenon that the biography most emphatically presents him, for Lockhart found in the problematical encounter of a brilliant, commanding, crude social presence and an Edinburgh gentility that lionized him with ruthless fickleness, the ideal matter of the literary form that always interested him most: the novel of manners, of complex social dynamics. Central to the encounter was the question of literary patronage. What permanent support did Burns receive from his lionizing countrymen, what did he deserve, how was the blame for relative neglect to be apportioned? The entire biography is a restrained but incisive exploration of these questions. In the pervasive presence of no other complex of questions is Lockhart's individual tone more evident.

Lockhart's measured criticism of Burns's anti-kirk satire is severe only when it condemns Ayrshire's New Lichts for patronizing the reckless young wit. A similar judgement accompanies the account of Burns's early move to Tarbolton. Gilbert Burns reports (in Currie's quotation), 'The seven years we lived in Tarbolton parish . . . were not marked by much literary improvement.'[66] In adapting the report, Lockhart emphasizes the lack of literary patronage: 'He was separated from his acquaintances of the town of Ayr, and probably missed not only the stimulus of their conversation, but the kindness that had furnished him with his supply, such as it was, of books' [pp. 27-28]. Patronage played an important part in the Kilmarnock edition: 'encouraged by the ray of light which unexpected patronage had begun to throw on his affairs, [he] composed, while the printing was in progress, some of the best poems of the collection' [pp. 87-88]. Mrs Dunlop's encouragement is stressed, and to Dr Blacklock's providential letter alone is attributed the transformation of mood which terminated Burns's Jamaican plans. Lord Melville and the Duke of Gordon would have been indulgent patrons had accident not intervened. But other delinquent patrons are treated severely for offering no 'interference from a higher quarter' even when 'it was known that Robert Burns, after being caressed and flattered by the noblest and most learned of his countrymen, was about to be established as a common gauger among the wilds of Nithsdale' [p. 288]. At the end as at the beginning, Lockhart urges the effect of literary patronage on Burns's circumstances and his spirits. At the end he finds Burns's countrymen at fault.

But the central moral question in the book is not to be measured by a measuring of patronage or neglect. However willing to excuse Burns at the expense of his countrymen, Lockhart measures the man himself by the degree of his intellectual and spiritual transcendence over the circumstances of social caprice. The area of ultimate moral concern is not social but personal. Lockhart surveys and judges social irresponsibilities, but he consistently moves beyond them to consider Burns as a supreme member of a tradition of tragic genius. This, the book's essential moral direction, may be seen in the structure of a single representative paragraph, one which embodies a thematic transition from social patronage to the personal spirit. It begins:

'It seems impossible to doubt that Burns had in fact lingered in Edinburgh, in the hope that, to use a vague but sufficiently expressive phrase, something would be done for him. He . . . all the while nourished, and assuredly it would have been most strange if he had not, the fond dream that the admiration of his country would ere long present itself in some solid and tangible shape.'

Thus far we see how the theme – the influence of patronage – enters the biography, through a pattern of recurrent inference. We also see an illustration of Lockhart's tone: sympathy for Burns's point of view, and criticism of those who fostered his mistake. But then the direction changes, and the paragraph moves on to suggest the way circumstance encouraged the self-indulgence of a nature in itself tragic:

'His illness and confinement gave him leisure to concentrate his imagination on the darker side of his prospects; and the letters which we have quoted may teach those who envy the powers and the fame of genius, to pause for a moment over the annals of literature, and think what superior capabilities of misery have been, in the great majority of cases, interwoven with the possession of those very talents, from which all but their possessors derive unmingled gratification.' [p. 169]

One thinks often of Savage and others cited by Lockhart in 'a long and painful' list of Johnson's subjects [pp. 291-2]. Burns's is the plight of 'unfortunate genius', the tragic paradox of the nature of genius itself, as conceived by an aesthetic of Sensibility. Sensibility is genius's measure and its burden. The poet's essential gift, measured by his strength and delicacy of feeling, places him in extraordinary and persistent moral or spiritual danger.

Spiritual is the better word. For if Lockhart judges sternly on occasion, his severity is not provoked by weaknesses of the flesh. Otherwise, the biographical critic would not cite as supreme evidence of Burns's art 'Tam' and 'The Jolly Beggars', and Peter Morris would not have disqualified teetotallers from Burnsian commentary:

'How can they ever sympathize with the misty felicity of a man singing

"It is the moon — I ken her horn!"

I think no man should be allowed to say anything about Burns, who has not joined in this chorus, although timber-tuned, and sat till daylight although married.'[67]

Rather, Lockhart's severity is directed at spiritual danger, at Burns's Faustian sins against his own nature: negativism, bitterness and spleen, desperate pride and spiritual darkness. The danger is evoked in such recurrent phrases as 'haughty spirit', 'darkness of mood', 'magnificent hypochondriacism', 'haughtiness of character', 'dark places of his spirit'. It is associated with its origins in the sensibility of genius:

'that jealous pride which formed the groundwork of his character; that dark suspiciousness of fortune, which the subsequent course of his history too well justified; that nervous intolerance of condescension, and consummate scorn of meanness, which attended him through life, and made the study of his species, for which nature had given him such extraordinary qualifications, the source of more pain than was ever counterbalanced by the exquisite capacity for enjoyment with which he also was endowed.' [pp. 148, 168]

When the same severity is applied to Burns's poetry, the haughty darkness of spirit becomes the sin of extreme satire. Poetry in which malicious indignation dominates is poetry deformed by the spiritual self-destruction of which it is born. The poems in which Burns celebrates the birth of his illegitimate child are to be condemned, not because they celebrate a sin of the flesh, but because they embody a hardening of the heart, a stilling of the conscience by false pride:

'and the fermenting bitterness of a mind ill at ease within itself, escaped (as may be too often traced in the history of satirists) in the shape of angry sarcasms against others, who, whatever their private errors might be, had at least done him no wrong.' [p. 50]

'The Holy Fair' is superior to other anti-kirk satires because in it 'unlike the others that have been mentioned, satire keeps its own place, and is subservient to the poetry of Burns'. The 'Epistle to Davie' is superior to 'Man was made to Mourn'. The latter expresses 'bitterly' and 'loftily'

H

'the indignation with which he through life contemplated the in-equality of human condition, and particularly, – and who shall say, with absolute injustice? – the contrast between his own worldly circumstances and intellectual rank.' But the 'Epistle' shows 'the same feeling strong, but triumphed over in the moment of inspiration, as it ought ever to have been in the plain exercise of such an understanding as his' [pp. 67-68, 74-75].

In this preoccupation with the sin of spleen, Lockhart's own bio-grapher may feel the intensity of Lockhart's own striving to exorcize a personal demon. The conceptions of spiritual good and evil which we have characterized seem rooted in a revulsion against Lockhart's own notorious capacities for self-destructive diffidence and bitter pride. And this ethic of sensibility and its spiritual dangers by which Burns is judged – self-punished, in Lockhart's presentation – is the ethic by which Scott will be extolled and Lockhart self-condemned. It is best summed up as an ideal of spiritual health (anti-Byronic and, hence, proto-Victorian) in a word Lockhart often uses: 'manly'. Exquisite sensibility passes the ethical test of true genius only when controlled by a manly character.

But Lockhart was not Dr Arnold. 'Manliness' is not the single ground of his absolution of Burns from the tragic sin of sensibility. The redeeming power is intellectual strength. True genius, as opposed to extravagant or selfish sensibility, is, in both Burns and Scott, an 'exquisite sensibility of mind' [p. 256] controlled by a strong under-standing. Under wretched conditions at Mt Oliphant, the young Burns carried burdens 'which would have broken altogether any mind where-in feelings like his had existed, without strength like his to control them'. His letters to Burness of Montrose are 'worthy of the strong understanding and warm heart of Burns'. From the outset Lockhart thus emphasizes Burns's 'gigantic understanding'; quoting Gilbert on the books at Mt Oliphant, he italicizes the following: 'no book was so voluminous as to slacken his industry, or so antiquated as to damp his researches.'[68] But this controlling intellectual power is manifest, in Lockhart's delineation, less in Burns's poetry than in his conversation, to whose brilliance and power Lockhart attributes Burns's extraordinary social conquests. 'The extraordinary resources he displayed in conver-sation, the strong vigorous sagacity of his observations on life and manners', caused even philosophers such as Adam Smith to feel inferior in Burns's presence. 'It was by that talent that he first attracted notice

among his fellow peasants, and after he mingled with the first Scotsmen of his time, this talent was still that which appeared the most
astonishing of all he possessed' [pp. 120-1, 36].

It is on Burns's conversation that Lockhart focuses his biography's
most masterful section: the analytical sketch of Burns's uniquely
problematical position in society. He is presented as the jealously self-
assured genius and wit, overwhelming 'the most cultivated under-
standings of his time in discussion'. Foreseeing from the beginning of
his triumph that none of it could last – this, too, is a testament to his
'gigantic understanding' – he moves 'across the street' to less respectable conversational circles in Edinburgh,

> 'where there was no check upon a tongue that had been accustomed
> to revel in the license of village mastery? where every sally, however
> bold, was sure to be received with triumphant applause – where
> there were no claims to rival his – no proud brows to convey rebuke,
> above all, perhaps, no grave eyes to convey regret?' [pp. 128, 131,
> 136-7]

Thus, the insistence on Burns's powerful understanding, the stress on
his conversational brilliance, the emphasis on the social nature of his
meteoric career – all are parts of the same thematic purpose. And in
terms of the same purpose, one can best understand Lockhart's treatment of the poetry.

The provenance of the poetry is directly traced to actual experience –
national, social, or personal. The process of composition is a swiftly
spontaneous crystallization of the same wit and ardent eloquence which
never deserted Burns under the circumstances of impromptu social
discourse. There is little emphasis on the *inventive* aspect of Burns's
genius. Indeed, for Lockhart, Burns becomes a pawn in the Byron-
Bowles controversy; he approves of the 'high and just contempt' with
which Byron treated those who charged Burns with a lack of imagination, with having written few poems of a 'purely imaginative character' [pp. 304-5]. For Lockhart, Burns embodies a very different idea
of inventive art: 'the art, namely, of recombining and new-combining,
varying, embellishing, and fixing and transmitting the elements of a
most picturesque experience, and most vivid feelings' [p. 304]. His is
not the poetry of private invention, but of an experience removed from
the normal only by its picturesqueness and the intensity of feeling with
which it is transmitted. Directly occasioned by social or personal
experience, it remained a part of that experience, a direct index of

sensibility and a moment in the history of a consciousness. Burns, Lockhart insists, was unusual in this respect. 'No man ever made his muse more completely the companion of his own individual life' [p. 250]. Lockhart never, however, professes the simple Romantic heresy of personality.

The strictures of New Critics and post-Eliot antipersonalists have long since forced literary biographers to a greater sophistication in deducing personality from personality's projections and masks. But the consequent caution and insight are not as extreme an advance on the Romantic biographer as one might suppose. Here is Leon Edel in 1957:

> 'However much a great work is independent of its creator, and may be judged independently, invisible threads remain – many more than anyone can discover and disentangle – which bind it to the fashioning consciousness. ... We dream our own dreams: no one else puts them into our heads. ... The act of imaginative writing is an act of expression as much as an act of communication.'[69]

But J. L. Adolphus was not unaware of the necessary distinctions in 1818. The reader is naturally curious with regard to authors' experience, Adolphus says:

> 'daily participation in their thoughts and feelings awakens a natural curiosity to be acquainted with the incidents of their lives, and to compare their manners and conduct as men, with the tone and character of their writings.'[70]

The sign of caution is the word 'character'; it denotes an individuating form or manner no more than analogous to the stamp or structure of a personality. Numerous critics and literary theorists of Lockhart's generation, while intrigued by the analogy, were aware it was nothing more. Hayley compares, as distinct entities, the moral and poetical 'characters' of Milton. The same distinction, writes Jean Hagstrum, obtains for Bowles and Johnson when they delineate in the 'literary character' of Pope 'a summary of subjective qualities of mind and heart, but only of those relevant to the literary qualifications of the author'. Stanfield insists that 'the biographer and critic, though borrowing lights from the department of each, do, as distinct characters, stand upon very different grounds'. Hence, while he urges that an understanding of provenance and genesis is something only the biographer can contribute, he distinguishes as cautiously as Adolphus: 'The professional character of the person is to be diligently sought for, and extracted from the spirit of individuality which animates an author or an artist's works.'[71]

The distinction between moral and professional character is common enough during the nineteenth century. But it appears to have sprung from two distinct motives. When Henry James insists that 'the life and the works are two very different matters, and an intimate knowledge of the one is not at all necessary for the genial enjoyment of the other', his reservation may be ethical rather than epistemological. His subsequent remark suggests so: 'A writer who gives us his works is not obliged to throw his life after them.'[72] It is the reservation felt by Tennyson, Thackeray, and Browning – expressed by Wordsworth regarding Currie's *Burns* – anticipated by Dr Johnson: 'the best part of every author is in general to be found in his book.'[73] Although he sees reticence as an ethical virtue in the biographer, Lockhart's distinction is epistemological. Defending Byron against personal attacks, he says:

'Two widely different matters . . . are generally, we might say universally, mixed up here – the personal character of the man as proved by his course of life, and his personal character as revealed in, or guessed from, his books.'

Some inferences may be drawn as to 'the character of an author from his book', and to profess an absolute separation between moral and aesthetic judgement is ridiculous. But he attacks 'the impudence with which things are at once assumed to be facts in regard to a man's private history, and the absolute unfairness of never arguing from the writings to the man, but for evil'. He deplores the confusion in the case of *Childe Harold*:

'we, in spite of all manner of disclamations and protestations, insisted upon saddling Byron, himself personally, with every attribute, however dark and repulsive, with which he had chosen to invest a certain fictitious personage, the hero of a romance.'[74]

The fault was, however, partly Byron's. What had begun as an imaginative creation became a dominant influence on the man; and if the Childe was not Byron, he was a distinctly personal creation:

'It is true enough that the thoughts and feelings embodied in this fictitious personage's character, as poetized by Lord Byron, must have at some time or other passed through Lord Byron's own mind, and subsequent events decidedly showed that many of them had been too much at home there.'[75]

On the basis of this relation between the 'character' of the work and the creative consciousness, Lockhart argues from the work to the biographical subject. He does so in one of two ways. He may approach the work as of moral persuasiveness, and measure its appeal by its effect on its maker; or he may approach the work as evidence of moral tone or capacity, and credit the maker with that tone and that capacity, though they may be manifest nowhere else. Illustrative of the first – the critical direction – is the severe treatment accorded the eighteenth-century novelists, whose license Lockhart fears. He is at his most puritanical here:

> 'The youthful admirer of Tom Jones finds that Fielding himself, originally placed by birth, connection, and education in the first class of English society, was a man so utterly lowered in his personal feelings, through long worship of pleasure. . . . And the mind that has been bewildered amidst Sterne's contradictions of fine sentiment and prurient filth, will find a salutary clue in the knowledge of a fact which all Sir W. Scott's good nature cannot prevent him from *hinting – namely*, that the tender and simple Yorick was, in his own person, a profligate man and a mean priest.'[76]

Illustrative of the other – the biographical direction – is the comparison of *Rasselas* and *Candide* with reference to the moral and intellectual characters of their authors: 'How soothing and elevating to turn from the bitter revelry of his [Voltaire's] cynicism to the solemn sadness of the rival work – its grave compassion.' His admiration for Johnson is focused on the comparison of literary and moral character:

> 'it may be worth while for some of those who smile at all the wisdom of our ancestors, and *inter alia* at him and his works, to consider whether, without calling for any assent to the abstract truth of his doctrines, the effect of them on the man himself as a man will not bear a comparison with the fruit of the other *sapientia*, as developed in any personal history they may choose to place by the side of his.'[77]

Against this background, we may avoid a misunderstanding of Lockhart's meaning when, in the conclusion to the *Burns*, he argues that the verses themselves,

> 'were some dross removed, and the rest arranged in a chronological order – would I believe form, to the intelligent, a more perfect and vivid history of his life than will ever be composed out of all the materials in the world besides.'

The history would be strictly a history of mind and feeling. The verses are successful attempts 'to clothe the sufficiently various moods of his mind in rhymes' [pp. 305, 31]. When used biographically, they justify the assertion that, for example, the dignity and piety of the 'Cotter's Saturday Night', the strained exaltation of 'To Mary in Heaven', the rhetorical solemnity of 'Scots Wha Hae' – all were as much parts of Burns's 'personal history' as the very different 'moods of his mind' clothed in 'The rantin' Dog the Daddie o't', 'Tam', and 'The Jolly Beggars'.

Burns, then, was unusual in the closeness with which poems reflected the circumstances of life which had occasioned them. From the outset Lockhart stresses the closeness by referring to biographical events and personalities in terms of the poetry with which they were associated. William Burnes is connected with the 'Cotter'; but it is not suggested that the 'Cotter' was simply a depiction of William Burnes. Rather, the poetic depiction of 'the saint, the father, and the husband' indicates the Burns children's feelings for their father. In the same way, the harsh *factor* of Mt Oliphant 'afterwards sat for his picture in the "Twa Dogs"'. And whenever such a close connection exists, it is of positive value: Burns was not simply inventing, but rather drawing from the realities of his experience. In 'Tam O'Shanter', the 'circumstances', the 'tragic memoranda', were not 'derived from imagination. Nor was Tam O'Shanter himself an imaginary character.' Concerning the songs Burns sent to George Thomson, the 'circumstances under which' they were written 'are all, or almost all, in fact, part and parcel of the poet's personal history' [pp. 12-13, 203, 250].

Emphasis placed on occasional provenance is responsible for what appears, in Lockhart's work, a foreshortening of the process of poetic composition. To be sure, the brevity of his narrative demanded compression. But it is clearly part of Lockhart's interpretation that for Burns, composition was a spontaneous act in close touch with occasioning circumstance. To incorporate this theme Lockhart had only to select and compress, for the legend of Burns's spontaneity and facility was very much alive. And though modern scholars are most sceptical of such anecdotes, they are unlikely to discover evidence on which to base substantial refutation. So far, the evidence for rejection seems composed almost exclusively of inconclusive discrepancies in Burns's letters. 'Tam O'Shanter' is assigned to an autumn day in 1790; on the 22nd of January 1791, Burns reports to Alex. Cunningham he has 'just finished' it. The truth, Chambers and Wallace suggest, is 'that the whole poem had been produced at a heat three or four months before, and that only a few corrections at most had lately been made on it by the author'. Another lyric had been sent to Clarinda, the 27th of December 1791; it was sent again to Thomson in September 1793 with the assurance that 'I have this moment finished the song, so you have it glowing from the mint'.[78] But it is more to our purpose to consider four anecdotes of spontaneous composition for which Lockhart is in some measure responsible.

The circumstances in the case of 'The Deil's Awa with the Exciseman' are characteristic in their implication of spontaneity as well as in the problem of their verification. Lockhart's account, attributed to the journal of exciseman Lewars, places the composition during the preparation for the capture of the smuggler 'Rosamond' in the Solway Firth. While impatiently awaiting Lewars' arrival with extra forces, Burns, the story goes, was urged to indite a song 'upon the sluggard', and did so, striding by himself 'among the reeds and shingle' and returning to chant the results to his raiding party. To accept this from Lewars, Lockhart must reject Cromek: 'At a meeting of his brother Excisemen in Dumfries, Burns being called upon for a Song, handed these verses extempore to the President, written on the back of a letter.' Chambers and Wallace give 'another account of the origin of the poem', from an old man who claimed he was 'one of that company that heard Burns recite the verses . . . in a house in the High Street of Annan'. The most striking thing about the three reports is the naive way in which each assumes an early spontaneous rendition was in fact an impromptu composition. One may wonder in vain about the origin of Cromek's assurance that the verses written for the President were actually composed on the spot; one may wonder why the old man believed that the Annan rendition was *extempore*. Significantly, Lockhart's is the only account that makes no such claim, though it implies it.[79]

There is what *appears* to be conclusive evidence in Burns's own words. Snyder claims that Burns 'said explicitly that he had composed the song "The Deil's Awa" at one of [Mr Mitchell's] Excise Court dinners'.[80] In making the claim Snyder is altering Burns's statement: 'Mr Mitchell mentioned to you a ballad, which I composed, and sung at one of his Excise Court dinners.' The comma following 'composed' surely leaves open the possibility that the phrase modifies only the

second verb, that Burns makes no reference to the location of composition, that, in fact, he may have encouraged ambiguity in such statements to foster the legend of spontaneity.

If we apply Snyder's criterion, the accounts are equally improbable.
Indeed, Lockhart's account of solitary composition on the beach may
well be less improbable than the picture of scribbling at dinner. But
what basis is there for choice, and why is choice necessary? Both
accounts refer to the same period: the Rosamond incident comes first –
in February; the dinner letter was close to, perhaps connected with,
the Rosamond capture. It is more consistent with probability to suggest
that the poem was born on the beach, composed over the intervening
period, and finally written down at the dinner.

The discrepancy with regard to the composition of 'Scots Wha Hae'
is less easily explained. Lockhart is brief:

> 'According to tradition, the tune played when Bruce led his troops to
> the charge, was "Hey tuttie tattie"; and it was humming this old
> air as he rode by himself through Glenken in Galloway, during a
> terrific storm of wind and rain, that the poet composed his immortal
> lyric in its first and noblest form.' [pp. 253-4]

This is from the account John Syme gave Currie of the 1793 Galloway
tour he and Burns took together. In using it, Lockhart compresses the
two occasions noticed by Syme into one, foreshortening the process, and
he removes Syme himself from the scene. Currie had apparently discovered the discrepancy: Burns had written to Thomson in September
1793 that the thought of the air and its association with Bruce had led
to the song 'in my yesternight's evening walk'. Currie had hidden the
discrepancy by revising 'my yesternight's evening walk' to 'my
solitary wanderings'.[81] Lockhart took the location and the storm from
Syme and the tune and the solitariness from Currie. If, as is now held,
the tour was actually in the year following the poem's transmission to
Thomson,[82] then of course Syme's is not the account of a composition
at all. But this does not mean that Syme was simply inventing or that
Lockhart was mendacious in accepting and trying to amalgamate the
discrepant elements of tradition. Syme had no reason to know of
Thomson's unpublished collection ('Scots Wha Hae' appeared in
1799), and may have reported what he thought to be the case: 'Next
day he produced me the following address of Bruce to his troops, and
gave me a copy for Dalzell.'[83] And as far as Lockhart knew, the tour
had antedated the letter to Thomson by two months.

In the case of 'Tam O'Shanter' a stronger case may be made. Snyder couples it with 'Scots Wha Hae' in his scepticism:

'There is no more reason for believing that "Scots Wha Hae" was composed in the midst of a storm on the "wilds of Kenmore" than there is for believing that "Tam" was written during an afternoon stroll with Jean and young Robert.'

He attributes the above to Lockhart and cites in refutation a letter in which Burns said "Tam" had 'a finishing polish that I despair of ever excelling'.[84] There is nothing in Lockhart's account to exclude later polishing; the extent of his concession to the theme of spontaneity may be simply the brevity of his statement: 'The poem was the work of one day' [p. 200]. Snyder, claiming that 'Burns worked hard over the poem, and did not merely toss it off during an afternoon's stroll with his family', is misrepresenting Lockhart. Lockhart relates that Burns 'spent most of the day on his favourite walk by the river, where, in the afternoon, [Jean] joined him with some of her children'. She found him, it continues, quoting from a Cromek MS version confirmed by M'Diarmid, 'busily engaged *crooning to himsell*' and did not interrupt him [p. 200]. That these facts do not exclude the possibility of prolonged work may be seen in Mrs Carswell's version. Burns, she recalls, had already written a prose version:

'one day, idling from dawn to dark by the full-foaming Nith . . . he had found the whole story turning from prose to poetry on his hands. Hour after hour he gave himself over to it, taut with the need to cope in a single unbroken effort with the heavenly coincidence of a sudden vision and verbal material ready to hand.'[85]

Daiches employs the same account more cautiously. Referring to it as 'the product (if tradition is to be trusted) of one day's truancy from the work and worries of his farm and his excise duties during one of his most troubled periods', Daiches argues that with more leisure Burns might have produced comparable poems.[86] The thesis at least suggests one practical answer to those who reject entire the legend of rapid facility in composition: farming and excise duties combined left little time for the laborious craft which they offer as an alternative.

Finally, there is Lockhart's ornately sentimental account of an ornately sentimental poem, 'To Mary in Heaven', rejected by Snyder because 'when Lockhart quotes a second person who quotes a third, the cautious reader will beware of believing any part of the resulting statement' – even though the second is M'Diarmid, editor of the *Dumfries*

Courier, and the third Jean Burns herself. Lockhart is evidently mis-taken in ascribing the poem to September, since the anniversary of Mary's death would have been in mid-October. This error led Scott-Douglas to challenge the harvest setting of Lockhart's anecdote. But at least an autumn setting is verified by the fact that Burns sent the poem to Mrs Dunlop on the 8th of November as 'a Song I made the other day'. Beyond this, Scott-Douglas's scepticism seems grounded in a terribly literal notion of poetic occasion. Because the poem apostrophizes a 'lingering star . . . That lov'st to greet the early morn', he argues that the poem could not have been composed at night and rejects the re-mainder of Jean Burns's reminiscence on that basis. Snyder follows him, clinging to the premise that Burns was not addicted to such poetic gestures: 'if Burns wrote a poem to the morningstar . . . while lying on a mass of straw in his barnyard during the early evening, he was making himself unnecessarily ridiculous.' The modern reconstruction exaggerates the original anecdote; Lockhart clearly suggests an ex-tended period which simply ended in that posture rather than originat-ing with the wrong 'beautiful planet'. The implication of occasional stimulus need not be taken so literally.

Otherwise, the anecdote is beyond verification or rejection. More significant is the general belief that whatever the poem's strained formality, it was occasioned directly by Burns's persistent and idealized devotion to Mary's memory. Hecht, with his dismissal of 'a veil of sentimental anecdotes', is the exception. But his speculation that the poem was occasioned by 'the purely literary necessity of finding a suitable text for a serious air' is challenged by the evidence that the poem was associated with Burns's almost hysterical remorse over Mary's death three years before. Snyder and Lindsay quote the refer-ence, in the December letter to Mrs Dunlop, to 'my ever dear Mary! whose bosom was fraught with Truth, Honor, Constancy and love', as well as to the poem itself as 'this distracted scrawl'. Daiches takes its solemnity to be of sufficient biographical reliability to warrant a scepti-cal view of recent attempts to make Mary 'a common prostitute'.[87]

The discrepancy between Snyder's emphasis on the elaborate finish of the poem and Burns's reference to 'this distracted scrawl' may serve at last to pinpoint the problem of evaluating Lockhart's recurrent theme of spontaneous composition. In the first place, the controversial anecdotes inevitably refer to first transcriptions or oral renditions, and they all record the same impression of occasional spontaneity, whatever the demonstrable inaccuracy of a few minor facts. In the second place, they, like their repudiators, ignore the possibility of prolonged composition before transcription or rendition, though the anecdotes allow time for such a process. The neglect of this possibility, one suspects from such phrases as 'distracted scrawl', may be traced to Burns himself and to a desire to stress his own spontaneity. Hence, it is possible that with this, as with other mythic exaggerations, Lockhart was actually recording, in the dominant themes of his biography, the biographical recreations of the mythmaker himself, Robert Burns.

III

The predominant themes of Lockhart's *Burns* give this biography a personal integrity not apparent to Carlyle. In his praise, however, Carlyle recognized a positive value of the book not noticed elsewhere: its form. Complaining of the negative, condescending tone of earlier biographers, Carlyle describes a misconception of biography in Currie and Walker:

'both err alike in presenting us with a detached catalogue of his several supposed attributes, virtues and vices, instead of a delineation of the resulting character as a living unity. This, however, is not painting a portrait; but gauging the length and breadth of the several features, and jotting down their dimensions in arithmetical cyphers. Nay, it is not so much as that: for we are yet to learn by what arts or instruments the mind *could* be so measured and gauged.'

Lockhart has done otherwise. He has 'avoided the method of separate generalities, and rather sought for characteristic incidents, habits, actions, sayings; in a word, for aspects which exhibit the whole man as he looked and lived among his fellows'.[88] In terms of the Romantic transformation of biographical theory, in terms of the new ideal of organic narrative, Lockhart was, for Carlyle, the first true biographer of Burns.

It is no wonder that abundant anecdotage, whenever it began to 'circulate', was not biographically recorded until what Snyder finds a suspiciously long time after the poet's death. It was an effect not of mendacious mythmaking, but of biographical theory, that details circulated orally so long before they were 'collected'. The theory, sketched in my first chapter, may be seen in clear, full form in the introduction of Currie's and Walker's predecessor, Robert Heron. His

Memoir (1797) opens with the 'philosophical' justification for biography, attacking the view that

'the mere, industrious accumulation of dates, anecdotes, and witticisms, of transactions in which no peculiarities of genius and character were displayed, or of obscure events by which the habits, thought, or action, were in no way remarkably influenced; can deserve to be ambitiously studied, or admired, as the perfection of biographical writing. The following memoir . . . has been composed under the direction of a very different, although perhaps not a more correct, critical principle.'[89]

The principle sounds promising enough, and Heron does promise to trace the gradual development of character and talents. But then he reveals the abstract scientific aim which undermines his promise: 'The writer's wishes will be amply gratified; if this TRIFLE shall be found to afford any exposition of the nicer laws of the formation and progress of human character, such as shall not be scorned as data by the moral philosopher.'[90] However different from each other, Heron, Currie, and Walker all saw themselves as analytic moralists or 'historians of mind'. Heron abstractly traced the 'progress' of life and character. Currie divided his attention between sociological speculation on the Scottish peasant and preachment on the curse of artistic sensibility. Walker offered the character-delineation of the man of genius 'as an important addition to the natural history of the human species'.[91] The organic narrative of a life was beyond their aims, and hence they failed largely to preserve the anecdotal materials for such biography. By the time a new ideal was recognized, the natural processes of tradition had long been operative commencing in the situation Cunningham describes at Dumfries when Burns died:

'Wherever two or three were together their talk was of Burns, and of him alone. They spoke of his history, of his person, and of his works – of his witty sayings and sarcastic replies, and of his too early fate, with much enthusiasm, and sometimes with deep feeling –'

and soon reaching the hopeless complexity he illustrates:

'Syme told the story, in a rather darker manner, to Sir Walter Scott, who thus related it in one of his criticisms. . . . I have heard a much gentler version of the story: indeed it has several variations, and a biographer has some latitude of choice.'[92]

In tracing the development of Burns's genius, Heron remains more plausible than Carlyle. But his 'tracery' subsists on a wholly abstract level. Under such and such influences, Burns 'slowly and unconsciously acquired a poetical temper of soul, and a poetic cast of thought'. He discusses one by one 'other features in his opening character, which might seem to mark him a poet', and traces from this opening 'the progress of his life and character'. The whole sketch has the paradoxical quality of the 'progress'; the hero is at once a fixed aggregate of psychological features independent of circumstances and a passive abstraction in the toils of circumstance. There is no evolution through the interplay of impulse and stimulus; the repetition of 'slowly' and 'gradually' is no substitute for narrative development. Heron's hero is static, his 'character' is his fate, and he becomes, in his arrogance, beyond help. He is the pawn in a struggle between abstract forces – 'the virtuous, the learned and the wise' and 'the gay and the dissolute' – for the soul of Burns. In the brevity of Heron's essay and the thinness of his temporal narrative, Burns's deterioration seems rapid and unbroken, and yet, during the increasingly severe assertions of moral decay, one senses only a condemnation of the 'foolish', the 'gross and vulgar' company which surrounded him and no implication of corrupt will in Burns himself. [93]

Thus, the severity of Heron's essay, as Hilton Brown has noticed, is 'fairer and less anti-Burns than is generally made out'.[94] Beneath the surface severity is an interpretation which seems to bypass Victorian excesses (Carlylesque or Wilsonian) and reappear in modified form in the modern period. We may consider melodramatic the depicting of Burns at his lowest as still of 'exalted mind', still 'not less than archangel ruined'; but such a conception originated in Burns's own admiration of the Miltonic Satan, and served to strengthen Lockhart's own emphasis on the dark, tragic side of Burns's terrible pride and bitter independence. More sound is Heron's insistence that Burns was the product of southwest Scottish rural life – parish schools, peasant piety, border tradition, the contradictions of eighteenth-century Scottish culture. Again, Heron insists on the 'studious bent' of Burns's genius, and asserts, like Lockhart after him, that Burns's 'plain common sense, or *mother-wit*' made the social conversationalist as prodigious as the poet. And from the unique circumstances of his social fame, Heron believes a significant part of his misfortune arose; there was a fatal lack of understanding on the part of both society and Burns:

'It seems to be forgotten, that a ploughman thus exalted into a man of letters, was unfitted for his former toils, without being regularly qualified to enter the career of any new profession; and that it became incumbent upon those patrons who had called him from the plough . . . to secure him, as far as was possible, from being overwhelmed in distress, in consequence of the favour which they had shown him, and of the habits of life into which they had seduced him.'[95]

But in spite of their failure, Heron insists, Burns's Ellisland life was marked by unimpaired intellectual and poetic activity. As for the latest years of rumoured degradation, it is Heron whom Lockhart quotes in support of the view that Burns's indulgences at their most extreme were never habitual, and that his moral sense was never deadened. Heron speaks as an admiring, judicious observer, with first-hand experience of the poet and his world, with no obligations to Burns's executors, and with direct access to Galloway tradition. His *Memoir* had for Lockhart at least the value Hecht assigns it: 'the reflection of a contemporary impression, seen in a dark and distorted mirror.'[96]

Cunningham thought Heron unkindest; Carlyle thought Currie most kind. Yet Heron's severity is conventional, while Currie's 'kindness' is strongly tinctured with condescension and distaste. His interest is more abstract than Heron's, his knowledge is indirect, and he speaks as one completely detached from the tragedy he describes. 'Currie,' writes the judicious Hilton Brown, 'was about as much in sympathy with Burns as he would have been with a witch doctor from the Congo.'[97]

The detachment is augmented by his abstract idiom. Burns's every fall is the culmination of a *psychomachia*:

'In Dumfries, temptations to the sin that so easily beset him, continually presented themselves; . . . and though he clearly foresaw the consequences of yielding to them, his appetites and sensations, which could not pervert the dictates of his judgment, finally triumphed over the powers of his will.'[98]

At Ellisland, rustic conviviality 'inflamed those propensities which temperance might have weakened, and prudence ultimately suppressed' [I, 193]. The dreadful phrase 'happy had it been' signals the onset of many a pious lamentation:

'happy had it been for him, after he emerged from the condition of a peasant, if fortune had permitted him to enjoy them [literary associations] in the degree of which he was capable, so as to have fortified his principles of virtue by the purification of his taste, and given to the energies of his mind, habits of exertion, that might have excluded other associations, in which it must be acknowledged they were too often wasted, as well as debased.' [I, 118]

The idiom is appropriate; Currie's interest is entirely general. The final 'character', an abstract disquisition on the curse of sensibility, concludes: 'These observations might be amply illustrated by the biography of men of genius of every denomination, and more especially by the biography of the poets' [I, 241]. Such is the motive of Currie's 'narrative'. Afflicted with the 'philosophic mind', he elucidates by deduction from the generic – the psychological or social pattern or institution. A letter is not explicated, but categorized: it 'displays the philosophic melancholy, which so generally forms the poetic temperament, and that buoyant and ambitious spirit, which indicates a mind conscious of its strength' [I, 101]. One need only commence such a passage as 'Those who have studied the affinities of mind, know that a melancholy of this description, after a while, seeks relief in the endearments of society . . .' [I, 102], to understand why there seems so little relation between Currie's documents and his experience of their subject, in Carlyle's phrase so little 'living unity' of subject and form.

Formally considered, Currie's *Burns* belongs to the decade of Hayley's *Cowper* and other successors to the Mason method. It begins with a speculative survey of Scottish peasant conditions, then quickly recounts Burns's entire life and gives his letter to Moore in full. Burns is born on page fifty-seven and, after an account of his forebears, again on page fifty-eight. On page fifty-nine he is six years old, and shortly thereafter a long passage from Gilbert's memoir takes us through his marriage. After a general commentary Currie transcribes the letter of Murdoch the boy's teacher, justifying his separate presentation of the three accounts as follows:

'The three relations serve . . . not merely to illustrate, but to authenticate each other. Though the information they convey might have been presented within a shorter compass, by reducing the whole into one unbroken narrative, it is scarcely to be doubted, that the intelligent reader will be far more gratified by a sight of these original documents themselves.' [I, 96]

The ideal of documentary integrity is the one Lockhart inherited. The difference is that Currie had no notion of narrative form or effective compilation.

Following a general picture of the poet at home, Currie introduces the Irvine letter, with no narrative setting, purely to illustrate early melan choly. Then comes an opportunity to renew his general speculation, for 'the philosophic mind will dwell with interest and pleasure' on institutions like the Tarbolton and Mauchline clubs Burns helped to establish; and 'if grandeur look down with a smile on these simple annals, let us trust it will be a smile of benevolence and approbation' [I, 107]. Currie's 'benevolence and approbation' balk at the dangers of refining the taste of peasants. Upon these he reflects generally, and then offers the following as biographical explanation:

'It cannot, however, be doubted, that by collision, the faculties of his mind would be excited, that by practice, his habits of enunciation would be established, and thus we have some explanation of that early command of words and of expression.' [I, 117]

Currie then returns to Mauchline, gives the poem on the 'lass of Ballochmyle' (1786), makes coy reference to 'youthful passions of a still tenderer nature . . . the history of which it would be improper to reveal, were it even in our power' [I, 124], adds the poem 'To Mary in Heaven' written years later at Ellisland. And even these must be justified as glimpses of the poet's 'character in its various aspects'. So ends Currie's major contribution, its *raison d'être* indicated in his summary:

'We have dwelt the longer on the early part of his life, because it is the least known, and because, as has already been mentioned, this part of his history is connected with some views of the condition and manners of the humblest ranks of society, hitherto little observed, and which will perhaps be found neither useless nor uninteresting.' [I, 127-8]

The 'views' have predominated; the correspondence now supersedes—such is Currie's term – the need for narrative.

Walker's appraisal, like Heron's, is at once more severe and more sympathetic; the most sympathetic Burnsian can share Hilton Brown's feeling that Josiah Walker had 'a remarkable insight into Burns'.[99] As concrete narrative, however, his account scarcely exists. In the first place he accepts Currie's 'masterly narrative'; in the second, his own experience of Burns has been transformed into a searching analysis of Burns's personality – an interpretation at once judicious and at first hand, and hence unique in Burns biography.

Walker is free of the misrepresentations of which the 'mythmakers' have been accused. He sympathises with Burns for a marriage lacking in intellectual stimulation, accepts Gilbert's assurances of constitutional

I

sobriety, and deplores the excise job. While he feels that Burns's imprudence frustrated designs for his advancement, he traces to the excise investigation the deterioration of Burns's 'temper and conduct', the disappointment (see the passage omitted by Snyder from the letter to Mar) which led Burns to give up all ambition 'in a rash and regard-less despair'.[100] He attributes to Burns the pride of young Sam Johnson, but sympathises with his jealousy of power and his hostility to any system which pays to birth and opulence the rewards owed to genius and virtue. Finally, he reaffirms that Burns's indiscretions were worse than those of other men only because of his eminence, that his disrepute was largely undeserved, that 'the world' hated not his sins, but his defiance of 'the world'. Visiting Burns in his last years, Walker had the impression of a certain coarsening, but he discovered in the poet's conduct 'no errors which I had not seen in men who stand high in the favour of society, or sufficient to account for the mysterious insinuations which I heard against his character'.[101] In some of these views Walker anticipates Lockhart, but in nothing more than in his tone of severe moral compassion. His conclusion would stand well with Johnson on Savage, and, what I believe comparable, Lockhart on Thomas Campbell:

'We must therefore, as far as possible, identify ourselves, in person and in circumstances, with the poet. We must conceive a being with unusual impetuosity of passion, goaded by the importunity of a vigorous organization, and inflamed by the seductions of a fervid and restless fancy, presenting numerous incentives, which escape the duller perception of ordinary men. We must then consider the circum-stances in which this being was placed; irritated by the pressure of hardship and disappointment; shaken in his reverence for a religious system, under the discipline of which he had been exposed to shame; thrown into employments unworthy of his genius, and unable to occupy or interest his mind; and invited by that obtrusion of oppor-tunity, which the simplicity of humble life creates, accompanied, in his case, with all the prurient sensibility which is generally confined to the indolent and pampered members of polished society. When these considerations have been fairly brought under our eye; when we have, by an effort of imagination, conceived our own character and circumstances thus put together, and thus put to trial, then is the moment to pronounce a verdict. The verdict must of course be, *guilty*; yet many of the partakers of his frailty may "blush as they give it in".'[102]

And yet, Walker is almost as remote as Heron and Currie from the Carlylesque ideal of a 'living unity' of narrative. The chief cause is signalled by his key transition: 'It was at this time,' Walker recalls, 'I became acquainted with the works and the person of Burns.'[103] 'This time' is the period of Burns's Edinburgh success; meeting Burns when the poet's short life was two-thirds over, Walker faced the formal dilemma confronted by Boswell and Lockhart in their major works. Walker describes the meeting and his first impressions; and as he does so, there appears for the first time a present sensibility behind the subtle speculative appraisal of motives and 'manners' which comprises his account. But the sudden appearance of the first-hand observer shocks the reader into revaluating Walker's earlier reflections and inferences. Those impersonal, detached observations are suddenly recognised as the partial experiences of a single observer, representing interpretations of later events applied to earlier incidents not experienced at first hand. The recognition is disquieting because this major shift in distance and perspective is neither revealed nor provided for by a modification of style and tone. The essential difference between earlier and later deductions is rhetorically unmarked.

It is impossible to document this claim fully. But we may show how deductive analysis overwhelms Walker's narrative. Take this reconstruction of Burns's resolutions upon leasing Mossgiel in 1784:

'These resolutions were as meritorious as they probably were sincere, while the subject had possession of his thoughts. But in a mind where every successive impression was so powerful, the very strength of the resolution contributed to its breach. It begot an easy and self-approving security, which, by tranquillizing his feelings, rendered them more open to the assaults of the next temptation. His satisfaction in the consciousness that the first step to amendment had been taken, made him careless about the rest.' [I, li]

The specific situation is lost in the conjectural analysis of a mental habit. The same habit – the temptation to slip into an 'easy and self-approving security' – reappears to inform other interpretations. In his first poetical success, Burns 'would probably have accomplished more, had his first encouragement been less sudden and less decided'. Although Burns's flatterers did not turn his head, they probably fostered his feeling that he had done enough, and so, at the time he did little more. The postulating of this habit controls Walker's 'description' of Burns's undertaking the farm at Ellisland:

'At this time Burns imagined himself busy in making arrangements for a future plan of life, upon which he was to enter, as soon as he had obtained the produce of his publication. In this, if he really bestowed much thought upon it, he showed little acquaintance with his own character, and little of that understanding which he certainly possessed.' [I, lvi, lxiv, lxxxii]

Such analysis, far more sophisticated than Currie's, recalls Johnsonian conjecture in *The Lives of the Poets*. And Walker, too, narrates as the generalizing 'philosopher of mind'. Consider how he explains the paradox that Burns's period of great anxiety, of 'amours' increasing in 'number and violence', of 'the tumults of hilarity and the toils of the field', was also the time of his greatest poetic creativity and achievement:

'It is not in its most quiescent state that the mind makes its noblest efforts. Many of the finest works have been produced in the intervals of anguish, in the pauses of agitation, in the intermissions of alarm. It is not during a permanent exemption, but in the moment of relief from pain, that the body enjoys the most delicious sensations and the mind its greatest alertness.' [I, lii]

Under such analysis the thin narrative is buried. Concrete glimpses of the individual Burns are infrequent. When Walker feels the need to observe that 'we are now arrived at a very critical period in the narrative', he is doing what his narrative cannot do for itself. From a reading of Walker's searching analysis one receives no clear impression either of Burns's development or of Walker's experience of him.

We have assessed Lockhart's predecessors in order to interpret Carlyle's praise of Lockhart's own *Life of Burns*. Having done so, we must recall Carlyle's reservations. He found Lockhart's book too cautious and derivative, having 'less depths than we could have wished and expected from a writer of such power'. The biographical persona, in current jargon, is uncommitted, diffuse; the narrative lacks 'personality'. The accuracy of this complaint is illuminated by a contrasting glance at the Burns of Lockhart's contemporary, Allan Cunningham.

Cunningham's narrative ideal is emphatically personal. Aware like Lockhart that he had few new materials to contribute to Burns's biography, he departed from Lockhart's decision to do a judicious 'compendium', to urge that the biographer's contribution should be an impressionistic personal rendition: 'like the artist who founds a statue out of old materials, he has to reproduce them in a new shape, touch them with the light of other feeling, and inform them with fresh spirit and sentiment.'[104] The 'fresh spirit and sentiment' are often extravagant enough to conceal his narrative. He took the need for sentimental originality so seriously that the result is inflation and often falsification.

Most noticeable are the ornate figures sometimes so extended as to compose wholly imaginary scenes in themselves. The transitions that give his narrative its deceptive fidelity to temporal sequence often depend on such figures: 'Having made this covenant with himself, he resumed his intercourse with the muse' – and produced 'Tam O'Shanter' [I, 245]. Narrative becomes allegory: 'The spirit of poesie led him, in much peril, through the prosaic wilderness around, and prepared him for asserting his right to one of the highest places in the land of song' [I, 44]. In the quaint scene of Robert's return from Edinburgh, his mother appears, tearful, on the threshold:

'"Oh, Robert!" He had left her hearth in the darkness of night, and he came back in the brightness of day; he went away an obscure and almost nameless adventurer, and he returned with a name, round which there was already a halo not destined soon to be eclipsed . . . he had now made his way to the mountain-top, his pipe was at his lips, and all the country round was charmed with his melody.' [I, 155]

More extreme is the account of society's betrayal: 'Whilst sailing on pleasure's sea in a gilded barge, with perfumed and lordly company, he was, in the midst of his engagement, thrown roughly overboard, and had to swim to barren shores, or sink for ever' [I, 203].

When speaking of Burns's relations with high society, Cunningham loses all restraint, and the resultant 'personality' is appropriate only in so far as Cunningham's anti-aristocratic spleen is equal to Burns's. One notes characteristic differences between Cunningham and Lockhart in descriptions of Burns in Edinburgh the first winter. The compressed formality of Lockhart's syntax is itself a restraining force; he achieves a general, yet concrete evocation of a social situation:

'In this proud career, however, the popular idol needed no slave to whisper whence he had risen, and whither he was to return in the ebb of the spring-tide of fortune. His "prophetic soul" was probably furnished with a sufficient memento every night – when, from the soft homage of glittering saloons, or the tumultuous applause of convivial assemblies, he made his retreat to the humble garret of a *writer's* apprentice, a native of Mauchline, and as poor as himself, whose only bed "Caledonia's Bard" was fain to partake throughout this triumphant winter.' [p. 109]

Cunningham is characteristically tempted to fanciful expansion, augmented by a *genre* picture of the Edinburgh lodging:

'When the company arose in the gilded and illuminated rooms, some of the fair guests– perhaps

> Her Grace,
> Whose flambeaux flash against the morning skies,
> And gild our chamber ceilings as they pass,

took the hesitating arm of the Bard; went smiling to her coach, waved a graceful good-night with her jewelled hand, and, departing to her mansion, left him in the middle of the street to grope his way through the dingy alleys of the "gude town" to his obscure lodging, with his share of a deal table, a sanded floor, and a chaff bed, at eighteen pence a week.' [I, 131]

It is predictable from such a contrast that the two biographers would differ in theme as well. Cunningham has his own axes to grind, and he risks narrative unity and coherence to indulge in indignant rhapsodies on Burns's behalf. [105] Cunningham's interpretation need not be assessed here. What is pertinent to our formal contrast is the ineptitude with which Cunningham incorporates recurrent motifs and extravagant digressions into a narrative deceptive enough already. General reflections arise repeatedly in different contexts, and the narrative becomes simply a connecting thread for extended digressions and hobbyhorsical rides. In addition, Cunningham seems unsure of how to locate and integrate documentary materials in his narrative. Cunningham seems unable to mark clearly in his four sections the particular stages of his narrative. He sums up, then reverts to earlier materials, losing the point of his summary. On page 126, for example, he cites the 'tone of despondency' in the letter to Moore from Edinburgh. On page 128 he sums up Burns's problem. On page 132 he is back making the same point, quoting from the same letter. On occasion he is so attached to surface chronology that he fails to organize around important thematic unities. The subject of Burns's jacobitism-cum-jacobinism arises in the anecdote of Burns and the minister of Dunscore. Cunningham allows the anecdote to remain in its place, while Lockhart saves the subject for the later chapter in which Burns's politics provide the emphasis.

But enough has been said to suggest some of the problems which even the biographer devoted to narrative concreteness and personality must solve, and to suggest that if Heron, Currie, and Walker were scarcely aware of them, Cunningham lacked the formal sophistication to solve them. Indeed, the modern efforts of Snyder and Ferguson[106] – one largely argumentative in form, the other sacrificing narrative for analytic exposition – suggest that the problems may be insurmountable. But it is the point of this chapter that Lockhart's, whatever the deficiencies and dangers, was the most practicable, efficient solution. That solution amounted to a flexible combination of compilation, progressive narrative, and thematic exposition.

Aware that his own opinions were remote by contrast with the testimony of biographical witnesses, Lockhart conceived his role as compiler-editor and, on occasion, jurist. In treating his sources, he holds the criterion of immediacy uppermost. He questions the accuracy of Gilbert Burns but adds: 'Gilbert's recollections, however on trivial points inaccurate, will always be more interesting than anything that could be put in their place' [p. 69]. The 'unfortunate Heron' is quoted frequently because he had 'mingled largely in some of the scenes to which he adverts' [p. 134]. When Cromek is the source of an extravagant account of the parting from Highland Mary, Lockhart manages adroitly to indicate its uncertainty as evidence without destroying its narrative value: he observes that the story is given by Cromek without authority and contains 'particulars which no one would willingly believe apocryphal', then mentions Cunningham's scepticism as well as the essential confirmation supplied by the discovery of the Bible [p. 81]. Allan himself is treated with caution; value is placed on the immediacy of his experience and the similarity of his own poetic background, but his anecdotes are clearly labelled as traditional. 'I envy no one,' Lockhart says ambiguously, 'the task of inquiring minutely in how far these traditions, for such unquestionably they are, rest on the foundation of truth' [p. 253]. Cunningham's recollections are given always in their proper person so that the compiler may use them as individual testimony without committing himself to their accuracy. To such accounts Lockhart subordinates his own voice; to the juxtaposition of their diverse views he applies, and then often suspends, his judgement.

Subordinate as he is, Lockhart fashions in his role as editor and compiler a biographical instrument (fully utilized in the *Life of Scott*) as clearly marked, personal, and dominant as Cunningham's. Though ostensibly he interferes little, he remains in control, and what evolves is a symposium of voices, quietly dominated by a judicious moderator. He marshals witnesses with a pleader's skill; and in the shape of an expertly managed inquiry, his investigation seems to present itself as the inquirer-compiler sits modestly by. This may be what Snyder has in mind when he finds Lockhart more misleading. Cunningham is so flagrantly personal that we easily detach ourselves from his experience as biographer; from Lockhart we rarely detach ourselves, for in his inquiry we detect no intrusive personality, but simply a mode of presentation, a principle of orderly arrangement. The impression is augmented by his painstaking citation of sources, in a small popular book, for almost every bit of evidence. Such documentation is no footnote fetish, but an important part of the *persona*, the inquiring tone, and a means of achieving a far stronger sense of authenticity than the contemporary reconstructive biographer, with his dogged omission of scholarly apparatus and his glib redaction of original testimony, can ever achieve. The first-hand accounts presented are, however, compiled with such skill that, while they may supplement, illustrate, validate, qualify, or contradict each other, they never simply coexist. The witnesses are presented, allowed the full effect of their individual views before they are questioned, and critically collated with modest caution.

The most obvious illustration of the dialogue procedure is supplied by the eighth chapter, the account of the earlier years in Dumfries. Here indeed, the form of inquiry temporarily almost replaces narrative. The question of Burns's political activities and sentiments and their effect on his expectations is placed in its historical context and set forth in dialogue among Scott, Peterkin, Gray, Findlater, with evidence supplied by Train, MacCulloch, and others, and with Lockhart's assessment of each view. The discussion leads to local electioneering and back to the question of drinking. Heron, Currie, and Walker are pitted against Gilbert Burns, Gray, and Findlater; and Lockhart concludes with an affirmation of belief in the good faith of all, and a cautiously critical attempt to weigh motives for the various exaggerations.

Were the *Life* as a whole of such a procedure, there would be no reason to praise its author for narrative art. Almost invariably, such units of inquiry and dialogue are carefully integrated into narrative sequence. The book is built in subject units which approximate chronological phases – units gathered around such centres as early home life, family, education, domestic labour, beginnings of poetry and early effects of his *penchant pour l'adorable moitié du genre humain*. In building such narrative units, Lockhart's usual procedure is to quote Burns's own account (from the Moore letter), then the account of one or more observers (Gilbert, Murdoch, Dugald Stewart), then to give his own understated summary and comment, to be followed when appropriate with an amplification (in documents) of a major topic, with a significant incident or dominant feature of personality, and with what appears a direct illustration from the poems themselves. Take for example the unit grouped around early education. Lockhart's description of William Burnes's desire for his children's schooling leads to Murdoch's account of William Burnes, and thence to his account of the school itself. Murdoch's failure to recognize Robert's talents introduces the part of the Moore letter beginning 'At those years I was by no means a favourite with anybody', describing his reading, and ending with the reference to the imbibing of 'Scottish prejudice' through the reading of *Wallace*. To give dramatic substance to 'Scottish prejudice', there ensues a passage from a letter to Mrs Dunlop, describing Burns's pilgrimage to the Leglen wood, incited by the same reading. The unit ends with the boys' removal from the school given in Gilbert's words, which also give the transition to Mt Oliphant life.

The procedure appears simple enough, yet the unity and authenticity it effects are unique in early Burns biography. Unique, too, is the way Lockhart suggests major themes simply by grouping. Here, for example, arrangement has suggested Robert's ambiguous relationships and arrogant independence, has depicted the contradictory directions taken by his complex education, has anticipated the ritualistic manifestations of patriotic imagination which were to characterize his tours, has introduced the strong humanitarian sensibility which displayed itself in a complete lack of social tact, and has suggested the irony of an extreme sensitivity contrasted with the external viewpoint to which it was invisible. But though these anticipations are accomplished, it is part of Lockhart's structural tact that he knows when and when not to generalize, when and when not to set aside narrative limits for wider expository development.

The rhetorical possibilities of biography consist in such alternatives as these. No biographical narrative with meaningful form can be ordered in absolute chronology; displacement is demanded by every event of thematic relevance to events past or to come. But every displacement is an act of interpretation. In the case of the letter to Moore, of course, the biographer of Burns confronted, in his most valuable document, displacement as a *fait accompli*. Some confusion inevitably resulted. Burns speaks of dancing school and of the awakening of his *penchant pour l'adorable moitié du genre humain* as belonging to his 'seventeenth year' and yet as having occurred at Tarbolton (where they moved in 1777, his eighteenth or nineteenth year). Gilbert dated the Tarbolton years accordingly; moreover, he and Currie crossed out 'seventeenth' in the M S. letter to Moore on Burns's reference to the intoxicating Kirkoswald summer. Chambers and Wallace place the trip in 1775, and Scott-Douglas can imagine 'no grounds whatever' for the change made by Gilbert and Currie.[107] One explanation is obvious: Burns himself is vague on dates, and places the summer well after the move to Tarbolton in the order of his letter. Gilbert could have responded to the obvious need for adjustment without ulterior motive. And yet the later placing of such experience has clear moral implications whether Gilbert recognized them or not.

Burns himself may well have recognized them. He obviously did in a more famous instance, and here he was aided and abetted by the structural skill of Lockhart. Of his desperate plans to emigrate to the West Indies and of the affairs which surround them, Burns repeats in his own notes that they were in 'very early life', in his 'very early years' before he was 'known at all in the world'.[108] As a result, Lockhart places the emigration plan soon after the move to Mossgiel. Scott-Douglas attacks his statement that Burns's 'letters show that on two or three different occasions, long before his poetry had excited any attention, he had applied for, and nearly obtained appointments of this sort'; but Lockhart does not say the letters were *written* that early. Ferguson is, as usual, more cautious on the problem of dating: 'The documents are lost which would settle the date at which Burns began seriously to consider emigration, but his mind was made up at the very beginning of 1786.'[109] The point of all this is its bearing on the chronology of the 'Highland Mary' episode. It is, to be sure, hard to see how the battle of extremists for Mary's virtue – Burns's Beatrice or John Richmond's doxy – hangs on the issue of two years and on the question of the affair's temporal propinquity to the fertile Jean Armour's achievements.[110] It is a narrow view of Burns's complex sensibility that assumes every ardent affair must have had the earthy quality of the affair with Jean, just as it is a singular puritanism which discounts the possibility of spiritual ardour on the basis of Mary's probable death in childbed. Be this as it may, Lockhart's construction of his third and fourth chapters clearly isolates Mary from the 1786 situation of sus - pense, angry grief, and concealment, and presents her story at a point in the narrative before the difficulties with the Armours. The suggestion that the Indian plans began early is, because of Mary's poetical associa - tion with them, a 'groundwork' for the implication that she was an 'early love' with the accompanying connotation of purity.[111] Yet Lockhart was simply participating in Burns's own deception – perhaps with the same motive of protecting Jean's feelings.

At any rate, such displacements, even mistaken dislocations, en - couraged the kind of licence in the use of documents which may be considered as an essential feature of Lockhart's formal skill. There could have been no reason other than formal ones for the characteristic liberties Lockhart takes with such major documents as Stewart's letter to Currie and Burns's letter to Moore; they were available and well known in print. His adaptation of Stewart's reminiscence amounts to nothing more than locating excerpts in the narrative. Even such a simple procedure, however, is indicative. The first excerpt belongs with the section on Burns's provincial recognition in the months preceding the trip to Edinburgh, and it contributes perfectly to the picture of this first social complexity to result from acclaim. The two Edinburgh excerpts are apparently separated in time, but their separation is more than temporal. The first depicts Burns in society; the second shows him on walks in the Braid Hills, gazing affectionately on cottages and the beauties of nature, and leads directly to his departure from the city. The final excerpt is used to supply a picture of Burns at home in Mauch - line during July. If Lockhart had printed the letter as a single whole, as had been done previously, he would have sacrificed the clear demarca - tions of narrative progression which such documents, carefully excerpted and set, supply.

Burns's letters to Moore are used in similar ways. In a section of the Edinburgh chapter, illustrating Burns's social triumph, we see speci - mens of Lockhart's amalgamating or 'telescoping' of excerpts from separate letters into single coherent texts. The first, which adds to a letter to Mrs Dunlop two paragraphs of a letter to a different correspon - dent, is copied from Currie. But the telescoping of excerpts to Moore is Lockhart's. He joins two passages from a January and a February letter with a hiatus, then adds for climax a passage from an April letter. All together make a coherent paragraph, in Burns's words, expressing his disenchantment with lionizing.[112] Other excerpts to Moore are placed elsewhere throughout the first four chapters as autobiographical nuclei of narrative units, with minor rephrasings to supply connectives and transitions. The passage recalling Burns's conversational jabs at Auld Licht divinity is set in the Mauchline chapter. Burns begins with a reference to an earlier period – 'Polemical divinity, about this time, was putting the country half wild' – and refers to his own jibes as in the future: 'I . . . used *a few years afterwards* to puzzle Calvinism.' Lockhart, setting the excerpt in the later context, omits the words I have italicized. He later uses a passage beginning in the Currie text, 'I now began to be known', and fits it into a specific narrative unit with the changed opening, 'From this time I began to be known'. Three sentences already excerpted for earlier use are omitted.[113]

Such excerpts are fitted together with other materials into larger narrative units with extraordinary skill. The third chapter, with its sketch of romantic involvements and frustrations, closes on a picture of desperation: 'the only alternative that presented itself to his view was America or jail.' The fourth opens with the decision made – 'Jamaica was now his mark' [pp. 86-87] – but, after the response accorded the Kilmarnock volume, suddenly set aside. The section that follows is framed in Burns's own words from the Moore letter: it opens with his statement that terror and exile were cut off by the Blacklock letter, and closes with the statement (following in the letter itself) that Black-lock's encouragement sent him 'posting away' to Edinburgh, that his 'baneful star' had 'for once made a revolution to the nadir'. These two statements of the same narrative fact, serving as terminal points, give the unit its total narrative effect. Between them are twelve pages whose descriptive purpose is to show Burns *at this period* of provincial success. Passages are chosen and grouped to suggest the reception of the poems and the poet. Heron's reminiscence begins with general survey; Stewart is referred to but not quoted; Gilbert's description of the re-sponse of Mrs Dunlop follows. The introduction of Mrs Dunlop having introduced the problematical position of Burns in a new social context, Stewart is quoted on Burns's early behaviour within and from the viewpoint of that society. But to fit better, the Stewart excerpt is re-arranged. Stewart speaks first of Burns's gloomy prospects, of his want of patronage and his hopes for the excise; in Lockhart's narrative, the social situation is depicted first, and following the Stewart excerpt

Lockhart returns to gloomy prospects and the excise. To cause the excerpt to fit, Lockhart reverses its order, effecting transitions at both ends without editorial intrusion, and establishing a pattern of alterna-tion between two topics – Burns's excise hopes and his difficult social situation – which later become interdependent. The displaced Stewart paragraph leads to Burns's letter to Aiken, speaking of both problems, presenting his state of mind at the time (confirming what Stewart had spoken of as observer), and suggesting the habits of thought and feeling which would complicate his social position and his hopes of patronage.

There follow two of the period's 'vagaries of the muse'. Both, how-ever, concern Burns in higher society, are addressed to two ladies of social rank; and Lockhart closes their description with a second of Stewart's remarks. He then reintroduces the narrative movement so as to suggest that it has not ceased at all – 'The autumn of this eventful year was now drawing to a close' [p. 97], reintroduces the suspense, the preparation for departure, the dramatic situation for the arrival of Blacklock's letter, quotes the letter, describes its delivery, and closes the unit with Burns's own words. The unit arrangement has achieved a coherent, progressive narrative form, permitted a descriptive sketch of Burns's life at a particular place and time, and simultaneously effected the parallel exposition of related themes.

This structural analysis could be applied to almost any of the units of which the biography is built, its chapters. By his mastery of chapter form Lockhart has managed to satisfy the demands of descriptive and expository unity within a predominantly narrative movement. More-over, a chapter-by-chapter analysis would also reveal the architectonics – the articulation of his conception of the life in significant form. A glance at chapter openings and conclusions would illustrate how narra-tive progression is stressed, how each unit has been given its own thematic focus, and how each unit builds to a climax of major signi-ficance in the biography's total effect.

But since these are claims to be substantiated with reference to two other, more ambitious works, they must be left here without further illustration.

4

THE FALLEN CHIEF.
A TRIO OF
BUONAPARTES

'Tis gone like a fairy revel; nor in the round of ever-rolling years will the like be seen again to humble and to exalt all that there is of pride in the heart of man. . . . If a Buonaparte or a Charlemagne appears once in a thousand years, it gives the world something to think of in the interim.

WILLIAM HAZLITT

Nations yet to come will look back to his history, as to some grand and supernatural romance . . . and when all the lesser tumults and lesser men of our age shall have passed away into the darkness of oblivion, history will still inscribe one mighty aera with the majestic name of Napoleon . . . now, God pity us, he sleeps sound beneath a thousand weight of granite, and shame on the mortal who dares deny that he was the greatest man of the last thousand years.

J. G. LOCKHART

If we seek *biography*, not hagiography, the story of a great life as it was actually lived, if we strive to understand Napoleon the human being, then we must bear in mind that Napoleon the Demigod was conceived at St Helena, came of age in 1830, and was solemnly canonized in 1840.

A. L. GUERARD

There never was and there never can be such a person as everybody's Napoleon.

J. M. THOMPSON[1]

4

THE FALLEN CHIEF.
A TRIO OF
BUONAPARTES

Had the *Life of Scott* never been written, Lockhart would remain one of the most skilful biographical artists of his time. Nor is it skill alone that makes him the most interesting of Romantic biographers. By coincidence he had, in his other two major subjects, a poet and a warrior who epitomized Romantic ideas of heroic personality and were inevitably elected to Carlyle's pantheon. Some men, it has been said, are born to become legendary.[2] No reputations provide better studies in nineteenth-century mythmaking than those of Burns and Buonaparte. Both men realized their mythic possibilities and exploited them.[3] Both, in meteoric careers, shattered social convention; to the early interpreter who sought to be just, both made moral paradox inescapable. Such an interpreter could not help but be as interesting as any biographer in his period.

But circumstance has added further interest. Lockhart's *Burns* and *Napoleon* are among the earliest British biographies written for a popular audience. In Britain, 'the age of broadsheets has gone', writes Lockhart the year of his *Napoleon* (1829), 'and that of cheap books has come'.[4] Of the three series with which it opened – Constable's, Brougham's and Murray's – Lockhart was present at the inception of 'Old Crafty's' mighty scheme; and when Murray followed Constable and Brougham in April 1829, Lockhart accepted one-third ownership as compensation for general editorship. His conception of the educational responsibilities involved is embodied in the *Burns*, for Constable, and in the *Napoleon*, which began Murray's Family Library. The soundness of his conception is evidenced by the survival of both in the Everyman's Library.[5] As the anonymous *Blackwood's* reviewer of Murray's project, Lockhart suggests a fearfully didactic ideal. Realizing amid revolutionary crisis 'the vast importance of such a scheme, if conducted at once with suitable skill and knowledge, and under the influence of salutary principles, moral, political, and religious', he pronounces: 'awful is the responsibility under which all that possess the means of influencing and directing the minds of multitudes of their fellow-citizens are placed.' But the primary obligation is intellectual honesty. Murray's Family Library is to be 'the first *Tory* series of cheap books', and, rather than condoning party pamphlets, its aim is an antidote to partisanship. Its early attempt to set a standard of impartiality and candour, reports the reviewer (disinterested reviewers bear him out), 'has commanded the eulogy of the Whigs themselves, from Caithness to Cornwall', and 'after this example, the attempt to convert popular histories into the vehicles of popular delusion and deceit, would hardly have much chance to be tolerated, whether by Tory, by Whig, or by Radical'.[6]

For Constable, Lockhart describes a model: 'you should get a readable abridgement of M'Crie's *Life of Knox*, leaving out all the controversial stuff and much of the angry feeling – the mere personal history, in short, of a great and good man.'[7] His own attempt was to be even more demanding; yet, 'to destroy at once all suspicion of vulgar views of partisanship in the conduct of the series',[8] he agreed to try a subject of unique difficulty. As an imperialistic threat, Napoleon had been the common enemy; as the tragic exile of St Helena, he had become an inflammable issue in domestic politics.[9] Radical Buonapartists were, no doubt, dissatisfied with the result, but Thomas Campbell's *New Monthly Magazine* praised the anonymous biographer for talent, good taste, and 'views . . . in general sound and impartial', and conceded that the book 'is written as it ought to be – not for a party, but for the people'. What must be Croker's wrath, observes Odoherty to Tickler and North (in Lockhart's *Noctes Ambrosianae*), 'in seeing such productions coming out of Albemarle street!' 'I expect,' replies Tickler, 'to find Johnson's Toryism, and so forth, treated as contemptible weaknesses in [Croker's] own edition of Boswell. Nothing like the march of intellect – it is taking all in.'[10]

But this was no general attempt on Lockhart's part to moderate the,

K

Toryism of Albemarle Street. He had come of age the year of Waterloo and was not of Scott's generation of British gentry, whose steadfast enmity and insular refusal to see anything but a dangerous imposter in 'Boney' had been major elements in British resistance.[11] Lockhart could understand the vituperation of his elders. Of the Croker who could snarl at 'the personal cowardice, the proneness to falsehood, the vulgarity of manner and language', 'the mean and audacious spirit of Buonaparte', Lockhart's Christopher North says:

> 'When he used to vituperate Napoleon, remember he was potent for evil. Yes, even at St Helena his name and his words were playing the devil continually all over Europe. He was then an enemy, and to have honoured him would, as the son of Sirach has laid down, have been the part of an idiot.'[12]

But in 1823, Lockhart had attacked 'this perpetual drumming at poor Buonaparte' and asked, 'Will nothing persuade all these rhapsodists to let a great man's ashes repose, at least until they have had time to cool in the urn?'[13] In 1818, when the Exile still fought the St Helena campaign, Lauerwinkel was ready to share Hazlitt's indignation over the 'venal pens' of 'that hardened prostitute, the hireling press', who had made of Napoleon a 'hideous caricature'. Attacking Gifford's coarse bigotry, he asked:

> 'who is so blind as not to see that mere wickedness, and extraordinary luck, could never possibly have elevated the son of an obscure gentleman of Ajaccio to the elevation which this prince of adventurers attained in the centre of civilized Europe? Nations yet to come will look back to his history, as to some grand and supernatural romance. The fiery energy of his youthful career, and the magnificent progress of his irresistible ambition, have invested his character with the mysterious grandeur of some heavenly apparition; and when all the lesser tumults and lesser men of our age, shall have passed away into the darkness of oblivion, history will still inscribe one mighty aera with the majestic name of Napoleon.'[14]

In 1829 Christopher North echoed the Baron's reverence: 'Now, God pity us, he sleeps sound beneath a thousand weight of granite, and shame on the mortal who dares deny that he was the greatest man of the last thousand years.' But the Baron had conceded that 'Napoleon was a wicked and unprincipled monarch', and perhaps this ambivalence was indispensable for Lockhart's success as Napoleon's biographer. He knew that Gifford's prejudice was 'founded in justice', but he knew, too, before Carlyle, that 'Loyalty, Discipleship, all that was ever meant by *Hero-worship*, lives perennially in the human bosom', and that

'there is something dignified and sacred in human genius, even though it be misapplied. The reverence which we feel for it is an instinct of nature, and cannot be laid aside without sin. He who is insensible to its influence, has committed sacrilege against his own spirit, and degraded himself from the height of his original elevation. It is clear that they who think Napoleon of a secondary class, do not belong to the first order themselves. The optics of a Lilliputian cannot take in the dimensions of a giant.'[15]

'Of veracious books, which give a sure or even remotely impartial picture of the man, there are remarkably few,' wrote Lord Rosebery.[16] But his prerequisites for impartiality – 'lukewarmness', 'a pair of smoked glasses' – may blind the biographer to the awesomeness of Buonaparte's career. Lockhart's closeness allowed him to sense the awe which transformed the man into myth, and yet to sense as well a moral law manifest in the tragic rise and fall. Pervading his biography is the elegiac feeling for lost greatness apparent in his earlier verses on Napoleon's death as reflected on the sensibility of the follower mourning his fallen chief:

> He hath been with him young and old;
> He climbed with him the Alpine snow;
> He heard the cannon when they rolled
> Along the silver Po.

The verses evoke

> Something that spake of other days
> When trumpets pierced the kindling air

and focus at last – and without judgement – on the Chief himself:

> What thoughts had calmed his dying breast
> (For calm he died) cannot be known;
> Nor would I wound a warrior's rest –
> Farewell, Napoleon.[17]

The mood returns when Lockhart reflects on the Battle of Brienne, fought where the boy Napoleon had attended military school:

'How strange must have been the feelings of the man who, having but yesterday planted his eagles on the Kremlin, now opened his fifteenth campaign amidst the scenes of his own earliest recollections – of the days in which he had never dreamt of empire.'[18]

It differs only in its quiet sadness from Hazlitt's

'''Tis gone like a fairy revel; nor in the round of ever-rolling years will the like be seen again to humble and to exalt all that there is of pride in the heart of man. Yet why complain of the void that is left? If such things happened every day, there would be nothing in them: it is enough that they survive in poetry and history. If a Buonaparte or a Charlemagne appears once in a thousand years, it gives the world something to think of in the interim.'[19]

Even sympathetic critics have made 'only passing mention' of Lockhart's book as 'little more than an abridgement, though a very clever abridgement, of Scott's book'; biographers have kept silent on its very existence.[20] It would be equally valid to discount all biographers of Scott between 1837 and 1932 as mere summarizers of Lockhart. The documentary historian equates originality with 'fresh materials', but even a superficial survey of Napoleonic biography suggests that such materials are often less influential than freshness and flexibility of mind and tone. To appreciate Lockhart's originality, we must compare three *Napoleon*'s, completed within twenty-six months, and necessarily dependent on the same principal materials. Scott had the primary sorting to do; but if Lockhart took advantage of it, so did Hazlitt.[21] Of course, Thibaudeau and de Bausset, put to full use by Hazlitt, were too late for Scott; and Lockhart alone had Napier's account of the Peninsular War, and (for his second edition) Bourrienne. The memoirs dictated to Gourgaud and Montholon at St Helena, the equally propagandistic *Moniteurs*, however suspect, were indispensable, as were Las Cases' *Mémoriale*, called by Henri Peyre 'the most skilful piece of self-advertisement undertaken by any general since Caesar',[22] and the heavily slanted memoirs of Savary, Fouché, and the Abbé de Pradt. More acceptable to all three were Ségur's account of the Russian campaign and the Baron Fain's *Manuscrits* for the two years following. None could satisfy the Romantic demand for self-exposure without the correspondence, which began to appear only in 1858. Lockhart's twentieth-century admirer, J. Holland Rose, himself lacked some of the most valuable of contemporary documents: the memoirs of Caulaincourt (1935), of Josephine's daughter Queen Hortense (1927), and of the faithful General Bertrand (1949–59), as well as the revealing correspondence of Marie-Louise, discovered in the 1950's and first used in Markham's 1963 biography. In short, it is irrelevant to charge Lockhart with a failure to use new materials.

Nor is it just to dwell on factual inaccuracies *per se*, when, as Rose observes, the works on which the early biographer had to depend were 'remarkable for their strong bias for or against Napoleon'.[23] But to what extent are the inaccuracies purely factual, and what proportion of these affect the essential picture, the interpretative balance, the shape and evolution of Napoleon's career? The fact that Napoleon was the fourth, not the second, Buonaparte child (two having died in infancy); the date Corsica became an actual department of France or young Buonaparte entered school at Paris; the fact that the visit to the Mount Sinai monastery was apocryphal – none has significance. Some of more importance cancel each other out.[24] Their correction would make a more accurate account of policy, but the evaluation of Napoleon's severity and sincerity as a ruler and diplomat would not be modified.

Some of the inaccuracies are more essential; some, the results of compression, contribute to the total effect. In Lockhart, Napoleon himself is credited with the plan of attacking La Grasse near Toulon, with being the sole officer second to Barras at Vendémiaire, with joining Lannes, Berthier, and Lallemagne at the head of the column that dashed across the Bridge of Lodi. In short, Lockhart foreshortens the swiftness and brilliance of Napoleon's rise, and in so doing supports the picturesque myth of Napoleon the fiery personal leader – at Lodi, at Arcola, under the walls of Mantua.

The modern historian will be less interested in the inevitable inaccuracies than in Lockhart's conduct as interpreter of 'the many controversial topics with which the Napoleonic story bristles'[25] – the questions of policy and motive, of Napoleon's true relation to political and philosophical struggles in a revolutionary age. It is here that a negative virtue – a determination to be the biographer (as he himself had recommended for the *Life of Knox*) – saves Lockhart from the fate of Scott and Hazlitt, even as it accounts for his comparative brevity. Neither Tory nor Radical, however circumspect, could in the 1820's have comprehended the complex relationship of Napoleon and the French Revolution. Yet both Hazlitt and Scott included histories of the Revolutionary epoch and considered the biography an appropriate occasion for extended invective and rhapsody on the entire historical phenomenon. The view Rose attributes to Lockhart – 'that the French Revolution produced floods of talk and unending confusion, until a stern and sensible soldier took it in hand'[26] – is really Scott's. For Scott the military despotism which crippled France was the inevitable outcome of the Terror of Jacobinism. Scott never loses an opportunity to point out that Napoleon had too much conservative good sense not to act on 'principles different from the brutal and persecuting spirit of Jacobinism', not to know that 'such a violence on the established rules of reason and morality . . . is too unnatural to remain long, or to become the basis of a well-regulated state' [III, 189, 171]. The French people, ready by 1799 to welcome back their legitimate monarchs, could not oppose the eighteenth of Brumaire:

> 'Thus were lost at once the fruits of the virtues, the crimes, the blood, the treasure, the mass of human misery, which, flowing from the Revolution, had agitated France for ten years; and thus, having sacrificed almost all that men hold dear, the rights of humanity themselves included, in order to obtain national liberty, her inhabitants, without having enjoyed rational freedom, or the advantages which it ensures, for a single day, returned to be the vassals of a despotic government, administered by a chief whose right was only in his sword.' [IV, 32, 54]

Hazlitt began with a lifelong faith to expound and a specific antagonist to attack. 'In Napoleon's career,' writes Herschel Baker, 'Hazlitt found a precedent and inspiration for almost all of his political ideals'; and his fall was for Hazlitt 'a personal grief and a public calamity'.[27] On hearing of Scott's project in 1825, he told Medwin he too would write a Life of Napoleon, and he wrote in rebuttal (while using his enemy as a major source). He quotes a 'great and admired writer, whose testimony in behalf of liberty is the more to be valued as it is rare' on the partition of Poland [II, 293]; and on the idyllic society of the Tyrol, he quotes 'one whom the same words of liberty and equality, used in any other connection and for any other purpose, would throw into the rage and hysterics of a fine lady who sees a toad or spider near her' [II, 352]. A final broadside at Scott blames the creative fancy for meddling in practical politics, in an author who 'writes fiction with the broad open palm of humanity – history with cloven hoofs!' [III, 215].[28]

Hazlitt had terrific obstacles to surmount, facts in ghastly refutation of his idea of 'the child and champion of the Revolution'. He concedes the difficulty in his Preface, and during the first half of the *Life* he is capable of bitter candour at Napoleon's expense. Of the Asian conqueror he reflects: 'So far from propagating new principles of civilization in the East, it was his object to crush and neutralize them at home; and instead of commencing and giving full scope to a new era in society, to patch up and lengthen out the old one, which had fallen in pieces from its own imperfections and infirmity' [11, 30]. He allows that true patriots must have cried out in bitterness when comparing the First Consul with the liberator of Italy and the scourge of royalty. But the young Buonaparte had been sincere – 'every one is sincere in the condemnation of wrong, till it comes to be his own turn to inflict it';

'as Buonaparte's power and reputation hitherto had been connected with the triumph of the broad principles of the Revolution, they would naturally still predominate in his mind, whatever designs might lurk there pointing to a different conclusion.' [1, 299, 318-19]

Pathetically, Hazlitt clings to his dream 'that the changes which were afterwards carried into effect were alien to his own breast'. But the pathos gives way, as growing indignation seems to repudiate earlier concessions, to Buonaparte's own *apologia*: (1) he had tried to give the French people a republic, but they were too frivolous and faithless to deserve one; (2) he had wished to be a Washington, but England could not rest until she destroyed him. [29]

More and more dogmatically, Hazlitt interprets the Revolution as simply and absolutely the negation of Legitimacy and Divine Right. And as those other 'tame and insignificant' questions arise, they are evaded or falsified on this basis: Napoleon's very existence was a challenge and a mock to the European monarchies. Every attempt to destroy him was the conspiracy of despots for revenge against the upstart. If Prussia, Spain, Russia are invaded, they are being offered a chance of liberation; if the natives oppose invasion, they are superstitious defenders of their own slavery, or pawns of English gold. All Allied efforts at peaceful negotiation are cynical; all Buonaparte's are sincere. In spite of this tissue of rhetorical evasion, self-contradiction, and contemptuous misanthropy, we are to believe that Hazlitt 'has sacrificed no principle to palliate his hero', that he 'was not the infatuated worshipper of an idol, but the champion of an historical character which he conceives unjustly and wantonly attacked'. [30]

There is little reason to accept Rose's suggestion that to Hazlitt's first volumes (1828) we owe the 'more favourable picture of Napoleon' in Lockhart.[31] If he read the volumes, his reaction must have been anything but increased liberality. He *is* stylistically closer to Hazlitt than to Scott. But his added liberality, his freedom from some of Scott's social biases, his detachment from a generation of older Tories, were nothing Lockhart had to acquire from an author who had always aroused his most vitriolic spirit. Rather, the difference in tone is due to a difference in purpose. While Hazlitt and Scott include much to dramatize the personality of Napoleon, both have other aims which, in Scott, distract and diffuse more than they falsify, and in Hazlitt, distort and evade more than they diffuse. Lockhart's purpose is to narrate and recreate. He avoids on the one hand a continuing denigration of the Revolution and on the other an extended defence of British policy. He shows no more respect for the Directory than Scott or Hazlitt, but his subject is Napoleon's growing contempt, not his own disapproval. His exposition of Napoleon's anti-Jacobinism is analytic: he notes Napoleon's hypocrisy in professing republicanism and then handing Venice back to the Austrian Emperor, but avoids further comment. He notes Napoleon's fear of popular uprisings – from the 'poor driveller' Louis XVI's weak tolerance of the 'rabble' in the Tuileries in 1792 to the refusal to allow a defensive national uprising in 1814. But it is always Napoleon's anti-Jacobinism, not Lockhart's, that is apparent; and when that anti-Jacobinism is opposed in the Tribunate by a Carnot, Lockhart gives that 'sincere republican' a full hearing [p. 206].

Two examples will suffice before we turn to more important controversies. Hazlitt concedes that Buonaparte's Spanish policy was Machiavellian and praises the popular resistance of the Spaniards, but he tries to excuse the invasion and the usurpation by stressing the degeneracy of Spanish royalty, by asserting that the bravery of the people was wholly misguided, and by treating British participation with contempt. He attacks 'indecision' and 'want of vigor in the Administration' for 'the dilatory advance and disastrous retreat of Sir John Moore'. With Moore's heroic death at Corunna, Hazlitt dispenses in these words: 'He was buried on the ramparts, and "left alone with his glory" – such as it was!' [11, 340-3]. Writing of the same expedition, Scott implausibly exonerates the English ministry. He stresses the vigour and boldness of their plan, and evades the question of responsibility for the procrastination – which is vaguely imputed to 'want of alertness in the different departments, which had been little accustomed to hurry and exertion' [VI, 144-6]. He praises Frere's faith in the

Spaniards (which Wellington was later to try and, says Markham, be 'quickly disillusioned'), and contrasts it with Moore's 'unfavourable idea' and his fears [VI, 145, 153]. Thus, Scott ends by giving the same negative impression of Moore as Hazlitt, though from an opposite point of view.

The Moore issue is a good test case. The battle between Moore and Frere became a major Whig-Tory struggle. The Tories defended the ministry by attacking Moore. Long after Moore's death, says Sir Charles Oman, 'the attitude of the critic or the historian who dealt with the Corunna retreat was invariably coloured by his Whig or Tory predilections'.[32] The most influential historian among Moore's defenders was Colonel William Napier, 'a violent enemy of the Tory ministry and a personal admirer of Moore',[33] who attacked Scott in his *History of the Peninsular War*. It is indicative of Lockhart's independence and moderation, as well as of his taste for colourful, dramatic historical narrative, that he based his own account of the Peninsular war on Napier far more than on Southey or Scott and, without Napier's specific rancour, accepted his view of Moore.[34]

The other example remains sufficiently controversial to have warranted a popular volume in 1957 – the actions and motives of Marshal Ney during the Hundred Days. For Hazlitt, Ney, 'the child of the Revolution', abandoned by his troops, 'yielded to the general impulse' and was accepted magnanimously back into the Chief's arms [III, 229] – 'threw himself', Croker had said, 'into the contemptuous embrace of Buonaparte'.[35] 'Well would it have been,' reflects Hazlitt, 'if all his qualms had ended here.' Hazlitt condemns Ney and Grouchy for the disaster of Waterloo. Scott, on the other hand, no doubt influenced by his hero Wellington,[36] sees Ney as 'a man of mean birth', lacking 'a delicate sense of honour or a high feeling of principle'. Ney's behaviour follows: 'Sensible of the incongruity of changing his side so suddenly, he affected to be a deliberate knave, rather than he would content himself with being viewed in his real character, of a volatile, light-principled, and inconsiderate fool' [VIII, 354]. A generous refusal to judge stands out in Lockhart's brief account.[37] He adheres to the fact that Ney and his soldiers 'joined the march of Buonaparte on the 17th at Auxerre', and refuses to speculate on the complexity or confusion of motives:

> 'Ney, in the sequel, did not hesitate to avow that he had chosen the part of Napoleon long ere he pledged his oath to Louis; adding that

the greater number of the marshals were, like himself, original members of the Elbese conspiracy. Of the latter of these assertions no other proof has hitherto been produced; and the former continues to be generally as well as mercifully discredited.' [p. 453]

It is in the area of what Scott calls Napoleon's 'enormities' that we would expect most difference in tone. Scott undertakes, in such cases, to examine evidence and motives, and pass judgement in tones of moral censure restrained by juridical formality, inciting Hazlitt to furious rejoinders against British anti-Buonaparte propaganda. Most prominent among controversial topics are the massacre and poisoning at Jaffa, the betrayal of Toussaint, the abduction and execution of Duc D'Enghien, and the similar treatment of Palm, bookseller of Nuremberg.

The first affords little room for candid disagreement. Nevertheless, Hazlitt, allowing the slaughter of the Turks and the poisoning of his own sick to be 'two of the ugliest charges ever brought against Buonaparte', claims they are 'as groundless as they were odious' [II, 37], and uses the occasion for a characteristic tirade against 'venal scribblers' by whose efforts the English government inflamed 'the national hostility and prejudices to a state bordering on madness' [II, 40]. Scott and Lockhart agree that the massacre 'will ever form one of the darkest stains on the name of Napoleon' [Lockhart, p. 100]. Both accept the charges as true, discount the suggestion that Napoleon was naturally cruel, and yet reject his own plea of expediency. Modern historians do not disagree. Nor, according to Thompson, is there any doubt that Napoleon gave the orders for a fatal dose of opium. 'The truth,' says Markham, 'appears to be that Napoleon suggested this form of euthanasia for the victims who could not be transported, but that he dropped the suggestion when his surgeons opposed it.'[38] Both Scott and Lockhart, doubting the carrying out of the order, comment only on intention, and accuse him, not of cruelty, but of indifference, presumption, or misdirected humanity. 'He doubtless designed,' says Lockhart, 'by shortening those men's lives, to do them the best service in his power' [p. 106].

A more significant test is provided by the three assassinations, which, however minimized by modern biographers (as by Napoleon himself), were of symbolic importance to contemporaries: the D'Enghien affair to Beethoven and the drawing-rooms of the Anna Pavlovnas, the Palm affair to the people what the D'Enghien affair had been to the nobility,[39] and the mysterious disappearance of Toussaint to those like Wordsworth who had responded with humanitarian exhilaration to the early Revolution.

To Hazlitt such victims are merely pawns in a cynical, anti-Buonaparte propaganda. The death of Toussaint, an English collaborator, was merely 'one of those topics on which the tropes and figures of political rhetoric at one time delighted to dwell' [II, 169]. The condemnation of D'Enghien was a justifiable blow against those who would assassinate Napoleon and think their royal blood made them invulnerable in return.[40] Palm, the martyr of a popular uprising against Napoleon, Hazlitt does not even mention.

The difference between Scott's and Lockhart's accounts is slight but meaningful. The affair of the Duc receives lengthy consideration from Scott. All Napoleon's evasions are rejected, and 'the murder of the young and gallant prince, in a way so secret and savage', is considered an indelible stain [IV, 330-1]. The fates of the 'unhappy African' and of 'one Palm, a bookseller', evoke less horror. Scott is not personally moved by the fate of popular heroes, and presents Toussaint as a ferocious despot little better than Buonaparte. Lockhart is influenced by Wordsworth, quoting the sonnet in full. Toussaint, who had won 'applause and admiration' by 'the wisdom and humanity of his administration', 'was shut up in a dungeon, where either the midnight cord or dagger, or the wasting influence of confinement and hopeless misery, ere long put an end to his life' [pp. 178-9]. In the D'Enghien affair Lockhart emphasizes the effect on Napoleon's fame, thinks Napoleon must 'have sincerely believed that the Bourbons were plotting against his life', and ends with the statement variously attributed to Talleyrand, Fouché, and Boulay de la Meurthe: 'It was worse than a crime – it was a blunder' [p. 202]. But it is in dealing with Palm's murder that Lockhart differs most. One recalls Lockhart's early interest in the rise of German nationalism, when he finds this 'deed as darkly unpardonable as the murder of D'Enghien', which 'arrayed against him, throughout all Germany, every feeling, moral and political, which could be touched either by the crimes or the contumelies of a foreign tyrant'. It is even less pardonable: 'the death of D'Enghien has found advocates or palliators – this mean murder of a humble tradesman, who neither was nor ever had been a subject either of France or Buonaparte, has been less fortunate' [p. 231].

This last distinction suggests a major difference in attitude among the three biographies: Hazlitt's sentimental exaggeration of the popular will; Scott's decidedly aristocratic attitude, which discounts popular movements and defends the Bourbons; and Lockhart's substitution for this element in Scott of a severity more broadly moral, less social in tone. Take, for example, the accounting for the miraculous return and the Hundred Days, which, as Queen Hortense noted, 'had something superhuman about it which stirred even the least interested observer'.[41]

For Hazlitt, 'the return from Elba . . . was a blow in the face of tyranny and hypocrisy, the noblest ever struck'; its success needs no 'dark and clandestine intrigues' to account for it.[42] Less partial modern biographers concede that 'there was hardly a class in the country, as Napoleon well knew, which was not anxious to be rid of the Bourbons'[43]; but whatever the potential of popular support, Hazlitt's stress on the spontaneity of the uprising now seems naive. Even Hortense concedes that many conspiracies were afoot. Sir Charles Petrie seems too close to Croker's 'All that was estimable in France either openly opposed, or secretly lamented Buonaparte's success' when he hypothesizes a *coup* with modern revolutionary counterparts.[44] But it is now generally concluded, 'The France of 1815 was not with Napoleon.'[45] Hence Hazlitt's desperate ecstasy has not lasted as well as Scott's Tory scepticism. But if Scott is nearer the truth than Hazlitt, he surrenders all detachment to become the advocate of the Bourbons and, as usual, the reviler of the Jacobin 'rabble'. The Allies had been romantically generous in 1814. Louis, in his 'good sense, humanity, love of justice, moderation, and other valuable qualities', was simply the victim of treacherous conspirators and incurable malcontents. 'Everything, indeed, which ought to have soothed and gratified the French people, was at last, by irritated feelings and artful misrepresentation, converted into a subject of complaint and grievance' [VIII, 217-18, 299, 279].

With this should be compared Lockhart's masterful sketch. It opens with Louis XVIII, 'advanced in years, gross and infirm in person', who, whatever his sincere desire to please everyone, was 'but ill-adapted' for a throne which even Napoleon had found insecure, and who began his reign by declaring twenty-five years of French history illegitimate. It passes quickly through a concise survey of a complex society in flux, giving fair expression to the motives and viewpoints of various segments. It recalls Lockhart the social novelist at his best:

> 'Were the comrades of Murat and Bernadotte to sit down in contentment as peers of France, among the Montmorencies and the Rohans, who considered them at the best as low-born intruders, and scorned,

in private society, to acknowledge them as members of their order? If we take into account the numerous personal adherents whom the Imperial government, with all the faults of its chief, must have possessed – and the political humiliation of France, in the eyes of all Europe, as well as of the French people themselves, immediately connected with the disappearance of Napoleon – we shall have some faint conception of that mass of multifarious griefs and resentments, in the midst of which the unwieldy and inactive Louis occupied, ere long, a most unenviable throne – and on which the eagle-eyed Exile of Elba gazed with reviving hope even before the summer of 1814 had reached its close.' [pp. 444-5]

The subsequent account of the landing and the march conveys in a small space a feeling for the whole event as a triumph of histrionics. One cannot help but feel exhilaration as Napoleon is greeted by spontaneous popular acclaim[46]; yet it is clear that he comes as a usurper who, while he owes something to the renewed hopes of those still believing him capable of constitutional rule, owes more to the support of the army. The entry into Paris is handled likewise; Lockhart does not suggest, with Hazlitt, that an ecstatic mob cheered Napoleon into the Tuileries, nor does he follow Scott's picture of bloodthirsty warriors, hired or coerced citizens, and 'devisers and abettors of this singular undertaking' cynically flattering the returned exile.[47] His account is neutral and dramatic. The only comment is implied by ironic juxtaposition: in the presence of the arch-intriguer, Fouché, Napoleon declares that 'it is disinterested people who have brought me back to my capital' [p. 455].

Even in their conclusions, Scott and Lockhart differ meaningfully. Scott's lengthy summation is impressively fair, but his historical perspective is limited. He stresses the Napoleonic policy which was to captivate the Julien Sorels – *la carrière ouverte aux talents*, and concedes Napoleon's use of revolutionary principles in the attempt to found a commonwealth. Lockhart's breadth of perspective is evident in his diction:

'He gave both permanency and breadth to the influence of the French Revolution. His reign, short as it was, was sufficient to make it impossible that the offensive privileges of *caste* should ever be revived in France. . . . He broke down the barriers everywhere of custom and prejudice, and revolutionized the spirit of the Continent. Such hurricanes of passion as the French Revolution – such sweeping scourges of mankind as Napoleon Buonaparte, are not permitted but as the avengers of great evils, and the harbingers of great good.' [pp. 505-6]

One who compares such a conclusion with the remarks of recent scholarly biographers will be astonished at how little has changed in over one hundred years.[48]

But what of the degrading aftermath, the final image of Napoleon as the aging, paunchy Prometheus on his South Atlantic rock? How is the amateur to judge early British views when modern academic historians cannot agree? One's final impression of Napoleon must be affected by the St Helena teapot-tempest. One can agree with Rosebery that neither side comes out well; nevertheless, the picture of the exiled, dying emperor evokes strong feelings. And if British policy (on the Bathurst-Castlereagh level, or the level of Sir Hudson Lowe) seems mean or petty, those impressions colour Napoleon's twenty-year relationship with his most steadfast enemies. If, on the other hand, one accepts the policy (with Rose and Fournier)[49] as justifiably firm, then Napoleon is a mendacious autocrat playing at intrigues with British politics for a final chance at the hapless Bourbons, and his entire diplomatic career is placed under a suspicious light.

'Even today,' Markham acknowledged in 1963, 'with the immense documentation of St Helena, it is difficult to determine whether it was due to the personality of Lowe or to a deliberate plan of campaign adopted by Napoleon.'[50] There is no doubt as to the plan; Napoleon told Las Cases, 'L'univers nous contemple!' and Las Cases understood, suppressing in the published Journal: 'We are possessed of moral arms only; and in order to make the most advantageous use of these, it was necessary to reduce into *a system* our demeanour, our words, our sentiments, *even our privations.*'[51] But to what extent were the privations invented? Two recent studies still diverge. The masterful debunker, Guerard, considers British precautions natural, and notes that Montholon found Sir Hudson 'able, courteous, and not un-friendly'. But Napoleon was set to wage a campaign against 'Perfidious Albion in the person of the Governor', and 'had the satisfaction of creating the legend of Sir Hudson Lowe as a brutal tormentor clanking his keys and glaring at his victim with a satanic sneer'. Markham, on the other hand, recalls Lowe's 'odious system of espionage', his morbid suspicion, his 'impertinent and shifty manner, and his petty annoyances', and Wellington's characteristically unsubtle appraisal that 'he was a damned fool'. 'It is impossible,' he writes, 'for an Englishman to read the Lowe-Bathurst correspondence without blushing for his country.'[52] Such has been the divergence since Lord Holland and the Duke of Sussex protested in the House of Lords.

Hazlitt and Scott omit no aspect of the controversy. Hazlitt accepts the picture supplied by Las Cases, O'Meara, and Antommarchi, and exaggerates ministerial intentions, The jailer who carried them out was a man 'equally devoid of decency and humanity, in whom the feeling of the insolence of office was happily seconded by a crawling servility' [III, 309]. The Emperor at Longwood is shown 'in the midst of persecutions of every kind, against which his serenity is his only shield', gradually drooping, destroyed by deplorable conditions, disease, and criminal neglect [III, 323]. Antommarchi's 'worthless and mendacious' book[53] supplies Hazlitt with a final chapter on 'The Death of Napoleon'.

How could the anti-Buonapartist compete with such materials? Scott had journals of English visitors, but they could hardly match in fullness and intimacy the memoirs of Napoleon's propagandists. He had Gourgaud's but this was scarcely dependable.[54] Giving 'the last phase' as extensive consideration as does Hazlitt, Scott adopts a lofty impartiality and a rhetorical sympathy for the prisoner: 'a noble lion imprisoned within a narrow and gloomy den' [IX, 175]. The grievances and complaints are enumerated. The grounds for ministerial policy are paraded, in Rosebery's impatient terms, 'with the same apologetic melancholy with which his own Caleb Balderstone sets forth the supper of the Master of Ravenswood'.[55] But most notable is the serenely idealistic position from which Scott judges, and from which both Buonaparte and Lowe fall far short of the 'rare and highly exalted' keeper and the philosophically serene prisoner of Scott's imagination. John Stuart Mill's charges are fair: (*a*) Scott's tone of impartiality and candour arises from 'a practice which he appears to have prescribed to himself from an early period – that of adopting such a mode of writing as should be best calculated to win the good word and good opinion of everybody'; (*b*) his adjudications are too abstract, too ideal, criticizing men in unique situations by absolute or irrelevant standards.[56]

Rose admires Lockhart's 'eminent good sense' in treating the St Helena episode.[57] 'The accusations . . . have been so often answered in detail,' Lockhart explains, 'that we may spare ourselves the pain of dwelling on transactions little worthy of filling a large space in the story of Napoleon' [p. 492]. The questions are then briefly and directly approached on the realistic assumption that Napoleon was a political prisoner – the same man who had imprisoned the Pope for four years and Ferdinand of Spain for five. Lowe's imperfections are of less concern than the fact that Napoleon degraded himself. Simply, undeniably, 'He never laid aside the hopes of escape and of empire. It was his business to have complaints' [p. 487]. Much beyond this Lockhart does not go. The career is ended, and the drama of the career is Lockhart's subject. 'The career of Napoleon,' writes Guérard, 'viewed from the standpoint of the professional dramatist, is a masterpiece of stagecraft; the character of Napoleon, if it were the creation of a fiction writer, would be pronounced shallow and uninteresting.'[58]

Guérard's terms recall us from questions of historical interpretation to those of literary form. The evocation of such a career is primarily a problem of narrative art. In few lives is the art of the biographer so essential. He must select, proportion, juxtapose, focus; he must illustrate the growth and fluctuation of ambition, convey an impression of the meteoric career, evaluate the role of circumstance, yet never lose sight of the concrete personality at the centre of it all. No mere acquaintance with the Kircheisen Bibliography will awaken such art; the unearthing of new memoirs or letters will be of moment only if they modify the viewpoint and if the modified viewpoint can be translated into form. As narrative art Lockhart's *Napoleon* is largely an independent work; its style and form are as responsible as its interpretative moderation for its survival as a popular biography.

In general, the demands of compression and coherence have dictated the character of syntax and diction, as well as the organization and location of narrative units. Initially Lockhart could eliminate much by excluding two types of composition responsible for the great length of Scott's and Hazlitt's works. Scott had explained to Lady Louisa Stuart: 'I have always endeavoured to regard Napoleon as a person upon his trial and I myself as one of his jury who was of course to condemn or absolve him.'[59] As jurist he felt compelled to collect and weigh every consideration, to expend pages on what might and should have been done, to adjudicate comprehensively among discordant viewpoints – in short, to lose the life's dramatic reality in commentary and judgement. Hazlitt's chief interest was in his 'speculative episodes' – in his efforts to bend every pliable incident to his thesis, to cloud in rhapsodic or vituperative oratory those 'powers of thought' which Crabb Robinson admired and which Scott, in his pedestrian conservatism, could not approach. To say that Hazlitt's *Life* is characterized by a 'swift-moving narrative'[60] is as inaccurate as to say that Scott achieves the coherence and directness of a novel. Scott's 'dashing style of composition, which precludes the possibility of compression and arrangement' has been described by W. H. Prescott:

'Instead of that skilful preparation by which all the avenues verge at last to one point, so as to leave a distinct impression – an impression of unity – on the reader, he is hurried along zigzag, in a thousand directions, or round and round, but never, in the cant of the times, "going ahead" an inch.'[61]

Hazlitt's value as a writer of Napoleonic narrative has been put by Crabb Robinson in a word: 'he is worthless.'[62]

Much cutting, then, was ready-made for Lockhart. But there remained the compression and manipulation, which a decade of editorial practice had taught him, and to which one *Quarterly* contributor paid characteristic tribute:

'Your manipulation of the article I furnished, and the highly improved form into which your critical shears have concided my rambling lucubrations has done me more good [than the money from Murray], and shown me practically how much condensation improves composition, how rambling and desultory writing is mended by arrangement.'[63]

The results in Lockhart's 'brief' *Napoleon* are long but unified paragraphs which do the work of entire loosely constructed chapters in Scott, and sentences which, for all their syntactical complexity, are direct and even elastic. Diction, too, while necessarily compressed and formal, is more precise if only through the elimination of Scott's rhetorical figures. 'I do not know,' he wrote Scott, 'by what magic you have contrived to enrich your language with such an overflow of new and bold imagery.' But to Blackwood, later, he complained of the 'eternal trash of imagery that disfigures Sir W. Scott's account of the French revolution'.[64]

In achieving a greater directness and immediacy than Scott, Lockhart seems to have been aware of two interdependent values of Hazlitt's splenetic rhapsody. Illustrative of the explosive political situation between Waterloo and the First Reform Bill, Hazlitt's *Napoleon* is also evidence that the effects of the burgeoning Napoleonic legend were by no means limited to the Julien Sorels or the rustic audience of Balzac's

Goguelot. Without sharing Goguelot's folk mysticism or Julien's ruthless romanticism, Hazlitt has outdone them both in expressing more naturalistic aspects of the legend. Lockhart was not deceived by the legend, but he knew that the romantic aspect of the career was an essential factor in any Napoleonic history – that, as Hazlitt says, 'renown is not a worthless shadow, but a real and substantial power' [III, 94] without which the career is inexplicable. With war a national adventure and leadership a function of morale, 'it was', Lockhart knew, 'urgently necessary that the name of Buonaparte should be surrounded with some blaze of almost supernatural renown'. This was to be purchased by such melodramatic feats as passing the Great St Bernard, and on such occasions 'Napoleon rarely failed to vindicate the prestige of his reputation' [pp. 142, 146]. Every drummer boy must be made to feel that *le petit Caporal* was a stern but solicitous father, a fellow-sufferer, not a ruthless despot, not the cold geometrician who could confess to Metternich that the loss of a million men meant nothing. To Lockhart, such devotion, even offered to a myth, was an admirable thing – not, as Scott insisted, the fruit of plebeian de-bauchery.

The biographer cannot simply describe such devotion; it must be concretely dramatized. And it is the second chief value of Hazlitt's narrative that, unlike Scott, Hazlitt includes every picturesque anecdote which renders immediate – with its legendary aura about it – the phenomenal personality he is presenting. It is not the backstairs Napoleon of Ludwig that he gives, but Napoleon at the front, leading the rush over the Bridge of Lodi – sadly caring for the wounded *enfants* on field or in hospital – dispensing *largesse* to the poor – joking with his counsellors – stirring his troops to ecstatic fervour before the battle.

But if such anecdotes come from the mythmakers, what is the critical biographer to do? To convey a true *impression* of the personality, he has to depend on materials which are suspect. To convey the force and marvel of the phenomenon (essential to its understanding), he must offend the scientific historian and exploit legend or apocrypha for its phenomenological or symbolic truth. Thus Lockhart includes the *Henry V* image of the General replacing the sleeping sentry and then stresses the effect 'such anecdotes as these flying ever and anon from column to column' had on the devotion of the troops [p. 59]. Like-wise, he quotes Savary's description of the escape from rising waters by the Red Sea, shows Napoleon in the hospitals, includes Napoleon's insistence that his horse be given up to the sick, puts Napoleon on the Bridge of Lodi with the vanguard, shows him asleep from exhaustion by the side of the rocky path gazed on by troops *en route* to Marengo, stresses the chatty presence of the returned Exile of Elba among his old soldiers, and dwells with emotion on Napoleon's grief at the death of his followers — Muiron at Arcola, Desaix at Marengo, Duroc at Bautzen — and on his parting from the Guard at Fontainebleau. Such anecdotes remain to puzzle but also illuminate when Lockhart concludes:

'His heart was naturally cold. . . . We doubt if any man ever passed through life, sympathising so slightly with mankind; and the most wonderful part of his story is, the intensity of sway which he exerted over the minds of those in whom he so seldom permitted himself to contemplate anything more than the tools of his own ambition. So great a spirit must have had glimpses of whatever adorns and dignifies the character of man. But with him the feelings which bind love played only on the surface — leaving the abyss of selfishness untouched.' [p. 504]

But they are not accidental — nothing is accidental in so highly selective a structure. Where space permits so few, those anecdotes chosen are selected, placed, and framed for all possible value, for the light they shed on character as well as the life they impart to incident, and for structural anticipation or confirmation of theme. Notice the description of the enthusiasm with which Poland greeted the 'liberator', the 'old nobles, quitting the solitary castles in which they had been lamenting over the downfall of Poland', crowding the Victor's levees, to adore him as conqueror and legislator. No comment is made by Lockhart; but the continuing narrative exploits the pathos of the scene and says all that need be said of Napoleon's motives and naive Poland's prospects:

'Having largely recruited his armies with brave Poles, who fancied him both a Solon and Caesar, Napoleon now moved forwards' [p. 244].

Many other transitions between anecdote and narrative might be cited in which an episode is given significant structural location. But for an illustration of scenic compression, in which description is fused with comment, mood, and anticipation, take the glimpse of the Imperial Coronation, diffused throughout Scott's pages but focused by Lockhart:

'Throughout the ceremonial his aspect was thoughtful: it was on a stern and gloomy brow that he with his own hands planted the symbol of successful ambition and uneasy power, and the shouts of the deputies present, carefully selected for the purpose, sounded faint and hollow amidst the silence of the people.' [p. 208] Occasionally, Lockhart achieves this scenic fullness in a way seldom taken by Scott or Hazlitt : the conflation of two or more anecdotes – possibly distinct versions – from diverse sources and viewpoints. Hazlitt quotes as distinct versions the statements of the young general departing for Italy:

'Some one taunting him with his youth on this occasion, he is said to have given the memorable answer, "In a year's time I shall be dead or old!" Or as it was variously reported afterwards, "In a year's time I shall have Milan," – *J'aurai Milan.*' [1, 199]

Lockhart's conflation conveys a fuller scene and a more fatalistic Napoleon:

'"In three months," said he, "I shall be either at Milan or Paris." He had already expressed the same feeling in a still nobler form. "You are too young," said one of the Directors, hesitating about his appointment as general. "In a year," answered Napoleon, "I shall be either old or dead."' [p. 24]

More complex in its effect is Lockhart's juxtaposition of Savary's hero-leader of 'imperturbable mind' with Bourrienne's voluptuous dreamer, the Asiatic potentate *in posse*: '"He spent whole days," writes his secretary, "in lying flat on the ground stretched upon maps of Asia"' [p. 99]. The use of the graphic Bourrienne is equally effective in the narration of the near-disaster of Brumaire. The secretary's suggestion of how near his master had come to the guillotine follows immediately in Lockhart upon Napoleon's imperial gestures. Finally, Bourrienne and Mme De Staël are fused into a single dialogue, with Moreau added from another source, for the scene following the inauguration of the Concordat at Notre Dame. We must see the three versions side by side:

Scott	Hazlitt	Lockhart
Some address, it was said, was employed to procure the attendance of the old republican generals. They were invited by Berthier to breakfast, and thence carried to the First Consul's levee; after which it became impossible for them to decline attending him to the church of	The military had a great repugnance to the new arrangement, and there was some art used in getting them to attend the ceremony at Notre-Dame. Berthier invited the principal to breakfast with him, whence he took them to the First Consul's levee, so that they could	It was not easy, however, to procure the attendance of some of the revolutionary generals of the true republican race. Berthier had invited a large party of them long beforehand to breakfast; he carried them from thence to the levee of the Chief Consul, and they found it impos-

Notre Dame. As he returned from the ceremony, surrounded by these military functionaries, Buonaparte remarked with complacency, that the former order of things was fast returning. One of his generals boldly answered, – 'Yes! – all returns – excepting the two millions of Frenchmen, who have died to procure the proscription of the very system now in the act of being restored.' [IV,179]

not excuse themselves from accompanying him. On their return, Buonaparte asked Delmas what he thought of the ceremony? He replied, 'It was an admirable *capucinade*. All that was wanting to complete it was a million of men who have sacrificed their lives to overturn what you are trying to re-establish!' This sarcasm did not go unpunished. [II, 167]

sible not to join in the procession. Buonaparte asked one of these persons, after the ceremony was over, what he thought of it? 'It was a true *Capucinade*,' was the answer. To another of these, whom he thought less sincere, he said with a smile, 'Things, you see, are returning to the old order.' 'Yes,' the veteran replied, 'all returns – all but the two millions of Frenchmen who have died for the sake of destroying the very system which you are now rebuilding.' These officers are said to have paid dearly for their uncourtly language. [p. 172]

Such comparisons invariably reveal the same distinctions of style. Contrasted with Scott, Lockhart achieves a consistently stronger, sharper colloquialism; contrasted with Hazlitt, he gives a more complex portrayal of Napoleon. Consider the accounts of the birth of Napoleon's son; here again, drawing from diverse sources, Lockhart gives a dramatic glimpse of the normal, solicitous husband (as in Hazlitt) combined with the proud dynast (as in Scott).[65] A comparable complexity appears in Lockhart's dramatic juxtaposition of the gleeful conqueror and the reflective fatalist early in the Italian campaign. Buonaparte meets the innocent, injured Grand Duke of Tuscany:

'The grand duke, in place of resenting these injuries, was obliged to receive Buonaparte with all the appearances of cordiality at Florence; and the spoiler repaid his courtesy by telling him, rubbing his hands with glee, during the princely entertainment provided for him, "I have just received letters from Milan; the citadel has fallen; – your brother has no longer a foot of land in Lombardy." "It is a sad case," said Napoleon himself long afterwards – speaking of these scenes of exaction and insolence, – "it is a sad case when the dwarf comes into the embrace of the giant; he is like enough to be suffocated – but 'tis the giant's nature to squeeze hard."' [p. 167][66]

The contrast of mood is striking, as is the manner in which a lengthy episode has been compressed into a revealing dramatic encounter, and distinct temporal perspectives are juxtaposed.

The anecdotes also reveal Lockhart's narrative treatment of dialogue, and his freedom in rephrasing and rearranging speeches. Nor are we justified in calling this dishonesty. The sources were available in print; the biographer could claim the freedom of the translator and could assume that in the French originals the dialogue was refabrication out of dim recollections. Compare the three adaptations of Montholon's anecdote: the encounter of the unrecognized Buonaparte with an old Hungarian officer after Lodi. Napoleon asked how things went with them:

Scott	*Hazlitt*	*Lockhart*
'Things are going on as ill and as irregularly as possible,' said the old martinet. 'The French have got a young general who knows nothing of the regular rules of war; he is sometimes on our front, sometimes on the flank, sometimes on the rear. There is no supporting such a gross violation of rules.' [III, 49]	The old captain could not deny but that they went on badly enough; 'but,' added he, 'there is no understanding it at all; we have to do with a young general, who is this moment before us, the next behind us, then again on our flanks; one does not know where to place one's-self. This manner of making war is insufferable, and against all rule and custom.' [I, 215]	'Nothing,' replied the old gentleman, who did not know he was addressing the general-in-chief – 'nothing can be worse. Here is a young man who knows absolutely nothing of the rules of war; to-day he is in our rear, to-morrow on our flank, next day again in our front. Such violations of the principles of war are intolerable!' [p. 33]

Or notice the rendering of the letter which greeted the marauding French at Count Rostophchin's country estate. It is not to Hazlitt's advantage to quote it, but indirectly he turns the censure back upon the *perpetrators* of the Scorched Earth policy. Scott relegates the quote to a footnote [VII, 128n]. Lockhart, by rephrasing with stress on the first personal pronoun and by abbreviation, gives force and point to the Mayor's personal sacrifice:

Scott	*Lockhart*
'Frenchmen,' this was the tenor of this remarkable intimation, 'for eight years it has been my pleasure to embellish this my family residence. The inhabitants, 1720 in number, will leave it as you approach; and it will be reduced to ashes that not one of you may pollute it by your presence.'	the following letter, affixed to its gates, breathed the same spirit which had dared to sacrifice Moscow: – 'I *have* for eight years embellished this residence, and *lived happily in it with my family*. The inhabitants of the estate, in number 1720, quitted it at your approach; and *I set fire to my house*, that it may not be polluted with your presence.' [p. 354]

Lockhart had the advantage of the anecdotal vividness of Napier and Bourrienne. But for the most part, the early biographer, seeking to present Napoleon dramatically but lacking the correspondence, was forced to depend on the ornate redactions of the Bulletins and the formal conversations in Las Cases and Thibaudeau. How could such materials be put to effective dramatic use? Scott's usual answer was to keep them out of his narrative. Hazlitt's hero is the magnificent *persona* created by Napoleon's own rhetoric, and so he includes such documents and 'conversations' in full. Lockhart's compromise is that of the artist; for it, the scientific historian would criticize him and the modern biographer find in him a precedent. Selection, sometimes simplification, is the rule; the purpose is not simply to abbreviate, but to bring within the conceivable limits of terse dramatic speech and to suggest, out of the formality of a proclamation, the impact of an actual dramatic encounter. Such is the effect of compression and revision on the harangue to revive the ardour of unsuccessful troops at Trent; or on the encounter with 'an old grenadier' before the dawn of the Sun of Austerlitz:

Scott	*Lockhart*
an old grenadier, approaching his person, swore that the Emperor should only have to combat with his eyes, and that, without his exposing his person, the whole colours and artillery of the Russian army should be brought to him. . . . In the proclamation which Napoleon, according to his custom, issued to the army, he promises that he will keep his person out of the reach of fire. [v, 76-77]	'Only promise us,' cried an old grenadier 'that you will keep yourself out of the fire.' 'I will do so,' answered Napoleon, 'I shall be with the reserve *until you need us.*' This pledge, which so completely ascertains the mutual confidence of the leader and his soldiers, he repeated in a proclamation issued at daybreak. [pp. 222–3]

And even when a speech cannot be dramatically set, Lockhart's condensation reduces the address to its essentials and gives the reported oration dramatic point.

We have considered primarily the use of anecdote for dramatic reality. But often Lockhart's narrative speeds on without pausing for specific scene or dialogue. Anecdotes involving minor figures are rare, and in scenes where they do appear, only Napoleon, as a general rule, is directly quoted. During the imperial middle years of Tilsit and Dresden, Lockhart scarcely pauses, not sharing Hazlitt's enjoyment of the imperial *parvenu* lording it over legitimate monarchs. The account of the Peninsular campaigns, properly subordinate in a biography of Napoleon, includes few scenes. These are artful decisions. Throughout the book composition controls style and interpretation, and Lockhart's is the structure, not of a political or military survey, but of an intensely dramatic career whose most striking segments are its rise and fall.

The biographer of Napoleon faces special formal challenges. Buonaparte's career was so miraculous an exploitation of circumstance that the opportunist seemed lost in the genius, and his own belief in a personal destiny seemed the only plausible explanation. If he was creature and conqueror of the French Revolution, to what extent should the biographer re-interpret the Revolution from a Napoleonic angle? Scott feels compelled to do so for almost two volumes; Hazlitt adopts a more Shandean structure, beginning with his hero's birth, and turning then to the history of Corsica and four long chapters on the Revolution before Napoleon's debut at Toulon. The revolutionary period appears in Lockhart's narrative only as it affects the young Buonaparte, as he responds to its violence and confusion. The second chapter opens with three paragraphs that summarize the European reaction to regicide, the French royalist insurrections, the First Coalition, and the resistance to invasion – leading up to Toulon and thus back to Buonaparte. Chapter Three offers a comparable illustration of proportion and dramatic focus, again opening with Napoleon, *en route* to Paris in search of an assignment, then giving a clear summary of the events following the downfall of Robespierre and leading up to Napoleon's service – the immortal 'whiff of grape shot' – in the rising of Vendémiaire.

During Napoleon's rise to military fame in Italy and Egypt, the problem is how and to what extent the biographer must include the course of Directorial policy and the state of France, as well as how to avoid suggesting that Paris was a mean turbulence on the periphery of Buonaparte's career. Following Brumaire and Buonaparte's emergence as a major European figure, the problem becomes how to encompass his relations with many regions without substituting a geographical order (as J. M. Thompson did in 1952)[67] for a biographical narrative. Each solution in its own way affects interpretation.

Compare Scott's handling of the end of the first Italian campaign with Lockhart's. Prior to Rastadt and the victor's triumphant return to Paris, the Directorial crisis and Napoleon's negotiations with Cobentzel are obviously inter-related. Scott, anxious as always to preserve a simple logical outline, carries through his discussion of Campo-Formio, sends the conqueror off to Rastadt, and then, in the next chapter, while Buonaparte seems to be back fighting in Italy, gives a complete history of the Directory's unpopularity, the royalist conspiracy, and the *coup* of Fructidor. This is characteristic of Scott's structure; one is baffled trying to fit awkwardly overlapping parts, retrospects, tangential discussions into a narrative pattern or a comprehensive causal sequence. Trying to do so, the reader frequently loses sight of the biographer's subject. Lockhart's solution is also characteristic. After the preliminaries of Leoben, the humiliation of Venice brings Napoleon to the discovery of documents linking Pichegru with the conspiracy. The notice of the Clichyen intrigue and Pichegru's importance justifies a brief explanatory interlude tracing the rise of the plot and the fall of Directorial prestige. Preparing for a *coup*, the Directors need military support, and this allows Lockhart to focus again on Napoleon and his relations with the Directory. But once the fact is past, Napoleon's negotiations, held up by the crisis, can continue to their end; and when Napoleon leaves Italy, the reader, not forced to scurry back after loose ends, is free to go with him.

If Scott has trouble controlling his ill-proportioned survey, Hazlitt's structure, dependent on when and whether he chooses to include evidence, is capricious. The departure of Napoleon from Egypt, for example, presents in itself an almost impossible problem. The Egyptian campaign was cut off from the events in Europe surrounding the emergence of the Second Coalition; and yet the hero is suddenly spirited from one sphere to another. Hazlitt, as later at Smorgony, does not wish to focus on the leader's desertion; hence, he exaggerates the incoherence by suddenly announcing that Napoleon left Egypt because he felt he was needed elsewhere [11, 52]. Scott pauses to survey Napoleon's 'situation and prospects', then narrates the return, then is forced into another lengthy retrospect. Lockhart, holding that 'all these details' – together with 'any minute account of the internal affairs of France during the period' – 'belong rather to the general history of the period, than to the biography of Buonaparte', compresses Scott's retrospect into three-and-a-half paragraphs [pp. 111-13]. In the midst of the last of these paragraphs – in the midst of a situation awaiting his decisive presence – Lockhart's Buonaparte arrives at Fréjus and electrifies Paris with the news of Aboukir.

Hereafter, Buonaparte is consistently at the centre of affairs. The problem of structural unity and proportion exists only with reference to areas in which Napoleon was not immediately involved. The most obvious instance is the Peninsular campaign. To this, Scott, as spokes-man for British resistance and near-worshipper of Wellington, gives undue stress. Hazlitt, motivated by Anglophobia and anxious to mini-mize Napoleon the Machiavellian, errs in the opposite direction.

Lockhart compromises in proportion. He also underlines the significance of the 'affairs of Spain' through assimilating them into broader situations.[68] Spanish affairs are one more popular national movement to oppose Buonaparte. They are an omen that Napoleon is losing the reins, losing his sense of reality, when he allows the hopeless involvement of a great army to continue and turns his attention elsewhere. Such is Lockhart's interpretation, and his structure embodies it.

But the Peninsular phase serves to illustrate something more. Structural solutions establish impressions of moral causality and justice. Two examples are supplied by Napoleon's two last military campaigns, those which show Hazlitt's hero as the defender of France against legitimist invaders. Hazlitt's Napoleon, an unforgivable upstart to his enemies, was not permitted to make peace. Scott's Napoleon, had he been sincere in desiring peace, would have found his enemies liberal and conciliatory. In the account of the 1814 invasion, Scott's Napoleon completes his military preparations and leaves for the front before we hear about the Allied armies, although in fact Schwartzenberg had crossed the Rhine on the 21st of December, and Napoleon did not leave the Tuileries until the 25th of January. Lockhart's order, dramatically more effective, creates a different impression. His account of the invading armies builds up to the departure of Napoleon, who thus ostensibly goes to repel the invaders of France – a meaning closer to Hazlitt's. The same diversity appears in the ordering of affairs preceding Waterloo. All three authors make clear that invasion was again imminent. In interpretation, Lockhart is in agreement with Scott. Yet, once again Lockhart's climactic structure effects dramatic sympathy for the plight of the Emperor. Scott outlines the civil affairs, then turns to the military preparations; Lockhart evokes the atmosphere of imminent invasion first, then shows Napoleon, under the shadow of attack, struggling to bring order to civil affairs before again being forced to rush to the borders of France.

Lockhart's apparent purpose in such reorderings is the achievement of a better narrative. He succeeds remarkably: 'The arrangement throughout is strictly *chronological,* and yet with such practised skill have the parts been put together, that we do not remember experiencing the jolt of one harsh transition from the first page to the last.'[69] But the coherence of which the artist was proud has logical implications which the historian might reject. What Mill describes as the danger of form in Scott is more applicable to Lockhart:

'that important branch of the talent of the narrator, which sir Walter Scott in his character of a romancer pre-eminently possesses, the art of so relating every incident that it shall serve to strike the reader not as an isolated incident, but as a part of the train of events – of keeping the whole posture of affairs, such as it is supposed to be in the story, constantly present to the reader's conception, and almost to his sight, – is a talent most delightful in a novelist, most dangerous when the subject is real history, and the author's view of the posture of affairs happens to be wrong. It is nothing less than the art of so dressing up a fact, as to make it appear to mean more than it does; of so relating and arranging the events to be related, as to make them tell a different story from what would be implied in the mere chronological recital of them.'[70]

To this the reply is obvious: without structure there is neither history nor biography, but only annal; without interpretation there can be no structure. But to what extent did Lockhart create his structure to embody the interpretation which inevitably emerges from it?

His purpose was to achieve logical clarity within a narrative form; the most convenient, effective way was through the marshalling of disparate factors in cause-effect relations with major events. Lockhart's narrative of the Peace of Amiens builds up to Britain's re-declaration of war; there is no pretence there was not 'considerable insincerity on both sides'.[71] Yet he naturally deals first with the positive measures of the Consular Administration and then turns to the examples of Napoleon's 'grasping ambition' – in Switzerland, in San Domingo, in the Near East – which led to British resistance, the explosive scenes with Lord Whitworth, and war. Hostilities thus seem due to the ambitious Buonaparte. Again, the glory of Napoleon's triumph at Austerlitz is magnified in Lockhart by the chapter climax which follows. As the immediate consequences of Austerlitz, Lockhart marshals a survey of political changes in the face of Europe, concluding with the Confederation of the Rhine and the creation of a new French nobility. Equally rapid, because constructed in the same pattern, is the series of catastrophes following the defeat at Leipsic. Here, too, the structure embodies the theme as he states it: 'Having once reached the summit of his greatness, the long-favoured child of fortune was destined to sink even more rapidly than he had ascended' [p. 395]. The catastrophes follow in quick succession, with transitions which suggest their virtual simultaneity and create the image of a desperate Colossus peering in vain over Europe for consolation: 'On the side of Italy the aspect of affairs was almost as dark. . . . As little comfort could Buonaparte derive if he turned to the Pyrenees. . . . Nor were even these the worst tidings' [pp. 396-7].

All subordinate or peripheral factors, then, are marshalled about major events in which Buonaparte was the dominant figure. All causal elements lead to his action; all related affairs exist only to impinge upon his decisions. At Elba, the eagle-eyed Exile sat overlooking the entire continent; at Wilna, Moscow, Smolensk, the Leader in his bivouac was the nerve centre to which came all tidings of a far-off world and from which went out imperial decisions. Speaking of biographical form, I have simply described the achievement of dramatic focus; Lockhart kept it always before him in his narrative. Because of the analytic control which the juridical Scott holds over his account, he remains at the centre of his book; because of a sustained personality of tone, Hazlitt is the dominant figure in his. Lockhart's presence is embodied in structure: events propel each other; rhetorical transitions take on logical inevitability; all is focused on Napoleon. Such is his centrality, so swift and all-embracing his career, that he is indeed, as Lockhart had conceived him ten years before,[72] a figure of almost supernatural romance, the Warrior-Prince whose glorious ambition feeds on his triumph until it is bloated and blinds him.

To support his tragedy of the Fallen Chief, Lockhart finds Napoleon's own obsession with his destiny, his star, an ideal structural symbol. He is critically aware that 'Napoleon's imagination was always ready to welcome a tale that savoured of fatality' [p. 415], yet the same kind of imagination dominates his own narrative – from the rise of the Sun at Austerlitz, to the star 'on which one spot of fatal dimness had already gathered' in which Napoleon trusted in 1812, to the ceremonial on the eve of Leipsic: 'Upon this scene the sun descended; and with it the star of Napoleon went down forever' [pp. 223, 336, 390]. Thereafter, Napoleon's inexorable loss of control is accompanied by his increasingly frenzied efforts to keep it; his destruction is a matter between him and the Fortune which has turned against him. Lockhart echoes the 'adage', 'Whom God hath doomed to destruction, he first deprives of reason' [p. 416]. As he recounts the abdication of 1814 – 'the real end', says Thompson, 'of Napoleon's career'[73] – an unbroken current of tragic sympathy flows from a prototype of gigantic, destroying ambition, 'the Scottish usurper', whose presence colours these pages. Lockhart quotes:

> I have lived long enough: my May [*sic*] of life
> Is fallen into the sear, the yellow leaf. . . .
> Come, put mine armour on; give me my staff.
> . . . The Thanes fly from me.

He imagines that on the night the deserted Chief is alleged to have swallowed poison, his meditations must have been those of 'the falling Macbeth':

> There is no flying hence, nor tarrying here.
> I 'gin to be weary o' the sun.[74]

It is this impression which remains of Lockhart's Napoleon – this, and the memory, not of a mundane self, but of a personalized force, a career made self-aware, a tragic parabola whose rise and fall are functions of a mysterious relation between soaring ambition self-blinded and moral law working through Fortune and the agency of lesser beings. By contrast, Hazlitt's bitter idolatry allows no such conception, and from Scott's diffuse survey no central narrative personality emerges.

To the charge that Lockhart's preconception is narrow or exclusive, one can only answer with Thompson's warning: 'there never was and there never can be such a person as everybody's Napoleon.' Peter Geyl said, to 'bring together the overwhelming multiplicity of data and factors, of forces and movements, and from them establish the true, one might almost say the divine balance' would be 'literally a super-human task'.[75] Could it be done, the result would be a portrayal at once superhuman and inhuman. Guérard the debunker would reject Lockhart's Romantic portrayal. It could hardly be discounted by the author of the most moving tragic Napoleon of this century, Jacques Bainville. Markham recently restated Lockhart's theme: 'The Greeks would have understood Napoleon's story as a simple case of Hubris followed by Nemesis; and perhaps it is better to leave it at that. . . . His sins were on the heroic scale – the sins of pride.'[76] Thompson concludes his study with the comparable words of Marshall Foch. Napoleon 'forgot that a man cannot be God; that above the individual is the nation, and above mankind the moral law: he forgot that war is not the highest aim, for peace is above war'.[77] Lockhart's is perhaps the first effective narrative of the tragic Napoleon.

5

THE MAKING
OF THE
LIFE OF SCOTT

... there is a hypothesis now current, due probably to some man
of name ... that Mr Lockhart at heart had a dislike to Scott,
and has done his best in an underhand treacherous manner to
dishero him!

THOMAS CARLYLE

Beneath the magnificent monument designed by his son-in-
law, Sir Walter has lain in urbane dignity. Perhaps it is time
that he rose from the tomb and re-assumed some of the characteristics of which Lockhart in his protective love divested him.

UNA POPE-HENNESSY

... the best example I know of unimaginative biography ... a
most satisfying piece of biographical photography ... a great
literary quarry.

HESKETH PEARSON

Carlyle, who admired the book sincerely, regretted that it was a
'compilation' rather than a 'composition'. This criticism is
difficult to understand. No one, if work examines the machinery,
shows more careful 'composition' than Lockhart's *Life of Scott*.

 Lockhart ... is the second greatest (I am sometimes inclined
to think the greatest) of all British biographers.

HAROLD NICOLSON

5

THE MAKING
OF THE
LIFE OF SCOTT

1. THE LIFE OF A 'LIFE'

In her eightieth year, from her house in Gloucester Place, Lord Bute's indestructible daughter and Walter Scott's age-long correspondent, Lady Louisa Stuart, watched the long-awaited volumes begin to appear. At 9 Manor Place, Edinburgh, her senior the Highland Bluestocking Mrs Grant was 'reading Sir Walter Scott's Life with lively interest'. To a friend, she wrote in mournful tranquillity:

'I pray tell me what you think of the life of Sir Walter Scott, which no doubt you have read, as well as all the world beside. Did you ever meet with a character so entirely lovable – such a happy combination of all that attracts our highest admiration and conciliates our warmest affection?'

– an affection whose warmth might have cooled had her family taken less effectual precautions to keep from her eyes Sir Walter's remarks on her pension. If Mrs Grant was spared an unpleasant shock, Harry Cockburn was agreeably surprised. He was struck by the honesty: 'nothing is kept back or misrepresented so as to exhibit Scott in a false light'; by the 'extraordinary revelation to the people of Edinburgh ... that there was a time when Lady Scott was pretty and agreeable'; by the generous treatment of Jeffrey and Edinburgh Whigdom. On the northern court circuit in the spring of 1838, he took the last 'sad sad volume', and recorded his feelings:

'I know no biography which gives a truer account of its subject. It is Scott to the life; at least so much so as any man can be exhibited to the public by words. . . . I see him in the Court, and on the street, in company, and by the Tweed. The plain dress, the guttural burred voice, the lame walk . . . all before me a hundred times a day.'

Francis Jeffrey, en route to London, wrote from Northallerton: 'I have been reading Sir Walter's last volume with great interest, and growing love for his real kindness of nature. . . . Poor Scott! could we but have him back, it seems to me as if we would make more of him. I have had strong pullings at the heart homewards again, and feel half as if I were too old for any other place now.'

In Keswick Southey saw the book as the close of his era: 'Of late, I have seen much of myself in a way that thus painfully brings back the past: Sir Walter's Memoirs first, then Joseph Cottle's Recollections of so many things which had better have been forgotten; and now these Memorials of poor Charles Lamb. . . . my thoughts and feelings have been drawn to the years that are past far more than is agreeable or wholesome.'

To Lockhart he wrote, 'It must have cost you much, but you will have the satisfaction of having produced the most compleat biography that has ever appeared of a great man.'[2]

Wordsworth began the book on a tour of the Italian Lakes with Crabb Robinson. The Diarist read 'as long as the light lasted' on 'a hot and disagreeable drive' from Como to Milan, read into the night, while the poet slept, at an inn at Bergamo, and was still reading in mid-August back in London. At the outset, it was 'a made up book, the writer, like his subject, carrying on literature as a trade, and being desirous above all things to make a large book for the sake of the large pay'. Having finished the third volume, he was sure the book 'must injure both the subject and the writer'. Going on he was 'glad to find the opinion of the world at large agrees with mine'; Wordsworth, he claimed, agreed that it was 'a degradation of the literary character of our countryman. Walter Scott was a trader.'[3] Poet and Diarist changed their views as the narrative darkened and deepened into stoic forbearance in misfortune. As Robinson later reached a grudging admiration of Scott's proud integrity, he could hardly fail to recognize the measured candour that made possible such a complex reaction as his. Certainly Wordsworth seemed aware of the moral courage demanded of the biographer when he sent Lockhart his approval:

M

'So much of Sir Walter's affairs having become objects of public investigation, nothing remained for you but to act as openly and sincerely as you have done in writing his Life. Whatever complaints may have been made upon this point will pass away, and ere long your mode of treating the delicate and difficult subject will meet with universal approbation.'[4]

Listening to partial observers, one would suppose that approbation was already universal. Maria Edgeworth is sure 'from all we have felt ourselves and from all we have heard from others' that Lockhart has handled his subject and himself 'with peculiar delicacy taste and judgement':

'we thought it impossible any publication could raise Sir Walter Scotts talents or character in public opinion or in private opinion more especially. And yet you certainly have raised high as ever biographer raised his hero – And you have done it without one word of puff or exaggeration or even full-faced eulogy – I am sure that Sir Walter Scott himself would say – "Well done – my good son."'

The indiscreet Boswellian Basil Hall, to whose Abbotsford journal Miss Edgeworth sharply objected, echoes her evaluation:

'the kind, and generous, and gentlemanlike tone which pervaded the whole book is what I admire still more – . . . . The book does you great honour in every way – is just what the old boy could have wished, and I cannot doubt, expected, at your hands.'

Morritt writes, 'You make men as well acquainted with Scott as ever Jemmy Boswell did with Johnson, and yet neither you or your hero ever suffer from it, as his did.' Others admire Lockhart's candour. The historian Lord Mahon acknowledges his peculiar dilemma:

'In writing the life of a near and dear relative it is most difficult to avoid the conflicting dangers of appearing either blindly partial to his merit or coldly insensible of it, as in speaking of living persons, how few are able to give both a true and graphic and yet a courteous and inoffensive mention! It appears to me that you have successfully avoided the two former dangers and combined the two latter advantages and that your work will fill a high and enduring station in British literature.'

R. H. Cheney defines the requisite tone:

'Nothing has struck me more in it . . . as [*sic*] the union it displays of the greatest candor with that affectionate veneration which the public requires of those who approach one of its former idols. No biography of a great man I am persuaded however ingeniously put together can be permanently popular if it is not written with this feeling.'[5]

But the fan mail cannot be wholly trusted. Cockburn records that 'Amidst much praise Lockhart gets much blame for his execution of this work'; and Lockhart thanks Haydon for approval which 'might well console me for all the abuse it has called forth both on him and on me'.[6] Both refer in part to the Ballantyne-Constable partisans,[7] but they refer also to those Cockburn called 'the idolaters of Scott', who, as Carlyle said, found 'far less reticence than was looked for' and 'received pain'.[8] Who were these? The Edgeworths, Morritts, and Baillies praised. Sir Walter's sons winced at the display of their upbringing, but young Walter wrote in April 1838 to express 'how deeply grateful both Charles and myself feel for the very able and delicate manner in which you have treated the important trust confided to you'.[9] It is the unsympathetic who have left records of their pain at Lockhart's can-dour. For Cockburn, Lockhart's 'trust' might have been carried out without

'a great deal of the useless and vulgar matter which pervades the work. . . . All of Scott's peculiarities could have been easily described without the injustice and offensiveness of not only exposing, but of expatiating on the exposure of selfish transactions and paltry thoughts, which were probably immaterial at the time, but are represented in this "Life" as fixed and essential parts of the man.'

For the malevolent Harriet Martineau, 'It is a curious instance of Lockhart's moral obtuseness that, while writing thus, he could make some most painful and needless disclosures in regard to Scott himself in that Life.' More especially for the public whose idol had been shattered, the effect was as George Ticknor described it from overseas:

'To the admirers of Sir Walter in America, who knew him only as they know Shakespeare, part of what is in Lockhart was an unwel-come surprise, much more so than it was in England, where the weaknesses of his character were known to many.'

Ticknor's reflection on the cause is a striking indication of the bio-graphical ethic by which the reticent Lockhart was judged culpably indiscreet:

'there is one thing he could have avoided; I mean printing some of the letters, and some parts of the private journal. No doubt the letters, generally, are the most delightful part of the whole work. . . . But in some of them Sir Walter is made to expose himself. There was no need of this and it has given great pain.'[10]

Most pained was the author of the book's most notorious review, Carlyle's 'American Cooper'.

This 'transatlantic Scott' would have had a bellicose British counterpart had Macaulay not refused to do an *Edinburgh* review because his opinion of Scott's character was hardly appropriate for a 'Scotch Review'.[11] This left Scottish opposition to *Tait's* and pro-Ballantyne *Chambers's*, which expressed pain at Scott's excessive desire for gain, at his 'absolute spirit of feudalism', and at 'a tale too long drawn out'.[12] In England the *Quarterly* remained silent, and its waggish Tory adjunct, Maginn's rebellious *Fraser's*, simply provided O. Y. with a platform for lambasting 'Epaminondas Grub, or Fenimore Cooper'. Among the rest, John Keble's enthusiastic review stands out, expressing admiration for Scott as a religious force and high praise for the biography.[13] In America, too, high praise was abundant. The *American Quarterly* praised the fulfilment of 'a pious duty' with 'an unwavering purpose of impartiality'. In the *North American Review*, W. H. Prescott pronounced it 'not the least' of Scott's 'good fortunes' in life

'that he left the task of recording it to one so competent as Mr Lockhart; who, to a familiarity with the person and habits of his illustrious subject, unites such entire sympathy with his pursuits, and such fine tact and discrimination in arranging the materials for their illustration.'[14]

He defended Lockhart against the charges of undue exposure. But the *Life's* two most provocative reviews question both aspects of his praise – the ethical and the formal.

Cooper's attack is so obviously a splenetic thrust at the *Quarterly Review* that it can hardly be taken seriously. The *Knickerbocker* itself published a devastating reply two months later. I am interested, however, in the implications of a valid point in Cooper's initial claim:

'the effect of this biography has been to lessen the blind respect for the character of Scott, which sprang up as a natural consequence of his unprecedented literary popularity, rather than as a consequence of investigation and facts, by exposing motives that are never admitted by the upright, and never avowed by the sensitive.'

The student of Lockhart and Scott, knowing blind respect to have been utterly lacking in their relationship, suspects that this lessening of 'blind respect' may have been part of Lockhart's aim. Cooper felt otherwise:

'in all those cases in which he has rendered Scott most obnoxious to the censures of the discriminating, he has been totally unconscious himself of the conclusions to which all right-thinking men must arrive. . . . in the very face of his own testimony, in the summing up of his case, he claims for his father-in-law a character for worth and probity, that is utterly irreconcilable with his own facts. This circumstance constitutes the predominant moral defect of the book.'

Because Lockhart includes evidence of political contrivance, literary mystification, and Tory subservience, Cooper charges 'obtuseness in matters of moral concern'. Because Lockhart passes judgement where reticence prevented full explication – brother Daniel, the Ballantyne connection, the implications of settling Abbotsford on young Walter a year before the crash – Cooper accuses him of mystification.[15]

The latter charge may be just. The former is more controversial and more interesting. One recalls Lockhart's comment that Boswell had seemed remarkably unaware of the implications of some of his materials[16]; Cooper is saying the same of Lockhart, and the impression is understandable. There is a discrepancy between the multiplicity of Scotts which Lockhart's materials illustrate and the essential Scott of his personal assessment. There were degrees of reservation in Lockhart's feeling for his subject which he scarcely allowed to appear in his personal conclusion. But the chief cause is Lockhart's refusal to comment where judgement seems called for. Is there any explanation? The explanation is in the biographical theory that formed the book. For this we may turn to the other of the most memorable reviews and to what seems a wholly distinct fundamental criticism.

The editors of the *Westminster* felt they could not withhold their review pending the publication of the last volume. Hence, Lockhart's most notable reviewer wrote without having read what Basil Hall called the 'magnificent seventh volume' and Maria Edgeworth called 'one of the most touching books I ever read in my life'.[17] Those who cite Carlyle's criticism neglect this crucial fact. From the vantage point of Lockhart's splendid, searching conclusion, Carlyle might well have traced in retrospect the organic form he had so far failed to find. He complains that

'To picture-forth the life of Scott according to any rules of art or composition, so that a reader, on adequately examining it, might say to himself, "There is Scott, there is the physiognomy and meaning of Scott's appearance and transit on this earth; such was he by nature, so did the world act on him, so he on the world, with such result and significance for himself and us"; this was by no manner of means Mr Lockhart's plan.'

There follows, after an absurd Carlylesque rhapsody on Silence, the description precious ever since to thumbnail historians of biography:

'His Work . . . is not so much a composition, as what we may call a compilation well done. . . . The truth is, the work, done in this manner too, was good to have: Scott's Biography, if uncomposed, lies printed and indestructible here. . . . The scattered members of Scott's Life do lie here, and could be disentangled.'

Harold Nicolson finds this hard to understand, while James Corson upholds its accuracy. It is my purpose to prove Nicolson right, yet account for Carlyle's impression.[18]

In the superficial accuracy of Carlyle's critique may be found the reason for the other charge of moral obtuseness. For the ethical charge of obtuse exposure and the formal criticism of uncomposed compilation are parts of the same judgement. The reviewer in the *Athenaeum*, anticipating Carlyle and Cooper, had recognized that a meaningful coherence could be attained only through the judicial omnipresence of the biographer. 'We are sorry to say,' he says of the first three volumes,

'that Mr Lockhart, in place of attempting a coherent, well-proportioned and philosophical biography, which should be entitled to a permanent place on our library shelves, seems to have aimed at (and surely has effected little beyond), collecting the materials for such a work.'

Reaching volume five he complains, 'There is no grappling with it, and all unity of purpose and effect is lost.' After volume six he still hungers in vain for 'high discourse': 'The philosophy of his life,' he observes, 'is still to be discussed.'[19]

Coherence, unity of purpose and effect, proportion: all mean interpretive personality, which it was Lockhart's intention, not to exclude – on the contrary, but to subordinate to copiousness, to liberality of proportion, even to a multiplicity of viewpoints and testimonial tones. Lockhart's judicial reticence is embodied in formal reticence. That this was deliberate is clearly recognized in a letter to Lockhart from one candid and wise friend, the Whig Lord Chief Commissioner Adam: 'I have not a doubt that this *honest reserve* of proceeding on your part, in giving the detail, will secure a just, splendid, and philosophic view of the character in your concluding chapter.' The result was as he predicted: 'Your concluding chapter,' he wrote twelve months later, 'which has been read over to me (oftener than once) is a masterpiece.'[20]

Subsequent biographers of Scott felt little need to search further for materials. Lockhart's copiousness of matter and abundance of witnesses made it easy to accept Carlyle's suggestion that the work was a storehouse from which numerous Scotts could be drawn. Biographers used it with the apology that, as Gladstone told Hope-Scott in 1868, the complete edition was too ponderous ever to enjoy wide circulation.[21] R. H. Hutton prefaces his popular E. M. L. epitome: 'There is hardly any other great source of information about him; and that is so full, that hardly anything needful to illustrate the subject of Scott's life remains untouched.' Norgate discards the notion of superseding Lockhart, whose work 'is and will always remain the magazine from which the great novelist's biography must be drawn.' The same year (1906), Andrew Lang, having earlier sifted the Abbotsford papers, gives this door-slamming analogy:

'The late regretted Mr David Carnegie, after twice crossing the Australian desert, summed up his results in the saying that no explorer need go thither again. The Abbotsford MSS. are not a desert, but Lockhart has omitted nothing in them which is of value, nothing which bore essentially on his theme. No explorer need go thither again, save to confirm his appreciation of the merits of Lockhart's work. All other books on Scott are but its satellites, and their glow, be it brighter or fainter, is a borrowed radiance.'[22]

The 'storehouse' may be thought of very differently. Corson echoes Lang with a difference – 'no amount of research which I have done on Scott has ever made me alter my conception of him as I had learned to accept it from Lockhart' – but complains that Lockhart's work stifled Scott research for a hundred years.[23]

Ethically distinct is Corson's charge that Lockhart deliberately prevented the publication of subsequent biographies. We shall consider later the tragicomic cases of James Hogg and Sir William Gell. Corson cites another, the proposed English edition of a *Life* by Donald MacLeod, and claims Lockhart 'threatened the publisher with legal proceedings and in February 1853 the book was withdrawn from circulation'.[24] A letter survives to indicate that Lockhart's role was not active. Richard Bentley had apparently paid court to Lockhart's influence by ostentatiously stepping *off* his proprietary toes. On the 2nd of January 1853 Lockhart wrote Bentley:

> 'On returning from Paris last night I found your note respecting a Life of Sir W. Scott by Mr Macleod of which I had never before heard. I have now looked into the advertisements and beg to thank you most warmly for the kind and courteous feeling that induced you to withdraw your name from the publication. It is however proper to lose no time in informing you that neither I nor any of Sir W. Scott's descendants have any pecuniary interest in my Life of the Poet.'[25]

But since the potentiality of other biographies is one of the conflicting circumstances which strongly conditioned Lockhart's procedures, we may postpone the subject. Whatever the *Life*'s restrictive influence, its exemplary place seems to have been fixed at the end of the century, attested to by Saintsbury, for whom '*no other biographer*' had 'reached quite this pitch of art', and by the *DNB* himself, Leslie Stephen, for whom the biography remained 'Lockhart's admirable life . . . next to Boswell's *Johnson*, the best in the language'.[26]

The publication of the *Journal* and *Familiar Letters* in the 1890's provided a new inspiration. But a more symbolic turning point in the life of the *Life* is 1906. Late this year, Lang's pious epitome of Lockhart was called 'shapeless and invertebrate stuff', 'a mass of affectation which would have made Scott's gorge rise', in a review called 'Not by Lockhart' by a youthful Lytton Strachey.[27] With the epoch-making appearance of *Eminent Victorians* Carlyle's disparagement of compilation seemed wittily reborn. If this event opened a new era in biography, it also broached a new biographical tone, a matter-of-fact corrective to reticence, an ironic antidote to reverence. The effect seemed to be death to the grand manner.

Strachey's attack was neither as broad nor as irresponsible as some of his friends and enemies have wished to believe. His rebellion was not against Boswell and Lockhart, both of whom he admired. The passage in which he urges the careful distinction between life-portrait and profile is not known as well as the famous preface:

> 'a biography should either be as long as Boswell's or as short as Aubrey's. The method of enormous and elaborate accretion which produced the *Life of Johnson* is excellent no doubt; but, failing that, let us have no half-measures.'[28]

But his epigram on eggs versus omelets stuck; and those 'numberless imitators' who proved by their efforts that 'Strachey's pen was a bow of Odysseus'[29] are well represented by Pearson, who, in 1930, called the *Life* 'the best example I know of unimaginative biography', and a quarter of a century later still considered it 'a great literary quarry'.[30] And although both Grierson and Nicolson have supported the case for Lockhart the artist of 'constructive genius' and 'consummate literary tact', Corson continues to side with Carlyle and the 'quarry' school. So much for the formal criticism. What of the ethical? The reversal in the ethics of exposure has been complete – or so it seemed to a fellow-Bloomsburian writing of Strachey in *The Death of the Moth*: 'at least it was possible to tell the truth about the dead.' To the fore, then, on the centenary of Scott's death came two swashbuckling liberators of the border laird from the idolatrous Lockhart. Donald Carswell attacked Grierson for subservience to Lockhart. His research 'was bound to reveal Scott as a much subtler character than the amiable, rather fatuous prodigy of Lockhart's portraiture', yet he piously restricted himself to a supplement.[31] Una Pope-Hennessy commenced her attack at the same time, accusing Lockhart of the sin of respectability. She urged an end to the 'urbane dignity' in which Scott had reposed under a 'ten-volume tomb': 'Perhaps it is time that he walked the earth again and reassumed some of the characteristics of which Lockhart in his protective love divested him.' Agnes Mure Mackenzie retorted in the grand *flyting* manner of *Blackwood's,* saying of Dame Una's book:

> 'Its glib chatter-about-Harriet, its arch-vacuity of standards in life or letters, its *refaned* patronage of anyone so ignorant as to be born before '87 and live out of London, are a quaint mixture of the evening paper and Mrs Elton talking about Jane Fairfax.'

Dame Una's mind was unchanged by this critical Bannockburn; in 1949 she argued 'that in Lockhart's most resolute and capable hands the perceptive genius, the bookish Borderer racy of the soil, the hard-working professional man, became the victim of the gentlemanly tradition'.[32] Christina Keith's posthumous *The Author of Waverley* (1964) carried the war of liberation a step further, claiming Scot as a native Bohemian never understood by the 'stiff', 'prim', 'priggish' Lockhart.

But in general the *Life* has outlived the anti-Victorians. The real crisis in its life came when the ethical criticism shifted from Lockhart's reticence as interpreter to his behaviour as textual editor. Here the assailants have been blessed by a word Lockhart used to describe his handling of documents: 'manipulation', with all its present connotations of cynical dishonesty.[33] The charges require only brief itemizing. Collation of manuscripts with Lockhart's versions of letters shows omission – this is commonplace – but omission without indication – this was, perhaps, typographical commonplace too. Collation shows correction or revision of spelling, syntax, punctuation, normalization of idiom or dialect. It occasionally shows 'contamination' of texts, telescoping of extracts into single 'letters'. Where originals survive, the diaries and journals show the same treatment to a lesser degree. Finally, in narrative incident Lockhart is charged with decoration, even fabrication.

Defenders are not lacking. They include, in addition to those who say simply, 'It wasn't as extreme as all that!' those who assert that standards were lax, scientific methods unknown.[34] This defence, while true, is singularly ineffectual, since it relegates the book and its method to the realm of antiquarian curiosities.

It is my hope to account for the method in more positive terms, to argue that the *Life* is a logical result of the conditions under which it was produced, and that its method was a remarkable implementation of the paradoxical theory of biography which insisted simultaneously on direct autobiographical exposure and the controlling presence of the biographer's own personality. Lockhart's editorial behaviour was largely a response to formal demands for coherence, for narrative continuity, for variety and freedom from repetitiousness, for compromise among narrative, expository, and dramatic structure. It was through manipulation that the compiler-biographer responded to those demands, gave his materials editorial unity in diversity, organic form.

This hypothesis will explain why Lockhart wrote as early as 1834 that he was about to begin composition, and what Sophia Lockhart meant when she wrote two years later, 'He has been arranging it so long in his mind that, now fairly commenced, he will not be long about it.'[35] My conclusions are based on collation of the Lockhart texts with the Grierson edition of letters, the Tait-Parker edition of the *Journal*, and the MS. memoirs and anecdotes sent Lockhart by Irving, Harriet Scott, Ballantyne, Morritt, Skene, Shortreed, Cadell, Gell, Moore, Rose, Dorothy Wordsworth, and Basil Hall. Perhaps any apology for a work textually unreliable, too long to read, about a novelist 'outgrown', is purely academic. But whatever the future of Lockhart's

Life, I must agree with Saintsbury and Nicolson that there is no more extraordinary literary composition in English biography.

II. INFLUENCES ON A *Life*

James Hogg and Henry Cockburn agreed that 'a son-in-law ought not have written the Life'.[36] But Lockhart's task was far more complex than that relationship alone could have made it. In view of the conflicting circumstances which surrounded the making of the *Life of Scott*, it is a miracle that the work was done at all – especially since Lockhart set himself such a comprehensive and rigorous ideal. The intensity of his prolonged effort to realize it may best be seen in his own statements on the work in progress.

Any notion that the work was slipshod bookmaking is quickly disspelled by the time-table. At Scott's death on 21 September 1832, Lockhart as literary executor was authorized to write a *Life*. The collection of materials began at once. In the Ballantyne pamphlet Lockhart indignantly denied having planned the work before Scott was cold in his grave,[37] but the evidence remains. On 6 October 1832, sending her own reminiscences and those she had already collected, Harriet Scott of Harden wrote: 'Walter told me you wished to collect something about poor Sir Walter's early life.' This letter came two days after Hogg's proposal that Lockhart write the *Life* in Hogg's name, and three days after young Walter forwarded materials to Lockhart, including the Ballantyne packet 'Open not, read not' and the Ashestiel fragment of autobiography, which Lockhart said came to light only after he 'had made some progress' in his 'narrative'.[38] Almost two years later (August 1834), Lockhart told William Blackwood: 'I am now about to commence writing my Life of Scott, a heavy and anxious task, for which I have hitherto been collecting and arranging the vast mass of materials.' But the process of arranging was not over. In March 1836 Sophia wrote to Cadell: 'Knowing how anxious you are for the "Life", I cannot help writing to tell you it is fairly begun, and Lockhart working as hard at it as ever you could wish' – this, in view of Sophia's distaste for the avaricious, hard-hearted publisher, no doubt with sarcasm. Her letters throughout 1836 show him hard at work, and she only hopes his health 'will stand the labour he takes'.[39] By the year's end he could predict to Willie Scott of Raeburn, 'The book will consist of six volumes three of which are now in the printer's hands. The publication however will not begin for some months as I wish the whole MS to be complete before I hazard that step.' On 24 April 1837 he was confronting 'the only *difficult* part of my task . . . the closing chapter of my book'. On 19 January the first and second volumes were 'nearly out of the printer's hands'; the first was advertised for 15 March, and on 2 May Cockburn had finished reading the second. Sophia died on 17 May, but publication continued, at least five volumes appearing by early fall. On 12 February 1838 Morritt wrote, 'I congratulate you with all my heart on being out of harness, and expect your seventh and last volume with great eagerness.' And on 21 February 1838 Lockhart wrote Croker: 'I have sent off the last of my proofs long ago to Edinburgh and am now enjoying great idleness – preparatory to resuming the role of reviewer which is an easier one than that of Author and a deal more safe as well as dignified.'[40]

Publication was not hazarded without painstaking scrutiny and discussion of proofs. The months following Sophia's death were filled with correspondence mixing personal condolence with critical comment or editorial exhortation. But the caution and discretion were powers delegated by one whose native detachment, increased after his wife's death, made him extraordinarily free from the timidity Haydon attacked in Moore as biographer of Sheridan; and appropriately to Haydon Lockhart expressed his own indifference: 'the work is now done, and I leave it to its fate. I had no personal object to gratify, except, indeed, that I wished and hoped to please my poor wife; and, since she is gone, I consider the whole affair with most consummate quiescence.' It was not all a negative integrity, however. He had felt a Boswellian faith in his subject: 'I trusted to the substantial greatness and goodness of the character, and thought I should only make it more effective in portraiture by keeping in the few specks. I despise with my heels the whole trickery of erecting an alabaster image, and calling that a *Man*.' More confidentially, he expressed it to the most candid of his elder counsellors, Commissioner Adam:

> 'I really could not have any pleasure in my task unless I carried with me throughout the strong and perfect faith that by *telling* the truth in all things I shall ultimately leave the character of Scott as high and pure as that of perhaps any man ever can appear after being subjected to a close scrutiny.'[41]

But Lockhart's responsibility to Scott and to truth was not a personal one, and his work was to include, not a single view, but many. If justice required honesty and restraint, effectiveness depended on convincing a contemporary world of truthfulness. Lockhart was more than ready to distrust his independence and elude petty hostilities: 'God knows,' he wrote Adam, 'I wish to avoid as far as possible all offensive topics and details, and I cannot but hope that time and the grave have softened away all the petty spleens and prejudices that may have been looked [*sic*] on former occasions.' To Laidlaw, three months earlier, he had expressed the same mixture of independence and self-effacement before elder survivors of Scott's society: 'I am glad that Cadell and the few others who have seen what I have done . . . are pleased, but I assure you none of them can think more lightly of my own part in the matter than I do myself. My sole object is to do him justice, or rather to let him do himself justice.' Justice will force him – 'a stern sense of duty' will induce him – to 'touch the few darker points in his life and character'. But the truth of the picture will be determined 'by you and the few others who can really compare the representation as a whole with the facts of the case'. Some will check the proof; Laidlaw will receive the volumes long before publication.[42]

The letter to Laidlaw replies to one of the 11th of January in which Laidlaw mentions some Scott correspondence he has withheld:

'I have still four or five letters from Malta and Naples which I will give to nobody but you and not to you either if I thought it at all possible that you would let them out of your hands. Although it seems to be well known that this powerfull [*sic*] mind went utterly out of joint it is not for you or me to print his letters written in that state.'[43]

In answering with a plea to see what use might be made of the letters, Lockhart is coping with a problem peculiarly his own, one which taxed all his diplomatic and editorial skill from the beginning, and one without an awareness of which we cannot recognize his art. His was not simply a Life *with* letters; it was a Life formed through correspondence. Lockhart's conception of Scott was less literary than social; Scott was the centre of a society grounded in paternalistic fidelity, the incarnation of a rural aristocracy which was no more – which Lockhart knew had never quite been. Appropriately, his biography presents Scott through a network of evolving and interconnected relationships, manifest in copious correspondence. Many correspondents were still living. Ellis and Erskine and Terry were dead. The huge correspondence with Lady Abercorn was not to be used – if indeed Lockhart saw those letters, and he may be referring to them in a letter to Skene: 'I have seventy-two to Morritt, every sentence of which is precious – perhaps as many to one fine lady, the whole whereof would hardly furnish one extract.'[44] But several principals were very much alive, and their relationships with Scott were living materials. Lockhart's undertaking was dependent on the trust and textual integrity of numerous self-appointed editors, some of whom took their duties very seriously. Lockhart describes his editorial apparatus to Miss Edgeworth:

> 'The enormous heaps of letters committed to me were all copied by ladies, and the originals forthwith returned; and I fear besides innumerable blunders of names and dates, which, in the most important of them, it cost me no small pains to correct, there may have been on the part of my dear Sophy and her assistants, many omissions or hints about omission which had come to hand on separate papers. I hope no very serious evil has been occasioned, but consider she who had been my secretary for years in preparing these Memoirs only lived to see, not to read, my first volume, and in her I lost the only person who could have put and kept me right as to a thousand little things.'[45]

But Sophy's ladies did not always have the originals. Joanna Baillie had trouble reading Scott's hand and left up to Lockhart what should be used; Tom Moore sent originals; Lord Montagu placed his entire collection in *Mrs* Lockhart's hands. Others sent transcripts with permission to extract; *copies* are mentioned, perhaps a single 'faithful transcript of two letters, which you may dispose of as you please'. One is unconcerned when Scott's former amanuensis George Huntley Gordon sends copies, 'each on a separate sheet and *no* writing on the *off* pages', or when the antiquarian David Laing copies Scott's letters regarding the Bannatyne Club. But Laidlaw discovers letters from the time of the *Minstrelsy*, and makes his daughter copy them. And others may have followed the helpful policy of Harriet Scott with Scott's last letter from Naples: she noticed 'a few words left out which I have put in a copy I took of it as it was not easy to read – and I would copy it again for you'. We know that Lockhart so distrusted at least one amanuensis that he could not use her transcripts.[46]

Charles Kirkpatrick Sharpe was not the only contributor who did his own editing: 'what I think may be of use to you shall be transcribed.' Lady Louisa Stuart picked out the 'most characteristic' letters. Some did extensive arranging. Cadell transcribed Scott-Cadell-Ballantyne correspondence into a narrative of publishing affairs. Joseph Train wove his transcriptions into a huge M S. account of his correspondence with Scott. Skene copied and interwove letters with his reminiscences, and even provided a 'contamination' for which Lockhart is blamed. The manuscript Skene sent in lieu of originals contains the 'contamination' already intact.[47]

Those who did submit without editing assumed thorough editorial caution on Lockhart's part. Lockhart had become accustomed to discretion in letters while Scott was alive; a letter to Sir Walter, concerning an influential political figure, has this note at the top of the first page: 'He said *no names* – for when the great unknown pops off all his letters will be printer's prop!'[48] Such a hint accompanies a surviving letter of the Scott-Erskine correspondence: 'This might have been an awkward Document had the biographer not done his duty – fairly and fearlessly.' Crofton Croker provided Lockhart with a similar precedent: when, years before, he had sought permission to publish a letter, Scott had approved *provided* he had a chance to correct it.[49] Morritt insists on a change in a letter of his own,

'which tho' entirely at your service I must beg you *not* to leave exactly as it stands. . . . the Earl of Darlington now Duke of Cleveland is mentioned by me in a tone, which though compatible enough with my own opinions when writing *confidentially* to Scott who knew them well, I cannot allow to be printed as a gentleman, without making myself responsible for a positive impertinence. . . . I will recast it as I wish it to stand or leave it out altogether in revising this proof.'[50]

All of this assumes that Lockhart was not denied his pleas altogether: 'Should you possess any letters of his of which, in your opinion, use might advantageously be made in a Memoir of his life, and be pleased to allow me copies or extracts of these, you would be conferring a valuable favour on your friend's surviving family; but this is a point on which I feel that I have no right to insist.'[51] Some who ordinarily opposed the publication of private correspondence found it impossible to refuse – Wordsworth, for one.[52] But Maria Edgeworth cannot have been alone in her refusal. Her letter is an excellent expression of the conservative view Lockhart was certain to encounter.

'The general rage for the practice upheld by venality and vanity leagued together on one hand and depraved curiosity and malice on the other threatens to destroy private friendship and all human confidence and to leave no *privacy* in this world, no *true* feeling – Every high or delicate sentiment which in their very natures cannot bear display are now dragged to light– blasted, withered by that horrid, garish eye of curiosity . . . though I am aware of all the use and advantage to biography and all the pleasure in getting thus at the private soul having the good and great drawn by themselves – and all that has been well said about seeing great minds in undress, yet the modern abuse of the advantage has overbalanced all this.'

She was persuaded to change her mind. She conceded to Sophia on the 7th of April 1837, 'Mr Lockhart makes such admirable use of all the letters – they so unfold to the reader Sir Walter Scotts mind from the earliest time.' Sophia herself may have been the effective pleader; only a note from Sophia, Cadell reports, would cause the indolent Will Clerk 'To *howk* and search, and rummage for more.'[53]

Maria Edgeworth was only one member of the influential group Lockhart acknowledges in the letter to Laidlaw. In the same letter he identifies a member of greater importance: 'I have waived all my own notions as to the manner of publication, etc., in deference to the book-seller, who is still so largely our creditor, and, I am grieved to add, will probably continue to be so for many years to come.' 'Cadell,' he specifies elsewhere, 'is at my request a copious annotator on my proof-sheets & I fancy he will keep a pretty strict watch over me when either Whigs or personal cronies of Constable are handled. But indeed I shall on all serious points take good care that I take him with me.'[54] That Cadell was an unreliable travelling companion has been a principal theme of Grierson's strictures. In the years before the crash, he notes, Cadell's position was 'an ambiguous one'. He was cannily instrumental in keeping Sir Walter for Constable at all costs. If Scott deceived himself, Cadell helped by encouraging him to accept loans, giving deceptive reassurances on the eve of disaster, and insisting on Scott's futile advance of £10,000. All this history had to be reshaped if, after the crash, Cadell was 'to clear the traces of the "bookseller" and gain exclusive control of the "bookmaker"'. At the time, Lockhart had warmly encouraged Constable: 'all literary men wish to see you hold up your head again; for they know how great is the debt that they all, as a body, owe to you personally for having thrown so much of new life and vigour into the conduct of the profession of which it is to be hoped you will long be an ornament.' Constable referred in reply to the 'kind expressions and good wishes for my future welfare which I know you have not been backward to express on more than one occasion of which I have heard with much gratitude'. It must have been later that Cadell 'inoculated' the biographer's mind with a 'false or partial view of the character and conduct of Constable and the Ballantynes'.[55] Cadell was cannily aware of his own position in the making of the *Life*: 'here is Lockhart', he wrote, 'telling about all of us to posterity. We will all be handed down as appendages to the great man.' Of the Ballantyne-Constable part of Scott's world, he alone survived, 'having cuckooed all these men out of their nests'. He alone could shape the history of Scott's business affairs. At the outset Lockhart's trust in him was considerable, as Basil Hall hints: 'I am truly glad to see you writing in such terms of Cadell & I feel well assured that you will never have reason to alter this tone. At least I never yet met a person with whom I have acted so confidentially & so long without a shade of suspicion.' When the shade crossed Lockhart's mind, it was too late. 'I dare say,' he wrote Murray in 1838, 'you have seen a Ballantyne pamphlet nominally against me but really against Cadell whose evidence as to the affairs of Constable & Co. I relied on & thought I might well do so as it seemed criminative of his own *house* at least as much as of the other parties.'[56]

Lockhart's reliance is seen in the proofsheets. He depended on Cadell for bibliographical facts and figures: marginal notes on the size of editions are signed 'RC'; blanks left for the actual debts of the various houses at the time of the crash are filled in by Cadell. In his role as Edinburgh agent, he 'saw to' Latin, Gaelic, and law phraseology. He was Lockhart's intermediary with Scott's Edinburgh friends, and through him their opinions and recollections were brought to bear on the work in progress. For one example, in the margin beside Lockhart's account of the advance printing of *Lenore* for Miss Belsches, Cadell has written: 'Thomson and other comrades doubt the separate printing.'[57]

Of greater complexity are the proofsheet revisions of passages relating to Cadell's role in the Scott-Constable dealings. Especially suggestive is the difficulty over the proof of the third chapter of the sixth volume. In it Lockhart deals extensively with 'commercial affairs' and recalls the warning of financial collapse in the autumn of 1825. He describes Scott's midnight ride for reassurance, allegedly from Abbotsford to Constable's house at Polton and back to Chiefswood in time for breakfast. Grierson has argued that the ride could not have taken place, a position soon (and persuasively) to be upheld by Edgar Johnson.

Evidently the 'Polton ride' is an adaptation to Lockhart's narrative[58] of some other 'Polton ride' at some other period – for while Lockhart conflated and even divided incidents, and while he often manipulated calendar time, he did not manufacture *ex nihilo*. What is of moment here is that it was Cadell who deceived Scott; and hence, the proofsheet attempts to mystify or generalize the account of the early warning must seem to be effects of Cadell's influence. A short paragraph appears in proof:

'It is proper to add here that the story about the banker's throwing up the book was, as subsequent revelations attested, wholly groundless. The incident on which the rumour rested occurred in the first week of November.' [VI, 100]

Several attempts were made at weakening the second sentence. Finally the whole sentence was vigorously crossed out, I believe by Cadell's pen, and Lockhart substituted the vague published sentence: 'Sir Walter's first guess as to its origin proved correct.' An excision in what follows further obscures the timetable. Lockhart's allusion to Murray had been followed by : 'with whom I had formed a very strict connexion in the preceding month'.

Such revisions, when they conceal Cadell's role, tend to increase the severity of Lockhart's presentation of Constable. There is, for a related example, the mystery of Lockhart's *second* meeting with Constable in London (January 1826), at which Constable proposed that Scott borrow £20,000 and forward it to London. James Glen has concluded that no such proposal was made, and Grierson has recalled that Scott's advances were made at the insistence of Cadell.[59] One must, then, find significance in the fact that this 'scene of the same kind a day or two afterwards' was written into the proofsheet by Lockhart after Cadell's reading [VI, 177].

This is not the only instance in the proofs of the birth of an incident by binary fission. In January 1837 Lockhart wrote to ask John Wilson Croker, longtime political mainstay of the *Quarterly*, if he could recall Scott's first dinner as guest of the Prince Regent at Carlton House. 'Can you recall for instance what song it was that the Prince sung – for Scott in a minor poem alludes to having heard him perform in that way & I take it on that occasion.' He wrote to Adam with the same request. Adam could not help on 'the subject of the songs': 'There was no singing at that dinner. Croker was not there, indeed I never dined with Croker at Carlton House.' Croker was not sure he remembered Adam's being there, either. Yet they claimed to be recounting the same dinner of twenty-two years before.[60] But they agreed as to the absence of singing, and the proofsheets show how Lockhart reacted. The account of the Prince's 'several capital songs' had made up part of the account of the first dinner. In the proofs, the brief paragraph has been cut out of its position and pasted in following the end of the account, where it is introduced by these words written in the margin: 'Before [Scott *deleted*] he left town he again dined [w *deleted*] at Carlton House, when the party was a still smaller one than before, and the merriment if possible still more free.' One dinner evidently has become two. Croker found the account 'disgraceful', but the account stood – in spite of Croker.

His influence was by no means disregarded in other areas. Among the Scott letters he forwarded to Lockhart were two of the 4th and 5th of February 1818, in which Scott tells Croker of the discovery of the Scottish Regalia. The second of these letters is known only in Lockhart's published version; the proofsheet version indicates Scott's hope that a traditional office associated with the Regalia might be revived in his favour. The passage has been crossed out. The excision must have been dictated by Croker, for Lockhart expresses to Croker his 'doubt about suppressing his hint as to the Knight Marischalship'. Lockhart requests further information. 'At all events tell me whether the P. R. at the time shewd any disposition to comply w Scotts request.' The embodiment of Croker's reply in the narrative must, to Croker, have seemed disturbingly indiscreet: Croker had blamed Lord Liverpool for the failure to appoint Scott. The passage was cancelled in proof; only a revised allusion to Captain Ferguson's appointment remains.[61]

But Croker's restraining influence was most apt to appear in the account of Scott's later political activities. Years later, Lockhart looked ahead to the time when an heir would sell Scott's complete journal 'for a larger sum than my book brought for the relief of his immediate representative. . . . Posterity will know that I at least endeavoured to avoid the offending of Scotts surviving contemporaries and you will not doubt,' he tells Croker, 'that I had to spare Tories about as often as Whigs the castigation of diarizing Malagrowther.' The problematical relationship of Croker, Malagrowther, and Malagrowther's Tory biographer may account for other signs of reticence in the proof-sheets.[62]

Lockhart dedicated the work to Scott's intimate friend, Morritt of

Rokeby – and with good reason. He had called on Morritt to help select the extracts from the journal to be used. He explained to Croker years later:

> 'Greatly feeling the responsibility imposed on me, in selecting for publication within a few years after his death, I had the whole Diary set into type in order that I might obtain the advice throughout of his most intimate friend Mr Morritt, and another person who knew very little of him [Dean Milman].'[63]

But Morritt had the opportunity to exert a considerable force for reticence on the biography as a whole. His letters to Lockhart make clear that he and Rose read and annotated Lockhart's proofsheets. For example, 'I sent you this morning the proofs of the whole 2nd volume with a swinging long letter enclosing also a sheet of references and comments noted on the margin.'[64] We cannot identify all of Morritt's alterations, but we can see that he was not ignored. It was Morritt who contributed the sceptical comment on Scott's report of '50,000 blackguards . . . ready to rise between Tyne and Wear' for which Cockburn credited Lockhart. It was Morritt who urged the cutting of two passages which 'clog the march of narrative' – the account of Joanna Baillie's *Family Legend*, and the extracts from Scott's 'Essay on Judicial Reform'; and they were cut. Occasionally he sought only to protect himself: to conceal his authorship of the account of Scott and Jeffrey in 1808, he has, he tells Lockhart, 'mystified and generalized' the description. Finding the letter in which he speaks impertinently of 'the Earl of Darlington now Duke of Cleveland', he insists it be changed.

In themselves insignificant, these indicate his general attitude. Consider his support of a cut urged by Cadell: 'it were better to suppress even the heart rending appeal here made to our posthumous sympathy than to expose this character to malignant comment, for subsequent inadvertency at a more sanguine moment.' His position is strong and clear in this directive to Lockhart: 'I would at all events not name Gillies, or indeed any innocent or unfortunate name in *private* transactions. I have on the same principle & stronger feeling begged quarter for other more distinguished names as you will see. Do not "make one *worthy* man" (or woman) his foe, or your own. "*Non est tanti*," for rogues, fools , & coxcombs lay it on & spare not; & there are plenty to season the book.'

One of Morritt's characteristic revisions involves a particular editorial licence for which Lockhart has been blamed. Among other 'improvements' of his documents, Lockhart has been charged with the cultural betrayal of 'correcting' Scott's Scotticisms. The charge seems most peculiar in the face of other evidence. One thinks of the strong cultural nationalism of Dr Peter Morris. One recalls this statement in a letter to Allan Cunningham: 'I shall never cease to have some difference of opinion w you as to the Scotch tongue – which nobody uses quite to my satisfaction but Sir Walter. . . . he alone writes what is all over Scotland Scotch National.' One thinks of Lockhart's enjoyment of Cockburn's style in the *Life of Jeffrey*: 'the locality of all his views with the Scotch of his style are to *me* among the attractions of the book.'[65] Why would Lockhart have yielded to the murderous snobbery of Anglicization in the case of his *ultimus Scotorum?*

The answer is simply that he did not. Morritt's sheet of 'References and Comments' identifies the ubiquitous editorial hand sprinkling 'shalls' and 'shoulds' through the proofsheets. 'Rose agrees with me in all the substitutions I have made of words and sometimes of collocations, except where he has dissented in red ink. They are chiefly in Scott's own letters, and are Scotticisms or at least not English, (shalls, wills, etc.) I would alter these that they may not be of example to our hackney writers, and confound the language by giving them authority and precedent like this.' Lockhart yielded to Morritt and Rose. He yielded to Morritt's pleas, too, in the excision of 'damns' from diary and letters: 'they are banished from print', Morritt argues, quoting Bob Acres on their obsolescence; 'nor would I print for another what he would not have printed himself.'

Applying the same principle, Morritt urged reticence in the depiction of Scott's mental deterioration during his last months. Laidlaw had vowed he would not send Lockhart his Malta and Naples letters if he thought they would be printed. Lockhart replied by expressing his hope 'to put together a picture that will be highly touching of a great mind shattered, but never degraded, and always to the last noble'.[66] Then came Morritt's plea: 'Do not print a line of the diary that indicates decay of mind, or relate except in a general way the painful close of the scene in which he only partook of the universal lot of all mortality. Facts serviceable to medical science may be *medically* told, but as Benjamin Constant told Lady Davy when she objected to some *superfluous improprieties* of his heroine as indecorous in his book, "Je mettrai cela dans une note."'

The result is obvious in the proofsheets. References to and manifestations of the mental effects of Scott's illness have been cut from letters, journals, narrative links, and reminiscences. The following is cut from Lockhart's narrative: 'His bookseller and printer had before them daily evidence that, whatever the origin of the ailment might have been, it had not left either the mind or the hand exactly what they had used to be' [VII, 202]. Also cut (and hence absent from the Grierson edition) is a long extract of a letter to Cadell on *Castle Dangerous* and *Count Robert*. It ends: 'I will talk to you about my plan when I see you, for which I am sufficiently eager, and will show you also what I have thought of as to Count Robert – but I fear it will always be liker mended china than whole. However, it must not be lost; but I wish to start with something on which I have bestowed the pains I am now taking. We must play our best bout at the ceasing of this long frost, and show, if we can, that Richard is himself again' [VII, 289]. Large cuts are made in Gell's and Cheney's accounts of Scott in Italy. 'He spoke of his last work with contempt,' says Cheney. '"Never read it," he said, "it smells of the apoplexy."' Lockhart prints: '"No author," he continued, "has ever had so much cause to be grateful to the public as I have. All I have written has been received with indulgence."' He suppresses: '"I was astonished at my own success. At first I wrote for amusement, and from the pleasure I had in spending money I acquired so readily, and surely no man's money was ever more his own than mine, for I made every halfpenny by the sweat of my own brain – latterly I wrote from necessity, and to satisfy my creditors; and my last thing has served my turn – for it cleared me"' [VII, 378]. Suppressed, too, is the opening of Dr Ferguson's account of Scott's homecoming:

'During Sir Walter's absence from this country, I heard from his family that he had lost all control over his appetite, and was at times so irritable and excitable, as to render him nearly unmanageable. He was tormented by an incessant desire to return home, but believed there was a conspiracy to prevent his doing so. This fixed wish extinguished every other; and he scarcely ever evinced the slightest desire to see or explore any of the objects which his situation presented.' [VII, 384]

Such suppressions are in keeping with Morritt's views – and, incidentally, with the views of other older members of the Scott circle whose influence was less directly felt. It will be suggested that Lockhart accepted only that advice with which he agreed. But the suppressions were not made earlier; Morritt had to state his case strongly and repeatedly; surviving correspondence shows Lockhart for years in the position of one begging permission to be honest and full in his use of materials. There is an admirable bit of evidence to show that on a crucial moral issue Lockhart might weigh Morritt's demands that the portrait be softened, and yet persist in his own judgement. On Scott's blacksheep brother Daniel, Morritt wrote:

'I think the facts of Scott's conduct on his brother Daniel's death though *truly* given do not leave a *true impression* of his feelings. The particular misconduct and stigma on poor Dan's character are not and should not be specified, but then, in justice to Scott, the detail of his refusal to see him, even *in extremis*, and his not attending the funeral or wearing mourning should also be suppressed, and only mentioned in *general* terms. I write this in justice to the tenderest and kindest heart I ever knew, which ever open to the *distress* even of an enemy, still recoiled from the *disgrace* even of a brother.'

Lockhart added Morritt's last phrases in the proof – but only after they had been fused with his own: 'Thus sternly, when in the height and pride of his blood, could Scott, whose heart was never hardened against the distress of an enemy, recoil from the disgrace of a brother' [II, 247].

Such were the powerful influences which augmented Lockhart's own more moderate reticence. There was, however, a strong stimulus to give rein to his natural candour. Lockhart knew that upon Scott's death the parasitical tourists and peeping Toms who had so infested Abbotsford would crash into print to capitalize on their peeps and eavesdroppings. Prevention was a possibility, and desirable from various motives. Someone had proposed to Laidlaw, for example, that he do a short *Life*. Young Walter writes Lockhart of the executors' dilemma:

'now we must either stand in poor Laidlaw's way or submit to have a poor meagre work written upon a subject, which is to us, one of the utmost importance in every point of view, both as regards the justice due to the memory of our poor father and as regards the benefit that may be derived from your future operations.'[67]

Walter is inclined to submit if Laidlaw is likely to make £1,000, but 'one Life begets many and you may chance to find Laidlaw published and republished with notes, additions and heaven [knows what]'. For confirmation of the prophecy one need only glance through Corson's bibliography. Whatever happened to Laidlaw's offer, he may have

reached a position similar to that of James Ballantyne, who explains to
Lockhart in October 1832:

> 'I hastily and imprudently committed myself, by pledging my
> exertions to the readers of the Journal [his own weekly] to recall and
> record, should my health permit me, sundry anecdotes of the de-
> parted, known only to myself. I beg leave to say, in three uncere-
> monious words, that I now trample upon this pledge, by which I
> now find, what I should have seen from the beginning, that I
> should thus enrich paltry scribblers at the expense of those who
> merit to know all that I can tell them on this interesting subject.'[68]

Ballantyne kept the faith, and his memoranda are widely and imaginatively used in the *Life*, together with those of many others who chose
to submit their materials to a single editorial and interpretative control.

Indeed, the comprehensive, multifaceted form of the *Life* may in
part have been determined by the actual and potential abundance of
such fragments, and by Lockhart's recognition that only by collection
and editorial manipulation could he control the inundation of Scottiana.
He had little choice. It meant the inclusion not just of the Morritts and
Adolphuses and Irvings, not just the Skenes and Ballantynes and Moores
(easily adapted and manipulated), but also of the notebook Hall kept
on his knee at Abbotsford meals and of Gell's condescending, sometimes
ghoulish reminiscence of a pathetic Scott in Italy. It meant including
concessions and explanations simply to anticipate, with sympathetic
delicacy, the charges and exposures certain to be made by others.
Morritt gives full expression to the strategy in one of his most valuable
letters:

> 'Go on then and I would stake my life on your success. You will have
> given us a standard work, and no temporary controversy will survive
> the newspapers and periodical magazines into which it may creep
> for you will so exhaust the materials that no bookseller will find any
> that can be separately profitable. Additional letters, and notices will
> always be left for future Curl's and Bowles's in the next generation,
> but like those of the last will wither and die of themselves after you
> have completed your labours, to which they will produce but a dull
> appendix. I feel that you are right in anticipating all injurious
> disclosure, and that nothing should be avoided that is assailable by the
> Edinburgh partisans of Constable and Ballantyne – You have done
> this well, and by truly exhibiting the mixed motives on which Scott
> really acted you have done him full justice.'[69]

To this extent, Morritt had been converted to candour.

Such strategy explains the strange episode of Sir William Gell, Scott's *cicerone* in Rome and Naples in the winter of 1831-2. A transcription of Gell's reminiscences, of which Lockhart printed three-fifths, was published in 1953 with the customary editorial aspersions on Lockhart and the assertion that Lockhart's omissions 'are, taken together, just as valuable and important as what Lockhart chose to print'.[70] They do make a peculiar picture of an invalid mind and a comically helpless body. The editor observes that the history of the reminiscences is obscure; it is less obscure than he makes it appear, and quite explicable in terms of Lockhart's design. The design was to control such effusions by employing them in the *Life*.

From Gell's letter of 4 April 1833, to the Countess of Blessington, it appears that he had planned to record his reminiscences before being requested to do so. He has been employing himself 'by the desire of the family, in writing those very same memoirs of Sir Walter Scott's residence in Italy, which you recommended to my attention'. Beginning with the expectation of 'only a page or two', he soon finds his manuscript burgeoning, and is surprised to discover 'the whole . . . by no means so barren of interest as I thought it would have been when I began the narrative'.[71] But there has been a complication: 'Miss Scott wrote to me by the desire of Mr Lockhart, to beg I would send him any reminiscences of Sir Walter, because I was "the last of his friends".' If Lockhart acted in part to prevent separate publication, the strategy succeeded; Gell's manuscript went 'to Hamilton to give to Mr Lockhart, for as the family had requested them from me, I could not well dispose of them to my own advantage, which I was told I might easily do'. He has been careful to keep a copy, 'and if Mr Lockhart does not use my materials, which I think he can hardly reject, as I have taken care to give due honour to his hero, they may appear hereafter separately'. Gell's 'due honour' includes the demonstration that Scott was stupid in classical languages, coldly insensitive to Greek and Roman antiquities, unable to get into or out of the carriage, and so absentminded as to try to have bound and sent home to Scotland the books lent him by his friends in Italy. [72]

The scene of this obscure comedy now shifts to Sussex Place, Regent's Park, in June of the same year (1833). Sophia has received Gell's memoirs and gone over them with close friends, the Maclean Clephanes of Torloisk. The daughter writes Sophia on their arrival home: 'I had no time to write to Mrs Cheney on the subject I promised, but Mamma did from Edinburgh.' The subject is Gell's memoir; the purpose to obtain an alternative view of Scott in Italy. But once again the request has been anticipated; Henry Cheney has seen Gell's memoir and found 'personally offensive' references to his brother Edward, to whom he has reported the discovery. Edward finds that he has been made 'the channel of several reflections on Sir Walter of which I am utterly incapable; moreover, this memoir is so ill-written and so irrelevant that I am almost sure Mr Lockhart will not publish it'. Edward is ready to submit his own faithful account of Roman conversations with Sir Walter for Lockhart to use 'in any manner he sees proper '. Miss Maclean Clephane, reporting all this to Sophia, would prefer Henry as narrator, but Edward will suffice as an antidote to Gell's deliberate malice:

> 'Depend on it, every prickle of it was meant, as well as all you mentioned of untrue and disagreeable on the more immediate subject of it. Do not suppose me as spiteful at the old sinner as he is at every one else. I have even a kind of good will to the man on ordinary occasions, but it enrages me that such a nasty snail should be able to leave his slimy track on such a laurel as that consecrated to your dear father's memory.'[73]

What was Lockhart to do? If he did not publish it, 'the nasty snail' would. If he did, Gell had stipulated that not a word be omitted. According to Gell's letters to Lady Blessington, he did – and one suspects it was no oversight – nothing:

> '[19 Nov. 1833] He has never thanked me for it, nor even acknowledged the receipt of it, nor sent me Sir Walter's works, which he ordered for me with almost the last sentence he uttered that was intelligible. . . .
>
> [22 Jan. 1834] As to Mr L- - -, I fear that he is not good for much, and I am certain he got the work. . . . I kept a copy of it, however, and I will send it to you. There are no remarks except such as tend to explain away and render ridiculous the total want of classical taste and knowledge of the hero, in a situation full of classical recollections, and *which I have added, that I might not seem insensible to its real merits* [italics mine] . . . if the Life is published by the said L- - -, without use and acknowledgement of my papers, the best way will be to sell it to the bookseller, and let it come before the public. . . .
>
> [9 March 1834] Since you wrote me on the 17th of February, you

will have received from Mr Bulwer the MS. of the notes on Sir Walter Scott, and may have, perhaps, disposed of it to some bookseller in London. . . .'[74]

For neglecting to enter into correspondence with this obsequious blackmailer, Lockhart has been damned for discourtesy.

But Gell's noble agent's opinion was apparently not too different from Lockhart's. N.P. Willis, dining at Lady Blessington's the year following, was told by the Countess that 'she had received from Sir William Gell, at Naples, the manuscript of a volume upon the last days of Sir Walter Scott. It was a melancholy chronicle of imbecility, and the book was suppressed.' It was suppressed because Lady Blessington reached a compromise with Lockhart, and then convinced Gell, who charged that the whole project was 'a dull piece of affected piety':

'By no means, however, publish my "Scottiana," as you seem to think that L—— is inclined to behave well about it, though his reasoning is poor and false, and inconclusive, as a history of Rome would be, which finished at the Antonines, or one of Buonaparte which ended at the taking of Berlin.'[75]

If Lockhart succeeded where he might easily have failed, he failed where he might have expected most cooperation. As Mrs Hughes wrote Sophia in the late summer of 1834,

'Considering the deep interest of the subject and the eagerness for knowing all that could be known of your father I have often wondered that there was not a multitude of lives and memoirs published by the ? booksellers: The announcement of *The Life*, of course, prevented any respectable publication; but I certainly did not expect that Hogg with all his obligations to Sir Walter and his family would have acted so impudently and one might say ungratefully. . . . He is so coarse that I am always as much disgusted as pleased with his works and it is like eating a good thing which has a disagreeable strong smell. . . . Can you lend me his Memoir of *your house?*'[76]

The account of Hogg's *Domestic Manners of Sir Walter Scott* is another unpleasant episode in the making of a *Life of Scott* that would command multiple viewpoints and include the mass of available materials. It is also a characteristic episode in the history of the sport of blackening Lockhart's name.

Hogg's daughter Mrs Garden recounts the generous help and encouragement given her father by Lockhart in the winter of 1831–2, the attempts to complete publication of Hogg's *Altrive Tales*, the promotional dinner, Lockhart's encomiastic speeches. She gives Lockhart's letters to Hogg about Scott, and his friendly, solicitous letter of 23 September 1833: 'God knows friends are dropping off so fast into the grave, that we need to think well before we suffer estrangement to arise among those that are left.' She then abruptly announces that, once Scott and Hogg were both dead, Lockhart of the 'scorpion pen' showed his true feelings and became 'not only the enemy but the virulent detractor of Hogg's good name' . . . 'without', she proclaims, 'any apparent cause'.[77] The cause is not apparent because she chooses to ignore it. It has been fully defined since and remains one of Lockhart's chief diplomatic failures in the making of the *Life*. As a tactless, vain, mildly entertaining book, it became one of the early publications which gave Lockhart additional cause for candour.

Hogg fell into company less scrupulous than Gell's. Hogg justifies his behaviour to Lockhart:

'Now you must know that from a jocular hint given in one of my *reminiscences*, I was applied to in all quarters even from a place called Albion [Albany] in America for something original [in] anecdotes about Sir Walter. I refused them all saying to every one of them, "If I can furnish anything original about him it must be to my friend Lockhart his legitimate biographer!"'

He claims Cochrane and McCrone, the London publishers, deceived him into the belief that Lockhart had said he had an overabundance of materials and approved of Hogg's helping McCrone. Even then, he stipulated that Lockhart see and edit the MS, but he concedes the naiveté of the stipulation and fears that McCrone has already made and will use a copy of his reminiscences. He is deeply hurt by Lockhart's contemptuous remarks about him and his MS to Cochrane and McCrone, who had, of course, everything to gain by exaggerating all such remarks to Hogg and thereby causing a complete rift.[78]

Lockhart's answer is eloquent in its friendly wrath. It portrays Lockhart at the business of trying to suppress irresponsible Scottiana. He recounts the interview with McCrone at which Hogg's manuscript was produced:

'I confess I was exceedingly hurt and angry not that you should have sent him such a M.S. – no – but that you should have sent it to them *unseen by me*. For I well knew that altho' you had always loved and respected Sir W. you could not write so many pages about him without saying things that would give pain to his children, and I

strongly suspected that, tho' on my representation, you would willingly strike out any offending passages, he would have made a copy for himself, and that some day or other all would be out. Did I not judge aright? You confess that he has made such a copy, and that you have no doubt all you wrote will be published, after *you are gone* – aye, after you are gone – after you can suffer nothing from my answer – Perhaps after I and all that could have answered you are gone also! – I cast my eye hastily over the M.S. and the first thing I lighted on was your statement about Lady Scott and opium! and then indeed I was wroth and abused you heartily. I said the next thing would be to get Sir Walter's valet and explain the secret history of his toilette. I felt that you had permitted yourself to put before the public a statement which would cause misery to my wife and her sister, and I perceived that there was no remedy – that it would be worse ten years hence than now. . . . On reading afterwards your M.S. I declined giving this man any opinion of its contents. They seem to me very unworthy of the subject and of the writer – And they contain among other things, several gross misstatements as to matter of fact – one of them what must be a mere dream of yours, and which directly impeaches the personal veracity of Sir W. Scott. . . . Is it thus that James Hogg talks *now* of Sir W. Scott – what would he have said had he been so charged in his lifetime by any man?'
The conclusion of this expression of his 'true feelings' – which Mrs Garden implied he kept hidden during Hogg's lifetime – is conciliatory. [79]

As far as Lockhart was concerned, this ended it, and six months later Hogg was writing for the money collected for the *Tales*, Lockhart answering with the friendly solicitous letter of September 1833, already quoted. Lockhart had taken seriously the assertion with which Hogg's earlier letter closed: 'The work as far as I am concerned is cancelled.' [80] Three months later, Hogg could not 'resist complying' with the request of S. DeWitt Bloodgood of Albany, NY, described Lockhart's 'violent rage at my intrusion on his sphere', and enclosed the MS, with permission to 'publish it in what shape or form or as many shapes and forms as you like'. He urged that sheets be forwarded to Cochrane to secure the British copyright to Hogg. Bloodgood brought out *Familiar Anecdotes of Sir Walter Scott* in the spring of 1834; it appeared that summer in England, and then Lockhart gave up and wrote Blackwood (18 August 1834):

'In Wilson's hands the Shepherd will always be delightful – but of the fellow himself I can scarcely express my contemptuous pity, now that his Life of Sir W. Scott is before the world. I believe it will however do Hogg more serious and lasting mischief than any of those whose feelings he has done his brutal best to lacerate wd wish to be the result. He has drawn his own character, not that of his benevolent *creator* and handed himself down to posterity – for the subject will keep this from being forgotten – as a mean blasphemer against all magnanimity.'[81]

The subject has kept Hogg's book alive, but the rest of the prediction has backfired. The book remains one more testament to the dark malevolence of Lockhart for those who trace every misunderstanding to this source. They read in the conclusion of *The Life* the stern reference to Hogg's death – 'it had been better for his fame had his end been of earlier date, for he did not follow his best benefactor until he had insulted his dust' – and ignore the gentler criticism of the rest: '*In pace requiescat.* There will never be such an Ettrick Shepherd again' [x, 225; III, 81].[82]

It was clearly not jealousy on Lockhart's part. Hogg concedes as much when he cites his precedents: 'I thought when Cunningham and Chambers had both given sketches of his life and character one who was a thousand times oftener in his company than them both should have as good a right'; two years later he could have added R. P. Gillies to his list.[83] Over Chambers, publishing a short life in his own *Journal*, Lockhart had no control. But what of Cunningham, publishing in the *Athenaeum*, or Gillies, who had turned often to Scott and Lockhart for help, in *Fraser's*? It is inconceivable that Maginn would have published Gillies' *Recollections* without Lockhart's blessing – note his flaying of Hogg.[84] And since Cunningham used materials which appear in expanded form as his contributions to Lockhart's *Life*, one suspects that the *Athenaeum* sketch had the cooperation of the other biographer to whom Cunningham refers:

'The task of truly delineating his life and genius requires an abler pen than mine, and the world need not be told, that such is to be found in the poet's own household. I shall content myself, therefore, with throwing hastily together such notices of his life and writings, as I think will be acceptable, till something worthier can be done.'[85]

One wonders whether Gillies received help in a tangible form. His footnote on Ballantyne, Hogg, and Scott's illness[86] suggests that Gillies had seen the Ballantyne memoranda or that Lockhart had edited his proofs. In either case, such cooperation repudiates Hogg's claim of jealousy.

But such materials in print increased the probability of others, and this encouraged candour in Lockhart. As Morritt says,

'Like you I would leave nothing unsaid that can be disadvantage- ously told by others, and I think you have not, but that you have often introduced such details very gracefully with a short expression of your own consciousness that they were only necessary for the im- perfect or impertinent versions already current.'[87]

A good example is the treatment of the anecdote concerning Mrs Scott and Jeffrey's criticism of *Marmion*. Cunningham prints an extreme version:

'Jeffrey, who, perhaps had not been consulted before publication, wrote a review at once bitter and complimentary, and it is said had the hardihood to carry the proof-sheets to Scott's dinner-table, and lay them before him. The poet, acting upon his own maxim of forbearance and gentleness, read the article, and saying 'Very well – very well,' returned it to the author. The poet's wife snatched it out of his hand, and glancing over it, exclaimed, "I wonder at your boldness in writing such a thing, and more at your hardihood in bringing it to this table!"' [p. 644].

Lockhart's apology for including the incident is characteristic: 'it has been printed already in an exaggerated shape, so I thought it as well to present the edition which I have derived from the lips of all the three persons concerned.' His version is at once more restrained and more idiomatic:

'[Mrs Scott] behaved herself with exemplary civility during the dinner; but could not help saying, in her broken English, when her guest was departing, "Well, good-night, Mr Jeffrey – dey tell me you have abused Scott in de Review, and I hope Mr Constable has paid *you* very well for writing it."' [III, 47]

Lady Scott's foreign accent calls to mind another rumour Lockhart could not ignore. Hogg asks, in coarse whimsy,

'Who was Lady Scott originally? I really wish anybody would tell me, for surely somebody must know. There is a veil of mystery hung over that dear lady's birth and parentage, which I have been unable to see through or lift up; and there have been more lies told to me about it, and even published in all the papers of Britain, by those who *ought* to have known, than ever was told about those of any woman that ever was born. I have, however, a few cogent reasons for believing that the present Sir Walter's grandfather was a nobleman of very high rank.'[88]

Chambers seems mainly responsible for suggesting the liaison between Lady Scott's mother and Lord Downshire, her children's British guardian. But not until Carswell recalled the rumour in 1930 were scholars impelled to seek the means of refutation.[89] Is the matter really closed by the discovery that Mme Charpentier's children were baptized as legitimate at Lyons in 1770 and 1772? Grierson and Corson conclude so. But Lockhart himself unwittingly complicated the evidence. Grierson can understand 'why Lockhart in part suppressed it, in part disguised it by a few attractive but misleading references to the French Revolution and aristocratic *émigrés*'. Corson notices Lockhart's 1848 footnote justifying his own earlier reticence; in it, he reports, Lockhart 'was content to state that no member of Scott's family had ever believed that Lady Scott and her brother were the children of Lord Downshire'. Lockhart amplified this assertion, however. His footnote concludes:

> 'Lady Scott always kept hanging by her bedside, and repeatedly kissed in her dying moments, a miniature of her father which is now in my hands . . . – I am assured the features have no resemblance to Lord Downshire or any of the Hill family.'

Either Lady Scott's attention was divided, or the man of the miniature was the man of her final words. The man is identified by Anne in a letter to Sophia; the MS. is unmistakable: 'Johnnie was amongst the last she mentioned at least I heard his name though I cd not make out the words also her father Ld Downshire.' The term might seem merely an affectionate reference to a kind guardian, were it not for Lockhart's extended footnote.[90]

Also unsuccessful was Lockhart's attempt to include with delicacy the story of Scott's early romance. For the attempt, another early Life was primarily responsible – a book based upon Cunningham, Chambers, and much original research. It was the important, ill-proportioned *Life of Sir Walter Scott* ascribed to George Allan but planned and begun by William Weir.[91] I have found no reference by Lockhart to the book outside of his simple acknowledgement in the *Life*. Lockhart might be supposed hostile to Weir's principal category of witnesses: an old nurse who must be trusted because she relates fifty-year-old recollections with such simplicity and minuteness; a servant who was ten years old in 1796 when he took his walking excursions with Scott; Edinburgh ladies with a grudge against Sir Walter.[92] Moreover, Weir wrote of Scottish law and Scott's Toryism from the perspective of an extreme Whig or Radical.[93] Finally, his mode of biography was one Lockhart rejected: the 'philosophical' Life, the abstract study in the history of mind replete with general conjectures, themes abstractly stated and then illustrated with anecdotes in purely expository form.[94]

In spite of the antagonism he must have felt, Lockhart had the book, and used it, at least to the extent of cutting out passages of Jeffrey's reviews to paste into his own manuscript. But there are more significant connections. For one thing, Weir anticipated Lockhart in some of his authorities – Cunningham, Chambers, a source close to the Ballantynes, old Shortreed and his account of the border 'raids', and, directly or indirectly, William Laidlaw. For another, materials of interest were supplied by Weir himself, and, though I think Corson implies a greater debt than really existed,[95] Lockhart made more use than he acknow-ledged. Allan (Weir) is cited only once, in reference to the 'brother apprentice' who was shown Scott's M S poem on the conquest of Granada. But the 'thunderstorm' incident in Scott's childhood may well have been adapted from Weir: 'there is a story,' says Lockhart.[96] The account of the murder of great-aunt Margaret Swinton is suggestively similar in wording [I, 113] ; the straightforward rejection of 'a story which I have seen in print, about his partaking in the dancing lessons of his brothers' [I, 124] is a direct challenge of Weir's veracity. The report of Scott's unwillingness to work at his apprenticeship and his playing surreptiti-ous chess with an office mate, concealing 'the board with precipitation when the old gentleman's footsteps were heard on the staircase' [I, 158], is accepted by Lockhart as plausible, and attributed to 'more than one of his biographers'. Its most specific source is Weir's anecdote. Weir records that the players 'were frequently interrupted by the in-opportune entrance of the old gentleman; when pop, crash, down went the chess-board and men into the desk, and the two delinquents assumed as grave and business-like deportment as their trepidation would admit of'.[97] Finally, Weir's account of Scott's futile love for Wilhelmina Belsches caused Lockhart to attend to the Greenmantle circumstances. He admits as much in his Preface, forestalling the charge that he was 'trenching upon delicacy':

'I should have been inclined, for many reasons, to omit them; but

o

the choice was, in fact, not left to me, – for they had been mentioned, and misrepresented, in various preceding sketches of the Life which I had undertaken to illustrate . . . after all, there was nothing to disclose that could have attached blame to any of the parties concerned.' [I, x]

Lockhart's attitude toward this and other innocent, but delicate matters is strikingly manifest in a much worked-over page in the proofs [I, 158]. The passage refers to Scott's correspondence with young Charles Kerr (Lockhart never names him):

I regret, that from the delicate nature of the transactions ~~on which his young friend~~ ✗ *the young friend not alluded to in the preceding sentence – which is required as the antecedent to this allusion*

dwelt upon in the earlier of these

~~chiefly dwells~~ in the earliest part of this correspondence, I dare not produce any detailed specimens of it – probably when another generation shall have passed away, and the names which I could not transcribe without awakening painful feelings have come to be mere syllables, the world may be gratified with an intelligible summary at least of a very strange and romantic history. I now allude to those letters (the answers to which, I fear, have ~~all perished) simply because I wish to~~ record the strong impression they have left on my own mind of high generosity of affection, coupled with calm judgment . . . ~~Indeed I would not alluded to them at all, but that I feel it my duty.~~

~~dwelt upon in these~~ *communication*

I dare not ~~quote them~~ *make a free use of them, But I feel it my duty*

The influences on Lockhart were many. But the responsibility and the achievement were ultimately his. A most misleading feature of the case made against him is that historians have taken the charges of Cook, Grierson, and Parker, even the partial exoneration offered by Principal Tait,[98] and simplified them into superficial, unqualified rejections of Lockhart's *responsibility* as a biographer. They equate an unscholarly handling of documents with biographical dishonesty, confusing the ethical issue with what was, for a biographer profoundly aware of the ethical implications of his role, simply a matter of raw materials. For such they were to Lockhart and his contemporaries; and as such, they were to be 'compiled' into an organic narrative. It is the purpose of what follows to demonstrate that Lockhart's use of his 'raw materials' was largely dictated by formal demands; that excisions, compressions, relocations, 'contaminations' – these and other 'sins' were seldom intended to distort or mislead, but were generally means for realizing Lockhart's aim: to make the materials tell their own story, paint their own picture, trace their own evolution, and even convey their own judgement.

III. THE FORMING OF A *Life*

Memoirs of the Life of Sir Walter Scott seems largely a string of letters and journal extracts until one counts pages. Since Lockhart minimized his own contribution, one is surprised to find that correspondence, autobiographical fragment, diary, and Journal comprise just half of the finished work. The most abundant materials, Scott's letters, make up just over a fourth. Lockhart is responsible for the notion that the work is overwhelmingly autobiographical: it is his aim 'to lay before the reader those parts of Sir Walter's character to which we have access, as they were indicated in his sayings and doings through the long series of his years' [x, 198]. The book 'will well deserve to be called his own book, not mine'. He calls the *Life* 'this compilation of his private correspondence' [v, 56] and speaks of 'the copious and candid correspondence from which it has been throughout my object to extract and combine the scattered fragments of an autobiography' [vii, 28]. Hence, it is natural to look first at the use made of these most abundant materials.

Before such an analysis can be meaningful, we must notice what correspondence he had and did not have. He did not, it appears, have Scott's letters to his wife, although he had a few pre-marital letters from Charlotte. As a result, Charlotte remains a dim figure until the poignancy of the Journal at the time of her death brings her to vivid life. The same would be true of Scott's dearest friend, Erskine, whose papers had been destroyed, were it not for Lockhart's own sensitive portrait of the man; but as part of a central correspondence in Scott's life, he scarcely exists. Skene appears in his own memoirs and in the Journal; but he too lacks dimension because, as Scott observes, they had held 'firmly established' their 'habits of non-correspondence'.[99] The abundance of 'Abbotsford copies' of letters to fellow antiquarians such as Rose, Heber, Surtees, and Percy suggests, when we note Lockhart's use of the voluminous Ellis correspondence, that for reasons of form and interest, Lockhart had to cut and eventually terminate his account of Scott's sustained antiquarianism. The *Life* suggests Lockhart did not have access to the correspondence with Lady Abercorn. A single reference hints otherwise: 'As early as 1803 I find him writing to the Marchioness of Abercorn' [III, 185]. Why were these letters not used? Grierson discounts the idea of a flirtation, and the letters themselves supply more obvious reasons: their concern with noble influence exerted on Scott's behalf and with the imprudent stewardship of his brother Tom, for example. The flirtatious correspondence with Lady Anne Hamilton Lockhart may not have seen. [100] It is clear from the pamphlet aftermath that he did not have all the Ballantyne correspondence, and, most serious for its effect on interpretation, he did not have the Constable correspondence.

Among the available correspondents, certain influential figures stand out. What is more, each of these correspondents was peculiarly appropriate to an epoch of Scott's life, and served to dramatize a distinct facet of his personality. As Lockhart recognized, Scott the letter-writer possessed an 'instinctive courtesy with which he uniformly adopted, in conversation, a strain the most likely to fall in with the habits of any companion' [III, 312]. The affectionate, playful pomposity of the young man is sketched in the few letters to his aunt Christie Rutherford and Will Clerk. The young married advocate, the 'Shirra', the amateur antiquarian, is illustrated by the Ellis series. A rather self-conscious *litterateur* is drawn into correspondence with the aging Swan of Lichfield, or shows himself in the long letters to Southey. Providentially, as the Ellis series wanes, two new and most valuable acquaintances are made, followed shortly by a third: Joanna Baillie, Morritt, and the actor-manager Daniel Terry. Each evoked in Scott a different tone within a single tonal range. The first two belong predominantly to the years of his most exuberant literary energy, the years of *Waverley*, *Guy Mannering*, *Rob Roy*, and the *Tales of my Landlord*. Later, appropriately, it is the man of the theatre who, as fellow-speculator in doomed financial projects and as agent for the chivalric adornment of Abbotsford, becomes central. He is joined by two new figures – two new epistolary *personae* of Scott – and a related third. First there is the head of the family to whom Scott bore quasi-feudal allegiance, the deceased Duke of Buccleuch's brother Lord Montagu. Second there is the young Hussar, Walter, the elder son who was to inherit the border barony. The third is one through whose mild epistolary presence Scott appears most amiable in his baronial role of benevolent landlord – his devoted steward and amanuensis Laidlaw. A significant pattern of relationships emerges, focusing on Abbotsford. Minor figures in the correspondence assume lesser roles in such patterns.

The uses of this many-voiced correspondence are various. In a narrative structure the most obvious function is narrative: the letters are Scott's accounts of the events in his life. Occasionally Lockhart arranges letters in a simple chronological series to fill out the narrative of a year or a season. More generally, however, he conceives of the letters as illustrative materials, and several major uses derive from this conception.

As in the *Burns*, Lockhart's division of his narrative is not into simple chronological units, but rather into periods or phases characterized by major events or interests or locations. Correspondence is frequently selected, edited, and grouped to illustrate 'the usual course of his existence' [v, 259] at a certain time, to give 'a curious picture of the man who was brooding over the first chapters of the Bride of Lammermoor' [v, 335], to show 'what his feelings were while this affair continued under agitation' [III, 205], to 'give us amusing sketches of his buoyant spirits at this period of gigantic exertion' [v, 6] – in short, to illustrate a complex of interest and activity together with the predominant tone of mind and emotion at a certain period. The result has been well described by John Rycenga as 'a kind of epistolary mosaic in illustration of a complex series of events or personal attitudes'.[101] Occasionally the period is focused on a single event – the appearance of the *Lay*, the finding of the Scottish regalia, the first abdication of Napoleon, or the death of Scott's mother. At such points, chronological order is sacrificed to portray intensively Scott's evolving awareness of the particular event. Most important, letters are selected and arranged to illustrate the relationships which made up Scott's life as a social being and determined the various roles of his active personality, to display the personality in a variety of situations and contexts until the reader, says Lockhart, will be

'much better acquainted with the man than he could have been before he took up this compilation of his private correspondence . . .; and a thousand little turns and circumstances which may have, when he originally read the book, passed lightly before his eye, will now, I venture to say, possess a warm and vivid interest, as inimitably characteristic of a departed friend.' [v, 56-57]

But how are such repetitious, haphazardly formed documents to be made to serve such functions? The modern biographer's answer would be simple: extract and paraphrase. In the early nineteenth century, we recall, the letter was prized as a whole, a manifest integrity complete with dramatic elements such as salutation and farewell, and in the original voice. While removing repetitious elements, the biographer had still to keep a remnant coherent within itself. If the narrative was to depend on a letter in sequence, then the letter might have to be reorganized to yield up proper transitions. If it contained transitional allusions mystifying in themselves, these were better edited out than needlessly, diffusely explicated. If a letter gave minor anticipation of the topic of a later narrative unit, the passage were best held over for use as part of a subsequent text. If the biographer was blessed with several letters on a single topic, all of the criteria so far implied could be brought to bear on the selection of one. If, however, he found a single topic diffused among several letters, each repetitious or tangential, he could, without violating the dramatic or tonal integrity of any one, compile pertinent extracts into a single text. To the biographer for whom the letter was not an inviolate documentary fact, but an ephemeral, ambiguous expression of its personal origin, the letter was a flexible unit in the rhetoric of biographical recreation. He knew that a letter could be a deceptive piece of evidence; that a letter addressed to an irrevocable other consciousness within the dynamic of a unique relationship, might well mislead if left unedited. It is irrelevant to accuse such a biographer of textual dishonesty; his loyalty was to the personality behind the document and to the milieu which preserved his image and supplied the impulse for its preservation.

This hypothetical sketch will help to explain the treatment of such a correspondence as that of Scott with the Ballantynes in 1813. On the one hand are those like Maria Edgeworth who cry, 'Give us none of these sordid accounts! We want the essential artist.'[102] On the other are those who criticize every omission of financial detail, or, more moderate, argue – as I would – that an honest illustration of Scott's consciousness in the summer of 1813 is impossible without an abundant representation of these epistolary pleas and reassurances and cries for help and demands for candour. Lockhart's is a feasible compromise. Some selection is necessary, and Lockhart has chosen to sacrifice specific terms and figures in order to include a variety of letters and notes conveying the shifting tone of the conflict and the variety of Scott's moods and attitudes. If one letter or passage of specific calculations is omitted, reference to those calculations is omitted elsewhere. Because references to the Drumlanrig postal service are insignificant, Lockhart avoids them, compressing the letter of 31 July [IV, 80-81] – actually written on two successive days – into one continuous text, which essentially it is.[103] When representing Scott's bargaining with Constable for an unwritten poem, Lockhart had a complex of three letters – two from Scott and one from Constable which crossed Scott's first and caused him to modify already complex terms. The result in Lockhart is an attempt to simplify and combine [IV, 73-74], avoiding inaccuracy by the addition to Scott's letter of the words 'in proportion'. The letter to Terry which follows is mainly intended to urge that tireless agent to look into an auction of ancient armour, but it also gives much advice to Terry the actor. In order that it may better fit the context, the letter is cut and compressed to focus on the current financial contrivances by which the purchase money for armour is to be supplied.[104]

The 1813 letters are edited to provide narrative coherence and clarity of emphasis. A fuller analysis of the uses made of the Ellis correspondence will reveal the same methods and aims. The analysis is made difficult by the editorial misfortunes of Grierson and his assistants,[105] but enough is clear to illustrate most of Lockhart's editorial techniques. His main purpose is evident in his introduction of the first series of extracts:

'I must not swell these pages by transcribing the entire correspondence of Scott and Ellis, the greater part of which consists of minute antiquarian discussion which could hardly interest the general reader; but I shall give such extracts as seem to throw light on Scott's personal history during this period.' [II, 56]

The principles of selection and omission follow. Extended comment and conjecture on ballad-collecting, Ritson, *Tristrem*, Leyden, 'Scoto-Celtick Bards', Merlin's Scottish genesis, and True Thomas are cut. What remains is ample for the purpose summarized at the close:

'The passages which I have transcribed appear sufficient to give the reader a distinct notion of the tenor of Scott's life while his first considerable work was in progress through the press. In fact, they place before us in a vivid light the chief features of a character which, by this time, was completely formed and settled.' [II, 67]

The letter of 25 May 1803 will illustrate the rearrangement of a text for narrative coherence. The letter follows Scott's return from London and Oxford and is introduced by Lockhart as a recollection of Oxford

[II, 109]. In the original [*Letters*, XII, 234], a passage on romances (omitted by Lockhart) precedes the Oxford section of the letter. Following the letter Lockhart discusses Longman's new edition of the *Minstrelsy*; unfortunately, Scott's news of the edition is buried in the middle of his letter. Lockhart's manipulation is purely formal: the Oxford description is moved to the opening and the news of the *Minstrelsy* to the close. Minor revisions support and clarify the changes already made. The opening of the Oxford section is replaced by Lockhart's own introduction; since the next sentence depends on a removed antecedent, 'Heber's' is substituted for 'his'. Since the discussion of romances is cut, its closing transcription is, too, and what follows is syntactically adjusted by an added expletive: '~~And now my dear Sir having done the needful let me tell you how~~ often [do] Charlotte and I think of the little paradise at Sunning Hill.' Innumerable similar reorganizations for strictly formal ends are found elsewhere in the Life; for one simple example, in the letter to Morritt of 16 May 1816, preceding Lockhart's discussion of *The Antiquary*, the paragraph on that novel is moved from the middle of a long letter to the end [V, 126].

The same letter to Morritt illustrates another aim – one Morritt himself had mentioned: the avoidance of repetition. Scott had mentioned five months earlier the 'declining health of my elder brother, Major Scott' [V, 113], and observed then that, although the brothers had enjoyed no intimacy, Scott was saddened by his decline. The letter of 16 May reports the Major's death and adds the same comment. To avoid repetition Lockhart has chosen the later version and the more moving occasion as more appropriate and cut the reflection from the earlier letter. Reporting to Ellis the death of his uncle Robert Scott – and characteristically Lockhart moves the comment on the loss to a position following the portrayal of the man – Scott adds a description of Rosebank, the Tweedside villa his uncle had left him [II, 160]. Two months later, recounting the sale of Rosebank, he gives the same description [*Letters*, XII, 258, 263]. Lockhart recognizes the earlier as the appropriate context and cuts the second description. Often what seem editorial reticences turn out to be simply cuts to avoid repetition, and essentially the same passages appear in later texts. The account of Scott's dinner with the Princess of Wales, 'a most fascinating woman', cut from the letter to Ellis of 3 March 1806, reappears in the letter of 7 April printed by Lockhart [*Letters*, XII, 281].

Excisions are prompted also by a desire for compression and focus, for the avoidance of unimportant or irrelevant topics. The letter in which Scott speculates on the editing of ancient Welsh poems and inquires into Ellis's editing of the Mabinogion [II, 179] has its antiquarian abundance pruned to permit focus on the just-published *Lay of the Last Minstrel* [*Letters*, XII, 270]. Unity of mood and subject is achieved when, from the letter conveying the 'cursed news' of Napoleon's advance in Spain [III, 139], Lockhart cuts the good news of Leyden in India [*Letters*, XII, 308]. Occasionally such compressions prevent premature introduction of subjects or events to be emphasized later. In each case Lockhart seems to have decided whether the subject warrants postponement. If not, he leaves the passage intact and risks digression. An example is the inclusion of letters on the laureateship in 1813, where he explains, 'To avoid returning to the affair of the laureateship, I have placed together such letters concerning it as appeared important' [IV, 105]. Or the allusion to the Countess Purgstall: 'As I may have no occasion hereafter to allude to the early friend . . . I may take this opportunity', and so on [VI, 372]. If postponement seems warranted, he omits the allusion. A notable example is the reference to the purchase of Abbotsford in the letter to Morritt of 1 July 1811 [III, 278]. The letter is occupied with two other subjects – *Don Roderick* and the death of Lord Melville. An initial allusion to Tweedside lairdship can only confuse the narrative and diffuse all emphasis [*Letters*, II, 507]. Lockhart cuts the passage, concludes his chapter with the subject of *Don Roderick's* publication, and opens a new chapter with the chronologically prior land question.

Such devices for narrative organization would scarcely evoke criticism today if Lockhart were not judged as an editor of letters and if he or his publisher had not violated the later convention of signifying every textual omission and emendation. Less easily accepted is another, more extreme editorial device utilized for the same ends. Also manifest in the Ellis correspondence, it is the device of amalgamating or telescoping extracts from separate letters into ostensibly single documents. Though not used generally throughout the *Life*, it proves a useful means of incorporating bits and pieces of otherwise insignificant or irrelevant letters. A simple illustration is the letter to Ellis of 19 May 1804, in which Scott describes his new situation at Ashestiel and urges the Ellises to come north for a visit [II, 158]. What appears to be a unified, coherent letter with indicated omissions is a descriptive portion of a letter written in March, followed by a continuation of the description which is the termination of the original 19 May letter, concluding with a portion of a letter of 4 May [*Letters*, XII, 243]. A similar instance clearly reveals the formal purpose of such contamination. In the narrative of the late summer of 1805, extracts from two letters – one written 17 October, the other 20 July – are combined as two parts of a single undated letter to follow a quote from a note to Ballantyne of 5 September [II, 212]! The note reports: 'I have had a visit from Rees yesterday.' The extract to Ellis begins: 'I have had booksellers here in the plural number. You have set little Rees's head agog.' The extract which Lockhart adds to this – 'I am interrupted by the arrival of two *gentil bachelors*, whom, like the Count of Artois, I must despatch upon some adventure till dinner time' – refers to a similar situation, but actually has no connection with the principal content of the previous extract. It fits neatly and supplies a brief, amusing sketch of one aspect of the Scotts' rural situation. Such 'telescopic' augmentation has no effect on meaning, but fabricates a single 'letter' which serves a fuller, more varied illustrative purpose.

But we note the narrative transition that follows and realize the dangers: 'Already, then,' says Lockhart, 'he was seriously at work on Dryden.' When? 'During the same summer'? The allusion to Dryden is from the 17 October extract. There is no motive here for deception. Throughout his narrative, Lockhart simply reveals an unconcern with exact dating: his aim, rather, is the organizing of period sketches, self-defining durations of experience, into a unified narrative. Superficially, his pattern seems annalistic; actually, a complex narrative form is always controlling the chronological inconsistencies and contradictions of life. To one who seeks the significant pattern of Scott's life, this technique of the novelist is invaluable; to the historian, it is unnerving. But there is no art more important in the *Life of Scott* than the flexible control with which Lockhart translates calendar time into the significant form of a temporal progress through life.

The risk at its most dangerous may be seen in a 'contamination' not recognized in the Grierson edition. The letter concerns the 'raid' with Leyden which produced 'a complete and perfect copy' of 'Auld Maitland' [II, 86]. Lockhart says merely that they went during the 'autumn vacation'. Actually, the letter which reports the 'Auld Maitland' raid is dated 10 May. The autumn 'grand tour' is described in a letter to Ellis of 17 October in the first person singular; this time Scott went alone while Leyden was expecting momentarily to depart for the East. The passage transferred from this later letter adds only a general description of the risks and hardships encountered in the raids, and to adapt it to the earlier situation Lockhart changed the personal pronouns from singular to plural. When he prints as of 'a few weeks later' other parts of the 17 October letter, he omits the passage already used. Moreover, the later extract dealing with Ritson is augmented by previously unused sentences from the letter of 10 May! The purpose can only be narrative coherence. Yet in the resultant amalgamation two 'raids' are literally made one.

Nothing is more graphically illustrative of Lockhart's conception of his materials as narrative components than this practice of amalgamation. The corrected proofs demonstrate the practice in action. Morritt had complained that the account of the Edinburgh production of Joanna Baillie's *The Family Legend* was too long. In the proofs the long letter of 30 January 1810 is followed by another of 31 January [III, 191], a continuation. The bulk of the continuation has been crossed out, but there remain two separate passages, which survive in the published work as a single 'P.S.' – the letters are written in – to the letter of the 30th. Again, in a later volume of the proof are printed *three* letters from Scott to James Ballantyne, whose purpose is to illustrate the relations of Scott and James, his critic, after the financial disaster. The Ballantyne sympathiser might find grounds for complaint in the excision from the proof of, among other things, Scott's thanks to James for his critical efforts; the fact remains that Lockhart set up the three letters in full. The need to compress, to reduce the mass of separate documents, led him to make careful cuts, and as a result the three letters, their distinguishing openings removed, have become one [VIII, 330].[106]

The correspondence with Ellis had many uses. It was succeeded in Scott's epistolary life by several voluminous correspondences, and with their appearance and growth Lockhart's editorial problems and alternatives increased. The problem of repetitiousness becomes more extreme when Scott writes long letters of almost the same date to Morritt and Terry and Joanna Baillie, or to young Walter and Lord Montagu and Maria Edgeworth. Some of the same solutions obtain; but it is noteworthy that Lockhart's theory allowed no cross-amalgamation, no violation of the individuality of a correspondence. The very abundance did, however, permit means of structural emphasis and variation. When a single event or situation or purpose appeared in similar letters to various correspondents, the compiler interpreted simply by his selection. Or, by grouping a number of letters to diverse correspondents on the same period or event, he could at once give structural emphasis and convey the complexity or intensity of Scott's response.

The first alternative may be illustrated by two examples late in the *Life*. Of the death of his dearest friend William Erskine, at the height of Edinburgh's reception for George IV, Scott speaks in several letters – to Terry, to W. S. Rose, to young Walter, to others in letters not preserved (Lockhart extracts from an untraced letter to an unnamed correspondent), and to Joanna Baillie.[107] For the only full account, Lockhart chose the letter to Joanna [VII, 65]; the choice is subtly appropriate. Erskine, a middle-aged 'man of feeling', a retiring widower, had been linked in scandalous rumour with a married woman. Full investigation proved the charges absurd, but Erskine died, apparently as a result of extreme 'medication' consequent on a nervous breakdown. Writing to an old friend, a poetess of emotional insight yet modest reticence, Scott is explicit enough to answer Lockhart's narrative need, yet restrained in his account of the scandal, and sadly affectionate in tone. The choice of the letter to Joanna gives Lockhart an account which is moderately frank and full, unaffected and yet delicate. On a later occasion Lockhart had a wider choice. Of young Walter's engagement in 1824 to a commercial heiress Scott writes to everyone. His devotion to his new daughter-in-law marks a high point of pride and prosperity. Some of the letters verge on smugness, some on jocular self-congratulation. Many go into detail on the financial settlement; some are severely critical of the mother, the Highland widow of a mercantile dynast, who opposed the match. Lockhart's choice is the letter to Lady Davy – Scott's bluestocking cousin Jane Kerr, late Mrs Apreece, 'a lion-catcher', says Scott, 'I could pit . . . against the world'. Comparison of this account [VII, 317] with those rejected reveals editorial deliberation and tact. Scott was fond of Lady Davy and could be frank with her. Yet he was critical of her own social ambitions and wrote to her of the match with some restraint. Lockhart's choice is made, one feels, for the letter's fullness and for its combination of discretion and whimsical frankness of tone.

Sometimes, rather than choosing a single letter, Lockhart groups overlapping accounts of single occasions; at such times, the choice and arrangement of letters seem dictated as much by Lockhart's sense of tonal counterpoint as by more obvious demands of narrative form. The reader of the *Life* may well wonder why Lockhart thought it necessary to recount the deaths, in a single week, of Scott's aunt, his uncle, and his mother in several lengthy letters giving the same information. He may wonder whether Scott had to be shown responding to the news of Napoleon's first abdication to several correspondents; or describing the raising and adorning of Abbotsford, not just at length to Terry, but at comparable length go others as well. The reader may balk at the lengthy overlapping letters to the Duke of Buccleuch and Joanna Baillie, which cover the same ground covered by 'Paul' in his *Letters to His Kinsfolk*. But Paul himself provides the Walpolian justification for such apparent duplication, and the tonal principle involved is well illustrated in the pair of letters. Compare these excerpts [v, 67, 73] :

'I imagine your Grace about this time to be tolerably well fagged with a hard day on the moors. If the weather has been as propitious as with us, it must be delightful. The country through which we have travelled is most uncommonly fertile, and skirted with beautiful woods; but its present political situation is so very uncommon, that I would give the world your Grace had come over for a fortnight.

Your fancy, my dear friend, will anticipate, better than I can express, the thousand sentiments which arose in my mind from witnessing such a splendid scene, in a spot connected with such various associations.'

To the Duke, as later to Lord Montagu, Scott is the friendly, devoted, but dignified bondsman; to Joanna, 'I am myself a poet, writing to a poetess' [v, 100]. Joanna is, in addition, a maiden-lady and a Whig, and hence letters to her on identical subjects could never actually duplicate letters to Morritt. However full the letter to Joanna, the analogous letter to Morritt will be uniquely valuable in its own way. Morritt was another country squire, a Tory M P, a close family friend, a classical antiquarian, and a literary consultant who shared the Waverley 'secret'. A glance at the variety of subjects and the ease of masculine intimacy in any one of many letters to Morritt would show their unique values.

In subject-matter the large correspondence with Daniel Terry is far more specialized, but for this reason if for no other it has unique tonal value; its very bulk portrays Scott's obsessive preoccupation. For Terry, the man of the theatre, is ideally cast as aid and confidant in Scott's own greatest spectacle, the building and decking out of the romance in stone by the Tweed. Here, as elsewhere, Lockhart justifies copious use of the correspondence in terms of the relationship it depicts and the dimension it adds to a sympathetic picture of the social Scott. He defines its tone:

'The intelligent zeal with which the actor labored to promote the gratification of the poet's tastes and fancies on the one side: on the other, Scott's warm anxiety for Terry's professional success, the sagacity and hopefulness with which he counsels and cheers him throughout, and the good-natured confidence with which he details his own projects.' [III, 311]

But the relationship has other implications and the correspondence more critical effect when juxtaposed with two other collections, whose use is similarly justified. The correspondents are very different, and Scott is on his dynastic dignity with both Lord Montagu and young Walter. In the late teens and early '20's, as Morritt fades temporarily from the epistolary *Life*, these two predominate with Terry; and the three correspondences combine in tonal effect to show a dignified, paternalistic Scott, an extravagant castle-builder, with no longer the same palliative presence of exuberant creativity. The hubristic rise and tragic fall that form Lockhart's compilation are dramatic effects of this piling up in repetitious abundance of Scott's letters to Terry on the finishing of Abbotsford at the same time he was corresponding most extensively with Montagu and 'Cornet Scott' and reaching his social zenith as Scotland's chief host for the King. Lockhart concedes that the Terry letters have, 'as many readers may think, rather too much of the "new bigging" and "the rigging o't"'; but he 'cannot consent to curtail such characteristic records' [VII, 88]. And the effect of such emphatic repetition and tonal juxtaposition is striking, especially since the narrative then moves with comparative rapidity through 1823 to a climax of dynastic glory at the completed Abbotsford of 1824 and 1825, followed by dark threats, mysterious concealments, and disaster.

But simultaneously there appears and prevails a very different type of document, and, as a result, a profoundly different Scott. We must consider Lockhart's uses of this new type of material before we can recognize his larger pattern.

The biographical providence that guided Scott in his choice of correspondents gave him his glimpse of Byron's journal at the turning-point of his fortunes.[108] Scott's 'Gurnal' commenced at the moment when his social roles were curtailed or compromised by financial exposure and ruin, and when the shattering of dynastic dreams forced him in upon himself. The coincidence is the kind of 'accident' which makes the biographer simultaneously thrill and despair. Moreover, the Byron transcript reached Scott as a direct result of the Murray-Lockhart connection, which took away Scott's closest literary consultant and simultaneously gave him the most valuable of his latest correspondents – both in the person of his biographizing son-in-law.

The 'Gurnal' accounts for only two-thirds of the explicitly autobiographical records Lockhart included. But the others are significantly different in kind. Of the first, the Ashestiel Fragment, we need only glance at the defiant reticence of its opening to realize the degree to which Scott himself had accepted a radically different ethic of self-exposure by the time he undertook a minutely circumstantial journal which he knew would be published. Whatever its virtues, the earlier account is formal and thin; one need only glance through Lockhart's 'illustrations' of the same period (1771–92) to realize its thinness.

Of Lockhart's use of the fragment, nothing beyond the obvious structural observations can be made, for the MS has temporarily disappeared. But the structural facts are meaningful. One wonders whether Lockhart thought of the document simply as a first-hand account of Scott's early years, or valued it equally as a revelation of the author in 1808 (when it was written), a portrayal of the poet of *Marmion* and of the British resistance to Napoleon. Certainly the juxtaposition of the cheerful, self-assured *persona* of the fragment with the manifestly later, sadder viewpoint dominant in the illustrative chapters creates a striking complexity of moods and perspectives.[109] Lockhart recognized this. He kept the tonal distinction by preserving the fragment intact and throwing his own additions and comments into separate chapters: 'This procedure has been attended with many obvious disadvantages; but I greatly preferred it to printing the precious fragment in an Appendix' [I, x]. To understand why, we need only recall the controversy which raged at the time, the critical warfare over Croker's Boswell and specifically the charge that, by interweaving other Johnsoniana, Croker had destroyed the personal integrity of Boswell's book.

But it is reminiscent of Croker's procedures – indeed, it recalls a procedure recommended by Lockhart – that Lockhart should include intact his second major document, the 1814 Diary. This is a record of a very distinct kind. The Ashestiel memoir is the result of the retrospective autobiographer's own proportion and selection. The printing intact of a two-month travel journal challenges proportion in the same way Croker challenged proportion when he included Boswell's Hebrides journal. But there are differences. Boswell's journal was already in print; Scott's had been printed only in brief extract. Boswell's was a preliminary picture of his subject on which he himself subsequently enlarged; Scott's was an extended, unconscious self-revelation.

It was as such that Lockhart defended its inclusion against the criticism that was sure to come. Wordsworth's opinion is representative: 'In your P. S. you allude to the length of the work as having been objected to, and I hope you will not be hurt when I say, that I have been somewhat of the same opinion. The Diary of his northern voyage ought, I think, to have been printed apart from the life'.[110] Lockhart's remarks in justification, which open and close the transcript, identify the criteria for inclusion. The Diary affords 'a complete and artless portraiture of the man, as he was in himself, and as he mingled with his friends and companions, at one of the most interesting periods of his life' [IV, 159]. The account dramatically illustrates a variety of 'characters' or roles:

'We have before us, according to the scene and occasion, the poet, the antiquary, the magistrate, the planter, and the agriculturist; but everywhere the warm yet sagacious philanthropist – everywhere the courtesy, based on the unselfishness, of the thorough-bred gentleman; – and surely never was the tenderness of a manly heart portrayed more touchingly than in the closing pages.' [IV, 325]

Hence, though the trip itself is of little narrative significance, the occasions it provides are as valuable dramatically as the situations Boswell was often forced to contrive for the display of his subject.

Allowing such a document to speak for itself, Lockhart exercised editorial control as he had with the letters. Davidson Cook, who has voiced the loudest lamentations over Lockhart's 'manipulations', has seen the 'five little paper books':

'it becomes my duty to report that Lockhart's text of the Diary is as unreliable as his treatment of the letters . . . that Lockhart instead of giving a faithful rendering of Scott's manuscript garbled the text and paid scant reverence to its authority.'

He cites, in addition to the prejudicial charge of 'mangling' or 'garbling', the sin of omission, such as in the cuts bracketed below:

'The keeper [here] is an old man-of-war's man, of whom Mr Stevenson observed that he was a great swearer when first he came [to the situation] but after a year or two of residence in this solitary abode became a changed man. [He has been many years here.] There are about fifty herd of cattle on the island [belonging to Lord Dundas's tenant].'

One hesitates on the basis of the evidence he gives to accept his condemnatory conclusions. No doubt his evidence is characteristic. But one finds hardly relevant the implication that 'despite his promise Lockhart could not resist the temptation to edit', that what was deliberate editorial procedure should be seen merely as an irresistible licentious impulse in a jaded editor. Finally, one's doubts are turned to complete uncertainty by Cook's concluding admission and conjecture:

'A portion of the Diary was printed in Forget-me-Not for 1826. The text in this annual is on the whole more in agreement with what Lockhart printed eleven years later than with Scott's manuscript, and must therefore derive from the same contaminated source, which one infers was a much altered copy of the Diary.'[111]

If the inference is valid, then obviously the 'contaminator' of his own Diary was Scott.

Here there is only conjecture. In the case of the great 'Gurnal', the Tait-Parker edition makes conjecture unnecessary. And here Lockhart has found a defender. Principal Tait, whose critical campaign was directed rather against his late-Victorian predecessor as editor, claims that 'Lockhart's departures from the MS are merely intended to smarten the style, and they do not affect the sense. Douglas, believing that he was following Lockhart's editorial methods which he did not understand, made violent and improbable changes' [*Journal*, p. viii]. I am concerned not with stylistic 'improvements', but with Lockhart's uses of the Journal. Yet my argument supposes that while Lockhart's 'editorial methods' were neither essentially dishonest nor irresponsible, they were free and flexible. His theory did allow for correction, for compression which conceals excision by closing over the gaps, and for amalgamation and chronological re-arrangement. Hence, I find Tait's defence as difficult to accept as Cook's condemnation.

Tait implies that errors in Lockhart's version are due to transcribers, and that by the time transcribers had reached March 1826, Lockhart realized he must decipher for himself [*Journal*, p. viii]. If this is true, are we to take his letter to Croker in 1843 as a simple lapse of memory or an attempt to deceive? He begins by ascribing some of the errors to Scott himself:

P

'I suspect every man that keeps a diary falls now and then into the sort of mistakes which you point out. I somewhere or other intimate in Scotts Life that I had discovered such errors of date in many places. . . . In fact, I did not examine into such things very closely unless when the Entry referred to occurrences of some intrinsic importance.'

But there was another source of error – a transcriber of the entire manuscript:

'when I was working at the book I had before me not the original very cramped & illegible MS of Scott but a transcript made by a young person from which I might when I chose clip out a fragment to stick into my page as I went on – & in copying two thick ill-written quartos he might again confound dates occasionally.'[112]

A glance at the facsimile makes clear that a transcriber might well confound more than dates. For example, the revision of 'manner' to 'manners', which incited J. F. Cooper's anger and supplied the basis on which his sympathizers charge Lockhart with malevolent deceit,[113] is easily accounted for in a MS where final *r*'s are indistinguishable from final *s*'s. Transcripts, we recall, did exist; there were in fact three: one for Lockhart's own use, one for Morritt, and one for Milman. It is impossible to measure the influence of Morritt and Milman on minor revisions as well as major excisions. But the proofs of the *Life* do show that on the eve of publication the Journal extracts were still being revised. Much of this late revision in proof consists of cutting, suggesting that Lockhart had acquired a reticence not felt earlier, or that, more probably, he bowed to the reticence of those who were reading his proof.

Of what nature are the excisions, whoever made them? Sufficient evidence of the purely euphemistic impulse to which we would condescend as 'Victorian' is seen in the proof, where some reader has struggled with Scott's term for Harriet Wilson [VIII, 135]: the original 'W- - - -' is there crossed out, as is the substituted 'courtezan', and the second addition 'punk' remains [*Journal*, p. 36]. Prudence of a more practical nature is manifest in the excision or modification of remarks about others: Scott's charges of 'liar' and 'cheat' against the Radical Aberdonian MP Joseph Hume are removed; the already mystifying references to the scandal over Richard Heber's 'unnatural practices' and sudden resignation from Parliament are cut, as are references to the advantageous marriage of Lockhart's neighbour, the painter Francis Grant.[114] Before one concludes, however, that an excision represents bowdlerizing, one must wait to see if the passage appears elsewhere in the Journal in a variant form. Such is the anecdote of the old lady expecting Celtic ravishment at Carlisle in the '45, an anecdote whose first appearance is cut, but whose second version remains [*Journal*, pp. 194, 260].

Of a related yet distinct category are the excisions involving Lockhart himself and the medical history of John Hugh. In such cases Lockhart must have acted from such a mixture of motives – both self-effacement and self-protection – that it is futile to seek specific explanations. And who could say what hand has changed (and for what reason) Scott's entry of 22 January 1826, beginning 'Lockhart would be worth gold just now', from 'but he too *would* be too diffident to speak broad out' to '*might* be too diffident' [*Journal*, p. 76]? Again, who can say what admixture of political prudence to natural reticence and rhetorical reserve causes Lockhart to play down his role as Scott's informal but industrious London gossip in the days of Malachi, the brief Canning power, the Catholic bill, and the struggles over Reform?

These last topics lead to significant alterations. As omissions they affect the presentation of Scott. The proofs show abundant evidence of protecting Whig and Tory alike from the barbs of 'Diarizing Malagrowther', a Malagrowther slower to sweeten and repent than the *Life* suggests. In the process of selective de-emphasis, the Malagrowther that was a real part of Scott is considerably softened [*Journal*, pp. 127-8]. Such editorial softening can be seen fully in later extracts. Scott's political belligerence, his irrational determination to do battle against Reform, resulted in such unpleasantly pathetic episodes as the 'Burke Sir Walter' incident at Jedburgh. The treating of such an episode was part of the discretionary tactic urged by Morritt to conceal Scott's mental deterioration. Lockhart cut the entry at the opening of October 1831, 'I would compound for a little pain instead of this heartless muddiness of mind which renders me incapable of any thing rationalal' [*sic*] [*Journal*, p. 744]. The 'temper' which 'sets strong toward politics, where I would be sure of making a figure' is minimized by excision, as are the entries describing 'slumbrous feelings', the repetitious reference to medical details, the signs of helpless idleness and the deterioration of a strong will. The treatment of the entry for 1 August 1826 illustrates Lockhart's practice of preserving coherence in such extracts. Cuts are bracketed:

'Yesterday evening [did nothing for the *idlesse* of the morning. I was hungry; eat and drank and became drowsy; then] I took to arranging [the] old plays, [of which Terry had brought me about a dozen,] and [dipping into them] scrambled through two.' [*Journal*, p. 209]

The detail of drowsiness after surfeit – Boswell might have kept it – is cut, and this might be judged a culpably protective reticence.

The passage serves to introduce a more common kind of excision. The major cuts exclude matter intelligible only with reference to passages already omitted. The '*idlesse* of the morning' had been described in the omitted entry of the 31st; references to Terry's visit had belonged to other unused entries, and hence references have been cut here. Moreover, the omission of Terry is characteristic of the cuts most frequently noted: of innumerable 'minor characters', of casual social incidents – cuts essential if all focus or unity was not to be buried in the multiplicity of Scott's every day. The majority of excisions of names of dinner guests and visitors and casual encounters serve no other end. But Lockhart saw that one cut leads to many, and he painstakingly removed all later references to eliminated antecedents. The omission of the visit of Count Davidoff in July 1826, for instance, requires subsequent alterations: Lockhart's 'July 2' amalgamates the end of the 2nd and the beginning of the 3rd, and omits 'my young Muscovite' at both ends. The 4th and 5th, containing more about the Count, are also omitted. The opening of the 6th is compressed: 'Returned last night [with my frozen Muscovites to the Capital], and suffered as usual from the incursions of the black-horse' [*Journal*, p. 195]. A more extensive specimen, amalgamating into plausible units worthwhile parts of entries not worth complete inclusion, comes later the same summer. 15 August is cut, and with it the arrival of young Walter and Jane; the 16th is kept and its opening is augmented with 'Walter and Jane arrived last night'. It includes a social call to Huntly Burn, to which, as a natural continuation of situation and mood, Lockhart appends the description of what was actually the *next* evening at Abbotsford, the entry of the 17th being otherwise omitted. Omitted from the 16th is the arrival of 'young Mr Surtees'. Thereafter, Surtees' attendance at various family occasions is carefully excluded, as, on 6 September, is his departure with Charles and Walter. The need for a ponderous annotative apparatus to identify such visitors is thus avoided [*Journal*, pp. 215-25].

Consistency seems the aim in another editorial practice. Scott's internal life in the Journal is a shifting spectacle of moods and impulses, of reflections and contradictions, of the inconsistencies and fluctuations of interior monologue. Lockhart was aware of this texture as a positive value in the Journal; a dominant theme in the *Life* stressed it. Scott's

'Diary shows (what perhaps many of his intimates doubted during his lifetime) that, in spite of the dignified equanimity which characterized all his conversation with mankind, he had his full share of the delicate sensibilities, the mysterious ups and downs, the wayward melancholy, and fantastic sunbeams of the poetical temperament.' [IX, 151]

In illustration Lockhart included entries such as that for 13 May 1827, 'a most idle and dissipated day' [IX, 61]. Yet often, a desire for consistency and coherence has edited this value out of existence. Minor details show the effect. Consider the cut (here bracketed) from 2 March 1826: 'First epistle of *Malachi* [is getting out of print, or rather is] out of print already'; or the correction of the toothache location on 5 April: 'Yesterday every tooth on [the left – no] the right side of my head was absolutely wal[t]zing' [*Journal*, pp. 121, 148]. The omission from the entry of 12 April of three sentences – three hesitant, conflicting turns in a hopeful but uncertain mood – shows the price paid for coherence.[115]

Perhaps the most extended example is the moving entry of 18 December 1825 [*Journal*, p. 45], in which Scott faces his tragedy and recounts its causes and consequences – only to have good news interrupt, throw him temporarily out of a sense of doom into uncertainty, and back again to reflection on the strangeness of his life. As with the correspondence of the same period, Lockhart tried to simplify the prologue of financial disaster, complicated as it was by sanguine computations, by deceptions on all sides, and interwoven with rumours and counter-rumours from London. The entry of the 18th dramatizes the shifting moods of the major participant. After Ballantyne's call, Scott believes unequivocally *Venit illa suprema dies*, and speaks bitterly, candidly, at times defiantly, of the certainty of ruin. But the day brings a counter-rumour that Hurst and Robinson have weathered the storm, and resignation and defiance give way to a weary uncertainty, a quiet astonishment at the inconsistencies of his life and fortunes. If Lockhart's cuts and rearrangements are deceptive, the deception lies principally in his removal of incidental and temporary effects. He

places the essential parts of the long reflection in a consistently conditional mood, removing the extreme self-accusation and despairing
uncertainty of the early parts. The added conditional clause in the
paragraph Lockhart moves to the opening signals the nature of
subsequent modal changes:

'For myself, [if things go badly in London,] the magic wand of
will be   then, faith,
the Unknown ~~is~~ shivered in his grasp. He must ~~henceforth~~ be
will be
termed the Too-well-known. The feast of fancy ~~is~~ over with
He shall
the feeling of independence. ~~I can~~ no longer have the delight
his
of waking in the morning with bright ideas in ~~my~~ mind, haste[n]
to commit them to paper, and count them monthly as the means
of planting such groves, and purchasing such waste[s], replacing
my dreams [of] fiction by other prospective visions of walks by
Fountain heads and pathless groves [;]
Places which pale passion loves.'

The final lines, incidentally, show that Lockhart includes Scott's awareness that 'land was my temptation'. The specific clause, however, together with the later claim that Abbotsford 'has been my Dalilah', is
omitted; and some editorial hand has cut from the proofs Lockhart's
own itemization of her support:

'He had, indeed, paid not much under 40,000 for an estate, which
did not at that time produce a rental of 700; he had expended on his
buildings, woods, and agricultural improvements, probably not less
than 40,000 more; and he had, since the splendid period of Abbotsford and the Novels began, kept open house in the style of a
munificent peer – at the rate, I presume, of about 10,000 per
annum.'[116]

Some of the verisimilitude of a day-by-day journal has been
sacrificed. Formal ends – unity, consistency, coherence – account for
the majority of editorial revisions. But the realizing of these aims
involves interpretation. Selection and rearrangement are frequently
controlled by Lockhart's sense of relative emphasis, and the resultant selective stress on a dominant mood or preoccupation obviously
constitutes editorial interpretation. One important example could be
traced through the Journal extracts almost from beginning to end. I

have remarked on the excision of casual visitors and social occasions, and such omissions are natural. But there is a more significant reason why Lockhart should choose to minimize the trivial, frequently cheerful everyday social business of Scott's journalized life. We noticed that a social Scott predominates in the correspondence. The journal is written to no defined audience; its new personality is a reflective solitary consciousness, and Lockhart has apparently made his selections with this in mind. Scott began journalizing in circumstances which forced an abrupt solitude fostered by ruin and exposure, by the breaking up of the Abbotsford-Chiefswood group, by the death of his wife. The interest of such a document at such a period is recognized by Lockhart:

'But for the revelations of his Diary, it would never have been known to his most intimate friends, or even to his own affectionate children, what struggles it cost him to reach the lofty serenity of mind which was reflected in all his outward conduct and demeanor.' [VIII, 218] Morritt was disturbed by the discrepancy. Referring to a cheerful, optimistic letter from Scott, of 6 February 1826, he wrote in the proof beside Scott's 'The blowing off my hat in a stormy day has given me more uneasiness': 'scarcely in the same tone as Gurnal.' Lockhart's answer in the same margin – 'no nor meant to be represented as such by me J G L' – refers him to the passage quoted above.[117] Given this discrepancy, the most moving peculiarity of the early Journal is Scott's struggle for stoic control over morbid thoughts and sensibilities – over what he recognizes as 'hysterica passio' – which he managed to conceal elsewhere.

Extracting from the 1826 Journal, Lockhart keeps this Scott – the locus of a lonely, inward struggle and of a deepening consciousness – dominant by keeping the long, pathetic entries of the May days following Lady Scott's death, and by cutting passages of the kind I have described throughout the ensuing June. From the 4th he omits a pleasant visit and thus emphasizes the tearful reflections that remain; the 5th and 6th are cut and with them the welcome visits of friends and affectionate relatives; from the 8th he cuts references to business meetings, and leaves sickness and mournful reflection ('gone – gone – forever – ever – ever'); the 10th – a day at court and work – and the 13th – a long record of walks and friendly calls and a satiric sketch of a clerical visitor – are both cut; but the 11th – alluding to bad dreams and a 'widowed bed' – remains. In July, excision has curtailed the impression of a busy social existence. From the 6th he cuts the cheerful visit to Sharpe and Clerk, and dinner out; from the 7th, a visit to Clerk's after dinner; from the 8th, another dinner. The omitted opening paragraph of the 10th reads, 'Slept too long this morning . . . . Terry and J. Ballantyne dined with me yesterday, and I suppose the wassail, though there was little enough of it, had stuck to my pillow.' The Journal for autumn gives the same impression of a varied, sociable season. Lockhart's selection gives an impression which the editorial interpreter felt was not only more valuable and moving, but also, apparently, more true a record of Scott's mind and mood. The same principle operates in later extracts. Cut from 1829 entries are the cheerful social evenings with the Skenes and Will Clerk, whose importance to Scott in these late Edinburgh years, reflected in no correspondence, is minimized almost out of existence. Characteristic is the fact that Lockhart cuts the 'merry', 'delightful' annual meeting at Blair Adam and skips to the news of the death of Terry and Shortreed [IX, 286].

Such selections illustrate vividly the editorial opportunities for interpretation, for the presentation of a reflective Scott in essential solitude, subject to the 'sad worry' of the old man arranging his papers and affairs. What remains to perplex the analyst is whether this striking transition from the multiple *personae* of the correspondence to the self-conscious reflective being of the Journal is simply a phenomeno-logical accident, a result simply of documentary chance, or a genuine psychological development. To what extent was the 'journal habit' itself a cause of such a transition? Scott himself suggests an answer. Resuming his journal in May 1830, after an interruption, he recalls, 'About a year ago I took the pet at my Diary, chiefly because I thought it made me abominably selfish; and that by recording my gloomy fits I encouraged their recurr[e]nce, whereas ought [*sic*] of sight, out of mind is the best way to get out of them' [IX, 300]. Perhaps this impatience explains why only 1826 and 1827 are complete in the Journal: 1828 breaks off in early summer, 1829 the same; 1830 is sketchy; 1831 is interrupted by the onset of a final illness, and the Journal ends in April 1832. Lockhart depends on the Journal chiefly for its first two years, and at the last uses it scarcely at all, its value having waned as Scott lost his taste for the habit. Indeed, it is only in using 1826 that Lockhart allows the Journal to set its own course. Partly as a result of this, the year 1826 – of unique biographical significance, though minor in literary importance – bulks so large in the *Life*. 1827, less than half as long, is still relatively large; 1828-31 together are only slightly longer than 1826.

The use of the Journal for 1826 involves little more than selection; 1827 is different. At the outset of 1827 Lockhart reassumes control, and uses the Journal, together with other materials, for a variety of illustrative purposes and organizational patterns. Structurally most complex, this year is technically most revealing. An initial group of Journal entries illustrates daily concerns and activities in the first half of the year. The entries record work, health, mood, and (to mark the temporal continuum) weather and seasonal shifts, punctuated by periodic travels between juridical Edinburgh and squirearchical Abbots-ford. Having established his chronology and created the sense of passing time, Lockhart shifts his narrative into an expository generality. Letters and Journal extracts illustrate various aspects of Scott's work and social experience during this period. The year is broken by Lockhart's move north for the summer; the narrator will, 'in my account of the sequel of this year, draw, as it may happen, on Sir Walter's Diary, his letters, the memoranda of friendly visitors, or my own recollections' [IX, 107]. In what follows, the diverse materials alternate to give a chronological record, an exposition of major events and situations, and a description of Scott's life at a certain period, closing with his own journalised summary. Through selection and arrangement Lockhart once again sustains a coherent expository form without losing de-scriptive fullness or predominantly narrative movement.

The composition of 1827 depends on the controversially free handling of calendar time which we have noticed before. Lockhart's interest is in the quality of personal experience in temporal setting, and he does not allow the accident of date to interfere. When he wishes to illustrate the 'ease' and 'heartiness' with which Scott resumed work upon returning to Abbotsford on 8 October, he gives (undated) as a single illustration the entry of 27 September before the trip began. Under 15 May, a date of return from Abbotsford to Edinburgh, he prints amalgamated, compressed parts of another 'return' entry not previously included – that of November 1826, evidently preferred for its more poignant reflectiveness and for its appropriateness to the mood of the later period and of the recurrent experience. Analogous is the handling, in 1828, of Scott's two stops at Carlisle on his spring trip to London. Lockhart avoids repetition by omitting one of the stops; yet the stop itself, an experience peculiar to this time at the place where Scott and Charlotte had been married over thirty years before, has an emotional unity independent of date and recurrence. The later entry would justify the assumption that Scott's state of mind and feeling was the same on both occasions; and with this justification, Lockhart has included under the later date the fuller, more touching account of the earlier stop [*Journal*, pp. 514, 556]. Likewise, other entries are shifted to places in the narrative, points in the evolution of mood, where they are reflectively or dramatically appropriate and effective. Under 23 October 1831 (the day of departure for Italy), Lockhart gives a final reflection of Scott's on a London 'misty morning', and continues: 'Dr Ferguson found Sir Walter with this page of his Diary before him, when he called to pay his farewell visit' [x, 107]. Ferguson may have seen a page, but not this one; for the passage is actually the beginning of the entry for 12 October, moved because it supplies such an effective final view of the city.

The principle is the same when Lockhart amalgamates fragmentary extracts into dramatically full anecdotes. Such a theory of anecdote, which justifies *placing* incident and reflection according to their structural effect and modal propriety, is, of course, simply one aspect of the proposition with which we began: that the principles guiding Lockhart's uses of his materials are primarily formal rather than ethical; that, however, the aesthetic and the moral fuse in the biographer's attempt to interpret a life by forming it. We have seen the proposition operative in the handling of letters and autobiographical records. There is a third kind of biographical material, comparable in importance. These are the memoirs, the diaries and bits of diaries, the germs of anecdotes, supplied by living contemporaries. The originals are not all to be found. However, I have compared with Lockhart's versions the manuscripts supplied by Irving, Rose, Skene, Ballantyne, Cadell, Morritt, and Tom Moore; while those provided by Gell, Shortreed, and Dorothy Wordsworth are available in print.

Lockhart's editorial freedom varied from case to case. Basil Hall, for example, sends what 'has been transcribed word for word as it was written' and implies that editing is *his* province:

> 'I have marked sundry passages . . . which must on no account be made use of . . . . I have had the copy made on one side of the paper only – so that if you should find anything in the Volume to suit you, nothing more is necessary towards its appropriation than the right use of a pair of scissors.'[118]

The only evidence of the way Lockhart used his scissors on Hall is supplied by the proofs, and there the revisions are few, slight, and strictly formal. Paragraphs of summary value are moved from opening to closing locations; those introductory in character are correspondingly placed. Excisions are to avoid repetitiousness. Gell agreed to editorial selection only under protest. Assuming that the Gell MS is what Lockhart received, we can observe the uses of that minor masterpiece of condescension and insensitivity. Many of Lockhart's excisions are of two related kinds: passages in which the exasperated classical antiquarian tries in vain to educate the Gothic romancier; and passages in which the conscientious cicerone has all he can do to keep Scott from seriously injuring himself – pictures of an absentminded old man stumbling in and out of carriages, trapping himself with his own walking stick until rescued by Sir William's servant, eating and drinking too much and falling carelessly, laughing stupidly and pathetically at his own helplessness. Such omissions are no loss. Other cuts involve facts given elsewhere in the final volume: Scott's inaccurate account of his financial ruin, and the intermittent delusion – mentioned by Lockhart earlier – that his debts had been wholly cleared. The only omissions one regrets are glimpses of a mind temporarily controlled by subconscious associations – the incoherent Stuart allusions, for instance, and of these the most memorable is included: Scott's grave rehearsal at the sight of the Lake of Avernus, of

> Up the craggy mountain, and down the mossy glen,
> We canna gang a-milking, for Charlie and his men.[119]

Other contributors were more willing than Hall and Gell to allow Lockhart editorial control. Adolphus assumed he was supplying raw materials for editorial selection, verification, and tonal discrimination:
'If you use any part of the pages I have sent, they can, if you like it, be thrown into the form of a letter to you, but I thought it might look whimsical to be telling you a number of things many of which you must know better than myself. . . . As to my own pages, you will of course be kind enough to see that, in anything you make use of, there are no blunders, and, what I feel of more importance, that nothing stands which may not be said by me with a certainty of giving no offence.'[120]
Richer still in what they imply of Lockhart's role are communications from Tom Moore and James Skene. Moore had tried the plan utilized by

Scott in submitting reminiscences of Byron and Burns to Moore and Lockhart respectively: a letter to the biographer.

> 'I tried my hand at the plan you suggested, but (though I squander-
> ed two whole days upon it) without any success, and I have just
> thrown my abortion into the fire . . . . Lest you should think, how-
> ever, that it is from any backwardness or want of zeal (which God
> knows, it could not be, where Scott, the mere man Scott – without
> any reference to his genius – is concerned) that I decline contributing
> any thing to you, I send the raw material of my Diary to be worked
> up – as much as or as little of it as you think right – in your own
> language. This was what Milman advised at first when we talked on
> the subject, and whether of any use or not, it is all, I feel, that I can
> do.'[121]

Skene's terms are similar:

> 'so far as the raw produce of my recollections in that matter can be
> acceptable you are certainly most welcome to them, as I can have no
> objection to their being laid under contribution, knowing that what-
> ever of essence or character they may chance to contain, will be
> readily extracted in passing through the alembic of your better
> judgement.'[122]

Saving Moore, whose materials were fully assimilated into Lockhart's narrative, we may look first at those of Skene and others, which did pass through that 'alembic' and yet remained ostensibly intact.

Characteristic minor revisions are apparent when we reconstruct Lockhart's editing of the letter from John Irving.[123] Writing of their high school experience under Dr Adam, Irving recalls Scott's remark-able memory. He offers in corroboration (the passage is 'quoted' from him) the fact that Adam

Irving MS	*Lockhart's Irving*
used generally to apply to him for the dates, and other particulars of battles and other remarkable events alluded to in Horace or other authors the class were reading, and as I happened to be better acquainted with Geography than the other boys, he used to call Sir Walter the Historian & me the Geographer of the class.	would constantly refer to him for dates, the particulars of battles, and other re-markable events alluded to in Horace or whatever author the boys were reading, and used to call Sir Walter the Historian of the Class.

The revisions, in part merely syntactical, stress Scott's position by removing all reference to Irving's. Irving's account of climbing and reading exploits is treated the same way. This sentence occurs early in

Irving's letter: 'We learned Italian together and could read it fluently';
this is a later one: 'The stories we told were as Sir Walter has mentioned interminable, for we were unwilling to have any of our
favourite Knights killed, and we copied such tales as we had read in
Italian, being a continued succession of battles and enchantments.'
Lockhart joins them to make a new sentence, and effects a causal
connection nowhere to be found in the original:

> 'The stories we told were, as Sir Walter has said, interminable – for
> we were unwilling to have any of our favourite knights killed. Our
> passion for romance led us to learn Italian together; after a time we
> could both read it with fluency, and we then copied such tales as we
> had met with in that language, being a continued succession of
> battles and enchantments.' [I, 133]

Skene's contributions were extensive; Lockhart found them 'equipped with a grace which he [Scott] himself, I think, would not have
surpassed'; and yet he edited. Skene later put parts of the account into
book form, and may have revised his earlier draft. The surviving MS is
considerably cut up. Hence, full comparison is impossible. But enough
remains to show us Lockhart working into Skene's text his own
recollections and images.

Skene MS[124]	*Lockhart* [II, 233]
Upon reaching Loch Skene at length, an Eagle rose majestically from the margin, and one cannot well picture anything more desolate than the features of this mountain loch as it then presented itself as if raised by enchantment to gratify the poets eye. It was but partially disclosed from under the thick folds of fog that rolled incessantly over its surface, at times rent asunder & giving some distant portion to view, as speedily closing again, and opening up in some other quarter, so as to show an uncertain glimpse of a projecting rock, a point of land, or an island bearing a few scraggy clumps of trees, and the cheerless scene of bogs and heath in the bosom of which it lay.	At length, as we approached the gloomy loch, a huge eagle heaved himself from the margin and rose right over us, screaming his scorn of the intruders; and altogether it would be impossible to picture any thing more desolately savage than the scene which opened, as if raised by enchantment on purpose to gratify the poet's eye; thick folds of fog rolling incessantly over the face of the inky waters, but rent asunder now in one direction, and then in another – so as to afford us a glimpse of some projecting rock or naked point of land, or island bearing a few scraggy stumps of pine – and then closing again in universal dark-ness upon the cheerless waste.

The revisions are purely stylistic; the effect achieved is of imaginative
concreteness and compression. A later example from the same extract
shows revision of broader significance. Skene writes simply: 'A
favourite excursion was St Mary's Loch and the Loch of the Lowes, and

of course a frequent one.' The point in the narrative is 1805; but into the extract Lockhart works himself and, with him, an anticipatory reference to Scott's later life. Skene now addresses the biographer:

'I need not tell you that Saint Mary's Loch, and the Loch of the Lowes, were among the most favourite scenes of our excursions, as his fondness for them continued to his last days, and we have both visited them many times together in his company.' [II, 234]

Such modifications hardly alter the central figure, though they affect the portrayal of biographical witnesses. Other changes in Skene's contribution are more centrally thematic. The account of the Edinburgh volunteer cavalry provides a good example.[125] Lockhart apparently feared that Skene's description of Scott's jovial clowning at drill would reflect poorly on the whole operation which he sponsored with such 'zeal' (Lockhart substitutes 'ardor'). Hence, to Skene's description he adds emphatically 'at every interval of exercise'. He omits the zany aftermath of one of 'Earl Walter's' jokes, which 'raised a laugh among a party that was standing around him so loud and so sudden, that it startled the horses, who, finding themselves at liberty, with one accord scampered off in all directions, oversetting various troopers in their dispersion'. This excision fits a pattern of omission. The effect of several cuts taken together is to minimize the reckless joviality of Scott's early Castle Street days. The survivors – Rae, Dundas, Clerk, Forbes, Mackenzie – in their 1837 dignity would scarcely have welcomed such anecdotes as the wild alcoholic return from Clermiston, or the hilarious, fire-burnt dinner at Castle Street.[126]

The same discretion is manifest when Lockhart makes changes in Skene's account of *Marmion*. 'One whole Canto, I think the Fifth,' writes Skene, was composed

Skene MS	*Lockhart* [III, 7]
on the drill ground at Portobello Sands, where they assembled at five o'clock in the morning, and where, during our evolutions, Sir Walter was often seen dodging up & down on his black gelding at the very edge of the sea in complete abstraction. He used to join me in the rear of the squadron when returning from exercises, and recite what he had been composing.	*In the intervals of drilling*, Scott used to delight in walking his powerful black steed up and down by himself upon the Portobello Sands, within the beating of the surge; and now and then you would see him plunge in his spurs, and go off as if at the charge, with the spray dashing about him. As we rode back to Musselburgh, he often came and placed himself beside me, to repeat the verses that he *had been composing during these pauses of our exercise.* [Italics are mine.]

In Skene's account of the beginning of *The Lay of the Last Minstrel*
Lockhart had to cope with discrepancy of evidence as well. He had
Skene's assertion that the *Lay* was begun while Scott was confined by a
horse's kick to his quarters in Musselburgh. He had Scott's own statement that the *Lay* had been started at Lasswade and proceeded at the
rate of a canto a week. He conjectured that what Skene had witnessed
was really a resumption, and modified Skene accordingly:

Skene	*Lockhart* [ii, 96]
It was upon that occasion that the Lay was begun, and at the close of the third day he had composed and fairly written out the whole of the three first cantos which he shewed me (I believe) in the state in which they were sent to the press without alteration.[127]	The scene and date of this resumption I owe to the recollection of the then Cornet of the Edinburgh Light Horse. Mr Skene found him busy with his pen; and he produced before these three days expired the first canto of the Lay, very nearly, if his friend's memory may be trusted, in the state in which it was ultimately published.

Lockhart must have recognized a favourite generalization playing
tricks with Skene's memory, controlling such recollections as 'the most
remarkable proofs of his facility of composition', showing 'that talent
to be a gift of nature, and not the result of practice in versification as is
generally the case'. He therefore made the claim more moderate: 'That
the whole poem was sketched and filled in with extraordinary rapidity,
there can be no difficulty in believing.'

Morritt's MS fills a notebook[128] which Lockhart used. Comparison
shows familiar practices: slight revisions of diction and syntax, rearrangements for coherence or for climactic effectiveness, and of course
the one special relocation which Morritt 'mystified' in proof: the account
of the dinner with Jeffrey and Scott, which Lockhart lifts out of
Morritt's narrative altogether, generalizes, and places (as by 'an old
friend of mine') prior to his first mention of Morritt's name [iii, 55].
Interpolated into the account of Scott's first London season is a paragraph of dialogue on his goodhumoured lion-playing [iii, 161]. One
passage will show, at their most extreme, the revisions which modify
Morritt's impression of Scott. Morritt is speaking of those who had
misunderstood the value Scott set on love and applause and loaded him
'with undesired eulogy':

Morritt MS	*Lockhart* [iii, 90]
It was on such occasions – and among those who hunted him as a lion that I have known him murmur in my ear,	It was on such an occasion that I heard him murmur in my ear, 'Author as I am, I wish these good people would re-

'Though I know I am & have been an author, I wish these good people would recollect that I began by being a gentle-man, and don't mean to give up the character.' Such continued to be his feeling through life, and this, with a slight prejudice common to many Scotchmen in favour of ancient and re-spectable family descent, constituted what is called his pride.

collect that I began with being a gentle-man, and don't mean to give up the character.' Such was all along his feeling, and this, with a slight prejudice common to Scotchmen in favour of ancient and respectable family descent, constituted what in Grub Street is called his *pride*.

The general occasion has become specific, the quotation of Scott is syntactically compressed, the anachronistic allusion to 'through life' is gone, the assertion of Scottish prejudice has become categorical, and the misunderstanding is traced to Grub Street.

We have here a first glimpse of Lockhart revising Scott's talk. The same practice is noticed by the editor of another of Lockhart's 'origin-als'. Robert Shortreed

'talked much to his children of his excursions with Scott, and his son John had the foresight to see that an account of their journeys at first hand might be interesting. Accordingly he wrote down, in a form not unlike the modern interview, all that his father had to say on the subject.'[129]

But as the editor concedes, Lockhart himself had 'many opportunities of hearing Shortreed's stories from his own lips, having often been under his hospitable roof in company with Sir Walter'. Moreover, the son's notes had been made thirty years after the father's experiences. Finally, parts of Shortreed's recollections had appeared in earlier Lives. All of these were justifications for Lockhart's editorial freedom:

'Lockhart's use of the material is just enough to bring out the individual value of the Dialogue on which he drew. It is curious to note how constantly he retouches the phrases of the original, condens-ing, re-arranging, even adding a further Scottish idiom to enhance the flavour.'

This last type of retouching is what one notices first. Shortreed made his father alternate between extreme dialect and formal English; Lockhart, an accomplished practitioner of 'Noctes Ambrosianae', managed to sustain a happy medium:

Shortreed-Cornhill	*Lockhart* [1, 223]
Aye! we had great doings and then Sir Walter had sich an endless fund o' humour and drollery as never was the like. We never travelled ten yards the-	Eh me, sic an endless fund o' humour and drollery as he then had wi' him! Never ten yards but we were either laughing or roaring and singing. Wher-

gither, that we warna either talkin' or roarin' and singin'. And he could suit himsel sae brawlie to the way of livin' o' everyone he was in the Company o', just aye did as they did, and never made him-sel the great man or shewed himsel off or apparently took the lead in the Com-pany.

ever we stopped, how brawlie he suited himsel' to everybody! He aye did as the lave did; never made himsel' the great man, or took ony airs in the company.

The collator comes next upon some surprising omissions. Shortreed claimed that Scott's 'raids' had little to do with ballad-collecting; that, with few exceptions, the ballads collected for the *Minstrelsy* came from the MS or subsequent gleanings of Dr Elliot of Cleugh-head. According to Shortreed, Scott was not the ballad collector, but the manners novelist in embryo:

Shortreed-Cornhill	*Lockhart* [I, 220]
J.E.S.: 'He was not aware at that early period of what was within him.' Father: 'No, vera likely not, but he was makin' himsel, he was laying the foundations o' his future greatness. . . . There's nae doubt that baith the Country and its peculiar manners sat for their picture at that time, tho' perhaps he wasna conscious to what purpose.'	how soon he had any definite object be-fore him in his researches seems very doubtful. 'He was *makin' himsel'* a' the time,' said Mr Shortreed; 'but he didna ken maybe what he was about till years had passed: at first he thought o' little, I dare say, but the queerness and the fun.'

Lockhart suppressed the passage where Shortreed asks his father, 'Then how did you occupy your time, for seeing Sir Wr. was saved the trouble of going about to collect the Ballads, you must have had a good deal on hand?' The father answers, 'Oh, we rade about visiting the scenes o' remarkable occurrences, and roved amang the fouk haill days at a time, for Sir Walter was very fond o' mixing wi' them, and by that means he became familiar wi' their character and the manners of the Country.' Shortreed's repeated insistence that Scott's collecting was done for him, together with his allusion to the curious notched sticks, is all cut. Of more immediate interest, leaving to students of the *Minstrelsy* the problem of Shortreed's accuracy, is Lockhart's formal modification. His single narrative unit has been constructed of rambling recollections of several annual expeditions. The Shortreed account shifts from year to year, recalling various visits to Cleugh-head and forays to other parts of the forest. In Lockhart, the random allusions to numerous occasions and hostelries are coherently organized into a few long narrative paragraphs with explicit connectives – 'Next morning', 'On reaching one evening', Shortreed's 'It was in that same season', and finally, 'It

Q

is a pity that we have no letters of Scott's describing this first *raid* into Liddesdale.' It is not clear in Shortreed how many raids were involved; but Lockhart's effective narrative composite seems to recount a single expedition.

The same freedom in building narrative units from unorganized anecdotal materials is evident in Lockhart's adaptations of the journal of Dorothy Wordsworth and the diary of Tom Moore. In the case of Dorothy, our study is complicated by an intermediate step: Lockhart's access to sources of her account. He had written Wordsworth requesting reminiscences, and the poet replied (27 April 1836):

'Your letter was duly received but I have hesitated about answering it on account of my intention to be in London in the course of a fortnight or so, when I could communicate in conversation all that I remember of your lamented Friend at the period of our first acquaintance. In this I should be aided by a journal which my dear Sister kept of that interesting tour, and which I would take with me.'[130]

Lockhart's footnote explains the subsequent genesis of his episode:

'I have drawn up the account of this meeting from my recollection partly of Mr Wordsworth's conversation – partly from that of his sister's charming *Diary*, which he was so kind as to read over to me on the 16th May 1836.' [II, 142n]

A collation of Lockhart's account with Dorothy's *Recollections of A Tour Made in Scotland* (1803)[131] reveals that William added impressions coloured or formed by later acquaintance and Scott's subsequent fame. It also shows words being transferred from Dorothy to William:

Dorothy's Recollections	*Lockhart* [II, 140]
but indeed Mr Scott is respected everywhere: I believe that by favour of his name one might be hospitably entertained throughout all the borders of Scotland.	'but indeed,' says Mr Wordsworth, 'wherever we named him, we found the word acted as an *open sesamum*; and I believe, that in the character of the *Sheriff's* friends, we might have counted on a hearty welcome under any roof in the Border country.'

At the outset Lockhart follows Dorothy's order and itinerary closely, yet in subtle modifications his hand is evident. The tourists experienced difficulties over rooming arrangements with the landlady at Melrose, who was impressed by the Sheriff and ignorant of the Lake Poet. Lockhart professes to quote Dorothy: '"the landlady refusing to settle anything until she had ascertained from *the Sheriff himself* that he had no objection to sleep in the same room with *William*"' [II, 140].

The italicization gives comic emphasis to the landlady's discrimination between the local celebrity and the stately, sombre poet called 'William.' Dorothy's journal reads simply: 'I could not persuade the woman to show me the beds, or to make any sort of promise till she was assured from the Sheriff himself that he had no objection to sleep in the same room with Wm.' The revision of a later conversation is likewise significant. The tourists pass a forest of 'fine old trees' near Fernie-hurst, and *Dorothy* observes

'The wind was tossing their branches, & sunshine dancing among the leaves, and I happened to exclaim, 'What a life there is in trees!'' on which Mr Scott observed that the words reminded him of a young lady who had been born & educated on an island of the Orcades, and came to spend a summer at Kelso and in the neigh-bourhood of Edinburgh.'

Lockhart changes the setting, attributes the exclamation (how often was William thus obligated!) to *Mr* Wordsworth, and gives a new direction to Scott's sentiment, which he quotes directly:

'The grove of stately ancient elms about and below the ruin was seen to great advantage in a fine, gray, breezy autumnal afternoon; and Mr Wordsworth happened to say, "What a life there is in trees!" – "How different," said Scott, "was the feeling of a very intelligent young lady, born and bred in the Orkney Islands, who lately came to spend a season in this neighbourhood!"' [II, 141].

Lockhart again turns the journalist's words into direct quotation of Scott when Dorothy remarks of their parting,

Dorothy	*Lockhart* [II, 142]
We wished we could have gone with Mr Scott into some of the remote dales of this country, where in almost every house he can find a home and a hearty welcome.	. . . neither their engagements nor his own would permit them to make at this time an excursion into the wilder glens of Liddesdale, 'where,' said he, 'I have strolled so often and so long, that I may say I have a home in every farmhouse.'

The coherent account which Lockhart ostensibly draws from Tom Moore's 'scraps'[132] is a selection and arrangement of several scenes and pieces of scenes [VIII, 61-66]. In Lockhart the visit begins at dinner; there follows 'Moore's account' of an after-dinner *tête-à-tête* concern-ing Byron's recent death, and including Scott's candid account of the Waverley Novels as his own:

'This frankness was met as it should have been by the brother poet; and when he entered Scott's room next morning, "he laid his hand," says Mr Moore, "with a sort of cordial earnestness on my breast, and said – *Now, my dear Moore, we are friends for life.*"'

There follows a long walk through the plantation, to Kaeside, to Melrose, to Huntly Burn, and back to Abbotsford for a jovial dinner with guests and music.

The journal scraps are far more diffuse. The visit begins with a walk and a talk, whose pertinent materials are included by Lockhart in the walk of the day following. The talk about Byron was not after dinner, but before, and was concerned exclusively with reports of Lady Byron's plans to remarry: 'Being even a W——,' said Scott, 'would be perhaps better than that.' The talk of Scott's own books was introduced by *Moore* after dinner and had no connection with the talk of Byron. Scott's expression of friendship the 'next morning', which Lockhart presents as a direct consequence of the *Waverley* discussion, actually was voiced a day later – the 31st, not the 30th – and had (in the diary) no explicit relation to previous talks. It came not 'when he entered Scott's room next morning', but 'Before we left the house, as I was standing alone.' Moore arrived the 29th of October 1825; the *tête-à-tête* took place that evening. On the 30th (Sunday) and 31st there were two walks and two dinners, the first (the Sabbath) without music. The conversation about Scott's ignorance of music, which Lockhart placed during the evening party in its appropriate place, actually occurred during one of the walks. Lockhart has thus composed two scenes or sequences, whose conversations are dramatically framed, out of four whose conversations spring up by chance. James Boswell had indeed joined hands with a narrative artist and a veteran of the *Noctes Ambrosianae*.

Lockhart's use of Moore and Dorothy Wordsworth illustrates strikingly the theory of anecdote we have previously noticed. For him, the anecdote is the brief prose matter of oral tradition; it is not a literal record of historical truth, not an end in itself. Narrative in setting and dramatic in form, it is illustrative in purpose. Assuming an anecdote to be true in essence, the biographer (close kin to the novelist of historical 'manners') can set that anecdote where its significance will be most effectively realized. At least two of Lockhart's chief contributors submitted anecdotes in full acceptance of such a theory. Both Skene and Ballantyne disowned all claim to temporal accuracy and circumstantial setting for their anecdotes. Skene says in his letter:

'Such as they are therefore you shall have them, but I must claim the privilege of a roving license, as I do not feel that I could with any chance of success tax my memory as to precision in dates, or even connectedness of narrative, but merely to note down at random such traits and facts as occur to my memory.'[133]

They expected this connectedness to be supplied by the narrator. James Ballantyne writes of his projected contributions:

> 'they shall all be authentic, and a large proportion of them eminently characteristic. You will, of course, desire to have no more than the mere materials, and indeed I hardly expect to be able to put them much into shape; but this is to bring no disparagement on my taste, for I shall give you them all unboulted.'[134]

Lockhart's 'boulting' of Ballantyne is a process fascinating to watch.

Ballantyne includes[135] an extended reminiscence of a conversation with Scott shortly after his return from Paris and Waterloo in 1815. To illustrate Scott's absentmindedness following his 1819 illness, Skene begins, 'When absent for a few days upon one occasion', and describes Scott's failure to notice that the drawing room has been refurnished in his absence. Lockhart places both anecdotalists at the 1815 return:

> 'Reaching Abbotsford, Scott found with his family his old friend Mr Skene of Rubislaw, who had expected him to come home sooner, and James Ballantyne, who had arrived with a copious budget of bills, Calendars, booksellers' letters, and proof sheets.' [v, 81]

The anecdotes follow, Skene's slightly edited, Ballantyne's given almost *literatim*, but introduced specifically as 'their next morning's conference'.

The 'boulting' of Ballantyne's anecdotes is always interesting. Ballantyne frequently quotes Scott directly; Lockhart does not hesitate to revise what is quoted or make direct quotation out of what is implied. Here is the beginning of the interview following publication of the *Lord of the Isles*:

Ballantyne MS	*Lockhart* [v, 26]
He gave me, I think, about a week after its publication before he questioned me on the subject. He then took me into his library and asked me what people were saying about the Lord of the Isles.	One evening, some days after the poem had been published, Scott requested James Ballantyne to call on him, and the printer found him alone in his library, working at the third volume of Guy Mannering. I give what follows from Ballantyne's Memoranda:— ' "Well, James," he said, "I have given you a week – what are people saying about The Lord of the Isles?" '

In what follows, Lockhart revises to remove a notable Ballantyne error. Ballantyne seems uncertain as to whether Scott had yet thought of novels as an alternative to poetry. But the time was 1815. Hence, the end of Lockhart's 'Ballantyne' differs from the original; Scott is the speaker.

Ballantyne	*Lockhart* [v, 26]
Since one thing has failed, we must just try something else – only the question is what that's to be.	Since one line has failed, we must just stick to something else: and so he dismissed me and resumed his novel.

The continuous passage of 'Ballantyne's' narrative which follows – 'An evening or two after,' interpolates Lockhart, 'I [James] called again on him' – is drawn from widely separated parts of the MS. The 'scene' in which James asks to borrow the copy of *The Giaour* on Scott's table and leads Scott to compare himself with Byron is actually an amalgamation of three separate anecdotes which James supplied 'unboulted'.

One who objected to such methods, William Laidlaw, criticized Lockhart's use of another Ballantyne recollection. The scene is that of the seriously ill Scott dictating *The Bride of Lammermoor* to Laidlaw and John Ballantyne, constructed by Lockhart from James's memoranda and John's account as Lockhart remembered it. According to Robert Carruthers, Laidlaw took exception to the published version:

'Laidlaw abjured with some warmth the old-wife exclamations which Lockhart ascribes to him – as, "Gude keep us a" – "The like o' that!" – "Eh, sirs! eh, sirs!" But he admitted that while he held the pen he was at times so deeply interested in the scene or in the development of the plot, that he could not help exclaiming: "Get on, Mr Scott, get on!"'[136]

In the remainder of the incident, Lockhart has supplied Scott not just with a statement, but with the homely wit that adorns it:

Ballantyne	*Lockhart* [VI, 62]
The dictation of Caleb Balderstone & the Old Cooper's best jokes, was often mingled with groans extorted by severe anguish. But when Mr Laidlaw endeavoured to prevail upon him to take a little respite, the only answer he could obtain was a request that he would see that the doors were carefully shut, so that his groans might not be heard by his family. 'As to stopping work, Laid-	I have often . . . heard both these secretaries describe the astonishment with which they were equally affected when Scott began this experiment. The affectionate Laidlaw beseeching him to stop dictating when his audible suffering filled every pause, 'Nay, Willie,' he answered, 'only see that the doors are fast. I would fain keep all the cry as well as all the wool to ourselves; but as to

law,' he said, 'you know that is quite out of the question;' & accordingly he went on working.

giving over work, that can only be when I am in woollen.'

Cadell, in his MS memoranda,[137] recounts an earlier visit of James to Scott in his illness, this one during the writing of *Rob Roy*. Here, too, Scott's speech has been vividly Scottified. To Ballantyne's question as to why the printers had had no copy for several days, Scott answers:

Cadell	Lockhart [v, 244]
Ah! James, do you think it possible for me to paint Rob Roys wife when I have such a pain in my guts –	Ay, Ay, Jemmy, 'tis easy for you to bid me get on, but how the deuce can I make Rob Roy's wife speak, with such a *curmurring* in my guts?

Cadell reports having once asked Scott 'how he managed to write so much each morning before breakfast'. Scott replied, 'I then I may say write down what I thought of before I got up. I generally lie for half an hour in a kind of simmer before I get out of bed – my work after that is easy.' In Lockhart the question differs, and the answer is expanded as well, possibly from Lockhart's own memories. Cadell is quoted directly: 'when is it that you think?'

'"Oh," said Scott, "I lie *simmering* over things for an hour or so before I get up – and there's the time I am dressing to overhaul my half-sleeping, half-waking *projet de chapitre* – and when I get the paper before me, it commonly runs off pretty easily. –"'

If this is the practice with anecdotes in single versions, what must it be when reminiscences conflict with each other? In the reports of the black morning on which Scott discovered he was ruined [VIII, 207-8], the contradictions are significant. Skene's account[138] is as follows:

'It was the middle of January 1826 he had been to Christmas at Abbotsford, and dined at my house the day he returned to town without having called at his own house to receive his letters so that he remained ignorant of the event till he went home at night. The whole afternoon he had been in particular good spirits.'

Lockhart infers from Scott's Journal that the discovery *preceded* the dinner. With this revision, Skene's testimony that Scott was 'quite in his usual spirits' becomes a significant example of Scott's fortitude and surface composure. Another change follows: since, in Skene, Scott did not yet know of the calamity, he had no reason to ask Skene to call on him the following morning. In Skene, the 'verbal message' – it is not quoted – comes 'next morning', and Skene reaches the house 'at seven in the morning, still dark, where I found him by candlelight seated at his writing table, surrounded with papers which he had gathered around him'. In Lockhart, the request is quoted directly and is made in a whisper as Scott parts with Skene the night before; the arrival time becomes 'about half-past nine', apparently because the Journal records that James Ballantyne arrived first. Skene's arrival is acknowledged by Scott with one of the most famous speeches in the biography. Its strength, it appears, is a result of Lockhart's revision:

Skene MS	*Lockhart*
'Skene this is the hand of a beggar. Constable has failed and I am ruined *du fond au comble.*'	'My friend, give me a shake of your hand – mine is that of a beggar.' He then told him that Ballantyne had just been with him, and that his ruin was certain and complete.

The proofs show a further revision. Following his explanation to Skene, Scott speaks of his absence from Court; in the proofs, slight revisions are made to suggest that rather than staying away, Scott does intend to go to Court that morning:

'He requested his friend to apologize for his absence from
going to stay
the Court, and added, "Don't fancy I am ~~staying~~ at home to brood idly on what cannot be helped. I was at work upon Woodstock when you came in, and I shall take up the pen the I get back from Court."'
~~moment you go.~~"'[139]

Thus even the process of 'remembering' had not ceased until the forming of the *Life* was completed, and the type was set.

IV. THE PERSONALITY OF A *Life*: LOCKHART'S SCOTT AND SCOTT'S LOCKHART

The materials for detailed study of reconstruction and recreation are available. The study undeniably illustrates what Ian Jack has called Lockhart's 'habit of mingling truth and fiction so that it is hardly possible to separate the two'. It may even lend support to Jack's prejudicially phrased inferences that 'in Lockhart's lack of concern for the exact truth it is possible to detect a sort of indifference', that 'not every detail about Scott mattered to Lockhart'.[140] Lockhart did not possess Boswell's positivistic passion for sheer verification. He held to the Wordsworthian distinction: 'Truth is not here, as in the sciences, and in natural philosophy, to be sought without scruple, and promulgated for its own sake, upon the mere chance of its being serviceable.'[141] His own guiding sense of the truth of Scott's life – and to this truth there is surely no indifference – is in full conformity with the Romantic conception of symbolic fact shared roughly by the authors of *A Letter to a Friend of Burns*, *The Statesman's Manual*, and *Sartor Resartus*. His aims are profoundly different from those of Boswell: his ambiguous antecedent had sought the immediacy and authenticity of dramatic scene, while he worked for the significant organicism of panoramic narrative. He is, for better or worse, a Romantic biographer, in his method as in his epistemology. To base judgement, therefore, on the conventional comparison of his work with Boswell's is as misleading as to insist that Wordsworth be judged as an eighteenth-century loco-descriptive poet or Byron as an Augustan satirist. This much we can conclude from the uses Lockhart made of his materials.

We cannot know the extent to which Lockhart formed and remade his own memories. Of these no manuscripts survive, but there are hints to be used with caution. Lockhart recounts a visit in 1814 to a friend's house in George Street, Edinburgh. From a window the young men watched, in a window on Castle Street diagonally opposite, a tire-less hand at work on an evergrowing heap of manuscript [IV, 151]. The hand is identified as Scott's, the manuscript as *Waverley*. The host of the occasion, having read the published account, wrote to express his gratitude to Lockhart for preserving the incident. His terms are significant:

'I perfectly well recollect the incident of *the hand* tho' I am afraid you have embellished it a little. Some literary grub, criticizing the works of Lockhart some 50 years hence, may accuse him of inaccuracy, & in support of his charges prove that in 1814 W. M.'s only uncle was in India, & that the said W. M. did not reside in George Street before Whitsunday 1818. In the summer of which year I imagine the [event?] alluded to took place.'[142]

The 'literary grubs' took more than fifty years, but they did make the discovery, ironically through this letter. Citing it to Lockhart's dis-honour, they fail, however, to notice that Menzies accepts the theory of anecdote implicit in the inaccuracy and rationalizes Lockhart's charac-teristic licence in handling calendar time: 'The anecdote however is so well introduced where it stands, as to make the Anachronism of no consequence.'

The modern critic, unable to accept the Menzies view, is still less willing to believe in one of the most moving deathbed scenes in biography [x, 193]; for here, too, there is the strong possibility of anachronism or temporal licence. And here, too, a disconcerting letter survives. Mrs Scott of Harden apologetically offers Lockhart this suggestion:

'When you write anything of the last very melancholy weeks at Abbotsford I think it will be most valuable to mention any of the few sentences he uttered when his mind was clear, of a religious tendency such as I heard he said occasionally, "Oh be virtuous! it is our only comfort in a dying state" – & anything of that kind, for there are wicked minded people who will take a *pleasure* in saying that he was not a religious man; & *proving the contrary will do much good.*'[143]

Those who cite it ignore its assumption that Scott *did* make such utterances and that his mind *was* on occasion clear. Hence, it actually does not 'prove' that Lockhart made up the deathbed scene. The fact that Sophia reported no lucid intervals during Scott's last days is not as conclusive as it may appear. One alert student observed that the scene is supposed to have occurred four days before Scott's death, leaving time for the forty hours mentioned by Sophia.[144] Harriet Scott was, after all, simply recording what she had heard attributed to Scott *before Lockhart*. Hesketh Pearson finds 'further evidence that the famous episode is fanciful' in the similarity of the dying injunction attributed to Lord Lyttelton by Johnson: 'Be good, be virtuous, my Lord; you must come to this.'[145] And Lockhart himself had written in his obituary of William Blackwood:

'He had then what no good man will consider as a slight privilege – that of contemplating the approach of death with the clearness and full strength of his mind and faculties, and of instructing those around him, by solemn precept and memorable example, by what means alone humanity, conscious of its own frailty, can sustain that prospect with humble serenity.'[146]

But it is possible that biographers ordinarily stage fewer scenes than their subjects; Scott, aware of his deathbed, was as capable of thanatoptic didacticism as Lyttelton or Blackwood or Lockhart. Miss Dougary supplies appropriate caution: 'It is conceivable that Lockhart may have wished to produce a death scene characteristic and beautiful, but the precedent of the Polton ride should not make us conclude on insufficient evidence that he did so.' It is equally possible that such a scene occurred weeks earlier. Those memories which involve Lockhart alone are beyond either verification or refutation.

The importance of this truth is recognized only when we calculate the proportions of a work which finally extended to some 900,000 words. After we set aside letters, diaries, autobiography, and the memoirs of others, there remains approximately one third that is Lockhart's narrative based on his own memory and observation. How much of this huge narrative actually represents first-hand observation and recollection is impossible to guess. For the 'personality' of Lockhart's narrative is largely a deliberate technical achievement, a result of the way he uses himself as a *dramatis persona*, or as the perceptive and judicial centre of the book. If and when Lockhart *invents* his presence as first-hand observer, he does so to make such passages more compelling because more immediate. He uses himself, as the novelist would, as a central consciousness.

Nicolson gives special praise to the skill with which Lockhart, controlling his own presence, avoids a break of continuity between the early Scott and Lockhart's Scott, between indirect and direct narration.[147] He is thinking of the contrast with Boswell. But the discontinuity, an accident of calendar time, has been minimized by the fusing of indirect and direct narration almost from the beginning of the work. 'We have no sudden sense of Lockhart's own appearance on the scene' – true, but not because he is unobtrusive in his entrance. He is not. He is as prominent as Boswell in his. We have no sense of Lockhart's sudden appearance simply because he has been there dramatically and judicially all along. As compiler-inquirer he has maintained evident command of the book's arrangement; materials have been presented as located and compiled in accordance with *his* quest. By a technique of deliberate anachronism, his own later point of view has been consistently present for the verification of early reports in accordance with later impressions. Even in recording impressions of Scott's youth Lockhart is reminded, Lockhart recalls, visits, describes, sees, hears, compares – in short, Lockhart gives from the outset a personal unity to the book and the life it records. A specific instance bears repeating; it occurs in the third chapter (1782):

'exactly as the schoolboy still walks before "her mind's eye," his image rises familiarly to mine, who never saw him until he was past the middle of life: . . . her description of the change on his countenance when passing from the "doggie of the mill" to the dream of Paradise, is a perfect picture of what no one that has heard him recite a fragment of high poetry, in the course of table-talk, can ever forget. Strangers may catch some notion of what fondly dwells on the memory of every friend, by glancing from the conversational bust of Chantrey, to the first portrait by Raeburn, which represents the last Minstrel as musing in his prime within sight of Hermitage.' [1, 112]

Lockhart has been present, too, in his manifest control of the testimony of witnesses to Scott's youth. We have noticed how Skene, in recalling an early expedition, is made to allude to Lockhart; and the presentation of memoirs as letters to Lockhart serves to impart reality to Lockhart as well as augment the portrait of Scott. Scott's account of his boyhood encounter with Burns (1786–7) already existed as a letter to Lockhart; hence, the early narrative made up of this letter [1, 150-2] belongs to the Lockhart-Scott relationship. Moreover, for better or worse, Lockhart has been the controlling sensibility in the depiction of minor characters. Most of them he later knew; hence his later viewpoint is present in the early delineation. One thinks of Hogg. But even in the case of characters – such as George Ellis – whom Lockhart could not have known, it is of the essence of his controversial skill that he can transform indirect impression and documentary fact into the sensational immediacy of first-hand observation. It was this that so struck John Cay about the first volume:

'I am old enough to remember many persons mentioned in it some of whom were dead and others fast declining before you came to Edinburgh – I have been a pupil of some of Sir Walter's teachers; and my father knew and received at his table in my youth, some of his friends – I am surprised then to understand how you have contrived to give so vivid a picture of persons, of whom you could only have heard.'[148]

The later sketches of those Lockhart had known – showpieces such as the vivid sketches of Scott, Constable, and Ballantyne, as hosts at table – are fuller but no more immediate, not distinct in kind.

After his own appearance on the scene in 1818, Lockhart can make fuller use of himself as central consciousness. The anecdotes he gives as his own are as skilfully set as those attributed to others. More valuable – for the Lockhart enthusiast the most memorable passages of the entire work – are the panoramic reminiscences of Scott's later life. Such extended views, like chapters in the *Burns* and the *Napoleon*, are descriptive units adapted to narrative movement. Each opens with Scott observed at a specific time and place and then smoothly expands into a general but concrete panorama based on the observations of several years: work, society, domesticity during Edinburgh winters; autumns and autumnal occasions and traditions at Abbotsford; summers of glory and important visitors at the peak of Abbotsford's pomp and circumstance. All are infused with the reflective sympathy that has been anticipated throughout the first half of the *Life*, and thus the rhetorical unification of the work is perfected. And all reveal the persistent and inter-related themes which unobtrusively form the entire narrative and thus define the personality of *Lockhart's* Scott.

The themes are all conditioned by a fact easily overlooked, one which marks an essential difference between *The Life of Scott* and its Boswellian antecedent. Lockhart's biography was a supplement to Scott's autobiographical introductions and notes. Lockhart knew – and he warns the reader – that such materials are not of absolute reliability. Nonetheless, they provide an indispensable link between the works of a powerful imagination and – Lockhart's continuation – a narrative of the growth of that imagination. Certain normative views of the creative process and of the sociology and ethics of the imaginative life assume thematic dominance. Scott's works become moments in the history of a uniquely imaginative life.

Scott and his biographer evidently agreed that in him 'imagination [was] visibly the predominant faculty' [VIII, 70], that the 'resolution to give imagination her scope', the 'filial reverence of imagination', is 'the ruling principle and charm of all his best writings' [X, 203, 207]. Scott belonged to the 'gifted, as it is called, but often unhappy class' of imaginative beings [IX, 63]. The best Waverley critics from Nassau Senior to Thomas Crawford, however, find their definitive conception of his genius in 'the manner in which his works unite the most irreconcilable forms' [VII, 110], 'the amalgam of romance and realism', the 'tension between reality and romance that seems fundamental to Scott'.[149] In his majestic conclusion, Lockhart recognizes the same theme in Scott's life: the interplay – sometimes lovable, sometimes tragic, always splendid – of 'the brilliancy of his imagination' [X, 219] and the real world, 'the positive obligations of active life' [X, 214], which he would 'fain accommodate' to it. Scott and his biographer agreed that such a divided consciousness is at once a blessing and a curse. But they seemed not always to share a single definition of 'imagination'.

The poet, says Lockhart [I, 155], showed his 'habitual modesty' in 'undervaluing' his imaginative powers; Scott's journal alludes in characteristic denigration to his 'magic wand', his 'dreams of fiction', his 'wishing cap', his 'castle-building' [VIII, 167]. 'I can see as many castles in the clouds as any man,' he boasts ironically; 'as many genii in the curling smoke of a steam-engine, as perfect a Persepolis in the embers of a sea-coal fire. My life has been spent in such day-dreams' [IX, 56]. Lockhart, for whom Romantic epistemology was more congenial, holds to a more philosophical conception. Imagination is a perceptive power, an impersonative power. Scott 'had before him a vivid image' [II, 14]; 'the powers of fancy and imagination had such predominant sway, as to make him in fact live three or four lives habitually in place of one' [VII, 62]. Knowledge 'had by degrees fed his imagination, until every the minutest feature had been taken home and realized with unconscious intenseness of sympathy' [II, 181]. Then he could 'repeople' the 'awe-inspiring haunt of his infancy' [II, 22], or 'repeople the past by the power of imagination' [V, 159]; as Scott himself recalled, 'since I was five years old, I cannot remember the time when I had not some ideal part to play' [VIII, 167]. *Old Mortality* demanded, says Lockhart, an 'energetic sympathy of imagination', and as long as a buoyancy of spirit, a creative gusto, was possible – contrast the image of the pale, pertinacious Napoleonist of 1826 [VIII, 58] – the mind could triumph in its impersonative power. Such is the theme, for example, of Lockhart's image of Scott composing *The Bride of Lammermoor* in physical pain: 'when dialogue of peculiar animation was in progress, spirit seemed to triumph altogether over matter – he arose from his couch and walked up and down the room, raising and lowering his voice, and as it were acting the parts' [VI, 62].

Lockhart has a stylistic conception of imagination as well. Not to be confused with inventive fancy, imagination is a descriptive power. He had identified it in Defoe: 'that man has the *strongest* imagination of any prose writer that ever lived. Such is his power that he can make plain matter of fact infinitely brighter than all the inventions in the world could ever render a fictitious event.'[150] In *Peter's Letters* he had attacked the current emphasis on invention; defending Burns against charges he was unimaginative, Lockhart defined imagination as a power of visualization and vivid rendition. The ideal novelist of *Peter's Letters* gives imaginative form and life to ideas and manners already in the store of his national audience. Such is imagination in the *Life of Scott*: 'I mean especially a power of *vivid painting* – the true and primary sense of what is called *Imagination'* [v, 303]. When an event 'had left a vivid impression on his mind', Scott would relate it 'so as to make us all feel as if we had the scene passing before our eyes' [vi, 162]. His was the magic of evocation: 'And so we rode by Philiphaugh, Carterhaugh, Bowhill, and Newark, he pouring out all the way his picturesque anecdotes of former times – more especially of the fatal field where Montrose was finally overthrown by Leslie. He described the battle as vividly as if he had witnessed it' [vi, 67].

But imagination must begin with a power and a will to perceive sharply and exhaustively and remember strongly. Of the genesis of fictive character, Lockhart remarks, 'thus did every little peculiarity remain treasured in his memory, to be used in due time for giving the air of minute reality to some imaginary personage' [v, 76n]. The will to capture and preserve 'minute reality' was fired by *genius loci*, and Lockhart's narrative appropriately localizes the moments of creative potency in Scott's imaginative life: the completing of parts of *The Lady* 'under the full influence of the *genius loci*' of the Trossachs [iii, 168]; the searching out of Hebridean locales for *The Lord of the Isles* [iii, 238]; the trip to Rokeby in search of 'minute details about the scenery and local traditions' [iv, 12], a search Scott justified to Morritt in terms Johnson and Reynolds would approve:

'whoever trusted to imagination would soon find his own mind circumscribed, and contracted to a few favorite images, and the repetition of these would sooner or later produce that very monotony and barrenness which had always haunted descriptive poetry in the hands of any but the patient worshippers of truth.' [iv, 18]

It is significant that such passages occur early in the *Life*. Predictably, the Romantic biographer stresses the origins of imaginative power. But the stress conveys a specific interpretation. For Lockhart, Scott's imaginative life reaches its peak of intensity during the early years when the ardent antiquarian and the border minstrel unconsciously take in the gigantic stores on which the novelist will later draw. There is a truth Lockhart could accept in F. R. Leavis's suggestion that Scott was a 'kind of inspired folklorist'. Thomas Crawford discovers essentially the same truth: 'antiquarianism, when developed to a certain level and in a certain direction, becomes itself a form of creation'. For Crawford as for Lockhart, Scott's is the genius of the creative antiquarian. The theory Crawford attributes to Una Pope Hennessy – 'namely, that the sources of some of the novels go right back to his antiquarian "raids" into Liddesdale between 1792 and 1798'[151] – is fully stated by Lockhart in the pervasively Romantic close of his chapter on the *Minstrelsy*:

'the taste and fancy of Scott appear to have been formed as early as his moral character; and he had, before he passed the threshold of authorship, assembled about him, in the uncalculating delight of native enthusiasm, almost all the materials on which his genius was destined to be employed for the gratification and instruction of the world.' [II, 115]

Many of the links between antiquarian and novelist had, Lockhart notes, been indicated in the posthumous edition of the *Minstrelsy*. This and his theoretic bias toward the early forming of imagination in 'uncalculating delight' and 'native enthusiasm' explain why Lockhart's narrative attends much to the genesis of the poems and little to that of the novels. Even the early works of literary scholarship receive greater attention, for they too belong to the formative process:

'His editorial labors on Dryden, Swift, and these other collections, were gradually storing his mind with that minute and accurate knowledge of the leading persons and events both of Scotch and English history, which made his conversation on such subjects that of one who had rather lived with than read about the departed; while, unlike other antiquaries, he always preserved the keenest interest in the transactions of his own time.' [III, 175]

The creative antiquary lived simultaneously in diverse worlds. Herein, for Lockhart, lies the paradox of Scott's imaginative life. We may borrow Edgar Johnson's words for Dickens and suggest that for Lockhart Scott's triumph is the triumph of imagination in the life of the world, the conversation of men, the 'transactions of his own time'; Scott's tragedy is the tragedy of imagination against the world, the usurpation of reality by romance, the infatuation with the dream of Abbotsford. Scott, more than any other poetic genius, adjusted his 'filial reverence of imagination' to his life as a member of human society. But even Scott, Lockhart implies, with all his energy of commitment to the active life, his essential sanity, his wonderful 'manliness' of sensibility, could not make the life of imagination other than the tragic thing it is.

The triumph of imagination in the world is imaged by Lockhart in patterns of emphasis on the kindliness of the social Scott, his openness to experience, the fertility and humanity of his conversation. All, in

Lockhart's view, are consequences of imaginative power and its healthy restraint; all illustrate Lockhart's Coleridgian theme: the sanity of true genius. 'The imagination that so completely mastered him when he chose to give her the rein, was kept under most determined control when any of the positive obligations of active life came into question' [x, 214]. He was kindliness incarnate; 'in the social relations of life, where men are most effectually tried, no spot can be detected in him' [x, 212]. Such is the theme, for instance, of the otherwise comic episode of George IV's Scottish visit (1822), wherein Scott the man of action holds sway:

'I believe no man, after long and intimate knowledge of any other great poet, has ever ventured to say, that he could have conceived the possibility of any such parts being adequately filled on the active stage of the world, by a person in whom the powers of fancy and imagination had such predominant sway, as to make him in fact live three or four lives habitually in place of one.' [VII, 62]

Lockhart's personal reflection adopts the terms of Keats's Moneta: other poets 'have seemed to me to do little more than sleep through their lives – and at best to fill the sun with dreams'. Scott's equal in energy and self-possession is to be sought 'in the roll of great sovereigns or great captains, rather than in that of literary genius' [VII, 63].

Indeed, energy is a touchstone for Scott's Romantic biographer. Lockhart the man, we know, was severely sceptical of Scott's turbulently worldly existence. While completing the *Life* he read a biography of Wilberforce and reflected to Croker:

'After my long labours on Scott's energetic and tumultuous existence – all excitement of one sort or other – I could not but feel very strongly the beautiful composing and sustaining effect of religion in Wilberforce, and wishing from my heart that Sir Walter had had more of that element mixed in him. Surely the decision and vivacity of our friend's nature wd have been gloriously embellished by that capacity of looking on worldly things from a serene point of view which no mere philosophy ever can give us.'[152]

But Lockhart the biographical *persona* appears to delight in the 'healthy elasticity of spirit with which he could meanwhile turn his whole zeal upon new or different objects' [IV, 158]. He loses no chance to illustrate 'buoyant spirits' in the early periods of his 'gigantic exertion' [V, 6], and seems to admire without reservation the speed with which Scott leapt from project to project: 'his spirits seem to have caught a

R

new spring of buoyancy, and before the last sheet was sent from his desk, he had crowded his brain with the imagination of another fiction' [v, 132]. He appears to marvel at the spectacle of a prolific writer week after week devoting 'all but a hardly imperceptible fraction of his mornings to out-of-doors occupations, and the whole of his evenings to the entertainment of a constantly varying circle of guests' [vi, 212]. The implicit thesis is that through 'a happily constituted and virtuously disciplined mind and character' [v, 311], the imaginative genius will triumphantly adjust 'the strength and splendour of his imagination' [vi, 160] to the achievement of 'sagacity, discretion, and gentleness' in 'all his intercourse with mankind' [vii, 128]. If, as Rycenga argues, 'Lockhart envisioned his biography, ultimately, as a moral exemplum',[153] then this is what it exemplifies. And as the narrative moves sombrely into the dark times of 'the muffled drum', the note of distinctly Romantic elegy sounds the loss of buoyant power, the setting of 'the full sunshine of ease' [viii, 58], the fitfulness with which old energies were aroused in the final years of authorial drudgery.

Amid a 'tumult of engagements' [iii, 76], then, the imaginative man acted out his preference for a life of action and passed what Basil Hall called 'the great trial ... [of] every-day life, and among every-day people' [vii, 314], with worldly 'liberality and sagacity' [iii, 116]. The triumph is best embodied in conversation. Much is made of Lockhart's refusal to Boswellize Scott, on the supposition, held by many of Scott's Edinburgh contemporaries, that 'the genius of the great poet and novelist rarely, if ever, revealed itself in his talk' [v, 297]. In fact, as we have seen in *Peter's Letters*, the character of Scott's talk became for Lockhart a Romantic index of his imaginative genius. Scott was the raconteur, the 'Prince of all Story-tellers', says Basil Hall [vii, 301]. Will Clerk was struck early by his unconscious conversational powers – the liveliness, 'the strange variety of his knowledge – and above all, perhaps, the portentous tenacity of his memory' [i, 163]. In 1808 Morritt found the raconteur unequalled in animation and apposite stories, 'but equally impressive and powerful was the language of his warm heart, and equally wonderful were the conclusions of his vigorous understanding' [iii, 89]. In 1823 Adolphus found that 'the great charm of his "table-talk" was in the sweetness and *abandon* with which it flowed' – a benign natural force – and emphasized in his memoranda the impersonative power:

'Not only was he inexhaustible in anecdote, but he still loved to exert the talent of dramatizing, and in some measure representing in his own person the incidents he told of, or the situations he imagined.' [VII, 167]

All of these are included by implication in Lockhart's distinction: 'it was impossible to listen to Scott's oral narration, whether gay or serious, or to the felicitous fun with which he parried absurdities of all sorts, without discovering better qualities in his talk than *wit* – and of a higher order' [V, 303]. They are summed up in *imagination*. And for all his protestations of diffidence about preserving such talk, Lockhart has filled his narrative with illustrations of Scott the imaginative raconteur, stressing always his natural delicacy in adjusting his talk to the conditions and the company, and thus confirming this theme of imagination triumphant in the human world.

In the cumulative juxtaposition of imaginative man and social man, however, we sense a growing tension. Even in the account of the royal visit of 1822, Lockhart allows the warning to sound in the midst of triumphant practicality: 'it was necessary to be an eye-witness of this royal visit, in order to comprehend the extent to which he had allowed his imagination to get the mastery over him as to all these matters' [VII, 62]. Side by side with the exuberant openness of the imaginative raconteur we are shown the rash secrecy of the poet for whom despotic imagination made frank and judicious adjustment to reality ultimately impossible. Behind the appearance of the man of affairs is the man of imaginative feeling: 'I often take a doze in the plantations, and while Tom marks out a dyke or a drain as I have directed, one's fancy may be running its ain riggs in some other world' [V, 335]. Such warnings prepare effectively for the full analysis of Scott's worldliness and commercial rashness as manifestations of the power of imagination. His respect for rank and ancestry is thus explained: 'his imagination had been constantly exercised in recalling and embellishing whatever features of the past it was possible to connect with any pleasing ideas, and a historical name was a charm that literally stirred his blood' [VIII, 72]. Likewise, his secret commercial involvements. That a man who prided himself on worldly practicality should have acted so recklessly Lockhart 'must always regard as the enigma of [Scott's] personal history' [VIII, 89]. But, had the 'marvellous combination of faculties' been otherwise, 'the imagination which has bequeathed so much to delight and humanize mankind would have developed few of its miraculous resources. . . . The enchanted spring might have sunk into earth with the rod that bade it gush, and left us no living waters' [VIII, 95]. The romancer's 'bright visions' inevitably 'left a dazzle sometimes on the eyes which he so gently re-opened upon our prosaic realities', and so the minstrel 'must pay the penalty, as well as reap the glory, of this lifelong abstraction of reverie, this self-abandonment of Fairyland' [VIII, 96].

The paradox has its central symbol. For Lockhart, from *Peter's Letters* to the *Life* and beyond, the paradoxical reality of Scott's life is inseparable from the fantastic dream of Abbotsford. 'I shall ever regret', he wrote, 'that Crabbe did not see him at Abbotsford among his books, his trees, and his own good simple peasants' [VII, 76]. Tom Moore told Lockhart that he parted from Scott in 1825 feeling 'that those only could learn to love him as he deserved who had seen him at Abbotsford' [VIII, 66], and Lockhart's narrative organization reflects this feeling. But characteristically, Lockhart evokes the most profound sympathy in precisely those images which attract his severest judgement. Lockhart knew the 'true Scotchman's' infatuation to be the dream of house-building; he could easily have agreed with Hawthorne's Holgrave that 'planting a family' is a prime cause of human misdoing, or with the Scottish author of *The House with the Green Shutters* that it is a peculi-arly dreadful Scottish form of *hubris*. Scott, like Constable, 'desired to plant a lasting root, and dreamt not of personal fame, but of long distant generations rejoicing in the name of "Scott of Abbotsford". By this idea all his reveries – all his aspirations – all his plans and efforts, were over-shadowed and controlled' [X, 202]. The spectacle of Abbotsford growing, of the realizing of this romance, is one to evoke not just pity but terror.

From the acquisition of the original 'small farm' near Melrose, the process was continually one in which Scott 'was preparing fresh embarrassments for himself' [IV, 73], eagerly acquiring newly available properties at outrageous prices, and sacrificing likewise 'control of some of his minor tastes' in Abbotsford's antiquarian adornment [IV, 74]. Lockhart's own appearance on the scene in 1818 is set amidst a full panorama of the Laird in his new estates, at the peak of his fortunes: 'The great poet and novelist . . . under his own roof, when his fame was at its *acme*, and his fortune seemed culminating to about a corresponding height' [V, 341]. But for him, as for Constable, 'Fortune had already begun to prepare a stern rebuke' [VII, 23]. The faithful retainer Lockhart could share with Scott the patriarchal dream, the 'romantic idealization of Scottish aristocracy' [x, 207], that was Abbotsford. Yet the stern moralist Lockhart could portray the infatuated laird at its gaslit completion in these words: 'With what serenity did he walk about those splendid apartments, handling books, expounding armor and pictures, and rejoicing in the Babylon which he had built!' [vii, 355]. And perhaps loyal retainer and judge join in a passage such as Maria Edgeworth's visit, when the witnessnarrator reflects: 'Never did I see a brighter day at Abbotsford than that on which Miss Edgeworth first arrived there' [vii, 162]. It ended. 'Thus a fortnight was passed – and the vision closed; for Miss Edgeworth never saw Abbotsford again during his life; and I am very sure she could never bear to look upon it now that the spirit is fled' [vii, 163].

Indeed, the biographer could scarcely bear it himself. Babylon it may have been; reckless daydream; infatuated effort to impose romance on sober reality. But the biographer's commitment to the ambivalence of his symbol lived on to haunt the man. On 2 May 1847 he wrote to Miss Edgeworth from Abbotsford:

'You my dear friend can imagine w what a heart I have reentered this house which I had not seen since the morning after your old friend's funeral in September 1832 – Everything in perfect order – every chair and table where it was then left and I alone to walk a ghost in a sepulchre amidst the scenes of all that ever made life worth the name for me.'[154]

It is, of course, this extraordinary combination of intense sympathy and severe judicial detachment that makes Lockhart's conclusion the masterpiece Morritt called it. It is dominated by the controlling theme of the entire work – the prevalence, dangerous, ennobling, endearing, of imagination and how it 'soon shaped out a world of its own – to which it would fain accommodate the real one' [x, 201]. The full conception emerges in a letter to the Lord Chief Commissioner Adam [1837]:

'He had various faults if I may venture to speak openly to you who knew him and loved him as well as anybody did – but I think they may all be traced to the same boundless energy of imagination that gave us his immortal works. This imagination exalted and embellished for him things which I never could bring myself to respect and worship as he did – rank – fortune – mere worldly distinction – even *down to* the investing w a chivalrous dignity objects which a tithe of his observation wd have made any man less under the sway of romantic association contemplate as (especially with reference to

Scott's own self-won position in the eye of all mankind) mere nothings.'[155]

It is the view, evidently, which William Wordsworth found embodied in the work's conclusion: 'If, as I suspect,' he wrote Lockhart,

'his admirable Works would not, at least many of them, have been produced, but for the spur of worldly ambition, the world at large will, for the sake of those Works, be little disposed to blame what you yourself must have reckoned weaknesses, as is evident from the mode in which you account for, and with no inconsiderable success, palliate them.'[156]

Those who think Lockhart softened his severity unduly in the published work are overlooking such statements in the conclusion as this:

'He appears to have studiously escaped from whatever could have interfered with his own enjoyment – to have revelled in the fair results, and waved the wand of obliterating magic over all besides; and persisted so long, that (like the sorcerer he celebrates) he became the dupe of his own delusions.' [x, 209]

The conclusion is, as a rhetorical action, only the most extraordinary manifestation of the complex relationship of Lockhart and Scott, for the understanding of which no brief comparisons with Boswell and Johnson will suffice. If it is true that Boswell's *Johnson* is inseparable from the autobiography of that enigmatic biographer, it is even more true of Lockhart's *Scott*, to the extent that Lockhart possessed profundities of intelligence and feeling unknown to Boswell. Rycenga appears right: 'Lockhart's *Scott* is not so personal a study as Boswell's *Johnson*.'[157] But this is only because the intricately reticent Lockhart's personal involvement is assimilated so fully into the narrative form and method of his work. The nature of the involvement and of the man is a subject for some biographer almost equally perceptive and skilful. Commentators have long been dedicated to the supposition that the chill diffidence which sporadically burst into sharp, even arrogant irony, must have been rooted in what J. I. M. Stewart recently called some 'deep self-distrust' concealing a 'buried goodness of heart and fineness of perception'.[158] A generation ago, Donald Carswell saw the enigma in historical terms, remarking on the overwhelming rapidity of change in Lockhart's generation:

'many minds, even of the abler sort, could not adjust themselves to it. Lockhart was one of them. He was not a child of the eighteenth century [one should add that Scott most assuredly was]; if he had been, he would have known where he stood [as Scott did] and made the best of things [what he most admired in Scott's "manliness"].

But he was born and grew up in the magnificent but uneasy years of the Romantic transition, and, having more learning and intelligence than insight, lived all his life in a state of unresolved conflict and frustration.'[159]

Lang supposed an 'ineradicable ply of nature which . . . ended in a malady of voiceless grief'; Miss Lochhead invoked a personal devil – a wild, mocking one. Those who find in Lockhart only a chill, arrogant stoicism are much farther from the truth than the fire and ice school – 'the fire within burned the more fiercely because he never permitted it to grow into a blaze'.[160] But they have good reason for their exaggeration: as Maria Edgeworth wrote to Lockhart himself, 'You open your mind to so few that it is the more necessary those few should tell you plainly their true impressions.'[161] Scott felt compelled to prepare his London friends for Lockhart's withdrawn hidalgo airs, protesting in letters to Mrs Hughes, to Joanna Baillie, to Samuel Rogers, and others that the nut was well worth cracking, however hard. Lockhart's own letters occasionally portray a weary pococurantism, from an early inclination to bitter discouragement –

'As for the affair itself having long since dismissed it from my thoughts, I shall not now suffer it to enter much into them. If good come – so: if not there will be very little disappointment –'

to the late and revealing letter on the occasion of his appointment to Auditorship of the Duchy of Lancaster:

'I never pushed for anything, nor moved in any degree for anything. . . . I am now verging on 50, have long since lost all that made life pleasant enough to be much worth caring for, & with that all the little ambition I ever had.'[162]

Nevertheless, other letters and remarks make clear that a true stoic-ism was really an anti-self which he found in Scott; his most emphatically expressed admiration for Scott is in these terms. On the occasion of Lady Scott's death he writes Sophia of her father's recovery of composure: 'What a blessing to have such a regulated manliness of heart & mind. The possession is even more enviable than his genius.' But Scott was only the supreme example; Lockhart's condolences to Croker on the loss of an only child invoke the same ideal: 'It is fortunate when those whose feelings are the most keen have possession of that strong sense of duty and that Energy of will without which the measure of their faculties would only add to that of their afflictions.' And thirty-two years later, sick and aging, he places Croker and Scott together:

'every line or every day has shown how completely in your case mind triumphs over matter. I have had the rare fortune to know well two great men and both have set the example of consummate manhood – to none more needful than my poor weak self – but enough of painful topics.'

He never wrote more revealing lines.[163]

The 'poor weak self' apparently could be strengthened only in submergence, possible only through biographical identification with the subject, the anti-self he describes. His sympathetic and wise modern apologist, G. S. Gordon, explains best why the inevitable way was through biography:

'He needed always, I should guess, to attach himself to a man or an institution: Blackwood's and Wilson; the Quarterly; Sir Walter Scott. Thus merged and only half identified, he would communicate firmly with the world. His deeper self – for there were profundities in Lockhart – shrank always from exposure.'[164]

In view of such a process and such an impulse, and of the complex ways in which Scott was indeed the centre of his biographer's experience and self-knowledge, it is surprising that there was any judicial detachment at all in his *Life of Scott*.

The evidence of severity is undeniable. For the most part, though, apparently as an obligation he owed his better nature, and in conformity with his definably Romantic conception of biographical decorum, Lockhart allowed his fidelity to govern his detachment. The dominant tone in the *Life* remains closer to the elegiac than to the judicial. It is the tone of the lone survivor, the last of the retainers. And suitably, at Dryburgh Abbey, in the final tonal gesture of his great biographical creation, Lockhart had himself buried at the feet of his *ain deir lord*.

APPENDIX TO CHAPTER 4.
MYTH-MAKING AT
MONT ST JEAN?

At two points in the 'Waterloo' chapter modern biographers, were they willing even to notice Lockhart's early 'epitome', might level the familiar charges of picturesque fabrication. It is best, then, to indicate here the evidence which proves that, whether or not guilty of error, he is innocent of myth-making.

And yet the subject was (and still is) ideal; fact is so shifting and unstable that the fancy is almost free to construct what it will. The Duke of Wellington knew this; he used to say, it is reported, 'he was accustomed to read so many conflicting descriptions of the battle that he would soon begin to believe he was not there himself'. Hence, when Sir Walter applied for aid with 'Paul's' letters on Waterloo (even the battle's name is no more accurate than that of Hastings), he was discouraged. The Duke wrote:

> The object which you propose to yourself is very difficult of attainment, and, if really attained, is not a little invidious. The history of a battle is not unlike the history of a ball. Some individuals may recollect all the little events of which the great result is the battle won or lost: but no individual can recollect the order in which, or the exact moment at which, they occurred, which makes all the difference as to their value or importance.

Scott naturally persisted, and Wellington naturally confessed to Sinclair in the following year that he was 'really disgusted with and ashamed of all that I have seen of the battle of Waterloo'.[1]

The Duke's analogy of the history of a ball is suggestive; for one thing that must have disturbed him in narratives of the Campaign was the representation of his own behaviour at Brussels just before action commenced. It disturbs his memory still, for the most eminent of recent military analysts, Major-General Fuller, reports that though Wellington's 'actions have been minutely analyzed by all competent historians of the campaign, the only certain fact which has emerged is that he was totally unprepared to face the situation'.[2] In short – as even his own biographers seem eager to concede – he 'was taken by surprise'.[3] To this charge, Wellington himself, when he read it in Las Cases, gave the practical answer: in effect, the more fools they for not taking advantage of it! I beat them! And Lord Ellesmere, on the Duke's behalf, gave (in answering a sympathetic British historian) the more theoretic one:

> We should like to know Mr Allison's definition of a surprise . . . we contend that Napoleon's line of attack was one embraced and provided for in the Duke's calculations, but which the circumstances of his position made it impossible for him, up to the last moment, to anticipate with precision.[4]

J. C. Ropes outlines those circumstances, answering those who criticize Wellington for remaining in Brussels too long. His duty was to protect the Low Countries, the King of Holland at Brussels and Louis XVIII at Ghent (and Lockhart points out that, even if Napoleon's aim were known to be the former city, there were three main routes approaching it), as well as his own supply lines with the Channel. As Wellington later pointed out, answering Clausewitz, the Allies were on the defensive against an enemy in frontier fortresses capable of concealing its plans until the moment of execution:

> The initiative, then rested with the enemy; and the course to be pursued by the Allied generals respectively was to be prepared to move in all directions, to wait till it should be seen in what direction the attack would be made, and then to assemble the armies as quickly as possible to resist the attack, or to attack the enemy with the largest force that could be collected.[5]

Lockhart's was an early attempt to refute the 'fiction of the Duke of Wellington having been *surprised* on this great occasion'[6] – but even more, to counteract the impression of irresponsibility, of social trifling in Brussels even as Napoleon moved. 'There never was, since the days of Darius,' wrote the author of *Vanity Fair*, 'such a brilliant train of camp-followers as hung round the Duke of Wellington's army in the Low Countries in 1815, and led it, dancing and feasting as it were, up to the very brink of battle.' And the popular impression of Wellington, the supreme allied commander, unable to tear himself away from 'a certain ball which a noble Duchess gave at Brussels on the 15th of June', strangely persists. Consider Thompson's misleading phrasing: 'Wellington was so out of touch with reality that he ordered his troops to concentrate on a curved front from Brussels to Nivelle, and lingered till 3 a.m. [the hour latens from book to book] on the 16th at the Duchess of Richmond's ball.'[7]

Wellington was out of touch with reality to the extent that he expected the attack on Brussels up one of the main roads west of the Charleroi-Quatre-Bras-Mont St Jean line; and he clung through life to the notion that, as he told Lady Salisbury, 'Napoleon committed a great mistake in endeavouring to cut in between the Prussians and the English. He ought to have gone along the direct road by Mons.'[8] Fuller, to be sure, calls this 'an extraordinary misconception of Napoleonic strategy, because such a move would have driven Welling-ton and Blucher not apart but together'.[9] But it would also, had Wellington made a premature move to concentrate on his left in the Nivelles area, have exposed the communications lines of the entire force from the southwest, and ultimately endangered their access to the coast. Besides, the Mons route was no mere obsession; a letter always quoted to show Wellington the trifler (from a tutor in the Richmond family) reveals that on the 13th Napoleon was reported to be at Mau-beuge, far to the southwest down the Sambre from Charleroi, but directly south of Mons. And in the letter – Lockhart's authority – which I shall transcribe below, it is clear that even on the 15th the threat to Mons seemed as real as the possibility that Charleroi was *not* the main action. It was not until late in the evening, according to the Prussian attaché Müffling, that the report came from General Dörnberg at Mons assuring Wellington that his right was clear and that the main French force had moved east.[10]

Having communicated the news from Mons, he suggested to Müffling that they go to the ball; nor was he out of touch there. Again modern scepticism seems not wholly justifiable – Petrie, for example, who says 'there is no truth whatever in the legend that Wellington attended this ball fully aware of the French Emperor's movements, but did so in order to reassure the public about the safety of Brussels'.[11] Wellington's own dispatch makes clear that there were two sets of orders – one to prepare to march, the other, following the news from Mons regarding Charleroi, to march to the left. He told Müffling 'towards Midnight' that he had already ordered a concentration at Nivelles and Quatre Bras; he told the Duke of Richmond in his study after supper that he *had ordered* a concentration at Quatre Bras.[12] But even if the name of the village was a later accretion to these reports, a movement toward Nivelles – toward the east – is sufficient to indicate that the Duke was not 'completely in the dark'.

Lockhart's authority also asserts that the Duke's attendance at the ball was a public gesture; this, too, Petrie seems to deny. Again, his words to Müffling remain; even the antagonistic M. Houssaye gives them: 'Mes troupes vont se mettre en marche. Mais ici les partisans de Napoléon commencent à lever la tête. Il faut rassurer nos amis. Allons donc nous faire voir au bal de la duchesse de Richmond, et nous monterons à cheval à cinq heures du matin.'[13] This motive the letter to Lockhart again asserts, as it also gives an additional picture of how little Wellington must have been able to enjoy the ball. 'Although the Duke affected great gaiety and cheerfulness,' Lady Hamilton Dalrymple wrote in her journal, 'it struck me that I had never seen him have such an expression of care and anxiety on his countenance. . . . Despatches were constantly coming in to the Duke.'[14]

But it is not my purpose to add a neophyte's petulance to this great argument. I mean only to introduce the document from which Lockhart's revised account came – a letter addressed merely to 'Dear Sir' in the Abbotsford scrapbooks of letters to Lockhart, dated London, 14 May 1830, from one whose signature I read 'M. Fitzgerald'. I can only assume this to be Maurice Fitzgerald (1774-1849), hereditary knight of Kerry, Member for Kerry in Irish and imperial parliaments until the Reform Bill struggle, personal friend of Wellington and Castlereagh, and Catholic Emancipationist, who, at the time of writing, had good reason to defend the Emancipationist Duke. If (as seems unlikely) Lockhart simply accepted the account with no further verification from the Tory friends of the Duke with whom he was in contact, he was guilty of incautious scholarship; but if, in adapting this very circumstantial report of a very confused day, he produced an uncertain or incomplete account, he remains in the august company of most who have attempted the task.

(Nat. Lib. Scot. MS 91 off 39-40)   London 14 May 1830

Dear Sir

Was ever the tenacity of false rumour so illustrated as in the misrepresentations which still circulate of the Duke of Wellington
having been *surprised* at a Ball in Bruxelles. It is also a curious
illustration of His Grace's indifference to vulgar Fame, that he
shall have suffered an error so long to prevail which he could dissi-
pate by a single sentence. Finding that error continued even in
your recent interesting compendium of the Life of Napoleon, I
cannot resist my desire to furnish you with a complete refutation of
the original falsehood – which some circumstances accidentally within
my knowledge enable me to do. – To authenticate the case for your
satisfaction, I shall explain how I happened to know any thing on
the subject – and then give you separately a simple statement of
the facts attending the breaking up of the English Army in Flanders.
– In the beginning of June 1815 I went with my friend Lord
Ormonde to see the combined Armies in Flanders before they
should take the field in the then approaching campaign. – We were
late for the general review of the British troops but saw separately
the Horse Artillery reviewed & the French Household Troops
manoeuvered by the Duc de Berri. – The Duke of Wellington was
so kind as to give us a letter of introduction to Marshall Blucher
which he expected would procure for us a review of the Prussian
Army. – He recommended me previously to see the works he had been
carrying on at Aeth [Ath ?], the famous little fortress where
Vauban tried his first ricochet shot. – This advice took us round by
Aeth, where I saw the Fortifications on the afternoon of Wednesday
the 14th & proceeded at daybreak on Thursday for Mons on our
route to Namur. – Being desirous to view the fortifications I went
to the quarters of the Commandant, a Dutch Engineer, to ask for
permission to see the citadel. On finding that we were proceeding to
Namur he said he could not suffer us to fall into the hands of the
enemy which we should do if we proceeded as the French Patrols
were within two leagues of Mons. – He then detailed the information he had obtained of the advance of the French – & their defeat
of the Prussians. – He wished us to observe silence on the subject
as it was important to keep the Population of Mons in ignorance as
long as possible, & he was then taking steps to let out the inunda-

tion on the surrounding ground. – We resolved to return to
Bruxelles and, on the way, mentioned the circumstances, only, to
Baron Allen commanding one of our divisions, and Colonel Aber-
crombie at Enghien. – On arriving at Bruxelles at about half past
four P. M. I immediately went to Head Quarters, and sent to the
Duke through Colonel (Sir Colin) Campbell, to say I had returned
from Mons, where I had heard of the defeat of the Prussians. –
Colonel Campbell told me that about half past one a General Officer
had arrived from Marshal Blucher, with an account of the advance
of the French – one previously despatched had probably been intercepted. – He brought me in answer that the Duke was then writing
General orders for the Army, but wished me to dine with him, I
was unfortunately engaged. – He then said he would see me at 'the
Ball'. I asked if the Ball had not been put off – Sir Colin answered
No – that it had been considered – and it being very desirable that
no Eclat should take place at Bruxelles it was better to let it go on,
that the general officers would even appear there, but would quietly
leave the room at ten o'clock precisely – and join their respective
divisions in march – that orders had been despatched at *two o'clock*
to the cantonments of the Army to break up and concentrate on the
Left. – At the Ball the Duke conversed with me a considerable time
on the information I had received at Mons – explained his estimate
of the amount of force moved against his Left & the object – all of
which was literally verified by the result. – He told me that his
whole Army would be concentrated on his extreme Left at 'Quatre
Bras', the following evening by eleven o'clock – The entire Army
was up before twelve at that point. –
The General Officers after taking leave of their friends left the Ball
Room almost unobserved *quietly* one after another at the appointed
hour. – The Duke retired at twelve & left Bruxelles as originally
arranged the following Morning (the 16th) at 6 o'clock. – On
Friday the 16th Col Campbell told me that if the Duke had to fight
a Battle to cover Bruxelles it would either be in a Position he approved in front of the Foret de Soignies [sic] – (Waterloo) – or in
a still stronger one on the Eastern side of the town – according to
circumstances. – Sir Pulteney Malcolm who commanded the naval
branch of service connected with the Army was desirous that as the
Duke of Wellington would probably not write a despatch till after
a Battle, Ministers should be fully informed of all that had occurred.

He accordingly urged strongly my proceeding to London with a short despatch from himself to the Admiralty – leaving it to me to add the details – on which we perfectly agreed.
[Fitzgerald claims he did so, and reported to the Cabinet, who had assembled in the House of Lords to hear him.]

II

No document remains, to my knowledge, to suggest the source of Lockhart's other innovation. But here one is simply faced with the coexistence of circumstancial narrative and categorical denial, and is forced to conclude either an unaccountable fertility of invention in the narrator or an unknown motive for repudiation in the subject. 'Picturesque but apocryphal' are the words Rose chooses to describe the account of Wellington's midnight ride – it was not midnight at all – to see Blucher at Wavre the evening before Mont St Jean.[15] Lockhart cites no specific authority in giving the story for the first time, but observes in a footnote:

The fact of Wellington and Blucher having met between the battles of Ligny and Waterloo is well known to many of the superior officers then in the Netherlands; but the writer of this compendium has never happened to see it mentioned in print. The horse that carried the Duke of Wellington through this long night journey, so important to the decisive battle of the 18th, remained till lately, it is understood, if he does not still remain, a free pensioner in the best paddock of Strathfieldsaye.[16]

Some will think immediately of the famous 'Polton Ride' – another midnight gallop in quest of reassurance – which Lockhart is accused of fabricating for the *Life of Scott,* and will infer that Lockhart's fancy took fire at such equestrian possibilities. I, for one, fully aware of his attitudes towards biographical document and anecdote, do not believe that he simply invented incidents, nor that, in the Wavre case, the officers mentioned made it all up. Nor do I believe that Justice Coltman, however many years later he recounted the conversation to his son, *imagined* he heard the story from Wellington at Strathfieldsaye in 1858.[17] Nor does it seem to me probable that the journalist Julian Charles Young simply *imagined* that Henry Pierrepont, immediately following a visit to Strathfieldsay, had given him the story circumstantially, even quoting the Duke:

The fact was, I wished to see Blucher, that I might learn from his own lips at what hour it was probable he would be able to join forces with us next day. Therefore, the moment Fitzroy [Somerset]'s back was turned, I ordered Copenhagen to be resaddled, and told my man to get his own horse and accompany me to Wayre, where I had reason to believe old 'Forwards' was encamped.[18]

On what basis does Maxwell assign the story to the 'category of the myth'?[19] In the first place, on the basis of the Duke's silence; but this is circular, since, unless the evidence of Lockhart, Coltman, and Young be discounted, the Duke was not silent. In the second place, on the basis of Ropes' repudiation of the story in his third edition; Ropes based his decision on the distance in time of the Coltman and Young reports from the reputed conversations (hardly enough to explain pure fabrication), and on the Duke's own disclaimer in conversation with Baron Gurney.[20]

Lockhart himself was to publish a disclaimer from the Duke – by way of Lord Ellesmere as reviewer – in the *Quarterly Review*, LXX (1842), 464. But Ropes rightly points out that Ellesmere's rejoinder is vague and incomplete, giving no alternative accounting for Wellington's actions during the evening of the 17th.[21] And the story was allowed to remain in the Family Library.

There is no sign of it, however, in present-day works. For its 'romantic' colouring – and its unprofessional indignity – it has been doubted out of historical existence. Just or not, the elimination cannot be evaluated here. But we can at least conclude that, apocryphal or not, the story was definitely in the air, and was not simply a new toy of Lockhart the maker of picturesque myth.

NOTES

NOTES TO THE PREFACE

1. Altick, *Lives and Letters* (N.Y. 1965), p 181; Nicolson, *The Development of English Biography* (London 1928), p 110; Garraty, *The Nature of Biography* (N.Y. 1957), pp 97, 99; Kendall, *The Art of Biography* (N.Y. 1965), pp 103, 105. Admirable exceptions are found in Edgar Johnson, *One Mighty Torrent* (new edn, N.Y. 1955), pp. 305–7; and J. A. Rycenga's valuable PhD dissertation, *Theories and Forms in English Biography 1836–1899* Northwestern University 1959).

2. Reid, *English Biography in the Early Nineteenth Century* (New Haven 1965), p 28 and *passim*.

3. Reid, p 163. His final chapter, 'Some Principles', is an extremely valuable essay. His interpretations of biographical theory in the period we have both studied differ basically from mine. Further dialogue, then, seems futile; hence, the paucity of reference to his book in mine.

4. Reid, p 165; Clifford, ed., *Biography as an Art: Selected Criticism 1560-1960* (N.Y. 1962).

NOTES TO CHAPTER 1

1. In the *National Review:* see *Men, Books, and Mountains*, ed. S.O.A. Ullman (Minneapolis 1956), p 136.

2. *Biographical Essays* (N.Y. 1949), p 16; cf. C.R.Sanders, *Lytton Strachey: His Mind and Art* (New Haven 1957), pp 194–5.

3. *Quarterly Review*, XLVI (1831), 18.

4. 'Lockhart wrote in the Boswellian tradition,' observes John A. Garraty *The Nature of Biography* [N.Y. 1957] p 98). Cf. Edgar Johnson: *The Life of Scott* 'makes no significant departure from the Boswell method' (*One Mighty Torrent* [N.Y. 1955] p 309). 'The Boswell Formula' is Sir Harold Nicolson's phrase: Lockhart 'adopted Boswell's method in the sense that he worked up his portrait on the impressionistic method' (*The Development of English Biography* [London 1947], pp 117–24. Fuller comparisons are found in Ian Jack, *English Literature 1815–1832* (Oxford 1963), pp 356–61; and J.A. Rycenga, *Theories and Forms in English Biography*, unpub. PhD. dissertation (Northwestern University 1959), especially pp 39–41. Rycenga's work was done at the same time as my own preliminary studies; I regret having missed it until much later.

5. Stephen in 'Scott', *DNB*. Lang, *The Life and Letters of John Gibson Lockhart*, 2 vols (London 1897), II, 123. The 'prince of all biographers, past, present, and to come' is Saintsbury's phrase: *Essays in English Literature: 1780–1860*, 2nd ser. (London 1895), p 389. George S. Gordon, 'John Gibson Lockhart', address at the University of Glasgow, 18 June 1930 (Glasgow 1944), pp 14–15. Rait, 'Boswell and Lockhart', *Essays by Divers Hands* (Trans. Roy. Soc. Lit.), n.s. XII (1933), 121. Grierson, 'Lang, Lockhart, and Biography' (Oxford 1934), p 17. Morritt, MS letter (1837), Nat. Lib. Scot. MS 932 No. 84.

6. H. Harvey Wood, 'Literature', in *Scotland*, ed. H. W. Meikle (Edinburgh 1947), p 163; on a more sophisticated level, cf. Kurt Wittig, *The Scottish Tradition in Literature* (Edinburgh 1958), pp 104, 155.

7. Coleridge, *The Friend*, 3 vols (London 1850), II, 9–10.

8. *Critical Review*, n.s. XII (1794), 83; *Annual Review*, III (1804), 470; Stanfield, *An Essay on the Study and Composition of Biography* (Sunderland 1813), p vi; Scott's 'Ashestiel Fragment', 26 April 1808, which opens Lockhart's *Life of Scott*; Watkins, *Universal Biographical Dictionary* (1821), quoted by Waldo H. Dunn in *English Biography* (N. Y. 1916), p.157.

9. *The Friend*, II, 227; Foster, *Critical Essays*, 2 vols (London 1868), I, 18, and II, 193–4; Stanfield, *Essay*, p 325 (misnumbered 335); Lockhart, *QR*, XXXV (1826), 149, 164. Cf. his remarks on 'the bed-chaplain style of Memoir', *QR*, LXXVI (1845), 464–5.

10. D'Israeli, *Literary Miscellanies* (London 1801), pp 120–1; Lockhart in *Blackwood's*, II (1817–18), 269.

11. For a full analysis of the interplay of such factors, see R. D. Altick, *Lives and Letters* (N. Y. 1965), pp 27–34; cf. Garraty, *Nature of Biography*, p 82; and G. H. Mead, *Movements of Thought in the Nineteenth Century* (Chicago 1944), pp 82–83.

12. Wayne Shumaker, *English Autobiography* (Berkeley 1954), p 22. D'Israeli's 'Dissertation on Anecdotes' (1793: the year of Boswell's *Johnson*) offers a timely defence of the collection and 'relation of detached and interesting particulars'. Such symptomatic events validate Garraty's suggestion that towards the *end* of the eighteenth century 'the telling of anecdotes became a literary form in its own right' (*Nature of Biography*, p 85; cf. Altick, *Lives and Letters*, pp 33–34).

13. Kenneth MacLean, *John Locke and English Literature of the Eighteenth Century* (New Haven 1936); Cassirer, *The Philosophy of the Enlightenment* (Boston 1962), p 94; Isaiah Berlin, *The Age of Enlightenment* (N. Y. 1956), p 19; Hume, Intro. to *A Treatise of Human Nature*.

14. G. S. Brett, *History of Psychology* (London 1953), p 403.

15. *Confessions*, trans. J. M. Cohen (Penguin edn 1953), pp 19, 65, 169, 262.

16. W. R. Sorely, *A History of English Philosophy* (Cambridge 1920), pp 205–7; G. Bryson, *Man and Society: the Scottish Inquiry of the Eighteenth Century* (Princeton 1945), Intro.; S. A. Grave, *The Scottish Philosophy of Common Sense* (Oxford 1960), p 1.

17. Lockhart, *Peter's Letters to His Kinsfolk*, 3 vols (Edinburgh 1819), I, 177.

18. Reid, quoted by Grave, *The Scottish Philosophy of Common Sense*, p 12; Stewart, from Grave, p 200; Cousin from Grave, p 3. Brown held to the intuitionism of the group, but urged restraints on the appeal to intuition: see his *Lectures on the Philosophy of the Human Mind*, 3 vols (Philadelphia 1824), I, 158–9.

19. Reid, *Essays on the Powers of the Human Mind* (London 1827), p 165; cf. Brown, Lecture XI; Grave, p 3.

20. Reid, *Essays*, pp 158, 164–65; Brown, Lecture XIII: 'On the Direct Evidence of Mental Identity'; W.R.Sorley, *History of English Philosophy*, pp 205–7.

21. Stanfield, *Essay*, pp vii, xv; Adolphus, *Biography*, p 15; Bisset, *Life of Burke*, 2 vols (London 1800), I, 3, 17–18; D'Israeli, *Literary Misc.*, p 27.

22. *Contributions to the Edinburgh Review*, 4 vols (Edinburgh 1844), I, 691.

23. *Literary Misc.*, p 63.

24. Adolphus, *Biography*, pp 20–21; Lockhart, *QR*, LXIII (1839), 151; *Life of Scott*, 10 vols (Edinburgh, 1902–3), X, 198.

25. *Boswell's Life of Johnson*, ed. G.B.Hill, rev. L.F.Powell, 6 vols (Oxford 1934), IV, 424–5.

26. *Journal of Henry Cockburn: 1831–1854*, 2 vols (Edinburgh 1874), I, 175; cf. Forbes, *Life of Beattie*, 2 vols (Edinburgh 1806), II, 176; *Crit. Rev.*, n.s. II (1791), 337–8; *Analyt. Rev.*, XI (1791), 376.

27. *The Prelude* (1850), II, 203–7, 216–19.

28. Everyman Edn. (London 1908), p 153.

29. *Collected Works*, ed. P.P.Howe (London 1933), VIII, 313.

30. *Private Papers of James Boswell from Malahide Castle*, ed. G.Scott & F.Pottle, 18 vols (Mt Vernon, 1928–34), VI, 16–17; X, 195–6. *Letters of James Boswell*, ed. C.B.Tinker, 2 vols (Oxford 1924), II, 340, 344. Cf. *The Hypochondriack*, ed. M. Bailey, 2 vols (Stanford 1928), II, 259.

31. *Confessions*, p 169.

32. Stanfield, *Essay*, p 25.

33. *A History of Autobiography in Antiquity*, trans. E.W.Dickes, 2 vols (London 1950), I, 62–63, 290.

34. *English Literature: 1815–1832*, p 357.

35. *Life of Scott*, I, 112.

36. *Life of Arnold*, 2 vols (London 1845), I, ix.

37. *Life of Scott*, X, 197.

38. *Romantic Narrative Art* (Madison 1960), pp 69–70.

39. *Tales and Novels*, 18 vols (London 1832), I, ix–x, xii.

40. Fielding, *Joseph Andrews*, III.i; Lockhart, Intro. to *Don Quixote* (Edinburgh 1822), I, lviii.

41. E.A.Baker, *History of the English Novel*, VII, 63–64.

42. *Blackwood's*, VII (1820), 361, 368–9.

43. Andrew Lang, *Life and Letters of Lockhart*, I, 72–73, 75, 79.

44. *Adam Blair* (Edinburgh 1822), pp 308, 338 (misnumbered 336). On Lockhart as novelist, see G.Macbeth, *John Gibson Lockhart* (Urbana 1935), p 30; Saintsbury, *Collected Essays and Papers* (London 1923), II, 7; Elton, *Survey of English Literature: 1780–1830* (London 1912), I, 413; M.Lochhead, *John Gibson Lockhart* (London 1954), pp 124–36; D.Craig, *Scottish Literature and the Scottish People* (London 1961), pp 174–78, 189–90. Craig has provided a much-needed modern edition of *Blair* (Edinburgh 1963). *Blair* is the novel compared at length with *The Scarlet Letter* by Henry James in *Hawthorne* (N.Y. 1901), pp 111–13.

45. *QR*, XLVI (1831), 10.

46. Nat. Lib. Scot. MS 3653: 12 Feb. 1838.

47. Stauffer, *The Art of Biography in Eighteenth Century England* (Princeton 1941), p 413.

48. Intro. to *Don Quixote*, I, liv; *Q R*, XXXIV (1826), 350, 353–72 *passim*; *Noctes Ambrosianae* No. I (by Lockhart), in *Blackwood's*, XI (1822), 368; also, *Blackwood's*, II (1817–18), 269; and IV (1819), 395. The last article is attributed to Lockhart by Macbeth (p 211); Blackwood's Contributors List (Nat. Lib. Scot.) gives it instead to Howison. I quote only phrases which represent Lockhart's consistent attitudes. The rest, an attack on the new psychological novel as a 'spurious sort of literature', Lockhart would not have written.

49. Lang, *Lockhart*, I, 77.

50. *Blackwood's*, XV (1824), 624.

51. *Annual Review*, III (1804), 470.

52. *Blackwood's*, IV (1818), 212.

53. *Q R*, XXXVII (1828), 87; *Blackwood's*, XXVI (1829), 561–62; *Q R*, XLVIII (1832), 394; *Q R*, XXXVI (1827), 269.

54. *Essays in Ecclesiastical Biography*, quoted by Dunn, *English Biography*, pp 159–60.

55. Stanfield, *Essay*, p 59.

56. George Gordon, 'Art and Ethics of Modern Biography', *The Lives of Authors* (London 1950), p 17.

57. *Monthly Review*, XXX (1799), 241–2.

58. Quoted by Dunn, *English Biography*, p 182.

59. *Critical Review*, XXXI (1801), 35.

60. Garraty, *Nature of Biography*, p 80.

61. *Critical Review*, XXXI (1801), 48.

62. [George Hardinge?], *The Essence of Malone or the Beauties of that Fascinating Writer extracted from his Immortal Work*, etc. (London 1800), *passim*.

63. *Q R*, XLVI (1831), 4–5.

64. *Q R*, LVII (1836), 275.

65. *Art of Biography in Eighteenth Century England*, p 517; Dunn, *English Biography*, p 68.

66. Stanfield, *Essay*, pp 259–60; Southey, *Q R*, XLVII (1832), 466; Jeffrey, *Contributions to the Edinburgh Review*, III, 507, 573; Scott, *Crit. and Misc. Essays* (Philadelphia 1841), I, 50; III, 18.

67. *Q R*, XXXIV (1826), 574, 591.

68. *Q R*, LII (1834), 443, 446–7.

69. *Q R*, LVII (1836), 331–2.

70. *Annual Review*, II (1803), 462.

71. *English Literature: 1815-1832*, p 365.

72. *Contributions to the Edinburgh Review*, III, 572–3.

73. *Q R*, LXXI (1842–43), 548, 560, 546.

74. Lang, *Lockhart*, II, 114.

75. Nat. Lib. Scot. MS 331 ff 239–40.

76. *Q R*, LXIII (1839), 403.

77. *Q R*, LXXVII (1845), 34.

78. Foster, *Critical Essays*, I, 103; Carlyle, *Crit. & Misc. Essays*, IV, 77; Jeffrey, *Contributions to the Edinburgh Review*, I, 464.

79. *Q R*, XXXIV (1826), 407; XLVI (1831), 316; *Contributions to the Edinburgh Review*, I, 477.

80. *Q R*, XLVIII (1832), 456.

81. *Contributions to the Edinburgh Review*, I, 464.

82. *Biography*, p 25.

83. *Q R*, XXVIII (1822–3), 470.

84. *Q R*, XXXIV (1826), 407.

85. *Q R*, XLVIII (1832), 456.

86. *Contributions to the Edinburgh Review*, I, 660–1.

87. *Q R*, XLVI (1831), 314, 316.

88. *New Monthly Magazine*, XIV (1825), 97–98; *Westminster Review*, IV (1825), 409–11; *Contributions to the Edinburgh Review*, I, 485, 511, 480; *Crit. and Misc. Essays*, II, 419, 443, 449.

89. *Crit. and Misc. Essays*, II, 418–19.

90. *Q R*, LXXIX (1846–7), 300.

91. Letter of 7 November 1845 to John Murray, pub. by A.L.Strout, in *Notes and Queries*, CLXXXIX (1945), 36–37.

92. *Life of Scott*, IV, 325.

93. Quoted by Hayley in 'Desultory Remarks on the Letters of Eminent Persons', *Life of Cowper*, III, xxvii.

94. *Contributions to the Edinburgh Review*, I, 420.

95. *Crit. and Misc. Essays*, I, 180–81; *Annual Review*, II (1803), 457.

96. *Crit. and Hist. Essays*, 3 vols (Boston 1900), I, 709–10.

97. 16 May 1825: Nat. Lib. Scot. MS 331 ff 239–40.

98. 17 November 1832: Nat. Lib. Scot. MS 923 No. 51.

99. Jeffrey, *Contributions to the Edinburgh Review*, III, 646; Stanfield, *Essay*, p 173.

100. *Life of Cowper*, III, ix.

101. *Works*, ed. Howe, XVI, 141, 139.

102. Nat. Lib. Scot. MS 1825 No. 19.

103. *Q R*, XIX (1818), 118, 124–5.

104. *Crit. and Hist. Essays*, II, 203.

105. *Q R*, XXVII (1822), 179; *Q R*, LXXII (1843), 517–19; *Q R*, LXXXIX (1851), 136.

106. Nat. Lib. Scot. MS 1821 f 40: 5 June 1840.

107. *Q R*, XLIV (1831), 209.

108. *Q R*, LVII (1836), 275.

109. *Q R*, LXXXV (1849), 33; *Q R*, LXXXVIII (1850), 226, 247.

110. *Annual Review*, II (1803), 457.

111. *Contributions to the Edinburgh Review*, I, 395.

112. *Annual Review*, IV (1805), 449.

113. *Annual Review*, II (1803), 457.

114. *Crit. and Misc. Essays*, I, 66–67.

115. Stanfield, *Essay*, pp 76–77.

116. Garraty, *Nature of Biography*, p 196; Scott, *Crit. and Misc. Essays*, I, 181.

117. 'A Letter to a Friend of Burns', *Prose Works*, 3 vols (London 1876), II, 9.

118. *Q R*, XI (1814), 73.

119. *Biography*, pp 21–23; cf. *Lives of the English Poets*, ed. G.B.Hill, 3 vols (Oxford 1905), III, 206–8.

120. 11 December 1836: Nat. Lib. Scot. MS 2890 ff 137–8; *Life of Scott*, VII, 28.

121. *Life of Scott*, III, 242–3.

122. Garraty, *Nature of Biography*, pp 98–99.

123. Stanfield, *Essay*, p 184.

124. Forbes, *Life of Beattie*, II, 176; *Critical Review*, n.s. II (1791), 3 7–8; *Analyt. Review*, XI (1791), 376.

125. *Life of Scott*, III, 243.

126. *Works of Peacock*, ed. Brett-Smith & Jones, 10 vols (London 1926), IX, 71–76; cf. E.J.Lovell, Jr., *His Very Self and Voice: Collected Conversations of Lord Byron* (N.Y. 1954), p xi.

127. Nat. Lib. Scot. MS 923: 17 November 1832.

128. *QR*, XLIX (1833), 112.

129. *Works*, XVI, 155–6.

130. *QR*, LIII (1835), 79–80.

131. *New Monthly Magazine*, XVII (1826), 113n; cf. *Works*, XI, 350.

132. *QR*, XLIX (1833), 117.

133. *Crit. and Misc. Essays*, III, 75.

134. R.W.Armour and R.F.Howes, *Coleridge the Talker* (Ithaca 1939), pp 201, 363, 334, 345, 232, and 236.

135. Stanfield, *Essay*, p 54.

136. See Hart, 'Boswell and the Romantics', *ELH*, XXVII (1960), 44–65.

137. See Boswell's *Johnson*, 5 vols (London 1831), I, viii, xii-xiii; Pref. to the 1835 edn (10 vols); G.B.Hill edn (1887), I, xxiii-xxiv; P.H.Fitzgerald, *Croker's Boswell and Boswell* (London 1880), pp 35–37; F.A.Pottle, *The Literary Career of James Boswell, Esq.* (Oxford 1929), p 177; M.F.Brightfield, *John Wilson Croker* (Berkeley 1940), pp 296-306. Brightfield is misleading in his representation of Hill and Pottle as Croker's defenders.

138. *The Idea of History* (Oxford 1946), p 147.

139. *Crit. and Misc. Essays*, III, 67–68.

140. *Crit. and Hist. Essays*, 3 vols (Boston 1900), I, 708-11.

141. *Notes and Queries*, CLXXXIX (1945), 36–37.

142. *QR*, XLVI (1831), 9–17.

143. Stanfield, *Essay*, p 54.

144. *QR*, LXXIX (1846–47), 274; *Blackwood's*, XVII (1825), 146.

145. *Sartor Resartus*, I.10, and III.7; *On Heroes, Hero-Worship and the Heroic in History*, Lecture I; *Past and Present*, II.16.

146. *Blackwood's*, II (1818), 673–4.

147. *QR*, LXXVII (1845), 40–41.

148. *QR*, LII (1834), 443.

149. His fullest discussion comes in correspondence with Croker at the time of the publication of Moore's diary (1853). Also suggestive is Croker's review of the *Memoirs of Lady Hester Stanhope* (*QR*, LXXVI [1845], 430ff). Mahon detected Lockhart's 'friendly superintendence' in the article (Nat. Lib. Scot. MS 930 No. 30), which contains a veritable treatise on editorial ethics. See also Lockhart in *QR*, LXXVIII (1846), 463–510 (the uses of General Nott's private letters); and *QR*, XLIII (1830), 81, 89.

150. *QR*, LVII (1836), 275.

151. 19 January 1837; printed in Abbotsford Notanda, in the 1871 edn of Robert Chambers, *Life of Sir Walter Scott* (pp 190–3).

152. *QR*, LXXVII (1846), 468.

The following are abbreviations used in these notes. '*P. L.*' alludes to *Peter's Letters to his Kinsfolk*, the 'Second Edition', 3 vols (Edinburgh 1819); 'Gleig' means Gleig's memoir of Lockhart, *Q R*, cxvi (1864); 'Lang' means Lang's *Lockhart*, 2 vols (London 1897); 'Lochhead' means Marion Lochhead's *Lockhart* (London 1954); 'Macbeth' refers to Macbeth's *Lockhart* (Urbana 1935); 'Oliphant' refers to Mrs Oliphant's *William Blackwood and His Sons*, 2 vols (N.Y. 1897); 'Cockburn' alludes to Henry Cockburn's *Memorials of His Time* (Edinburgh 1910). The bibliography of this 'lively piece of contemporary history' (Oliphant, I, 219) requires a few words. Miss Lochhead has fun claiming that the question of the mythical 'First Edition' may not be closed (p 50); but there is no real question. The work was contracted on 5 April 1819 – '£500 for the first Edition' (Nat. Lib. Scot. MS 4004 f 169). It was being written during April (Scott, *Letters*, v, 331–2). It appeared, then, as a 'Second Edition' in mid-July; the *Scotsman* review was 17 July. The editors of Scott, *Letters*, must be noticing the 'Third Edition' (i.e., the *second*!) when they give October as the date of publication (v, 322n). The original plan called for the third volume 'to be written chiefly by Wilson' (see Mrs Gordon's *Christopher North* [1879], p 179n); and Lockhart claimed later that *P. L.* 'were not wholly the work of one hand' (*Life of Scott*, VI, 92). But Wilson was notoriously dilatory; Lockhart's Edinburgh survey extends well into the third volume; and parts of the volume are *prima facie* Lockhart's recollections of his home city of Glasgow. He might have considered Scott as one of the 'hands'. At the planning stage he went by invitation to Abbotsford, taking 'all my own ears and Dr Morris's also to catch what may drop from you concerning things so interesting to all, and so little understood by either of us' (MS 3890 ff 65–66).

1. *P. L.*, III, 134–36; *Blackwood's*, XV (1823–4), 102–3.
2. Cockburn, p 197.
3. Lang, I, 96, 112–14, 118; *Redgauntlet*, Letter IX; *P. L.*, II, 28–29.
4. Hogg, *Poetical Works of the Ettrick Shepherd*, 5 vols (Glasgow 1831), v, cxviii.
5. Lang, I, 92; Lochhead, pp 34–35.
6. Lang, I, 124.
7. *P. L.*, I ,8. Subsequent refs are in the text.
8. Cockburn, p 300; Lang, I, 124.
9. *Letters . . . by members of Sir Walter Scott's family to their old governess* [Miss Millar] (London 1905), pp 58–60; Scott, *Letters*, v, 407n. 'Papa' changed his mind about the severity, writing the same month to Lockhart, 'the general turn of the book is perhaps too favourable both to the state of our public society and of individual character' (*Letters*, v, 430).
10. *The Scotsman*, 17 July 1819, p 231; Michael Joyce, *Edinburgh: The Golden Age* (London 1951), p 145.
11. *Early Letters*, ed. C.E.Norton, 2 vols (London 1886), II, 240: 11 Nov. 1823.
12. *A Gallery of Literary Portraits* (Edinburgh 1845), pp 438–9.
13. Cockburn, p 302.
14. Gleig, pp 461-2; W.M. Parker, *Q R*, CCLXXXIX (1951), 369.
15. Scott, *Letters*, v, 430; *Life of Scott*, VI, 91.
16. *Blackwood's*, XV (1823–4), 102; Strout thinks the review was Wilson's,

but I am relying on the tone of certainty in John McNeill's letter (17 October 1824) to Lockhart: 'It was a most audacious thing in you to review Reginald Dalton yourself and not content with what you had said of the book to add a note also in praise of the review' (Nat. Lib. Scot. MS 925 No. 33). Moir, MS 4724 ff 199–200.

17. Lang, I, 128 (letter to Haydon, 11 July 1838).

18. 31 October 1819: Nat. Lib. Scot. MS 3890 f 311. Cf. Oliphant, I, 101ff. Additional evidence belongs to the history of the annual *Janus* (1826). The history can be reconstructed from correspondence in the files of Messrs Oliver and Boyd, who have kindly allowed me to see it. The prospectus (received 13 February 1825) is in Lockhart's hand. On 31 August Lockhart is waiting for Wilson but promises, 'The moment you wish the printing of your volume to begin I have plenty of MS at your service for that purpose.' Other letters show Lockhart repeatedly badgering Wilson for contributions.

19. *Sir Walter* (London 1932), pp 239–40.

20. *Christopher North*, p 193 & n; Oliphant, I, 159; Macbeth, pp 175–6.

21. Christie, quoted by Lang (I, 37) from Gleig.

22. Oliphant, I, 195.

23. Quoted by Lang (I, 131); cf. Lockhart's remark in *Noctes Ambrosianae*, XV: 'Pope was decidedly the Z of Queen Anne's time – his dunces were the progenitors of the present Cockneys.'

24. Strout, 'Writers on German Literature in *Blackwood's Magazine*', *The Library*, March 1954, p 35; G.B.Tennyson, *Sartor Called Resartus* (Princeton 1965), pp 135–40; Macbeth, pp 147–8; Morgan and Hohlfeld, *German Literature in British Magazines: 1750–1860* (Madison 1949), p 116; for Lockhart on the 'contented ignorance' of the *Edinburgh Review* in this area, see *Blackwood's*, IV (1818–19), 211–13; XV (1824), 619.

25. Macbeth, p 150; Miss Lochhead's suggestion (p 45) that Lauerwinkel treats 'the venerable Dr Playfair' as 'a kind of spiritual Deacon Brodie' is un-fair. Scott conceded that the article was 'extremely well-written' (*Letters*, V, 204). Lang, also disapproving, describes it as 'a model of polished vigour' (I, 183–4). Lockhart assured Murray that, while severe, the article was 'not only merited and unanswerable, but so written as no gentleman need be ashamed to have signed it' (Oliphant, I, 166). Lockhart's defenders need not be so timid.

26. Gleig, p 461.

27. H.J.Smith, *Oliver Goldsmith's The Citizen of the World* (New Haven 1926), pp 3, 5–9, 52.

28. *The Persian Letters*, trans. J.Robert Loy (N.Y. 1961), p 108.

29. *The Citizen of the World*, ed. Dobson, 2 vols (London 1891), I, 6.

30. Voltaire, *Contradictions*, in Smith, *Goldsmith's Citizen*, pp 12–13.

31. *Citizen of the World*, I, 24; cf. II, 1–2, 276.

32. *Persian Letters*, p 162.

33. *Citizen of the World*, I, 6.

34. *QR*, IV (1810), 82.

35. *Cambridge History of English Literature*, XI, 163.

36. *Letters from England by Don Manuel Espriella*, ed. J.Simmons (London 1951), pp 15–16.

37. Letters X, XXVI, XXVIII. Where some human source is cited, the source is seldom given dramatic reality. 'At Staines we crossed the Thames – not by the new bridge, now for the third time built, but over a crazy wooden one

above a century old. We inquired the reason, and heard a curious history,' etc. (p 43). His tendency to generalize is sometimes dramatically fitting. For instance, his horror at British industrialism makes particularity a burden: 'A sick stomach will not digest the food that may be forced down it, and the intellect is as little able to assimilate that for which it has no aptitude' [pp 196–7]. He is an interesting character, but an inappropriate ironic device.

38. *Edinburgh Review*, XI (1808), 383.

39. Quoted by Simmons, *Letters from England*, pp xxii-xxiv.

40. *Edinburgh Review*, XI (1808), 371–2; cf. *Letters from England*, pp xxi-xxii.

41. Cf. Lockhart, *Blackwood's*, IV (1818–19), 613: 'Dr Morris (for he is the author) has adopted a somewhat ambitious title to his Letters – yet we must not rob Peter to pay Paul.' *Paul's Letters*, the actual letters home of a travelling observer, have no relation to the ironic genre.

42. *Edinburgh Review*, XLIV (1826), 253ff; *Blackwood's*, I (1817), 38.

43. Lang, I, 107; the letter to an unknown correspondent is in the Knollenberg Collection of Yale University Library; I am grateful for permission to quote it.

44. Nat. Lib. Scot. MS 934 Nos 36–37 are from Chenevix to Lockhart, 18 August and 6 November 1826. I assume Chenevix is the 'Litterateur et chimiste irlandais, d'origine française', who died in 1830 (*Nouvelle Biographie Generale*, Paris 1855). Although Chenevix returned corrected proofs with the November letter, the article seems to have gone no further. Whatever transpired during the London confrontation, the next letter is from Spurzheim himself, who asks for the article to send Chenevix, who will 'revise the whole and return it'. He 'hopes that you have no reason to change your last decision' (18 May [1827?]: MS 934 No. 38). Apparently Lockhart found reason. The craniologist's only *Quarterly* appearance during this period is not flattering: *QR*, XXXIX (1829), 1–41.

45. *Blackwood's*, III (1818), 405ff.

46. Cf. *The Craniad; or, Spurzheim Illustrated; a Poem in Two Parts* (1817), attributed by the *Dict. Anon. and Pseud. Lit.* to Jeffrey and John Gordon, MD. The *Blackwood's* review in its entirety reads: 'The Craniad is the worst poem we have now in Scotland. The author has it in his power at once to decide the great craniological controversy: let him submit his skull to general inspection, and if it exhibit a single intellectual organ, Spurzheim's theory is overthrown' (I [1817], 288).

47. *Works*, XVI, 187–9.

48. *Fraser's*, LXI (1860), 692–3.

49. *QR*, LVII (1836), 182. On authorship, see Brightfield, *PMLA*, LIX (1944), 500.

50. *Blackwood's*, III (1818), 146, 300.

51. *Blackwood's*, IV (1818–19), 430.

52. *Blackwood's*, III (1818), 428; Lockhart claims the review in his first puffery of Peter – see IV (1818–19), 613. Cf. Macbeth, p 181.

53. Williams was later Charles Scott's tutor and headmaster of the new Edinburgh Academy. The Master of Balliol, writing of his pleasure in the book, tells Lockhart, 'I could not help recognizing the connection between Dr Morris and our portly friend of Ystraed Meirie' (Lang, I, 225n). Cf. refs to Bramble in *Blackwood's*, IV (1818–19), 621.

54. A long letter to Croker (MS 1819 f 20) and a dissertation (in *Janus, or*

the Edinburgh Literary Almanack, 1826) bear witness to Lockhart's serious interest in comparing the two university systems.

55. Postscript to the 'Third Edition', III, 365. He cites a journal given a 'rapturous reception' by 'these very Scottish Whigs . . . two or three years ago', by 'the American Simond – a book in which liberties of the very same species are taken with, in many instances, the very same individuals of whom I have spoken; – and in which, in spite of all the praises it received, that offence was really committed – which has been falsely, and blindly, and stupidly, alleged against me'. The ref. must be to *Journal of a Tour and Residence in Great Britain during the Years 1810 and 1811*, by a French Traveller (Edinburgh 1815) – Simond had lived in America for twenty years, hence Lockhart's epithet. His preface contains interesting reflections on the problem of editing such a first-hand account for publication, comparable with Don Espriella's ingenuous confessions of tampering.

56. Cockburn, *Life of Jeffrey*, 2 vols (Edinburgh 1852), I, 237n.

57. Gleig, pp 464-5; Saintsbury, *Collected Essays and Papers* (London 1923), II, 7; Lochhead, p 136.

58. See Lockhart's substantial contributions to the brilliant *Blackwood's* series of imaginary conversations, the *Noctes Ambrosianae*. It is now known that Lockhart contributed almost twenty of the seventy-one dialogues and supplied materials for several more. See A.L.Strout, in *MLN*, LI (1936), 493–504, and *The Library*, June 1957; and R.M.Wardle, in *TLS*, 9 October 1937, p 735, and *MP*, XLII (1944–5), 9–17.

59. *Blackwood's*, IV (1818–19), 614.

60. Cf. the letter to Christie of 3 January 1816: '*The Examiner* has well characterized Wordsworth as a poet – who, had he written but half of what he has, would have deserved to be immortal' (Lang, I, 102); to Croker eighteen years later: 'I can never but believe him the greatest poet of our time except Scott' (MS 1820 f 114); and Lang, II, 336; *Blackwood's*, XVIII (1825), 417.

61. *Life of Scott*, VI, 91.

NOTES TO CHAPTER 3

1. Lindsay, *Robert Burns* (London 1954), pp 1, 281; Muir, 'The Burns Myth', in *Robert Burns: Essays by Six Contemporary Writers*, ed. W.Montgomerie (Glasgow 1947), p 7; Linklater, *The Ultimate Viking* (N.Y. 1956), p 34. The following abbreviations are used in the notes. 'Letters' refers to *Letters of Robert Burns*, ed. J.De Lancey Ferguson, 2 vols (Oxford 1931); 'Brown' to Hilton Brown, *There Was A Lad: An Essay on Robert Burns* (London 1949); 'Chambers-Wallace' to *Life and Works of Robert Burns*, ed. R.Chambers, rev. W.Wallace, 4 vols (Edinburgh 1896); 'Cunningham' to *Works of Robert Burns, with his Life*, by Allan Cunningham, 8 vols (London 1834); 'Currie' to *Works of Robert Burns, with an Account of his Life*, by James Currie, MD, 2nd edn, 4 vols (London 1801); 'Daiches' to David Daiches, *Robert Burns* (London 1952); 'Ferguson' to De Lancey Ferguson, *Pride and Passion: Robert Burns 1759–1796* (N.Y. 1939); 'Hecht' to Hans Hecht, *Robert Burns: The Man and His Work*, trans. Jane Lymburn, 2nd rev. edn (London 1950); 'Lindsay' to Maurice Lindsay, *Robert Burns* (London 1954); 'Lockhart' to [J.G.Lockhart], *Life of Robert Burns*, 1st edn

vol. XXIII of Constable's Miscellany (Edinburgh 1828); 'Lockhart/S-D' to
Life of Robert Burns by John Gibson Lockhart, ed. W. Scott Douglas, 2 vols
(Liverpool 1914); 'Snyder, *Life*' to *The Life of Robert Burns*, by Franklyn
Bliss Snyder (New York 1932); 'Snyder, *SP*' to Snyder's article, 'Burns and
his Biographers', in *SP*, XXV (1928), 401–15; 'Walker' to *Poems by Robert
Burns, with an Account of His Life* [by Josiah Walker], 2 vols (Edinburgh
1811).

For a discussion of the texts of Lockhart's work, see 'Lockhart/S-D':
Appendix E. All manuscript references are to MSS in Nat. Lib. Scot.

2. J. C. Furnas, *Voyage to Windward* (N.Y. 1951), pp 147–8, 150;
Stevenson, *Works*, 25 vols (London 1911), III, 43–76; J. De Lancey Ferguson,
'Some Aspects of the Burns Legend', *P Q*, XI (1932), 263.

3. Lindsay, p 281.

4. S. G. Smith, 'Immortal Mummery', *Saltire Review*, II, 6 (1955), p 20.

5. Hamish Henderson, 'Enemies of Folksong', *Saltire Review*, II, 5 (1955),
p 20.

6. 'The Burns Cult', in *At the Sign of the Thistle* (London 1942), p 168.

7. Brown, p 11.

8. *P Q*, XXIII (1944), 158.

9. *Robert Burns: Essays*, etc., ed. Montgomerie, pp 5–7.

10. Catherine Carswell, *The Life of Robert Burns*, 2nd edn (London 1951),
p ix. Her justification is interesting to the theorist of biography: 'open as it is to
mistake, a committed opinion (so long as it be free from the mischief of self-
seeking or ill-will) has more of the stuff of life in it than a series of conflicting
suggestions offered noncommittally'. See also Longaker, *Contemporary
Biography* (Philadelphia 1934), p 246.

11. To Donald Carswell, 5 December 1927: *Selected Letters of D. H.
Lawrence*, ed. Diana Trilling (N.Y. 1958), p 267.

12. Snyder, *Life*, pp 488–9.

13. Longaker, *Contemporary Biography*, p 246.

14. Snyder, *Life*, p 130.

15. Snyder, *Life*, p 354.

16. Snyder, *P Q*, p 412; *Life*, pp 299, 318. Cf. p 351 n 31: 'The story was
not put into circulation till long after Burns's death' – by which he appears to
mean that it was not recorded in print until then. Most oral tradition can thus
be proved specious. See Meikle, 'Burns and the Capture of the Rosamond',
Burns Chronicle, 2nd ser., IX (1934), 47; Snyder, 'Burns and the Smuggler
Rosamond', *P M L A*, L (1935), 510ff.

17. Ferguson, p 132.

18. Snyder, *Life*, pp 374–5; cf. Ferguson, p 129. The account of the report
in Chambers-Wallace (IV, 219n) is critical, but more cautious and plausible.

19. Snyder, *Life*, p 396; Cunningham, I, 313–14; MS 935 No. 91, 28
September 1834: Train to Lockhart; Snyder, *P M L A*, L (1935), 510ff.

20. Lockhart, pp 73–74; Ferguson, p 83; Snyder, *Life*, p 185; *Letters*,
II, 42–43.

21. Snyder, *Life*, p 354; *SP*, p 409; the Peterkin essay – *A Review of the
Life of Robert Burns and of Various Criticisms on His Character and Writings*
(Edinburgh 1815) – is available in *Early Critical Reviews on Robert Burns*, ed.
John D. Ross (Glasgow 1900), 160–211; Lockhart, p vii and chap. VIII:
Peterkin is cited p 215; Gray and Findlater are quoted at length (pp 235–9).

22. MS 935 No. 131: 2 May 1837.

23. MS 935 No. 41 (1828).

24. *PMLA*, L (1935), 510.

25. MS 3905 f 160: 19 November 1827. 'I have to request as a particular favour that you will write me a letter describing your personal recollection of Robert Burns, the occasion of meeting him & this as soon as you can for I am far advanced with my little book about him –.' Scott, *Letters*, X, 401, 427; *Journal of Sir Walter Scott*, ed. Tait and Parker (Edinburgh 1950), p 554.

26. Lockhart, p 212; Ferguson, p 127.

27. Snyder, *Life*, pp 332–3, 429; Snyder cites Ferguson, 'New Light on the Burns-Dunlop Estrangement', *PMLA*, December 1929, pp 1106ff.

28. Snyder, *SP*, pp 413–15; *Life*, pp 327, 244, 309, 488.

29. MS 935 No. 91: 28 September 1834; MS 935 No. 131: 2 May 1837.

30. *Private Letter-books of Sir Walter Scott*, ed. W. Partington (N.Y. 1930), p 234; MS 931 No. 56: 12 October 1825.

31. MS 926 No. 89; MS 331 ff 269–70: 29 January 1827.

32. MS 3905 f 160: 19 November 1827; Scott, *Letters*, X, 392; MS 1553 f 1: January 1828.

33. *PMLA*, L (1935), 510.

34. *Robert Burns: His Associates and Contemporaries*. The Train, Grierson, Young, and Hope Manuscripts, ed. R. T. Fitzhugh (Chapel Hill 1943), pp 18–19. Cf. the treatment of Train's dogmatic detractors in Fitzhugh's 'Burns's Highland Mary', *PMLA*, LII (1937), 829–34.

35. *Journal of a Tour in the Highlands made in the Year 1787 by Robert Burns* (London 1927), p 7. Scott-Douglas, in *Works of Burns*, 6 vols, IV, 264, also assumes the existence of an 'extended transcript'.

36. Snyder, *Life*, p 244.

37. Lindsay, p 161; Ferguson, 'Burns's Journal of His Border Tour', *PMLA*, XLIX (1934), 1107.

38. *Journal of a Tour in the Highlands*, facs., p 14; Snyder, *Life*, p 245.

39. *Journal of a Tour in the Highlands*, pp 11–12; Lockhart, pp 156–7; Cunningham, I, 172.

40. MS 1828 No. 179: 26 May 1853.

41. Snyder, *Life*, p 449.

42. Burns to Agnes M'Lehose, 28 December 1787.

43. Snyder, *Life*, pp 450, 236.

44. Lindsay, pp 155, 162.

45. MS 331 f 273. Cf. Cadell's control of the printing of the *Life of Scott*.

46. *Crit. and Misc. Essays*, I, 260–1.

47. *Peter's Letters*, I, 118.

48. De Quincey, *Collected Writings* (1896), II, 130–1; Hazlitt, *Complete Works*, V, 128–32; H. C. Robinson on Books and their Writers, ed. E. J. Morley (London 1938), I, 220; Noyes, 'Wordsworth and Burns', *PMLA*, LIX (1944), 827.

49. A. L. Strout, 'John Wilson, "Champion" of Wordsworth', *MP*, XXXI (1933–4), 383–94; see *Blackwood's*, I (1817), 261–6; II (1817–18), 65–73, 201–4.

50. Lang, I, 136.

51. *A History of Modern Criticism* (New Haven 1955), II, 5.

52. *German Literature in British Magazines 1750–1860* (Madison 1949), p 106, No. 2131; Strout, 'Writers on German Literature in *Blackwood's*

Magazine', *The Library*, March 1954, p 37 (Strout's volume designation 'IV' must be a misprint for 'III'); *Blackwood's*, III (1818), 497–511.

53. *Blackwood's*, IV (1818), 4.

54. *Ibid.*, and III (1818), 419, 510–11.

55. *Reminiscences of Scottish Life and Character* (Edinburgh, Foulis, n.d.), p 85.

56. *The Correspondence of Arthur Hugh Clough*, ed. F.L.Mulhauser, 2 vols (Oxford 1957), I, 151.

57. *Blackwood's*, III (1818), 500.

58. *Peter's Letters*, I, 164.

59. Lockhart, p 300; MS 331 ff 269–70: to Constable 29 January 1827.

60. MS 1553 f 110: 27 April 1830; *Peter's Letters*, III, 326, 328; Cockburn, *Memorials*, p 53; Ramsay, *Reminiscences*, pp 172, 175; *Autobiography of Dr Alexander Carlyle of Inveresk* (London 1910), p 232.

61. *Lectures on the History of Literature*, II, 96; I, 346.

62. Originally preface to the series 'Horae Hispanicae', *Blackwood's*, VI (1819–20), 482–83.

63. *Peter's Letters*, III, 326.

64. 'Noctes' 46, *Blackwood's*, XXVI (1829), 399; *QR*, XLV (1831), 374.

65. The evidence for Lockhart's authorship of the poem is summarized in *TLS*, 27 February 1959, p 119.

66. Gilbert Burns in Currie, I, 71.

67. Lockhart, p 308; *Peter's Letters*, I, 115–16.

68. Lockhart, pp 23, 120–1, 19; Lockhart/S-D, I, 60.

69. *Literary Biography* (Toronto 1957), p 49, pp 42–43.

70. Adolphus, *Biography*, p 14.

71. Hayley, *Life of Milton* (1794), p cxxix; Hagstrum, *Samuel Johnson's Literary Criticism* (Minneapolis 1952), pp 38, 45–47; cf. Abrams, *The Mirror and the Lamp*, p 233; Stanfield, *Essay on Biography*, p 321. Cf. 318–19, where he praises Johnson for the *Lives*, but insists on the separation of the functions of biographer and critic.

72. Quoted by Edel, *Literary Biography*, p 44.

73. For Wordsworth's view and Lockhart's disagreement, see *QR*, XLVI (1832), 22. Of Johnson's remark to Mrs Cotterell, reported by Seward in *Biographiana*, Hill says it is actually an allusion to Rambler 14 (*Life of Johnson*, 6 vols, I, 450n).

74. *Blackwood's*, XVII (1825), 133.

75. *Ibid.*, p 136.

76. *QR*, XXXIV (1826), 370.

77. *QR*, XLVI (1832), 26–27.

78. Chambers-Wallace, IV, 38–39.

79. Cromek, *Reliques of Robert Burns*, 4th edn (London 1817), p 448n; Lockhart, pp 218–19n; Lockhart/S-D, II, 77n; Chambers-Wallace, III, 320n.

80. Snyder, *Life*, p 396; *Letters*, II, 113. Cf. Chambers-Wallace, III, 321n: 'It is not at all impossible that Burns may, with such verses in his mind, have made the first rough draft of his own poem while waiting for Lewars on the Solway shore, and read finished copies of it at an Exciseman's dinner in Dumfries and a convivial gathering in Annan.' One is increasingly struck by the continued value of Chambers-Wallace as a source-book for the study of Burns.

81. Such is the conjecture of Chambers-Wallace, IV, 38.

82. See Snyder, *Life*, p 438 n 27; *Letters*, II, 245. But Ferguson says else-where there were excursions 'in 1793 and 1794.' – both years (Ferguson, p 131).
83. Chambers-Wallace, IV, 20.
84. Snyder, *Life*, pp 420, 327.
85. Catherine Carswell, *Life of Burns*, pp 370–1.
86. Daiches, p 292.
87. For the preceding two paragraphs, see Snyder, *Life*, pp 309–10; Lock-hart, pp 184–5; Lockhart/S-D, II, 19–21 n; Chambers-Wallace, III, 110; Carswell, *Life of Burns*, p 362; Ferguson, p 148; Lindsay, pp 93–94; Hecht, p 169; Daiches, p 342.
88. *Crit. and Misc. Essays*, I, 260.
89. Heron's *Memoir* is reprinted by Hecht (see p 259).
90. Hecht, p 259.
91. Walker, I, xiii-xiv.
92. Cunningham, I, 343, 313–14.
93. Hecht, pp 263–4, 270, 274–5.
94. Brown, p 55.
95. Hecht, pp 276, 260ff, 263, 273.
96. Hecht, p 255.
97. Brown, p 56.
98. Currie, I, 199. Subsequent refs are in the text.
99. Brown, p 106.
100. Walker, I, xci, xcv, xcviii, ci. Lockhart differs from 'almost every one of his biographers', including Scott, in finding no evidence that Burns felt his hopes permanently blasted. He cites the letter of Findlater to Horne as well as the fact that Burns was acting supervisor during the last year of his life (pp 222–7). Snyder (*Life*, p 401) takes a similar view. He ends his excerpt from the letter to Erskine of Mar with the 'friendly advice' of Corbet. Immediately following is this: 'Mr Corbet was likewise my steady friend: so between Mr Graham and him I have been partly forgiven; only, I understand that all hopes of my getting officially forward are blasted' (Chambers-Wallace, III, 414). Both biographers disregard Burns's own statement.
101. Walker, I, xc-cxv, *passim*.
102. Walker, I, cxx-cxxi; cf. Lockhart on Campbell, *Q R*, LXXXV (1849), 81.
103. Walker, I, lxviii. Subsequent refs are in the text.
104. Cunningham, I, 2. Subsequent refs are in the text.
105. Cunningham, I, 58–59; cf. 52ff with Lockhart, pp 55f; also Cunning-ham, I, 179–80, with Lockhart, p 149.
106. A glance at the sub-topics in Snyder's table of contents indicates the prevalence of an expository order within the general chronological outline. Ferguson's preface explains his own relinquishing of time sequence 'in favour of the relationships of everyday life in which Burns most clearly revealed his personality' (p v).
107. Chambers-Wallace, I, 45–46; Lockhart/S-D, I, 38n; for the letter to Moore, see *Letters*, I, 104.–16.
108. Burns's allusions are in a note to 'The Highland Lassie O' and in a letter to George Thomson in 1792. See Chambers-Wallace, I, 341.
109. Lockhart, pp 80–82; Lockhart/S-D, I, 110–11n; Ferguson, p 191.
110. The question seems to be whether the Mary episode was an interlude in

the fertile Armour affair. Chambers-Wallace, I, 339–40; Lockhart/S-D, II, 234–42; R.T.Fitzhugh, 'Burns's Highland Mary', *PMLA*, LII (1937), 829–34.

111. Such is Scott-Douglas's thesis (Lockhart/S-D, II, 111-12).

112. *Letters*, I, 104–16. Added to the 15 January 1787 letter to Mrs Dunlop are two paragraphs from the December 1786 letter to the disgraced Rev. Wm.Greenfield. See Currie, II, 41; *Letters*, I, 59; Lockhart, p 138. For the telescoping of excerpts to Moore, cf. Lockhart, p 139; Currie, II, 43 & 48; *Letters*, I, 70 & 76. For the climactic excerpt see Currie, II, 69–70; *Letters*, I, 85. Note Lockhart's habit of italicizing documents for stress.

113. Lockhart, p 55, and cf. Currie, I, 39; Lockhart, p 63, and cf. Currie, I, 52.

NOTES TO CHAPTER 4

1. Biographies of Napoleon are identified simply by authors' names. Scott, *Life of Napoleon Buonaparte*, vols VIII–XVI in *Misc. Works* (Edinburgh 1861); vol. refs observe numbering for the individual work – I–IX. Hazlitt, *The Life of Napoleon Buonaparte*, vols XIII–XV in *Complete Works*, ed. Howe (London 1931); referred to as I–III. Lockhart, *The History of Napoleon Buonaparte*, is ordinarily cited in the Everyman edn (London 1906); ref. to the 1st edn (2 vols, London 1829) or the modern edition of J.H.Rose (Oxford 1916) is specified as such. No attempt is made to compare the several 'editions' systematically, beyond the noting of some significant augmentations of the 2nd edn. Earl of Rosebery, *Napoleon: The Last Phase* (1900: N.Y. edn 1930); J.Holland Rose, *Life of Napoleon I*, 2 vols (London 1902); August Fournier, *Napoleon I*, 2 vols (London 1912); J.M.Thompson, *Napoleon Buonaparte* (Oxford 1952); Albert Guerard, *Napoleon I* (N.Y. 1956); F.M.H.Markham, *Napoleon and the Awakening of Europe* (N.Y. 1954), and *Napoleon* (N.Y. 1963), are distinguished as *Awakening* and *Napoleon*. The following influence my discussion throughout: F.J.MacCunn, *The Contemporary English View of Napoleon* (London 1914); Guerard, *Reflections on the Napoleonic Legend* (N.Y. 1924); Pieter Geyl, *Napoleon, For and Against* (New Haven 1949); and Henri Peyre, *et al.*, *The Myth of Napoleon*, No. 26 (Fall-Winter, 1960–1) of *Yale French Studies*. The opening quotes are from Hazlitt, II, 270–1; Lockhart, *Blackwood's*, II (1818), 673, and XXV (1829), 798; Guerard, *Napoleon*, p 192; Thompson, p v.

2. Thompson, p 398.

3. Guerard, *Reflections*, p 189: 'The Napoleonic legend is an epic romance which was ready before it had discovered its hero.'

4. *Blackwood's*, XXVI (1829), 415.

5. Scott recalls to Lockhart (30 October 1828) the time 'you were giving [Constable] so much good advice in laying down his grand plans about the Miscellany' (*Letters of Scott*, XI, 28). Constable's correspondence in 1825 justifies his remark to Scott on 30 August: 'Mr Lockhart takes a deep interest in the Miscellany. His advice has already been of the greatest use to me, and I am anxious also to confer further with him about it' (*Archibald Constable and His Literary Correspondents*, III, 325). Cf. R.Altick, *The English Common Reader* (Phoenix edn, Chicago 1963), pp 267–73.

6. *Blackwood's*, XXVI (1829), 413–16.

7. *Archibald Constable*, etc., III, 315.

8. *Blackwood's*, XXVI (1829), 416.

9. Napoleon continued to hope that he could bring down the Liverpool government, and that the opposition would bring him back to the borders of Europe. Rose (II, 486n) wishes he 'had space to give a whole chapter to the relations between Napoleon and the Whigs, and to show how their champion-ship of him worked mischief on both sides in 1803–21, enticing him on to many risky ventures, and ruining the cause of Reform in England for a generation'.

10. *New Monthly Magazine*, XXVII (1829), 244–5; *Blackwood's*, XXV (1829), 798.

11. Rosebery, p 75. Cf. MacCunn, p 83: 'Never has the British contempt for foreigners stood the country in better stead.' The Imperial coronation left Hazlitt almost alone; 'it disgusted the main body of the Whigs and drove a Jacobin like Cobbett to unreasoning fury' (pp 80–81). But Coleridge noted with indignation in 1828 an 'apparent revolution in the *Fashion* of estimating the character, and aims of Napoleon' (*Unpublished Letters*, ed. E. L. Griggs [New Haven 1933], II, 409). And the change of sentiment which allowed even Tories to applaud the Orléanist revolution of 1830 must have affected the recollection of the imperial anti-Bourbonist, then safely dead.

12. *Q R*, XIV (1815), 55, 95–96; XVI (1816), 209; XIV (1815), 93; *Blackwood's*, XXV (1829), 798.

13. *Blackwood's*, XIII (1823), 284.

14. *Blackwood's*, II (1818), 673. Cf. Hazlitt, II, 251. Hazlitt is correct in saying (II, 187) that 'Buonaparte in his public and private character was uniformly held up as a monster of ambition, cruelty, and lust'. MacCunn, p 70, mentions characteristic pamphlets and broadsides; even Lord Whitworth conceded, at the time of the Peltier trial, that 'if Bonaparte had recourse to war, his action must be attributed to the irritation kept alive by the press' (MacCunn, pp 62–63).

15. *Blackwood's*, XXV (1829), 798; II (1818), 673.

16. Rosebery, pp 243, 19.

17. *Blackwood's*, IX (1821), 367–8.

18. Lockhart, p 407. Cf. the difference in mood and viewpoint of Scott, VIII, 50.

19. Hazlitt, II, 270–1.

20. Macbeth, *Lockhart*, p 196; Saintsbury, *Essays and Papers*, II, 9; Lang, II, 44; no ref. in Lochhead. Contemporary reviewers treated it as an independent work (see *The Athenaeum*, 6 May 1829, p 279). Howe (in Hazlitt, I, 355) refers to a review in *The Atlas* which explains that 'Sir Walter's was entirely taken up with unwieldy documents and long descriptions, and Mr Hazlitt's was a mere tissue of dissertations, or a series of essays, the facts and points of character being either obscured or wholly omitted in both, and now, for the first time, introduced into the two small volumes of the Family Library'. In the late 1840's, Maria Edgeworth wrote to Lockhart: 'I am glad there is a new edition of Sir Walter's Memoirs compressed into cheap form. – If it have the spirit preserved in it *as preserved and heightened* the spirit of the Life of Napoleon is in your *powerful compression* of Sir Walter Scott's Memoirs of Bonaparte, I shall delight in seeing the work' (Nat. Lib. Scot. MS 936 f 36; ital. mine).

T

Before beginning, Lockhart wrote apologetically to Scott for permission; Scott replied the 30th of October 1828 (*Letters of Scott*, XI, 28): 'Your scruples about doing an epitome of the Life of Boney, for the Family Library that is to be, are a great deal overdelicate. My book in nine thick volumes can never fill the place which our friend Murray wants you to fill, and which, if you don't, some one else will, right soon. Moreover, you took such pains in helping me when I was beginning my task, which I afterwards greatly regretted that Constable had no means of remunerating.' On the 2nd of December Scott wrote again (*Letters*, XI, 57): 'I hope you mean to come down at Christmas. . . . I want to speak to you about your *novum opus* and how I am to help it forward.' Lockhart spent approximately the first three weeks of 1829 with Scott. He wrote Murray from Abbotsford the 4th of January: 'I have found Sir Walter Scott in grand health & spirits, & have had much conversation with him on his hill-side about all our concerns' – conversation, no doubt, about the *novum opus*, for on the 8th he again wrote: 'I am getting on with "Napoleon", and shall have a good store of MS for the printer when I return, which will be very soon' (Smiles, *A Publisher and His Friends* [London 1891], II, 273–4).

21. I am accepting as authoritative the findings of R.E. Robinson in *William Hazlitt's Life of Napoleon Buonaparte: Its Sources and Characteristics* (Genève et Paris 1959). He is critical of Howe's 'Note on Sources' (Hazlitt, I, 356), which I have also used. He concludes that 'Hazlitt's dependence upon his source materials was characteristically so direct as to make the greater part of the biography little more than patched-together excerpts or summaries from his sources, with each long episode usually taken from a single work written with a strongly pro-Napoleonic bias' (pp 14–15). He finds that 'Hazlitt plagiarized Scott's narrative for about fifty-two pages of his text'.

22. Peyre, 'Napoleon: Devil, Poet, Saint', *Yale French Studies*, No. 26 (1961), p 25.

23. p vii in the Intro. to the 1916 (Oxford) edn of Lockhart.

24. Listed by Rose (Intro., pp vii-x). He stresses the weakness of the Waterloo chapter, suggesting that the author seems weary. I suspect Lockhart saw little reason to give *another* full account of the battle. Moreover, he treated everything following the first abdication as anti-climax.

25. Rose, Intro., p v. Rose characterizes Lockhart's as an attempt to 'steer a middle course between the diatribes of Gifford [and Croker] and the St Helena legend' (p vi). Between these extremes, there is, in fact, room for virtually all Napoleon biographies.

26. Rose, p vi. Cf. MacCunn, p 33: 'English writers echo the views of a German, quoted by Mr Alger, who compared the lawlessness of France to a brawl in a beer-shop – Bonaparte came along and said, "Stop that," and his first act was to extinguish the lights.'

27. *William Hazlitt* (Cambridge 1962), pp 328–30.

28. Lady Holland reports to her son (4 Sept. 1826) the rumour that Scott 'is busily employed upon the Life of Napoleon, which from him will only be a libellous romance, as he has not the materials or candid qualities to be the historian of so recent a period' (*Elizabeth, Lady Holland to her Son 1821–1845* [London 1946], p 52).

29. Hazlitt, II, 160. Cf. Robinson, *Hazlitt's Napoleon*, p 22. Here is the view held in Parliament by Whitbread and Fox, and by the *Edinburgh Review*: 'Our wars with France have only served to aggrandize her and change her

government from a tumultuous democracy to a regular, enlightened and well-disciplined military despotism' (1807) – MacCunn, pp 91–92.

30. Howe calls it a not inaccurate account of the facts, set forth in the preface to the posthumous edition of 1830 (I, 353–4). Far less evident than any idolatrous reverence for Napoleon is the dogged ungenerosity Hazlitt shows for everyone else – people and monarchs, opponents and supporters, Prussian, Spanish, Russian, British, and French.

31. Rose, Intro., p xi.

32. *A History of the Peninsular War* (Oxford 1902), I, 596–7.

33. *Ibid.*

34. Napier's narrative was published by Murray during a time when Lockhart was chief literary adviser. Lockhart certainly takes exception in his *Napoleon* to Napier's discounting of the Spanish resistance and his sympathy for France's defensive position. But the whole structure of his narrative of Napoleon sending his armies to Spain, rushing to Erfurt, returning to plan and lead the Spanish advance, is from Napier – and it is superior as narrative in proportion and focus to Scott and Hazlitt. Lockhart omits, of course, Napier's severe treatment of Frere.

35. *Q R*, XIV (1815), 70. Cf. Markham, *Napoleon* (1963), pp 216–21.

36. Sir Charles Petrie, *Wellington* (London 1956), p 209: 'Both Ney and his wife made passionate appeals to Wellington to intercede with the King of France, but he refused, and it is difficult to blame him. "It was absolutely necessary," he said to Lady Salisbury in 1838, "to make an example."' Such had been the view acquired by Scott's 'Paul' on his 1815 trip to Paris and Waterloo (*Misc. Works*, V, 315).

37. If Lockhart is more severe than Scott, his severity is not social but moral. The same distinction has already been made with reference to their judgments of Burns. For Lockhart, Napoleon is guilty of pride, of inordinate ambition – one recognizes the criteria of classical conservatism. But he is not condemned for vulgarity.

38. Markham, *Napoleon*, pp 51–52. Thompson (p 130) accepts Miot's figure of three thousand massacred. Guerard says twelve hundred: 'not cruel by nature, he was free from squeamishness' (p 34). Thompson says there is little doubt he gave the orders for a 'fatal dose of opium'.

39. Fournier, I, 420.

40. Hazlitt, II, 224: the affair, he says, 'would probably have never come to anything but for an intercepted letter'. Of this and other letters, Rosebery says (pp 29–36) *aut Las Cases aut diabolus*. Napoleon never mentioned it to Gourgaud, and corrected O'Meara to Montholon, who explained it was the note written during the trial. Of course, Tolstoy's Bezukhov, apparently acquainted with Napoleon's will, praises the emperor's greatness of soul in taking upon himself the full responsibility for the deed.

41. *The Memoirs of Queen Hortense* (N.Y. 1927), II, 189.

42. Hazlitt, III, 220. In the note on p 228, Hazlitt is perhaps again attacking Scott: 'It is a rule in philosophy to admit no more causes than are sufficient; and the army being sufficient to bring back Buonaparte, the Tories who are great philosophers when it suits them, hold themselves bound to maintain (be the fact as it might) that in this, as in the other instances, the inhabitants took no part in it.' The Tories, as MacCunn indicates (p 55), had always exaggerated the unpopularity of Napoleon.

43. Thompson, p 373; Guerard, p 165.

44. *Wellington*, p 186; *Q R*, XIV (1815), 74.

45. Guerard, p 175; cf. Thompson, pp 375–76. Markham (*Napoleon*, p 214) really evades this question.

46. Cf. the use of the two anecdotes – in Lockhart only – of the farm labourer and the old soldier (pp 448–9).

47. Hazlitt (III, 231) says: 'On alighting, he was almost squeezed to death by the crowd of officers and citizens who thronged about him, and fairly carried him up-stairs in their arms.' Cf. Scott (VIII, 359): Napoleon 'entered amid the shouts of armed columns, who, existing by war and desolation, welcomed with military acclamations the chief who was to restore them to their element. The inhabitants of the suburbs cheered in expectation of employment and gratuities, or by the instigation of their ringleaders, who were chiefly under the management of the police, and well prepared for the event.'

48. Thompson, p vi: 'His greatest conquest was not Europe, but the French Revolution. His most lasting monument is not the Arc de Triomphe or the flags at the Invalides, but the laws and institutions in which he adapted the ideas of 1789 to the traditions of the monarchy,' etc. Cf. Markham, *Napoleon*, p 254.

49. Rose, II, 489. Fournier (II, 442n) supports Rose against Rosebery. What finality is possible when such diversity persists, for example, in the interpretation of the Gourgaud letters? For Rose (II, 517), they are 'frank' admissions that the St Helena situation was far from disagreeable; for Rose-bery (p 63), they are the 'dutifully mendacious letters' of a good son trying to cheer his mother by 'painting everything at St Helena in rose-colour'.

50. Markham, *Napoleon*, p 231.

51. 29–30 Novembre 1815; Las Cases, *Le Mémoriale*, ed. Marcel Dunan (Paris 1951), I, 274. Rose, II, 509.

52. Guerard, p 183; Markham, *Awakening*, p 167. In 1963, Markham augmented his evidence considerably (pp 233–4).

53. So called by Rosebery, p 41.

54. Rosebery, pp 55–57.

55. Rosebery, p 97.

56. *Westminster Review*, IX (1828), 253, 258.

57. Rose, *Intro.*, p x – no doubt coloured by his reaction to Rosebery.

58. Guerard, *Reflections*, pp 180–1. Contrast Markham (1963), p 254.

59. Scott, *Letters*, X, 237–8.

60. E. A.M. Dougary, *The Materials and Technique of Biography*, unpub. thesis, University of Edinburgh (1942), p 72.

61. *William Hickling Prescott*, ed. Charvat & Kraus, American Writers Series (1943), pp 17–18.

62. *Henry Crabb Robinson on Books and Their Writers*, p 356.

63. Nat. Lib. Scot. MS 935 f 34: 28 October 1833.

64. MS 3904 f 48: 9 February 1827. The letter's enthusiasm is motivated, no doubt, by the desire to cheer and encourage Scott during months of grief and drudgery. MS 4025 ff 78–79: 17 November 1829.

65. Scott, IV, 368–9; Hazlitt, III, 10; Lockhart, p 320.

66. Cf. Hazlitt, I, 224. Scott's association of the two anecdotes, to which Lockhart is indebted for his juxtaposition, misses the pointed contrast, is weakened by Scott's unnecessary and lengthy connective (III, 88).

67. See Thompson's justification, p vi.

68. Spain was simply the most striking example of Buonaparte's threat to the principle of nationality; that principle – in Spain, Austria, Russia, and Germany – was finally, says MacCunn (p 109), to destroy him. Cf. Lockhart, p 300. Has the effect of Napoleon's imperialist threat on literary and cultural nationalism been fully recognized?

69. *Blackwood's*, XXVI (1829), 798.

70. *Westminster Review*, IX (1828), 274.

71. P.W.Seton-Watson, *Britain in Europe 1789–1914* (N.Y. 1937), p 18.

72. *Blackwood's*, XXV (1829), 798.

73. Thompson, p 358.

74. *Macbeth* V.iii.22–23, 48–49; V.v.48–49.

75. Thompson, p v.

76. Markham, *Awakening*, p 175; cf. *Napoleon*, p 254.

77. Thompson, p 404.

NOTES TO CHAPTER 5

No notes could acknowledge my indebtedness to James C.Corson and Edgar Johnson for their generous counsel and encouragement during the writing and revision of this chapter. Ian Jack has also been most kind and helpful. I am grateful to Frederick W.Hilles for permitting me to study his set of author's proofs of the 1st edn of the *Life*, and to Richard D.Altick for having arranged the opportunity. A few pages are revised from my article, 'Proofreading Lockhart's *Scott*: the Dynamics of Biographical Reticence', *Studies in Bibliography*, XIV (1961), 3–22. The chapter, already of unwieldy length, must stop short of a study of the history of Lockhart's textual revisions following 1837. It takes as standard the 10-volume 2nd edn; the 'making' of *this* work (pub. 1839) is ultimately the subject of the chapter, and refs in the notes to the *Life of Scott* are to the so-called 'Edinburgh Edition' reprint of the 2nd edn. Other abbreviations are used in the notes. 'Scott, *Letters*' signifies the 12-vol. Grierson edition (London 1932–7). '*Journal*' signifies the Tait-Parker edition of Scott's *Journal* (Edinburgh 1950). Grierson's 'Lang, Lockhart, and Biography', the Andrew Lang Lecture, 6 December 1933 (Oxford 1934) appears as 'L.L.B.'; his *Sir Walter Scott, Bt: A New Life* (London 1938) is called '*New Life*'. Refs to 'Carlyle' are to his review of the first six vols of the 1st edn, reprinted in *Crit. & Misc. Essays*, IV, 22–87. 'Carruthers' stands for the 'Abbotsford Notanda' printed in the 1871 edition of Chambers's *Life of Scott*. 'Cockburn, *Journal*' is the *Journal of Henry Cockburn*, 1831–54, 2 vols (Edinburgh 1874).

1. Carlyle, p 32; Una Pope-Hennessy, *Sir Walter Scott* (London 1948), p 15; Pearson, *Ventilations* (Philadelphia 1930), p 133, and *Walter Scott* (London 1954), p 285; Nicolson, *Development of English Biography* (London 1947 edn), pp 117 & 119.

2. *Lady Louisa Stuart: Selections from her Manuscripts*, ed. J.A.Home (Edinburgh 1899), p 272; *Memoir and Correspondence of Mrs Grant of Laggan*, 3 vols (London 1844), III, 315–16, 323; Cockburn, *Journal*, I, 134, 174–7; *Life of Jeffrey*, 2 vols (Edinburgh 1852), II, 298; *Life and Correspon-*

dence of Robert Southey, 6 vols (London 1850), VI, 335. I also quote from a letter of Southey to Lockhart transcribed by the late Alexander Mitchell in one of his notebooks, materials for a Life of Lockhart, now in the Nat. Lib. Scot.

3. *H. C. Robinson on Books and their Writers*, pp 524.–48 *passim*.

4. *Letters of William and Dorothy Wordsworth: The Later Years*, ed. E. de Selincourt, II (1831–40), 927.

5. MS 923: 10 November 1837 and 14 January 1838 (Edgeworth); MS 932 No. 65: 19 April 1838 (Hall); MS 932 No. 84 (Morritt); MS 930 No. 36: 21 March 1837 (Mahon); MS 923 No. 172 (Cheney).

6. Cockburn, *Journal*, I, 174; letter of Lockhart to Haydon, 11 February 1838, quoted in Lang, II, 182.

7. No attempt is made here to evaluate Lockhart's treatment of these figures. They are certain to receive belated justice on a grand scale in Professor Johnson's forthcoming biography of Scott; they have generally received fuller justice than Lockhart himself. Corson asserts that 'most of the resentment' which the work aroused 'was caused by Lockhart's treatment of the Ballantynes'. But the specific 'resentments' he cites reflect rather the distaste at the revelation of Scott's 'covetousness', his mercenary view of his art. Cooper's resentment, for instance, had little to do with the Ballantynes; his letter to his wife makes this clear: 'Well, I have read the Ballantyne's books, and Mr Lockhart is flat on his back.' Cooper had earnestly tried to put him there, and was bound to find any alliance effective. 'They not only show that Scott ruined the Ballantynes, but they show that he knew the entire situation of his affairs, James Ballantyne furnished a monthly statement to him, and they show that Mr Lockhart is a cool, calculating knave' (*Corresp. of James Fenimore-Cooper*, 2 vols [New Haven 1922], I, 384–5). Others had prejudged the case out of no fervent sympathy for James and John. Thackeray reported on 30 July 1840 that he had been reading 'the Banantyne Controversy wh proves Scott to be a rogue', but did not know their right name and did not get around to the *Life* itself until sixteen years later (*Literary and Private Papers of W. M. Thackeray*, ed. G. N. Ray, 4 vols [Cambridge 1946], I, 460; III, 327n, 633; IV, 438), The impossibility of Lockhart's pleasing everyone is vividly demonstrated by the fact that the pro-Ballantyne Chambers's *Edinburgh Journal* [VI (1837), 220] thought John had been used fairly while James had been mistreated, while Grierson holds 'that John has had less than fair play – James perhaps more' (L.L.B., p 17). Cf. James Glen, 'Sir Walter Scott's Financial Transactions', in vol. I of Scott, *Letters*; and less recent but more readable, the judicious Stephen essay, 'The Story of Scott's Ruin', *Studies of a Biographer* (London 1899), II, 1–37. In Lockhart's defence there is Charles Dickens in *The Examiner*, mocking the claims Cooper accepted so easily (*Works*, Nat. Lib. edn, XVIII, 6–23, espec. 17–18). Carlyle's defence is better known: 'Several men, as we hear, cry out, "See, there is something written not entirely pleasant to me!" Good friend, it is pity; but who can help it? They that will crowd about bonfires may, sometimes very fairly, get their beards singed; it is the price they pay for such illumination; natural twilight is safe and free to all' (*Works*, XXIX, 31).

8. Cockburn, *Journal*, I, 174; Carlyle, p 29.

9. MS 1555 f 117; cf. Mrs Grant's praise of young Walter's candour in allowing his father's admonitory letters to himself to be published so fully (*Mem. and Corresp.*, III, 319–20).

10. Cockburn, *Journal*, I, 174–5; H. Martineau, *Biographical Sketches*

(N.Y. 1869), p 31; Ticknor, *Life, Letters and Journals*, 2 vols (Boston 1909), II, 188–9.

11. *Life and Works of Lord Macaulay*, Edinburgh edn, X (1910), 8–9.

12. *Chambers's Edinburgh Journal*, VI (1837), 219–20; VII (1838), 6.

13. Keble, *Occasional Papers and Reviews* (Oxford 1877), p 4.

14. *American Quarterly Review*, XXII (1837–8), 203; *North American Review*, XLVI (1838), 432–3.

15. *Knickerbocker*, XII (1838), 349–66; 'Wamba's' answer is on pp 508–20. Cf. XI (1838), 380–6, and *Lippincott's*, VIII (1871), 625–9. Cooper's biographer James Grossman (*James Fenimore Cooper* [1949], pp 127–9) comments on Cooper's charge that a *Life* like Scott's was a planned posthumous deception: 'Cooper had arrived at a literary truth which we accept today but usually value differently. A great "Life" is in part something manipulated and contrived, an act of creation. Lockhart, like Boswell, had a subject who was himself a writer, among other things, of lives, and who lent himself with a sympathetic skill, not unlike that of a professional model's, to making a work of art out of his own. Depending on our point of view, we can label the portrait of such an accommodating sitter "the real thing" or – if we have Cooper's horror of manipulation and contrivance – a "fraud".'

16. *QR*, XLVI (1831), 8.

17. MS 932 No. 65; MS 923: 14 January 1838.

18. Carlyle, pp 26, 28–29; Nicolson, p 119; Corson, 'Scott Studies – I', p 30.

19. *The Athenaeum*, 1837, pp 396, 741; 1838, p 12.

20. MS 924 No. 23: 30 April 1837; No. 24: 24 April 1838.

21. Hope-Scott quotes Gladstone in his reply, 10 April 1871, published in the 1871 reissue of Lockhart's abridgement: *Narrative of the Life of Sir Walter Scott*, a compression of eighty-four chapters into eighteen. Corson ('Scott Studies – I', p 30) remarks on the substitution of 'Narrative' for 'Memoirs' that the longer work was 'merely' a compilation, while the shorter was an actual presentation. Detailed comparison reveals a kind of truth in this. Lockhart's exertion of a greater degree of personal control over the shorter work follows logically from his having to reorganize and compress into eighteen units, each a model of narrative coherence, each representing new choices, new emphases, new connectives (generally substituting narrative transitions for editorial or expository ones). Exclusion requires both simplification and interpretation. Comparison shows that as groups of letters disappear and narrative becomes more predominant, the narrator becomes more prominent as well. Greater selectivity in journal excerpts minimizes the texture of daily life. But most interesting, comparison shows vividly how remarkable a 'compilation' the longer work is. Such seems to be the feeling of Miss Dougary in *Materials and Techniques of Biography* (thesis, University of Edinburgh 1942), pp 102–5.

22. Hutton, *Sir Walter Scott*, E.M.L. (London 1902), p v. Norgate, *Life of Sir Walter Scott* (London 1906), p ix; Andrew Lang, *Sir Walter Scott* (N.Y. 1906), pp vii-viii. Ruskin, at work on *Fors Clavigera* in 1873, reports to Norton he is writing 'almost a life of Sir Walter Scott, and an important analysis of Frederick. Merely digests of Lockhart and Carlyle, but useful. My great mental gift is Digestion, and my great bodily defect, Indigestion – it's odd enough' (*Letters to C.E. Norton*, 2 vols [Boston 1904], II, 66–67).

23. 'Scott Studies – I', p 28.

24. 'Scott Studies – I', p 31.
25. MS 3649: 2 January 1853.
26. Saintsbury, *Essays in English Literature: 1780–1860*, 2nd ser. (London 1895), p 400. Stephen, *Hours in a Library* (London 1874), pp 218–19; *DNB*, XVII, 1043, 1049.
27. In *The Speaker* for 20 October 1906, pp 82–83: see C.R.Sanders, 'Strachey's Conception of Biography', *PMLA*, LXVI (1951), 299.
28. *Biographical Essays* (N.Y. 1949), p 16.
29. Guy Boas, *Lytton Strachey* (Eng. Assoc. Pamphlet 93, 1935), p 15.
30. *Ventilations* (Philadelphia 1930), p 133; and *Walter Scott*, p 285.
31. Carswell, *Sir Walter* (London 1932), p v; and *New Statesman and Nation*, n.s. XVI (1938), 626–8, where he called for a wholly new Life rather than Grierson's 'Supplement'. The same year W.M.Parker called for a revised and enlarged edition of Lockhart (LE, *TLS*, October 1938, p 627). For Corson's reaction see 'Scott Studies – II', pp 112–13.
32. *The Laird of Abbotsford* (London 1932), p 9; *Sir Walter Scott* (London 1948), p 16. A.M.Mackenzie in *NS&N*, 12 March 1932, p x. In fairness to Dame Una it should be noted that she contradicted herself: 'coming late on the scene Lockhart accepted the Scott who had traditionalized himself' (p 15).
33. Cook, 'Lockhart's Treatment of Scott's Letters', *The Nineteenth Century*, CII (1927), 382–98; Grierson, L.L.B.; 'Sir Walter in his Letters', vol. I of Scott, *Letters*. Cf. Lockhart to Cadell 20 June 1836: 'the perhaps dismalest thing for me (if I were to think of myself at all in the matter) is that very likely, when all his letters are thrown open to an unscrupulous after age, my manipulation may be thrown overboard entirely.' He considered them *his* materials; to Croker (10 April 1852) he still spoke of 'my Scott papers'. Cf. Dougary, p 111; F.A.Pottle, *Yale University Library Gazette*, II, 3 (January 1928).
34. Cf. R.S.Newdick, *The First Life and Letters of Charles Lamb* (Columbus, Ohio, 1935), p 27; also, H.M.Jones on Moore's use of Byron's letters in *The Harp That Once* (N.Y. 1937), p 275.
35. Lang, II, 114–15.
36. Hogg suggests (4 October 1832) that in order to write with freedom inaccessible to a son-in-law Lockhart take Hogg's 'name and forthright egotistical style' (MS 924 f 83). Cockburn, *Journal*, I, 174.
37. *The Ballantyne Humbug Handled* (Edinburgh 1839), p 7.
38. MS 1554 ff 55–56, 59; MS 924 f 83.
39. Oliphant, II, 124; Lang, II, 114–15; Lochhead, pp 202–4.
40. To Scott of Raeburn, 11 December 1836 (MS 2890 ff 137–8); Letter to Lord Chief Commissioner Adam (through the kindness of its owner, Dr Corson), 24 April; Letter to Laidlaw, 19 January (Carruthers, p 190); Lochhead, p 204; Cockburn, *Journal*, I, 134. Crabb Robinson speaks of the 5th on October 11th, and the same date Cadell writes Major Walter that vol. V goes off better and carries the others with it (MS 1555 f 65). Morritt, MS 935 ff 42–43; Lockhart, MS 1821 f 1.
41. Haydon, *Corresp. and Table-Talk*, 2 vols (London 1876), II, 102; Lang, II, 182–3; letter to Adam, 24 April.
42. Carruthers, p 192.
43. MS 924 No. 76.
44. Skene, *Memories of Sir Walter Scott* (London 1909), p 20 (9 Feb. 1834).

45. Quoted by Sir Robert Rait in 'Boswell and Lockhart', *Essays by Divers Hands*, n.s. XII (1933), 123–4.
46. MS 931 No. 14; MS 924 No. 39; MS 929 No. 96; MS 935 No. 61; MS 934 No. 111; MS 935 No. 45B, No. 3B; MS 932 No. 62–63; MS 929 No. 71; for Lockhart's distrust of Mrs Hughes, see Scott, *Letters*, I, 402n.
47. MS 935 No. 65; *Lady Louisa Stuart*, pp 268–70; MS 854; MS 3277; Scott, *Letters*, I, 255n, 314–15; Skene, *Memories*, pp 23, 26–28; MS 924 ff 41 ff.
48. MS 3907 f 56: 9 August 1828.
49. MS 934 No. 52B; MS 927 No. 24: 27 January 1837.
50. MS 932 No. 84.
51. *Letters from and to Charles Kirkpatrick Sharpe*, 2 vols (Edinburgh 1888), II, 479.
52. See Newdick, *Life and Letters of Lamb*, pp 20–21. Wordsworth's letters have been edited by Lockhart or the writer himself: see *Life of Scott*, II, 143–4, and 247–50, and cf. the texts in de Selincourt.
53. A.J.C. Hare, *The Life and Letters of Maria Edgeworth*, 2 vols (Boston 1895), II, 545; MS 923 No. 51-52: 17 November 1832; MS 936; Lang, II, 115; MS 923: 25 May 1847.
54. Carruthers, p 193; letter to Adam, 24 April.
55. *New Life*, pp 1, 205, 253, 259–60, 240; Scott, *Letters*, I, xliv, xlix; L.L.B., pp 13–15; MS 331 ff 269–70; MS 331 f 271.
56. Carruthers, p 193n; Lochhead, pp 211–12; Hall: MS 932 No. 51: 20 September 1832; Lockhart to Murray: MS 1821 f 4: 18 August 1838.
57. Cf. 'Proofreading Lockhart's *Scott*', pp 12–13. The proofsheets represent different stages. The seven volumes are now bound as six; the fourth contains 1st edn vol. IV (incomplete) with author's corrections, together with 'last proof' of vol. V. My refs ignore present binding and number vols by 1st edn Refs here are to Proofs, I, 415; VI, 224; II, 184; II, 315.
58. Ian Jack seizes on my term 'narrative adaptation' ('Proofreading', p 13) in his 'Two Biographers: Lockhart and Boswell', p 283, and finds it 'surely an understatement'. The term was culpably vague. But such 'adaptations' are not, I think, explained simply by reference to what Jack calls Lockhart's 'indifference to precise truth'. The positivistic presuppositions of Drs Jack, Corson, *et al.*, are, I believe, inadequate for the understanding and assessment of Lockhart's art. I take it, moreover, that no historian – including Boswell – can escape from a 'habit of mingling truth and fiction so that it is hardly possible to separate the two'; cf. Boswell's 'reconstruction' of anecdotes of Johnson the youth. For my farfetched hypothetical reconstruction of a 'Polton Ride', see 'Proofreading Lockhart's *Scott*', p 13n.
59. Scott, *Letters*, I, xciii; L.L.B., pp 35–36; *New Life*, p 260 & n.
60. Croker Papers, Clements Library; Nat. Lib. Scot. MSS 924 & 927.
61. For deleted passages see 'Proofreading Lockhart's *Scott*', pp 15–16.
62. MS 1828 No. 179: 26 May 1853; cf. 'Proofreading Lockhart's *Scott*', pp 16–17.
63. MS 1828 No. 179.
64. Quotations of Morritt that follow are all from letters in MSS 932 & 935.
65. MS 1553 f 110: 27 April 1830; MS 1828 f 112B: 10 April 1852.
66. MS 924 No. 76; Carruthers, p 192.
67. MS 1554 f 69: 2 January 1833.
68. *Ballantyne Humbug*, p 9.

69. MS 932 No. 89.
70. *Reminiscences of Sir Walter Scott's Residence in Italy 1832*, ed. G.H. Needler (Toronto 1953), p ix, superseded by Corson's edn (London & Edinburgh 1957), which retains the Needler intro. Subsequent refs are to the later edn.
71. *The Literary Life and Correspondence of the Countess of Blessington*, by R.R.Madden, 2 vols (London 1855), II, 69–70.
72. *Ibid.* Cf., e.g., Gell, pp 16–17, 21.
73. MS 1554 ff 89–90: 19 June 1833. Edward Cheney's letter to Anne (MS 1554 f 93: 26 June 1833), accompanying his own reminiscences, must have arrived within forty-eight hours of Anne's death.
74. *Blessington*, II, 74–80, *passim*.
75. *Blessington*, II, 11, 87.
76. MS 1554 ff 148–9: 17 August 1834.
77. *Memorials of James Hogg*, ed. by his daughter Mrs Garden (Paisley, n.d.), pp 247–55, 285–9.
78. MS 1554 f 75: 20 March 1833.
79. MS 1554 f 77: 22 March 1833.
80. MS 1554 f 75.
81. MS 4039 f 83: 18 August 1834; other quotes are from A.L.Strout, 'James Hogg's *Familiar Anecdotes of Sir Walter Scott*', *SP*, XXXIII (1936), 462–3, to which article I am indebted throughout these paragraphs.
82. One expects biographers of Hogg to blame Lockhart severely – e.g., J.E.H.Thomson in *Domestic Manners* (Stirling 1909), p 46: 'The truth is that Lockhart regarded himself as the high priest of the Scott cult, and, in consequence, the judge of the correct and orthodox way in which worship was to be offered to the immortal memory.' Such extravagances are common in Lockhart commentary. But one is surprised to find Dr Corson more sympathetic to Hogg than Hogg's own biographer, A.L.Strout. 'Scott Studies – I', p 27: 'Hogg's *Domestic Manners* is a wholly delightful work and contains much valuable information. . . . Hogg loved Scott in a way that Lockhart never did.'
83. MS 1554 f 75. Chambers's *Life* first appeared in his *Edinburgh Journal*, 6 October 1832 (pp 641–53). Writing to Chambers, Cunningham avows a limited aim: 'I have no intention of expanding or even of correcting, my own hasty and inaccurate sketch. Mr Lockhart will soon give a full and correct life of that wonderful man to the world' (William Chambers, *Memoir of Robert Chambers* [N.Y. 1872], p 219). Gillies' *Recollections* appeared in *Fraser's*: XII (1835), 249–66, 502–15, 687–703; XIII (1836), 104–20.
84. *Fraser's*, X (1834), 125–56.
85. *Athenaeum*, 1832, p 641.
86. *Fraser's*, XIII (1836), 104n.
87. MS 932 No. 89.
88. *Domestic Manners*, p 82.
89. Scott, *Letters*, I, lx; *New Life*, p 47; 'Scott Studies – II', pp 109–11; *Chambers' Journal*, II (1833), 204-5; Allan [and Weir], *Life of Scott*, pp 146–7.
90. *New Life*, p 53; 'Scott Studies – II', p 109; *Life of Scott*, I, 263–64n or *Narrative*, pp 73–74n. Anne to Sophia: MS 1552 f 179: 21 May 1826.
91. 'Scott Studies – I', p 25; cf. Allan [and Weir], pp 338–9, 350n.
92. Allan [and Weir], pp 12, 117, 145, 104–5.
93. Cf. the attack (p 64) on the 'judge-made' criminal law of Scotland.

The survey of the state of political feeling (pp 100ff) is more severe than Cockburn's (*Memorials*); and cf. Cockburn, pp 111–15, on the political trials and the yeomanry cavalry to which Scott belonged.

94. Joanna Baillie noticed, after the reading of one volume, that Lockhart had 'skilfully set . . . before our eyes' the 'special providence' working in Scott's early development (MS 931 No. 42: 5 March 1837). Weir speculates abstractly on this theme often. He is inclined to generalize and then deduce specific interpretations (e.g., pp 18–19, the school). He is fond of constructing trends in 'the history of mind' (cf. 1786–90, on p 52).

95. 'Scott Studies – I', p 26.

96. *Life of Scott*, I, 87. Weir (pp 13–14) locates the incident in the city and sets it as an *illustration* of the child's *temper*: 'Even when a child, he was pleased and happy in a thunderstorm. A violent tempest of this kind happening to break over the town one afternoon, shortly after Wattie began to run about on crutches, the children were collected into the nursery by their scarcely less frightened attendants. He was no where to be seen; the family became alarmed at his absence; and the domestics were despatched in all directions in search of him. No word however could be heard of Wattie, until accidentally one of the men-servants had occasion to go to the back garden, where to his surprise he found the child lying on his back, clapping his little hands at every flash of lightning, and crying "bonnie, bonnie". He was carried into the house drenched with rain, and screaming vexation at being disturbed.' Lockhart sets the incident among the crags in the locality of Sandy-Knowe and Smailholme Tower: 'There is a story of his having been forgotten one day among the knolls when a thunderstorm came on; and his aunt, suddenly recollecting his situation, and running out to bring him home, is said to have found him lying on his back, clapping his hands at the lightning, and crying out, "Bonny! bonny!"' at every flash.' *Weir* characteristically adds a 'philosophical' gloss: 'It seems to us that even in these trifling incidents may be discerned traces perhaps of a slight degree of that irascibility necessarily attendant upon protracted sickness, but at the same time of a temper inclined to drollery, bold and fearless, determined to keep its own under every disadvantage, and claiming kindred with the grand and beautiful.'

97. Allan [and Weir], p 53.

98. W.M. Parker, CCLXXXIX (1951), 367–82; CCXCII (1954), 426 ff. Tait, *Journal of Sir Walter Scott* (Edinburgh 1950), p viii: 'Lockhart's departures from the MS are merely intended to smarten the style, and they do not affect the sense.'

99. Scott, *Letters*, XII, 38.

100. Scott, *Letters*, I, lxiii–iv, 134, 149–50.

101. J.A. Rycenga, *Theories and Forms in English Biography 1836–1899*, unpub. PhD diss., Northwestern University, 1959, pp 75–81. Rycenga surveyed the uses of the correspondence at the time I did, and while we differed in primary concern, we reached some of the same general conclusions. His analysis of 'almost entirely epistolary' chapter XLV is admirable. He shows: 'Seventeen letters – six to young Walter – arranged with a feeling for focus, event, circumstantiality, contrast, variety of personalities and sensibilities – the chapter is a varied transcript, as whole and as satisfying as Boswell's reporting of Johnson's conversation, of Sir Walter's life through a busy, diversified Scottish summer. In only thirty-four pages, with a minimum of intrusion, Lockhart demonstrates what compactness and significance a well-manipulated

discursive biography can possess. And there are literally dozens of similar epistolary mosaics' (p 80).

102. MS 923: 25 May 1847: 'Do pray leave out all the *Accounts* in Scotts life – only make one clear general statement & let there be an end of all that – Posterity will care nothing about Ballantyne or Constable or any one of them but Scott himself –.'

103. Scott, *Letters*, I, 432–3.

104. Scott, *Letters*, III, 285–90, 295–7.

105. The misfortunes are recorded in the preface to vol. VII. The discovery of the Ellis originals came too late for the early volumes. In XII, the editors print from manuscripts the *parts* of letters not in Lockhart; hence, parts of documents are distributed among different volumes, some from Lockhart's 'manipulations', some from originals. Grierson's transcribers missed quite a few extracts which *do* appear in Lockhart. E.g., the letter of 14 Sept. 1809 (Lockhart, II, 135) is printed from MS in XII, 312–15, as 'for the first time'; 25 November [1802] appears in XII, 225, with the note that 'Lockhart omits this letter altogether' (not so).

106. Proofs, II, 260–7; VI, 324–5.

107. *Letters*, VII, 259, 231, 227, 220–4.

108. MS 1828 No. 179 (26 May 1853): 'Moores diary was suggested by Byron's – so was Scott's.'

109. Cf. Rycenga, p 98, on the device of 'multiple focus'.

110. *Letters of William and Dorothy Wordsworth: The Later Years*, II, 927.

111. LE in *TLS*, 22 August 1936, p 680.

112. MS 1822 f 117.

113. Cf. Lounsbury, *James Fenimore Cooper* (Boston 1882), p 160; *Journal*, p 266. Lockhart (MS 1822 f 117) cites the Cooper passages to illustrate errors in transcription.

114. *Journal*, pp 140, 190, 199, 726–77.

115. *Journal*, pp 152–3: 'If this work answers – if it *but* answers, it must set us on our legs: I am sure worse trumpery of mine has had a great run.' These three sentences follow: 'Well, I will console myself and do my best! But fashion changes, and I am getting old, and may become unpopular. But it [is] time to cry out when I am hurt.'

116. Proofs, VI, 112–13.

117. Proofs, VI, 221.

118. MS 932: 9 October 1836.

119. Gell, p 22. Page 5 has a fascinating slip; Corson attributes it to Gell, but it is characteristic of Scott. Gell reports talk about Laing's attack on 'Ossian' MacPherson. Scott tells Gell he received a threatening letter from MacPherson (for his review of Laing in 1805). MacPherson died in 1796; Scott's 'letter' derives from an unconscious identification he had long felt with Dr Johnson, and his 'answer' (reported to Gell) is Johnson's: 'I answered him,' said Sir Walter, 'that if we met I would prove which was the better man, but if he were the stronger I would have recourse to the law, for that at all events I would maintain that a barefaced lie was a lie, to the last day of my life.' Cf. *Boswell's Johnson*, ed. Hill (1887), II, 298; and Bailey Saunders, *The Life and Letters of James MacPherson* (London 1894), pp 304–7.

120. MS 926 No. 4: 23 March 1837.

121. MS 924 No. 40: 10 October 1837.

122. MS 924 No. 34: February 1834.
123. MS 934: 15 May 1833.
124. MS 924 No. 34: February 1834; *Memories*, p 20.
125. *Memories*, p 12.
126. MS 924 No. 35: 7 March 1834.
127. MS 924 No. 34, and *Memories*, p 16.
128. MS 916. Worth comparison, as representative, are the original and published versions of Morritt's account of Scott in search of local colour at Rokeby. Characteristically, Lockhart has placed the account of 'one of his visits' in the setting of a specific visit, set the scene, and turned indirect discourse into direct quotation of Scott:

MS 916	*Life of Scott*, IV, 17
I was struck as every body must have been with the almost conscientious fidelity of his local descriptions in the works he had published or was pre-paring, & the more so when in one of his visits at Rokeby I observed him noting down even the peculiar little wildflowers & herbs that acci-dentally grew round & on the side of a bold crag in the scene around his intended cave of Guy Denzil in the then unwritten poem. He had indeed previously conceived the outline of his story & called on me to ride with him & furnish him with a good robber's cave & a romantic church, as he often said I was always furnish-ed here with whatever could be wanted for a romance, & had only to look about for the articles in my assortment. These at least were found in the old slate quarry of Brignal, & the ruined Abby Church at Eggleston. Still I thought violets & primroses as poetical as briars or woodbine, & as he was not swearing to the truth of his song I laughed at his scruples.	I had, of course, had many previous opportunities of testing the almost conscientious fidelity of his local de-scriptions; but I could not help being singularly struck with the lights which this visit threw on that char-acteristic of his compositions. The morning after he arrived he said, 'You have often given me materials for romance – now I want a good robber's cave, and an old church of the right sort.' We rode out, and he found what he wanted in the ancient slate quarries of Brignall and the ruined Abbey of Egglestone. I ob-served him noting down even the peculiar little wild flowers and herbs that accidentally grew round and on the side of a bold crag near his intended cave of Guy Denzil; and could not help saying, that as he was not to be upon oath in his work, daisies, vio-lets, and primroses would be as poetical as any of the humble plants he was examining. I laughed, in short, at his scrupulousness ; . . .

129. 'The Making of the "Minstrelsy." Scott and Shortreed in Liddesdale', *Cornhill Magazine*, n.s. LXXIII (1932), 269–80.
130. *Letters of W. and D. Wordsworth: The Later Years*, II, 795–96.
131. *Journals of Dorothy Wordsworth*, ed. E. de Selincourt, 2 vols (N.Y. 1941), I, 386–87.
132. MS 911 ff 60–62.
133. MS 924 No. 34.
134. *Ballantyne Humbug*, pp 9–10.
135. MS 921 ff 159–207.

136. Carruthers, p 152.
137. MS 854.
138. MS 924 No. 35; *Journal*, pp 69–71.
139. Proofs, VI, 213–14.
140. Jack, 'Two Biographers: Lockhart and Boswell', pp 282–5.
141. 'Letter to a Friend of Burns', *Prose Works* (London 1876), II, 10.
142. MS 935 f 12: 10 October 1837.
143. MS 935 No. 58. Grierson, *New Life*, p 299.
144. Dougary, *Materials and Technique of Biography*, pp 126–7.
145. *Walter Scott*, p 283.
146. Oliphant, II, 133.
147. *Development of English Biography*, p 119.
148. MS 924 No. 93: 12–13 April 1837.
149. Thomas Crawford, *Scott* (Edinburgh 1965), pp 29–30.
150. Lang, I, 116.
151. *Scott*, p 20.
152. MS 1821 f 3: 26 April 1838.
153. *Theories and Forms in English Biography*, p 41.
154. MS 936 f 54: 2 May 1847.
155. letter to Adam, 24 April 1837 (courtesy of Dr Corson).
156. *Letters: The Later Years*, II, 927.
157. *Theories and Forms in English Biography*, p 39.
158. *New Statesman and Nation*, XLVIII (1954), 186.
159. *Sir Walter*, p 211.
160. Lang, II, 409; Lochhead, pp 18, 310 (quoting Charles Whibley).
161. MS 923 No. 51: 17 November 1832.
162. MS 3900 f 165: 9 April 1825 (to Scott); MS 1822 f 133: 15 November 1843 (to Croker).
163. MS 1552 f 173: 16 May 1826; MS 1819 f 15: 1 June 1820; MS 1827 No. 86: 31 January 1852.
164. *John Gibson Lockhart*: Commem. Address, U. of Glasgow, 18 June 1930 (Glasgow 1944), pp 14–15.

NOTES TO THE APPENDIX

1. Sir Herbert Maxwell, Bt., *The Life of Wellington* (London, n.d.), 2 vols, II, 50–51.
2. J.F.C.Fuller, *A Military History of the Western World*, 3 vols (New York 1955), II, 502.
3. Maxwell, II, 8.
4. Thompson, *Napoleon*, p 379; *QR*, LXX (1842), 477.
5. Lockhart, p 468; J.C.Ropes, *The Campaign of Waterloo* (N.Y. 1893,) pp 74–75; Petrie, *Wellington*, p 193.
6. Lockhart, p 468n. 'This great occasion' may refer to the campaign or the social climax of the 15th. In the letter to Lockhart transcribed below, the author is answering the specific charge that he was surprised at a ball.
7. *Vanity Fair*, chapter XXIX; Thompson, *Napoleon*, p 378.
8. Maxwell, II, 5.
9. Fuller, II, 502 note 4.
10. Ropes, p 76; Petrie, p 195; Fuller, II, 503. Müffling is quoted by Max-

well (II, 9). I have not seen elsewhere Oman's charge that Wellington's ignorance was due to Dörnberg's negligence. *Cambridge Modern History*, IX, 626.

11. Petrie, p 196; cf. Ropes, pp 80–81.
12. Maxwell, II, 12, 14; Petrie, p 197.
13. 1815. *Waterloo* (Paris 1898), p 146.
14. Maxwell, II, 13; Petrie, pp 196–7.
15. Rose, Intro. to Lockhart's *Napoleon* (1916), p ix.
16. Lockhart, pp 471–72.
17. Ropes, p 241.
18. J.C.Young, *Memoir of Charles Mayne Young* (London and N.Y. 1871), pp 165–7.
19. Maxwell, II, 45–46.
20. Ropes, p 242.
21. Ropes, pp 238–9.

ACKNOWLEDGEMENTS

Grateful acknowledgement is made to the following persons and institutions for permission to quote from materials in copyright or in manuscript. Frederick W. Hilles, Yale University, for his set of page proofs of the 1st edn of Lockhart's *Life of Scott*; James C. Corson, Lilliesleaf, Melrose, Scotland, for Lockhart's letter to Commissioner Adam; *Studies in Bibliography*, Fredson T. Bowers, editor, for pages (revised) of my article 'Proofreading Lockhart's *Scott*,' in *SB*, 1961; Elizabeth A.M. Dougary, for her 1942 PhD thesis (Univ. of Edinburgh), *Materials and Techniques of Biography*; to Oliver and Boyd Ltd, for the Tait-Parker edn of Scott's *Journal*; to A.D. Peters & Company, for Hilton Brown's *There Was A Lad*; to Thomas Nelson & Sons Ltd, for J.C. Corson's edn of Gell's *Sir Walter Scott's Residence in Italy 1832*; to Constable Publishers, for the Centenary edn of the *Letters of Sir Walter Scott*, ed. by Sir Herbert Grierson; to William Hodge & Co Ltd, for Hans Hecht's *Robert Burns*, trans. J Lymburn; to the Clarendon Press, Oxford, for R.G. Collingwood's *The Idea of History*, and for Ernest de Selincourt's edn of *Letters of William and Dorothy Wordsworth* : to Mr John Carswell and Chatto and Windus Ltd, for Catherine Carswell's *The Life of Robert Burns*; to John Murray (Publishers) Ltd, for Donald Carswell's *Sir Walter*, and for two articles by W.M. Parker in the *Quarterly Review* (CCLXXXIX, 1951; and CCXCII, 1954) on Lockhart, and for the article 'The Making of the "Minstrelsy"' in *Cornhill Magazine*, LXXIII (1932); to MacGibbon & Kee, for Maurice Lindsay's *Robert Burns* (1954 edn); to Cornell University Press, for *Coleridge the Talker*, edd Richard W. Armour and Raymond F. Howes (1940); to Sydney Goodsir Smith and Hamish Henderson, and to the Saltire Society, for Smith's and Henderson's articles in *Saltire Review*, vol. 2, nos. 5 and 6; to the University of Wisconsin Press, for Karl Kroeber's *Romantic Narrative Art*; to the Editors, *ELH*, and the Johns Hopkins Press, for pages (revised) from my article 'Boswell and the Romantics,' in *ELH*, XXVII (1960); to the Editor, the *University of Edinburgh Journal*, for James C. Corson's essays, 'Scott Studies, I and II', in the *Journal*, 1955 and 1956; to Basil Blackwell,

Publisher, Oxford, for J. M. Thompson's *Napoleon Buonaparte*; to H. van Thal, for Una Pope Hennessy's *Sir Walter Scott* (1948); to Penguin Books Ltd, for the J. M. Cohen translation of Rousseau's *Confessions*; to the Editor, *Studies in Philology*, for A. L. Strout's 'Hogg's Familiar Anecdotes,' in *SP*, XXXIII (1936); to Mr John Arthur Rycenga and Northwestern University Library, for Mr Rycenga's PhD thesis (1959), *Theories and Forms in English Biography*; to the Trustees of the National Library of Scotland, for manuscript materials in Abbotsford, Blackwood, and other collections, and to Mr James Ritchie, Deputy Keeper of Manuscripts, for kindly helpfulness over the years; to George Weidenfeld & Nicolson Ltd for Felix Markham's *Napoleon* (1963); to William Sloane Associates, for James Grossman's *James Fenimore Cooper* (1949); to Yale University Library for Lockhart's letter of 14 December 1825 concerning phrenology (in the Knollenberg Collection).

INDEX